THE BIOREGIONAL IMAGINATION

D1479294

The

EDITED BY TOM LYNCH,

Bioregional

CHERYLL GLOTFELTY,

Imagination

AND KARLA ARMBRUSTER

Literature, Ecology, and Place

MAPS BY EZRA ZEITLER

THE UNIVERSITY OF GEORGIA PRESS   ATHENS AND LONDON

© 2012 by the University of Georgia Press
Athens, Georgia 30602
www.ugapress.org
All rights reserved

Set in Adobe Garamond by Graphic Composition, Inc.
Printed and bound by Thomson-Shore

The paper in this book meets the guidelines for permanence and
durability of the Committee on Production Guidelines for
Book Longevity of the Council on Library Resources.

Printed in the United States of America
16 15 14 13 12 P 5 4 3 2 1

LIBRARY OF CONGRESS CATALOGING-IN-PUBLICATION DATA
The bioregional imagination : literature, ecology, and place /
edited by Tom Lynch, Cheryll Glotfelty, and Karla Armbruster ;
maps by Ezra Zeitler.
        p.   cm.
    Includes index.
    ISBN-13: 978-0-8203-4171-2 (cloth : alk. paper)
    ISBN-10: 0-8203-4171-1 (cloth : alk. paper)
    ISBN-13: 978-0-8203-3592-6 (pbk. : alk. paper)
    ISBN-10: 0-8203-3592-4 (pbk. : alk. paper)
    1. Bioregionalism in literature. 2. Ecology in literature. 3. Place
(Philosophy) in literature. 4. Ecocriticism. I. Lynch, Tom, 1955–
II. Glotfelty, Cheryll. III. Armbruster, Karla. IV. Zeitler, Ezra J.
    PN98.E36B56 2012
    809'.9336—dc23   2011037753

British Library Cataloging-in-Publication Data available

To Peter Berg, who led the way (1937–2011)

CONTENTS

ACKNOWLEDGMENTS

The seeds for this essay collection on literature, ecology, and place germinated in cyberspace. Cheryll, who wanted to teach a class on bioregional literature and criticism, posted a query to the e-mail list of the Association for the Study of Literature and Environment (ASLE). Tom then e-mailed Cheryll, suggesting that we edit an anthology on the subject, whereupon we invited Karla to join the team. Our first step was to test the waters by organizing a conference panel on bioregional approaches to literary study; accordingly, we posted a call for papers to the ASLE e-mail list. We received so many strong proposals that we formed not one but three well-attended conference panels at the 2007 ASLE conference in Spartanburg, South Carolina. Building on the success of those panels, we used e-mail to solicit essays from colleagues whose bioregional work we admired and to announce an open call for paper proposals. Via e-mail and Skype conference calls, we vetted proposals and corresponded with contributors. To create common ground and foster conversation among the essays, we set up a Google Docs site, where we uploaded a half-dozen core readings in bioregionalism and where contributors could read one another's drafts, making possible many of the cross references in the final essays. While we took the opportunity to meet face-to-face with many of our contributors and with Judy Purdy of the University of Georgia Press at the 2009 ASLE conference in Victoria, B.C., we happily acknowledge our indebtedness to the Internet. We have found it to be a marvelous tool for people working in far-flung locales, from Spartanburg to Reno, from Adelaide to Torino, enabling them to enjoy a frequent meeting of minds, allowing the rich compost of ideas from throughout the world to fertilize the bioregional practice of living-in-place. If this use of the placeless Internet to foster place-consciousness seems suspect, we would like to point out that the pages of *CoEvolution Quarterly* and *Whole Earth Review* during the 1980s were filled with articles on both bioregional thinking and the promise of a subversive, newfangled tool called the personal computer.

The University of Georgia Press has been supportive, exacting, and professional. We feel very fortunate in our choice of publisher. Acquisitions editor Judy Purdy shepherded the project through its early stages, and Nancy Grayson saw the book through to completion. Our thanks to them for being prompt, clear, helpful—and patient. Two anonymous outside reviewers offered an effective mix of inspiring praise and constructive criticism, and we appreciate their meticulous reports that raised the bar and pushed us to make the book better than it otherwise would have been. We also wish to thank the staff at the University of Georgia Press, particularly Beth Snead, Jon Davies, and John McLeod, and our copy editor, Dawn McIlvain Stahl, for their fine work.

Our universities offered crucial support, which we gratefully acknowledge. The University of Nebraska, Lincoln, funded a research assistant and awarded a grant that helped defray expenses. At the University of Nevada, Reno, the College of Liberal Arts Scholarly and Creative Activities Grant Program provided a grant, and the English Department funded a summer research assistant. Webster University underwrote photocopying and contributed a grant from the Dean of Arts and Sciences. Our research assistants deserve special mention. Tom's assistant, Tracy Tucker, tracked down core bioregional readings and helped set up the Google Docs site. Cheryll's assistant, Kyle Bladow, collated, proofread, and formatted the manuscript and annotated the Bioregional Booklist. Our sincere thanks to Tracy and Kyle—it's been a privilege to work with you. We count ourselves extraordinarily lucky to have engaged the services of cartographer Ezra Zeitler and indexer Sandra Marshall, both of whom are masters of their craft.

The Association for the Study of Literature and Environment facilitated this project in more ways than space permits us to enumerate. To show our appreciation, royalties from the sale of this book go directly to ASLE to further its mission "to promote the understanding of nature and culture for a sustainable world by fostering a community of scholars, teachers, and writers who study the relationships among literature, culture, and the physical environment." In the profession we would like to thank John Tallmadge for his enthusiastic support of this project and Lawrence Buell for graciously allowing us to adapt his book title *The Environmental Imagination*. To the contributors to this collection, thank you for working with us to make this book!

Tom would like to thank his colleagues and the many students who participate in the Place Studies interest group in the UNL English department. They have perpetuated a lively intellectual community in which the sorts of ideas discussed in this volume can be explored and debated. He has been fortunate at Nebraska to inherit a long tradition of commitment to regional studies. He would also like to acknowledge his family. His wife, Margaret Jacobs, is a model of blending the life of a scholar with the equally though differently rewarding role of parent and partner. His two boys, Cody and Riley, keep him grounded and remind him why concern for sustainability is not just an intellectual exercise. And he would also like to mention his border collie, Xena, whose need for a daily outing forces him away from the computer screen and out into the local terrain, regardless of weather.

Cheryll would like to thank Peter Berg and Gary Snyder for their inspiring ideas, David Robertson and Rob Thayer for their time, Eric Rasmussen for ably chairing the UNR English department, and colleagues and friends in the department. She thanks students in her graduate seminar on regionalism and bioregionalism, who influenced her thinking and created fond memories. The best things in Cheryll's life usually involve her husband, Steve; daughter, Rosa; and the mountains and deserts nearby—she thanks them for being there.

Karla thanks her family: her husband, Pete; her daughters, Lila and Lucinda; and her canine and feline companions. Each has provided invaluable support as well as much-needed reminders about what is most important in life (love, play, food, walks, and snoozing in a warm spot on the bed). She is also grateful to her students, whose energy, curiosity, and optimism are a crucial source of inspiration, and to her colleagues, whose friendship and generosity in sharing the administrative work of the department made it possible for her to take on this project during a term as chair. And finally, she recognizes the subtle but crucial influence of the human and nonhuman members of her adopted community of Webster Groves, Missouri (more specifically, Tuxedo Park): after taking a connected sense of place for granted as a child and then losing it as she moved around the country in pursuit of an education and job, she treasures each interaction that reminds her of the ways that she knows—and is known in—her new home.

THE BIOREGIONAL IMAGINATION

TOM LYNCH, CHERYLL GLOTFELTY, AND
KARLA ARMBRUSTER

Introduction

On a September evening in eastern Nebraska, several hundred
community residents gather at Spring Creek Prairie Audubon Center, a restored tallgrass prairie, for a "Twilight on the Tallgrass" celebration.
As people wander the trails, they encounter stations where they learn about
native insects, birds, wildflowers, and medicinal plants. At one station,
local writers read from their prairie-inspired work. Nearby, a Winnebago
tribe dance troupe gets into costume for a performance of traditional pow-wow dances. Outside the visitors' center, a local astronomy club sets up
telescopes they will later use to show visitors a close-up of the night sky.

In South Dakota, a rancher replaces his herd of cattle with bison, then
writes a book recounting the pains and delights of the experience. His book
is chosen as a One Book South Dakota selection and subsequently read,
discussed, and debated by tens of thousands of citizens around the state.[1]

In North St. Louis, a predominantly African American community,
crowds gather every Saturday morning from June through October for the
North City Farmers' Market. In this neighborhood, where gas stations,
convenience stores, and liquor stores long ago crowded out the grocery
stores, and some residents have no way to travel to distant supermarkets,
the stands selling fresh produce are a much-needed source of healthy food.
Just as importantly, the market brings neighbors together and provides a
source of community pride. Although traditional rural farmers participate,
many of the produce stands feature vegetables, herbs, and fruit grown in

1

nearby urban gardens. Another vendor, a student-run garden at Washington University, fosters connections between North City and the university population. The market also features health screenings, healthy-cooking demonstrations, and entertainment by local artists.

In downtown Reno, Nevada, residents gather on the banks of the Truckee River to cheer kayak racers in action. The Truckee, which had deteriorated into a trash-filled eyesore, is now the main artery pumping life into a downtown revitalization effort that links Reno residents with their watershed and has enhanced urban life throughout the community. Reno's historic Riverside Hotel, which had been boarded up for years and slated for demolition, has been renovated to provide affordable studio and living space for artists, whose works are installed throughout the city. Once a place to be avoided, the Truckee River has become the focal point of community life.

At the White House in Washington, D.C., the First Lady, joined by the secretary of agriculture and a group of school children, tears up a part of the lawn and replaces it with an organic garden. Vegetables from the garden are later served to visiting dignitaries at the White House and donated to a local homeless shelter.

Although the word *bioregional* may never have been uttered during any of these activities, nor even be familiar to many of the participants, these anecdotes all illustrate the bioregional imagination at work.

WHAT IS BIOREGIONALISM?

As part of the development of the environmental movement during the 1970s, a school of thought emerged calling itself bioregionalism. Located primarily in western North America, especially California and British Columbia, this movement included thinkers such as Peter Berg, Raymond Dasmann, Gary Snyder, and Stephanie Mills. Their motivation was to address matters of pressing environmental concern through a politics derived from a local sense of place, an approach they felt would effectively complement efforts focused at the national and international levels.

Hence bioregionalists began to create a sort of parallel culture and to redefine the locus of their work, moving away from existing but for the most part arbitrary political boundaries (nations, states, counties, cities, etc.) in favor of those that emerged from a biotically determined framework, primarily based on natural communities or watersheds. In a recent study, *LifePlace: Bioregional Thought and Practice*, Robert L. Thayer Jr. defines a bioregion as follows:

> A *bioregion* is literally and etymologically a "life-place"—a unique region definable by natural (rather than political) boundaries with a geographic, climatic, hydrological, and ecological character capable of supporting unique human communities. Bioregions can be variously defined by the geography of watersheds, similar plant and animal ecosystems, and related, identifiable landforms (e.g., particular mountain ranges, prairies, or coastal zones) and by the unique human cultures that grow from natural limits and potentials of the region. Most importantly, the bioregion is emerging as the most logical locus and scale for a sustainable, regenerative community to take root and to *take place*. (3)

In addition to establishing a particular way of delineating place, bioregional thinking also implies a political and cultural practice that manifests as an environmental ethic in the day-to-day activities of ordinary residents. As Doug Aberley has explained in his succinct history of the movement, "Bioregionalism is a body of thought and related practice that has evolved in response to the challenge of reconnecting socially-just human cultures in a sustainable manner to the region-scale ecosystems in which they are irrevocably imbedded" ("Interpreting" 13). As Aberley goes on to explain, however, "it is a difficult task to provide a definitive introduction to bioregionalism" because "its practitioners protect a defiant decentralism" (13). There are, that is, no designated leaders, no figure whose theoretical musings are accepted as gospel, though inevitably some people have had more influence than others. Still, there is no official bioregional program or ideology; rather, there is an evolving dialogue about a set of ideals and ideas continually tested by practice and, as would seem proper, continually inflected by the particularities of diverse places and cultures. Bioregional thinking may be expressed quite differently in San Francisco, California, than in Ferrara, Italy, and such flexibility has given the movement surprising durability.

Bioregionalism emerged as a proactive force in the environmental movement because it saw traditional environmentalism as too reactive, forever rallying around the next disaster or impending crisis. Granted such disasters require a response, but bioregionalists prefer a more positive orientation, one that seeks to head off environmental crises by attempting to both imagine and create human communities that live sustainably in place. Although the label *bioregionalism* does not have wide currency, the ideas that constellate around that term—community, sustainability, local culture, local food systems, "green" cities, renewable energy, habitat restoration, ecological awareness, grassroots activism—have become widely adopted around the world, in no small part due to the efforts and example of bioregionalists. In recent years, the bioregional movement has continued to inform a variety of other expressions of emergent new localisms, including community-supported agriculture, the slow-food movement, antiglobalization efforts, and postcolonial reconceptualizations of place and identity.

By foregrounding natural factors as a way to envision place, bioregionalism proposes that human identity may be constituted by our residence in a larger community of natural beings—our local bioregion—rather than, or at least supplementary to, national, state, ethnic, or other more common bases of identity. Bioregionalists ask questions such as the following: What does it mean to be a resident, not of Vancouver, British Columbia, but of *Cascadia*? Not just of Nebraska, but also of the *tallgrass prairie*? Not just of California, but of the *Shasta bioregion*? Not simply of Milan, but of the *Po River Watershed*? Not of Nevada, but of the *Great Basin Desert*? The answers to such questions are rich with ecological, political, cultural, and even literary significance, the consequences of which we are only beginning to understand. Such shifts in perspective, bioregionalists propose, can have a major and ecologically positive influence on how we choose to relate to the world around us and, indeed, for who we imagine ourselves to be. And as this book attempts to show, literature is very much part of such a shift, helping people reimagine the places where they live and their relations to those places, as well as reflecting the unique bioregional character of specific communities.

In the discourse of bioregionalism, several key terms recur, most notably *dwelling*, *sustainability*, and *reinhabitation*.

Kirkpatrick Sale titled his 1985 book advocating bioregional philosophy and practice *Dwellers in the Land: The Bioregional Vision*. In explaining the term *dwelling*, Sale argues that

> the crucial and perhaps only and all-encompassing task is to understand *place*, the immediate specific place where we live. The kinds of soils and

rocks under our feet; the source of the waters we drink; the meaning of the different kinds of wind; the common insects, birds, mammals, plants, and trees; the particular cycles of the seasons; the times to plant and harvest and forage—these are the things that are necessary to know. . . . And the cultures of the people, of the populations native to the land and of those who have grown up with it, the human social economic arrangements shaped by and adapted to the geomorphic ones, in both urban and rural settings—these are the things that must be appreciated. (42)

To readers familiar with twentieth-century European philosophy, the term *dwelling* certainly hints of Heidegger, who used the term extensively and in an analogous way. (Heidegger, however, is never mentioned in Sale's book, so his influence, if present, is once- or twice-removed). For Sale, to *dwell* means to live mindfully and deeply in place, to be fully engaged to the sensory richness of our immediate environment. In this context, and gesturing again towards European philosophy, bioregions can be seen as more phenomenologically real than politically constructed places. Different bioregions look, smell, taste, sound, and feel different. We sense the transition between bioregions with our whole bodies. Crossing from Nebraska into Kansas has no sensible effect, but the shift from the tallgrass prairie to the shortgrass prairie is vividly apparent to all the senses. More common than the term *dwelling*, however, is the less formal *living-in-place*, which Berg and Dasmann explain means "following the necessities and pleasures of life as they are uniquely presented by a particular site, and evolving ways to ensure long-term occupancy of that site" (Andruss 35).

The last phrase suggests another key concept in bioregional discourse: *sustainability*. Typically, this term refers to the practice of living within the ecological limits of a place in a manner that can be continued by future generations with no deleterious impact on the environment. In recent years *sustainable* has been used to describe everything from agriculture to architecture to poetry. Indeed it has become so widely used that (like *green*) it has been co-opted to describe activities that are far from sustainable. Canada's Suncor Energy, for example, has the audacity to call itself a "sustainable" company even as it ravages Canada's boreal forest to mine tar sands, which are converted into oil that will be burned to add carbon dioxide to the atmosphere. Surely few activities are *less* sustainable than that. Still, in spite of its misuse, *sustainability* is a valuable term that is worth fighting for. Making the long-term ecological consequences of our behavior—at the personal, social, and cultural levels—a matter of moral deliberation is surely an ethic worth maintaining.

Perhaps the most distinctive key term in bioregional discourse is what Berg and Dasmann refer to as *reinhabitation*, that is, not only "learning to live-in-place," but doing so "in an area that has been disrupted and injured through past exploitation" (35). Berg and Dasmann were considering the task of learning how to live in northern California when they wrote this description, but few places on earth, alas, remain uninjured by human activity, and so the principle of reinhabitation can be applicable nearly anywhere, even, and perhaps especially, in urban settings. The idea is not simply to minimize harm to the environment, not simply to be able to sustain the current circumstances, but to find ways of living that repair the environmental harm caused by previous behavior. Reinhabitory practices might involve restoring native plant communities, redesigning landscaping with an eye to indigenous plants and habitats, restructuring transportation facilities to have as little negative social and ecological effect as possible, founding remanufacturing businesses to make new products from byprod-ucts and discarded materials, retrofitting homes to conserve energy or, bet-ter yet, to produce energy, converting brownfields to gardens, working for social justice and valuing cultural diversity, and even reimagining what a bioregionally inspired local literary tradition might consist of.

Admittedly, these kinds of living-in-place activities are not the norm in the twenty-first century. Most of us live lives that have become increasingly detached from our places. We have become, as a number of recent theo-rists, such as Setha M. Low and Denise Lawrence-Zúñiga, term it, *deter-ritorialized*. We increasingly inhabit a global monoculture, consuming the same food, watching the same movies, reading the same books, wearing the same clothes, listening to the same music, surfing the same Web, thinking the same thoughts, from Canberra to Kathmandu.

Bioregionalism is certainly, in part, a response to this process. And one of the tools bioregionalists often employ to *re*territorialize their lives and places is mapping. Liberated from the control of the official cartographers of states and nations, map making can be an empowering tool of reinhab-iting and reimagining place, allowing us to visualize in a nearly infinite array of contexts and scales the multiple dimensions of our home places. In his book *Boundaries of Home: Mapping for Local Empowerment*, Aberley argues that maps can not only reveal socially unjust patterns of environ-mental harm and the degradation of plant and animal communities but also help us to visualize strategies for resistance and a hopeful vision for the future (4–5). Maps can mingle the contours of the land with the human imagination in powerful and productive ways. Mapping is so much a tool of bioregional thought and practice that we felt inspired to present maps with the essays in this collection.

CRITIQUES OF BIOREGIONALISM

There are, we are well aware, some critiques of bioregionalism. Indeed some of those criticisms are articulated in several of the essays that follow. Even as we wish to promote aspects of bioregionalism and are interested in exploring bioregional approaches to the creation and analysis of litera-ture, we have not shied away from rigorous debate regarding its tenets. We would like to address two frequently raised concerns, the perceived anti-urban bias of bioregionalism and the relationship between the bioregional and the global.

One common critique of bioregionalism is that it has been too focused on rural and pastoral places and too concerned with agrarian issues, and so has ignored the urban environment, the very place where the majority of humanity actually lives. We believe this criticism is largely unfounded, or at least exaggerated. Certainly some bioregionalists, perhaps especially Wendell Berry, have been involved in "back to the land" sorts of activities and celebrate rural places and agrarian culture. And some of the essays that follow do examine the literature of such activities. But many other bio-regionalists, including Peter Berg, have fostered "green city" efforts. Berg's Planet Drum Foundation, founded in 1973 and based in San Francisco, has been at the forefront of the global green-cities movement. In 1989, Planet Drum published a volume titled the *Green City Program for San Francisco*, and today Planet Drum is involved in helping Bahía de Caráquez in Ec-uador work toward its stated goal to be an Ecocity. Bioregionalists have long promoted bike- and pedestrian-friendly cities, light rail transporta-tion, community-based renewable energy, urban gardens, and a literary attention to the natural characteristics of urban places.

Admittedly, the city-country polarity is a tension within the bioregional community. It is, after all, an ancient tension in human history, and it seems rather unfair to expect bioregionalists to entirely resolve it any time soon; but we sense that within the tradition of bioregionalism this tension has been mostly a productive one. An example might be an exchange that took place in the pages of *CoEvolution Quarterly*. The winter 1981 issue was devoted to the topic of "Bioregions" and included the by now often reprinted "Where You At?" bioregional quiz (Charles et al. 3). The quiz included questions such as:

· Where does your garbage go?
· Name five native edible plants in your region and their season(s) of availability.
· Name five grasses in your area. Are any of them native?
· What spring wildflower is consistently among the first to bloom where you live?[2]

Some readers, not surprisingly, felt this quiz was unduly biased towards rural places. And so the following issue included an urban rejoinder, the "Wha' Happenin'?" quiz (Bennett et al. 97). It contained questions such as:

· How many days till your next garbage pickup? What Mafia clan is responsible for it?
· Name five varieties of nonheterosexual behavior in your neighborhood.
· Imitate five sounds of the street that you ordinarily tune out.
· What's your nearest neighborhood association, and when does it meet?
· Identify the three blocks of your neighborhood where you're most likely to step in dog shit.

As this urban retort suggests, there is certainly some tension among bioregionally inclined city and country dwellers, but that tension can be a productive and, as we think the humor here suggests, even a playful one. Nevertheless, the fact that only the first quiz was reprinted in *Home! A Bioregional Reader* does, admittedly, suggest a bias in the direction of the rural. But it is clearly not the case that bioregionalists have ignored city living. Bioregionalism is about the integration of city and countryside within a common and shared bioregion or watershed.[3]

Another criticism of bioregionalism and other locally based environmental movements has been recently and cogently articulated by Ursula K. Heise in her book *Sense of Place and Sense of Planet: The Environmental Imagination of the Global*. Heise finds the turn to the local as exemplified in bioregionalism to be too limited in scope. The kinds of in-depth experiences of place advocated by bioregionalism, she argues, are increasingly difficult in an age of globalization and are inadequate to the worldwide task we face (55). "The focus on the local," Heise argues, "can . . . block an understanding of larger salient connections . . ." (62) Those of us who have seen local newspapers filled with letters to the editor that, because of a cold snap in winter, decry the idea of global warming, can sympathize with Heise's concern for the limitations of local perceptions. She advocates instead *eco-cosmopolitanism*, a term adapted from Mitchell Thomashow's "bioregional cosmopolitanism." Heise describes eco-cosmopolitanism as "an attempt to envision individuals and groups as part of planetary 'imagined communities' of both human and nonhuman kinds" (61). Although she does not cite Peter Berg in this regard, Heise's notion of an eco-cosmopolitan is strikingly similar to Berg's notion of a "planetarian," articulated as early as 1983 in his essay "Bioregion and Human Location," evidence that from its very inception bioregionalism has always included a sense of planet.[4] As we read it, the shift from place-based bioregionalism to eco-cosmopolitanism is not an either/or proposition, but a matter of emphasis. Heise clearly does not advocate abandoning a sense of place, but rather warns that the cultivation of such a sense is no panacea and that we must add a much greater degree of global awareness to local and bioregional understandings than has typically been done, especially in the United States.

We wholly concur that a localized sense of place is incomplete unless augmented by a sense of how that place is integrated into the wider biosphere and the global network of cultures and economies. But we also suggest that a sense of the global is likewise incomplete without an awareness that the globe is an amalgamation of infinitely complex connections among variously scaled and nested places, and that many of those places are most usefully considered as bioregions.[5] Author Kevin Kelly, cofounder of *Wired* magazine, employs the metaphor of fractals to express the local-global relationship in his introduction to "The Big Here" quiz, an on-line update of the classic "Where You At?" quiz discussed above: "You live in the big here. Wherever you live, your tiny spot is deeply intertwined within a larger place, imbedded fractal-like into a whole system called a watershed, which is itself integrated with other watersheds into a tightly interdependent biome. . . . At the ultimate level, your home is a cell in an organism called a planet. All these levels interconnect." Patrick Murphy, one of the first ecocritics to study international nature-oriented literature, likewise affirms the usefulness of local engagement. He draws on the work of Mitchell Thomashow and Robyn Eckersley to posit a "simultaneity of identification, giving priority to the local, in order to provide the experiential basis for the appreciation of the global" (41).

In his recent book *Eaarth*, Bill McKibben—certainly a leading figure in fostering a global effort to mitigate the crisis of climate change—reinforces this understanding. In response to what he has glumly come to believe is the inevitability of climate change, McKibben says our response should be not resignation but "increased engagement." And, he emphasizes, "Some of that engagement will be local: building the kind of communities and economies that can withstand what's coming. And some of it must be global: we must step up the fight to keep climate change from getting even more powerfully out of control, and try to protect those people most at risk, who are almost always those who have done the least to cause the problem" (xv). As with the supposed opposition between city and country, we sense that the division of the local and the global is a false dichotomy that limits the possibilities for imagining environmentally responsible global citizenship.[6]

This book, we trust, is a small contribution to the integration of the local and global. Although it's true that most of the essays tend to focus on the "local," they are drawn from places around the globe, and many of the essays make explicit, or at least implied, connections to one another. To take an obvious example, the coal industry described by Wes Berry in Kentucky, through its implications with global warming, influences both the north circumpolar regions, as described by Pavel Cenkl, on one side of the globe, and the Australian arid regions, as described by Libby Robin, on the other side.

As a sociopolitical and cultural movement, bioregional practice is rich and multifaceted. One key dimension involves the creation of art, including literature, that fosters the sort of bioregional imagination that inspires and grows out of practice. In Aberley's historical overview, he points out that "[s]torytelling, ancient and new ritual, myth-making, theater, dance, poetry and prose all became the languages of bioregional expression" ("Interpreting" 24). From the beginning, the bioregional movement in North America incorporated literary expression into its toolkit for celebrating and cultivating relationships with specific bioregions; for example, the "bundles" of bioregional lore that Planet Drum Foundation produced in the 1970s, and the related collection, *Reinhabiting a Separate Country: A Bioregional Anthology of Northern California*, all included literary expressions. Perhaps the most obvious testament to the role of literature in bioregionalism is the career of one of the movement's key figures, Gary Snyder, who has contributed immeasurably to our sense of what it means to live mindfully in a place; his longtime residence in the Shasta bioregion of the Pacific Northwest inflects both the comprehensive bioregional vision he outlines in nonfiction books such as *The Practice of the Wild* and *A Place in Space: Ethics, Aesthetics, and Watersheds* and the bioregional aesthetic he expresses in poetry collections such as *Axe Handles* and *Danger on Peaks*.

Despite this history, the role of literature in promoting and inform-ing bioregional ideas and practice has been examined in only a limited way by literary critics. In *LifePlace*, Robert L. Thayer Jr. proposes that "a distinctly regional art, aesthetics, literature, poetics, and music can evolve from and support bioregional culture" (94). Thayer includes some anal-ysis of this process, but he is a landscape architect, not a literary scholar, and his discussion is thereby limited. No collection of bioregional liter-ary criticism exists.[7] The recent interdisciplinary anthology *Bioregionalism*, edited by Michael Vincent McGinnis, explains the theory and practice of bioregionalism, with essays from scholars in history, political science, geography, education, regional planning, and public policy. But it lacks any contribution from literary scholars. Bioregionalism is about creating place-based communities, or, cultures-in-place, yet, curiously, it is exactly the *cultural* dimension of bioregionalism that has been undertheorized and only minimally explored. We hope this collection of essays will help to fill that intellectual gap.

IMAGINING A BIOREGIONAL APPROACH TO LITERATURE

In his influential work of ecocriticism, *The Environmental Imagination: Thoreau, Nature Writing, and the Formation of American Culture*, Lawrence Buell emphasizes that the environmental crisis is "a crisis of the imagina-tion" (2) and that solving this crisis depends on finding better ways to imagine nature and humanity's relation to it. He argues that literature and other creative arts not only reflect but also influence the ways a culture imagines itself and its place in the natural world. Peter Berg and Raymond Dasmann once defined a bioregion as both a "geographical terrain and a terrain of consciousness . . . a place and the ideas that have developed about how to live in that place" (36). Building on Buell's work, as our title respectfully indicates, we start with the premise that imagination is one key to developing new and better ideas about how to live in our specific places, including a sense of how our individual bioregions are embedded in a larger global biosphere. Literature and other arts function as vital expressions of cultural values that can ignite emotion, change minds, and inspire action, and our contributors explore some of the many ways a bioregional imagination both produces and is shaped by specific works of literature, photography, film, and other art forms.

In "Postmodern Environmental Ethics: Ethics as Bioregional Narrative," the philosopher Jim Cheney points to the myths and rituals of indigenous people as models of bioregional narratives that reflect and maintain sustainable relationships between humans and their natural environments; these myths and rituals, he argues, locate the people associated with them "in the moral space of defining relations" and incorporate natural entities into their sense of moral community (126). This idea that indigenous people who have lived mindfully and sustainably in particular places for long periods of time have something to teach us through their stories and related practices is widespread among bioregionalists.

But most people need more than the stories and rituals of those who inhabited their places (or perhaps other places) before them, under very different cultural and physical conditions. Reinhabitation requires the development of new approaches to living in a specific place. Perhaps the simplest way stories, poetry, and other place-based art can support such a process is by providing information about the places where they are set. As Buell suggests in his discussion of an American tradition of bioregional writing extending back to the nineteenth century, the work of writers such as Susan Fenimore Cooper and Celia Thaxter reflects a careful attention to the natural and cultural histories of their bioregions, offering knowledge of local flora, fauna, weather, and cultural practices that grew out of those local biological contexts. Henry Thoreau, whose literary works display an equal passion for accurate observation of natural phenomena, is perhaps an even better example. Right now, botanist Richard Primack is using Thoreau's detailed notes about the blooming dates of hundreds of plant species in the Concord, Massachusetts, area to study the effects of global climate change on the current flowering times of the same plants (Nijhuis).

Literature and other imaginative arts can also reflect, develop, celebrate, and protect the unique character of the bioregions that produce them. In "Living by Life: Some Bioregional Theory and Practice," writer Jim Dodge makes the case that bioregional practice falls into the two broad categories of renewal and resistance (10). As several contributors to this volume demonstrate, literature and stories can play a crucial role in renewing a sense of place among residents. Bioregionally specific books seldom become nationally known even among ecocritics, but they often enjoy a dedicated local readership. Banking on the popularity of regional literature, even big-chain bookstores such as Barnes & Noble feature a local interest section (typically located near the store's main entrance) whose titles include a mix of genres, from field guides to fiction. These texts enable residents of a place to recognize their bioregions as culturally and ecologically distinct and value them as such. In fact, it is the imagination that transforms mere space into place, as Serenella Iovino argues in her essay in this volume on Italy's Po Valley, and environmentally devastated regions like the one she describes especially need writers and other artists to lead the way in reimagining them as meaningful places worthy of attention and love. Other works of literature go beyond renewal and inspire residents to resist environmentally harmful practices. Rick Bass's *The Book of Yaak*, for example, not only testifies to the unique biotic and cultural character of Bass's home, the Yaak Valley in northwestern Montana, but also urges readers to speak out to their government representatives on behalf of the valley, which is threatened by extensive clear-cut logging. Though Bass includes nonresidents in his implied audience, he tells the inspiring story of how residents—both environmentalists and loggers—are working together to develop sustainable alternatives to clear-cutting and explains how all of his readers are implicated in the forces destroying the Yaak, elaborating on some of the economic and political connections that tie places together.

Works of literature and art can also provide models for how to reinhabit a bioregion or otherwise transform our relationships to places. A fine example is Freeman House's *Totem Salmon*, an account of a grassroots effort to restore the salmon population to the Mattole River in northern California, and thus to restore the ecological health of the entire watershed. If bioregional perception is more a certain kind of attention to place than a sense of identity that divides one place from another, as Ruth Blair suggests in this volume, bioregional literature reflects and inspires that kind of attention. *The Inland Island*, Josephine Johnson's memoir of restoring to ecological health a thirty-nine-acre former farm in southwestern Ohio, provides a striking example of a bioregional attention to place that considers nonhuman as well as human members of the community, the ugly as well as the beautiful, and above all refuses the false comfort of seeing her land as an "island" disconnected from other places around the globe. And there is a role for speculative works of literature, such as Ernest Callenbach's *Ecotopia* or Ursula K. Le Guin's *Always Coming Home*, which sketch out alternate modes of existence that can help us imagine both high-tech and low-tech ways to synchronize lifestyles to place.[8]

One might go so far as to argue that human imagination and stories create bioregions and other places, organizing human perception as people "recognize" and label the natural and cultural features that they use to define their places. However, for those pursuing bioregional reinhabitation, it's important to realize that every bioregion is already filled with stories and modes of discourse, not all of them obviously supportive of bioregional values. As Bart Welling emphasizes in his essay in this volume on Janisse Ray, literature such as Ray's memoirs of living in the American South can remind the environmentally inclined reader of the values and practices, including modes of discourse, that ordinary working people who live in that place embrace. A truly democratic bioregional reinhabitation would need to engage with and (in some cases) reimagine those practices, as Welling argues. In Leslie Marmon Silko's classic work of Native American literature, *Ceremony*, her protagonist, Tayo, has the profound revelation that the "world [is] made of stories, ... always changing and moving" (88). Art and literature can help us listen to the many voices that produce those stories and imagine—and reimagine—what it might mean to live adaptively in our places as they change.

If these are the ways that literature and art can function to produce and enrich a bioregional imagination, one might also ask how bioregional literature itself might be defined. It's helpful to compare bioregional literature with the more widely recognized category of regional writing. As Tom Lynch argues in *Xerophilia*, bioregionalism moves away from common regional designations such as "West," "Southwest," and "Northwest"; from a bioregional perspective, these terms have "no internally inherent meaning, but only describe a place by reference to its direction from some other, presumably more central, place. By contrast, bioregions are internally coherent rather than externally defined by their relationship to a distant urban reference point" (22). Lynch points out that conventional regional literature is most often composed for an audience of outsiders rather than for the residents of the region and thus is more likely to be a "literature of tourism" that highlights the odd and exotic and relies on generalities and stereotypes. As he explains, the authors of this literature tend to be "former residents of the hinterlands [who] move to the big city and write stories about the colorful if rapidly fading life they left behind" or "writers from the big cities [who] may move (often temporarily) to the hinterlands to write stories about their new abodes for the amusement and edification of an audience back home" (27). Bioregional literature, by contrast, is more likely to be oriented towards those who live in that bioregion. As Lynch puts it, "the implied reader is more likely to be a neighbor than a dweller in a remote city" (28).

Lawrence Buell also differentiates modern bioregional literature from traditional regional writing in *The Future of Environmental Criticism*, arguing that the former displays a "sense of vulnerability and flux" that is less pronounced in the latter (88). To support this point, he discusses Thomas Hardy's 1887 novel *The Woodlanders*, in which the "villagers' basic life-rhythms have scarcely changed for years and seem unlikely to do so in the future," despite disasters that befall individuals (88). In contrast, he offers Graham Swift's 1983 *Waterland*, in which the residents of the East Anglian fenlands experience the world as a less stable and more porous place and are clearly affected by the "shock waves" from political and technological developments of the wider world, often in ways that affect their whole region (88). As Buell argues, this sense of vulnerability in the face of worldwide forces of change means that "the bioregional horizon must extend beyond a merely local horizon; the locale cannot shut itself off from translocal forces even if it wanted to" (88).

A great deal of what might be termed *bioregional literature* has a significant impact on readers; bioregional literary criticism has an important role to play in enlarging the audience for and extending the life of these texts by keeping them on the radar. At the Planet Drum Foundation in San Francisco, a poem by Lew Welch is displayed on a wall of the office:

> Step out onto the Planet.
> Draw a circle a hundred feet round.
> Inside the circle are
> 300 things nobody understands, and, maybe
> nobody's ever really seen.
> How many can you find?
>> *Ring of Bone* (1973)

When asked about the poem, Peter Berg replied simply, "poetry changes consciousness." An important role of bioregionally minded critics is to identify literature such as Welch's poem that raises bioregional and biospheric awareness. By drawing attention to these imaginative works, critics and teachers "release the energy and power stored in poetry so that it may flow through the human community," to quote from William Rueckert, who coined the term *ecocriticism* (qtd. in Glotfelty and Fromm 109).

One might well ask how bioregional criticism differs from ecocriticism. Ecocriticism arose out of the desire to better understand how literature could make a difference in our environmental predicament: how it has contributed to the problem and might contribute to the solution. In the introduction to *The Ecocriticism Reader*, Cheryll Glotfelty defines *ecocriticism* as "the study of the relationship between literature and the physical environment" (xviii). More recently, in *Ecocriticism*, Greg Garrard proposes that ecocriticism is "the study of the relationship of the human and the non-human, throughout human cultural history and entailing critical analysis of the term 'human' itself" (5). Given bioregionalism's focus on what Stephen Frenkel has described as "developing communities integrated with ecosystems" (289), bioregional criticism clearly shares ecocriticism's general goals. However, its focus is more narrow, concentrating on how literary works relate to specific bioregions or contribute to bioregional practice and imagination. While the terrain of bioregional literary criticism remains largely unmapped, this volume charts several important paths.

Literary critics can contribute to the bioregional imagination by enlarging the boundaries of what counts as bioregional literature, drawing out the bioregional implications of texts that have not been seen this way before. They can also help to shape the ways readers approach texts, encouraging them to use categories and concepts that highlight bioregional issues and concerns. Indeed, many of the essays in this volume demonstrate that the way a reader approaches a text can make all the difference in whether or not its value for bioregionalism is unearthed.

Bioregional thinking consistently emphasizes practice and the ways theories and concepts emerge from the ground up. Consequently, bioregional literary criticism can encourage readers to connect the texts they read with their own lives, places, and practices, helping them imagine how to move, both physically and imaginatively, from the word to the world. Working against larger cultural impulses to experience literature and other art as simply entertainment, escape, or intellectual or aesthetic exercise, bioregionally concerned critics cultivate an awareness of the implications of these creative expressions for readers' lives in the here and now.

Bioregional literary critics can also challenge us to see the bioregional value in texts from a diversity of places different from our own. Stories of how humans can, as Cheney puts it, "be in the world" (119) sustainably necessarily differ from place to place, and it is important to go beyond the characteristics, values and practices currently associated with bioregionalism—thus far largely a development of the industrialized North and Australia—when defining bioregional literature. Perceptive critical readings of stories, poetry, and other art forms from diverse bioregions around the globe can productively expand many readers' sense of the crucial differences (both natural and cultural) between places and of the possibilities for bioregional literature and imagination.

Through the way they read bioregional literature, and the context within which they place those readings, literary critics can remind us of how our places are intertwined with other places and of the responsibilities that we owe to other places and the beings who inhabit them. As Mitchell Thomashow suggests in "Toward a Cosmopolitan Bioregionalism," those of us who have the privilege of becoming "rooted" in a place have a particular obligation to think of those caught up in the diasporas caused by war, global inequities and, more and more commonly, global climate change (123). And several contributors to this volume make the excellent point that staying in place has never been a sustainable lifestyle in large areas of the world, such as certain desert or Arctic regions. As Ursula Heise argues, we cannot ignore or eradicate the implications of globalization and modern technology and must develop a sense of place that embraces rather than retreats from a sense of planet.

And critics can use literature to help us reimagine bioregionalism itself. For example, works of criticism that explore texts by African American and Chicano writers may challenge (white, middle-class, North American) assumptions about what it means to live responsibly and responsively in a particular place and thus help cultivate an awareness of environmental justice and its importance to the democratic aspirations of the bioregional vision. A bioregional perspective, in turn, can remind readers and critics that texts grow out of the specific places that produced them (and their writers)—though certainly some texts make that more obvious than others. As Cheney emphasizes in his essay on the postmodern bioregional narrative, a bioregional approach to literature challenges the notion of universal truths and values—not in a nihilistic way that rejects truth and value in general, but rather by valuing contextual discourse, which is grounded in and expressive of the diversity of specific places, over what he calls totalizing discourse, which ignores diversity and "assimilate[s] the world to it" (120). By reflecting and respecting the context—both cultural and natural—of specific places, bioregional literature and criticism make a powerful statement that where you are matters.

MAPPING THE ESSAYS IN THIS VOLUME

The essays collected herein are grouped into four sections. Each begins with the prefix *re*. In this, we're reminded of the mantra "reduce, reuse, recycle." The contemporary era is often characterized by the prefix *post*, as in postmodern, postindustrial, and postcolonial. Whereas *post* defines an era by its break from the past, as we use it, *re* envisions not a simple return to the past but, rather, a creative salvaging, a new-old process that reorients us toward elegant adaptation.

Essays in the first section, Reinhabiting, narrate experiments in living-in-place and restoring damaged environments. In these efforts to create or re-create a life place, stories, writing, and publishing projects play an important role. Ideas guide actions, and actions in turn beget theory, or, ecosophy. The pieces in this section, then, show theory emerging from lived experience—growing from the ground up. The essays in section two, Rereading, practice bioregional literary criticism, drawing critical attention to certain texts—due to their strong ties to bioregional paradigms—and stimulating new ways of thinking about works less obviously bioregional. Place-conscious readings of texts explore the complex dynamics of language systems and ecosystems and of people and the more-than-human communities in which, like it or not, we are embedded. Section three, Reimagining, features theoretically inclined essays that in one way or another push bioregionalism to evolve—by expanding the bioregional corpus of texts, by coupling bioregional perspectives with other approaches, or by challenging bioregionalism's core constructs. We value these and other essays in the collection for their original thinking and ability to spark debate; intellectual diversity ensures that the bioregional field will not become a monoculture. Having opened the collection with essays on praxis—in the community and in the watershed—we conclude the volume with a return to praxis, this time in the academy. Teaching is an ancient form of bioregional practice, connecting generations, renewing culture, and sharpening the (in)sight of student and teacher alike. Section four, Renewal, includes four essays on bioregional pedagogy within the context of English courses, beginning with

local habitat studies and concluding with musings on the globally connected environment of the World Wide Web. Concluding this anthology
of original essays is Kyle Bladow's "Bioregional Booklist," which reviews
selected books and articles representing the origins, core tenets, tensions,
applications, and recent developments in bioregional thought.

We invite the reader to go straight to the essays; however, for those who
would like a sneak preview, the following abstracts provide a glimpse of
the terrain ahead.

I. REINHABITING

The first two essays reflect the influence of Gary Snyder, Pulitzer Prize–
winning poet and probably the best-known exponent of bioregionalism.
Thanks to the seminal influence of Snyder, who joined the faculty of UC
Davis in 1986, Davis, California, in the 1990s became a Camelot of bioregional culture and thought. In "Big Picture, Local Place: A Conversation with David Robertson and Robert L. Thayer Jr.," Cheryll Glotfelty
recounts highlights of an interview she conducted with Snyder's colleagues
David Robertson and Robert Thayer, important bioregional authors and
activists in their own right. Robertson and Thayer recall their own paths
to a bioregional framework, describe the Putah-Cache Bioregion Project,
which they spearheaded, and discuss art, culture, and literary criticism in
a local and global context.

In his personal essay "Still under the Influence: The Bioregional Origins
of the Hub City Writers Project" John Lane charts his trajectory as a native
of Spartanburg, South Carolina, who in 1978 headed west after college,
landing in Port Townsend, Washington, where he worked for Copper Canyon Press, early publishers of bioregional ideas. Returning to Spartanburg
and inspired by a conversation he had with Snyder, Lane sought to foment
a literary and environmental revolution in his hometown. Among other
activities, he cofounded the Hub City Writers Project, which has published
the work of four hundred local authors in fifty books that together "reveal
a place to itself."

Like John Lane in Spartanburg, Rinda West in Chicago has worked
in her community to realize bioregional goals. Founded in 1993, Chicago
Wilderness, an enormously successful coalition of more than 250 conservation organizations devoted to studying, restoring, protecting, and managing the natural ecosystems of the Chicago region, is an exemplary model
of one approach to reinhabitation. Rinda West's "Representing Chicago

Wilderness" analyzes the communication strategies of Chicago Wilderness's various publications pitched to different audiences. These publications and related volunteer activities seek to transform people's alienation from nature into a bioregional vision. The very name "Chicago Wilderness" redefines wilderness as the natural areas near our own neighborhoods, places that require active human assistance to preserve habitat and promote biodiversity.

Strategies of habitat restoration likewise come to the fore in "'To Become Beavers of Sorts': Eric Collier's Memoir of Creative Ecology at Meldrum Creek" by Norah Bowman-Broz, who reads Eric Collier's 1959 Canadian settler memoir, *Three Against the Wilderness*, through the lens of Félix Guattari's theory of ecosophy, expounded in *The Three Ecologies*. Collier's "bioregional restoration narrative" recounts his and his wife's efforts to restore the Meldrum Creek watershed by "becoming beavers" to repair broken beaver dams. Attuned to all three of Guattari's ecologies—the environment, social relations, and human subjectivity—the Colliers' success demanded detailed site-specific knowledge and cross-species thinking and resulted in strengthening the local community, an approach that would serve us well today.

If beaver dams are good for a river, hydroelectric dams can kill it, or at least kill the salmon. Chad Wriglesworth traces the confluence of poetry and place in the heavily dammed Columbia River Basin in his essay, "The Poetics of Water: Currents of Reclamation in the Columbia River Basin." In the 1930s and 1940s songwriters and novelists celebrated federal reclamation projects in the watershed, but since World War II, poetic resistance has mounted. Wriglesworth shows how the poetry of William Stafford, Ed Edmo, Elizabeth Woody, and Sherman Alexie enacts, documents, and resists the damming of the river and the loss of salmon runs, suggesting that poetry and public art may even be re-creating the river by contributing to policy change.

Like Bowman-Broz and Wriglesworth, Serenella Iovino focuses on a damaged watershed. The Po River Valley, Iovino's adoptive home, is one of the most industrialized, polluted, and contentious regions in Italy; today, it is less a *bio*region than a *necro*region, she observes in her essay, "Restoring the Imagination of Place: Narrative Reinhabitation and the Po Valley." Iovino believes that bioregionalism offers tools for restoring and revivifying such places. Drawing from Gregory Bateson's idea of an "ecology of mind," she formulates a philosophical construct of *narrative reinhabitation* and considers how the place-embedded works of Gianni Celati and Ermanno Rea restore imagination to the Po River Valley, opening the possibility of transforming this necroregion into an evolutionary landscape.

Bart Welling's essay, which concludes the section, describes an attempt—by author Janisse Ray—to reinhabit a different degraded region, the American South. Laying a foundation for bioregional literary theory, Welling in "'This Is What Matters': Reinhabitory Discourse and the 'Poetics of Responsibility' in the Work of Janisse Ray" evaluates the strengths and limitations of what he calls *reinhabitory discourse*, namely, a bioregionalist author's attempt to reinhabit not only a place, but the traditional discourses of that place, thereby opening up a genuine dialogue with the people who live there. Welling analyzes the way that Janisse Ray's two memoirs of growing up and returning to the American South employ tropes of southern hospitality and Judeo-Christian iconography, modeling what Donna Haraway in her work on "material-semiotic" encounters labels "response-ability."

II. REREADING

The Rereading section begins with three essays that study the poetics of writers with strong bioregional leanings (even if they don't use the term, per se). Christine Cusick's "Mapping Placelore: Tim Robinson's Ambulation and Articulation of Connemara as Bioregion" studies the narrative mapping project of Tim Robinson, a contemporary writer who moved to the Aran Islands in Ireland in 1972. He became deeply interested in the region and concerned that its placelore was becoming forgotten, so he set about mapping the Connemara bogland by physically walking it, closely observing its flora, fauna, and topography, and, importantly, recording the stories of local inhabitants. Cusick suggests that Robinson's attention to "a bioregional epistemology of place" enables him to maintain hope in human nature's "capacity for recovery."

What literary forms best serve the bioregional imagination? Narrative mapping? poetry? the novel? Harry Vandervlist suggests that the late Jon Whyte's unpublished *Minisniwapta*—an experimental, concrete poem about the Bow River—is one example of what a "bioregional poem" might look like in his contribution to this collection, "The Challenge of Writing Bioregionally: Performing the Bow River in Jon Whyte's *Minisniwapta: Voices of the River.*" Printed on a long ribbon of accordion-folded paper, *Minisniwapta* was intended to be the third in a projected five-volume epic, encyclopedic poem sequence that would present a comprehensive imaginative vision of the Canadian Rockies, near Banff. Vandervlist draws on Tim Cresswell's *Place* and a range of bioregional thinkers to illuminate how *Minisniwapta* reimagines conventional notions of place, river, and time.

In "Figures of Life: Beverley Farmer's *The Seal Woman* as an Australian Bioregional Novel" Ruth Blair's reading of Farmer's 1992 novel *The Seal Woman*—a "meticulous exploration" of Queenscliff, Australia—prompts Blair to speculate what a *bioregional novel* might be: a vehicle "through which the creative imagination and language form our relationships with place," especially via metaphor and myth. Blair rethinks the *local* in non-binary terms, not as a designated place in opposition to something larger, but rather as "naming a kind of attention." Bioregionalism is rather new and scientific sounding, Blair observes, but its discourse is ancient and has always included storytelling.

Demonstrating the potential of a bioregional perspective for critically re-reading literature from earlier periods, Heather Kerr, in "Melancholy Botany: Charlotte Smith's Bioregional Poetic Imaginary," offers a new reading of the popular eighteenth-century British Romantic poet Charlotte Smith. Concepts that are pertinent to bioregional criticism—that is, relations between the local and the global, political versus ecosystemic boundaries, imaginative and physical types of belonging—enable Kerr to analyze Smith's "melancholy poetics" and paradoxical "outsider-belonging." In broad strokes spanning multiple works across several microregions, Kerr couples the two discursive sets of sensibility and science to characterize Smith's "bioregional poetic imaginary."

Bioregionalism raises awareness of the multiple ways that regions are defined. "The Nature of Region: Russell Banks, New England, and New York" by Kent C. Ryden examines the implications of regional definitions on our reading practices as he first situates the novels of Russell Banks in the cultural region of New England, where Banks's work appears to be a neorealist critique of popular images of New England. He then reads the same novels in the context of the ecological region of the Northern Forest, where the wintry environment constrains economic opportunity, and where Banks's working-class characters are impoverished by their attachment to place.

The final pair of essays in this section are not grounded on earth, but rather make methodological forays to the speculative bioregions of imaginary planets and futuristic time horizons. David Landis Barnhill advocates a critical methodology that examines the "social structures, economic systems, and political power" that shape our bioregional habitats. These elements align bioregionalism with utopianism, he claims in his essay "Critical Utopianism and Bioregional Ecocriticism," in which Barnhill explains that critical utopianism aims to imagine not a perfect society but a "more perfect" one, whose articulations may be "self-reflexive, multivocal, and fragmented." Barnhill envisions a "utopian bioregional literary criticism" and applies it to Ursula K. Le Guin's speculative fictions *The Dispossessed* and *Always Coming Home*, the latter being her most fully realized vision of a bioregional utopia.

Despite their obvious differences, what do all bioregions have in common?, asks Daniel Gustav Anderson in "Critical Bioregionalist Method in *Dune*: A Position Paper." Today all bioregions are subject to the economic context of globalization, he argues, reading Frank Herbert's sci-fi novel *Dune* as an allegory of the exploitation of places and the subjugation of people by global—or, in this case, intergalactic—capital. Anderson proposes *critical bioregionalism* not as a critical lens through which to read texts as aesthetic objects but as a philosophy of praxis that harnesses the revolutionary energy of texts to build a bioregionally sustainable radical democracy.

III. REIMAGINING

The first two essays in the Reimagining section recommend that bioregional literary studies build a diverse canon and join forces with other critical approaches. In her essay—"'Los campos extraños de esta ciudad'/ 'The strange fields of this city': Urban Bioregionalist Identity and Environmental Justice in Lorna Dee Cervantes's 'Freeway 280'"—Jill Gatlin evaluates bioregionalist theory from the perspective of environmental justice. Her reading of Cervantes's urban poem "Freeway 280" analyzes how race and class inform a person's relationship to place. In the poem, an impoverished minority community produces urban bioregional knowledge that is crucial to sustainable regional life and food justice. Gatlin argues that including urban and minority literatures in the bioregionalist corpus both avoids producing "totalizing and potentially violent regional stories" and stands to help bioregionalism "reach its transformative potential though coalitional activism of diverse communities."

Erin James's "Bioregionalism, Postcolonial Literatures, and Ben Okri's *The Famished Road*" broadens the purview of bioregional literary criticism by asking what insights a bioregional reading of a postcolonial text might yield. James takes up Ben Okri's novel *The Famished Road*, set in the Yoruba homeland of Nigeria, a novel that has been criticized for its seeming lack of place specificity. James's analysis of the novel's postmodern form, supernatural spirits, meteorological and biological accuracy, and tropes of migration and uprootedness bring postcolonial and bioregional studies together, enriching both and illuminating "how place is imagined and lived in around the world."

The next two essays, each from a different side of the earth, challenge bioregionalism's tendency to privilege "staying put." Libby Robin's survey of place-conscious writing in Australia includes diverse ecological and economic "countries," including the wheat belt, the highway, islands, littoral zones, and desert. Reflecting on Australia's arid Red Centre in her essay, "Seasons and Nomads: Reflections on Bioregionalism in Australia," Robin argues that in some places nomadism is the best way to dwell or live-in-place, thus challenging bioregionalism's traditional advocacy of rootedness. "Bioregional thinking needs to embrace multiple ways to create communities," she contends, finding in the work of René Dubos a promising coupling of a global imagination with local, personal empowerment and direct contact with nature in diverse places.

As in the Australian outback, in the circumpolar North, labor—such as hunting and herding—often requires migration and mobility across the land, a pattern that bioregionalists who are attached to concepts of rootedness should note. Pavel Cenkl's piece, "Reading Climate Change and Work in the Circumpolar North," highlights writing by Inuit author Rachel Qitsualik and Sámi poet Nils-Aslak Valkeapää to explore the intricate relationship between people and place in the Arctic. Cenkl argues that it is through *work*—and critics' attending to work in literary representations of the region—that the inherent dynamism and fluidity of the North can best be observed.

The last pair of essays in this section likewise emphasize the inherent dynamism of ecosystems, the authors seeking to destabilize bioregionalism's seeming fixity on balance and boundaries. In "Douglas Livingstone's Poetry and the (Im)possibility of the Bioregion," Dan Wylie argues that the place-based poetry of marine biologist Douglas Livingstone—widely regarded as South Africa's premier poet—challenges traditional models of bioregionalism in several ways: the poems are intersected by global influences, evince little interest in utopian schemes of balance and harmony, and are as interested in humans as in nature. Reflecting on the littoral zone, Wylie finds the *ecotone* to be a more useful paradigm than the "container-like" bioregion, since the concept of the ecotone highlights flux, dynamism, porosity, turbulence, pluralism, mixing, conflict, and convergence.

Departing from bioregionalism's persistent focus on place, the final essay in this set considers species. The feral, which Anne Milne defines as both the domestic-going-wild and the wild-becoming-domestic, has been valued in philosophy, performativity, and psychoanalysis for its "beautiful resistance." In bioregional discourse, however, the feral often figures as an unwelcome or invasive intrusion. In "'Fully motile and AWAITING FURTHER INSTRUCTIONS': Thinking the Feral into Bioregionalism" Milne urges bioregionalism to welcome the feral as a reminder of the dynamism of ecosystems, "a dynamism that challenges the smug stagnation of knowing what should be there." She discusses the Canada goose, *Gulliver's Travels*, and Natalie Jeremijenko's project *Feral Robotic Dogs* as opening up possibilities for a feral bioregional imagination.

IV. RENEWAL

Thinking about species in a bioregional context continues to be the focus in the first essay of the concluding section, which includes four essays on bioregional pedagogy. In Laurie Ricou's seminar in English titled "Habitat Studies," each student becomes a scribe for a local species of plant or animal, researching its presence in literature, reading scientific studies of it, encountering it in the field, discovering its contemporary and historical uses, learning its names in different languages, and writing about it. In time, students "become" their species and learn to perceive the world from the standpoint of that plant or animal. "Out of the Field Guide: Teaching Habitat Studies," an innovative essay that positions the reader as one of Ricou's students, raises fundamental questions about language, perception, identity, and place.

Wes Berry, a Kentuckian teaching Kentuckians, has been influenced by Wendell Berry's work and Wes Jackson's call for universities to teach "homecoming." Aiming to cultivate bioregional awareness in his students, Berry begins his writing and literature courses by airing Kentucky myths and then proceeds to investigate the concrete realities of energy supply and demand, particularly the regional practice of mountain top removal (MTR) coal mining. As he explains in his essay, "Switching on Light Bulbs and Blowing Up Mountains: Ecoliteracy and Energy Consumption in General Education English Courses," by semester's end his students become aware of their own energy use—and inclined to conserve energy—realizing how their lifestyle choices connect them both to their own and to other places.

Connectivity takes on a digital dimension in Laird Christensen's "Teaching Bioregional Perception—at a Distance," in which he describes his distance education course on bioregional theory and practice. His far-flung students cultivate bioregional perception by grounding their case studies in their local bioregion, each producing both a deep history of his or her place and a narrative map of its borders. As unlikely as it may seem to teach bioregional precepts in cyberspace, Christensen makes a compelling and inspiring case that doing so is not only possible, but has distinct advantages.

Recognizing the electronic milieu that twenty-first-century college students inhabit, Kathryn Miles and Mitchell Thomashow, at Unity College in Maine, wondered whether place and community are relevant to the "Net Generation." Their contribution, "Where You at 20.0," describes a course they cotaught titled "The Future of Life on Earth" in which they investigated their students' environmental perceptions. Miles and Thomashow endorse the model of interconnectedness facilitated by the Internet and respect their students' intuitive grasp that we are all part of the same worldwide web and that *how* we live is as important as *where* we live.

Finally, we offer a "Bioregional Booklist," annotated by Kyle Bladow, to point readers to foundational books and key essays that reward further reading.

NOTES

1. Dan O'Brien, *Buffalo for the Broken Heart: Restoring Life to a Black Hills Ranch* (New York: Random House, 2002).

2. See p. 395 in this volume for the full text of the "Where You At?" quiz.

3. Frankly, if any area has been slighted in bioregional thinking and practice it has not been the city but the suburbs, and the absence of essays in this collection addressing the literature of suburbia certainly reflects that neglect. Almost by definition, suburbs seem anti-bioregional. And we offer the bioregionalism of suburbia as a topic for further exploration.

4. Indeed, it was Berg's participation in the 1972 U.N. Conference on the Human Environment in Stockholm (or rather the frustrating institutional blocks that *prevented* him and other nongovernmental representatives from participating) that led Berg to establish the *Planet* Drum foundation in 1973 (editors' emphasis).

5. Richard Evanoff's *Bioregionalism and Global Ethics* and Huey-Li Li's "Bio-

regionalism and Global Education: A Reexamination" argue that bioregional and global perspectives can and should work together.

6. The *WiserEarth.org* website, described as "a social network for sustainability," furnishes good examples of globally connected local NGOs working on issues of "social justice, indigenous rights, and environmental stewardship." *WiserEarth* provides infrastructure for locally based nonprofits to network and collaborate.

7. For early forays in bioregional literary criticism and theory see Armbruster; Kowalewski; Lindholdt; Lynch; and Robertson. See also the works cited by the contributors to this volume.

8. See David Landis Barnhill's essay in this volume for a discussion of critical utopias and *Always Coming Home* in particular.

WORKS CITED

Aberley, Doug, ed. *Boundaries of Home: Mapping for Local Empowerment.* Gabriola Island, B.C.: New Catalyst, 1993. Print.
————. "Interpreting Bioregionalism: A Story from Many Voices." McGinnis 13–42. Print.
Andruss, Van, Christopher Plant, Judith Plant, and Eleanor Wright, eds. *Home! A Bioregional Reader.* Philadelphia: New Society, 1990. Print.
Armbruster, Karla. "Bringing Nature Home: Josephine Johnson's *The Inland Island* as Bioregional Narrative." *Reading under the Sign of Nature: New Essays in Ecocriticism.* Ed. John Tallmadge and Henry Harrington. Salt Lake City: University of Utah Press, 2000. 3–23. Print.
Bass, Rick. *The Book of Yaak.* Boston: Houghton Mifflin, 1996. Print.
Bennett, Steve, Ruth Loetterle, Jay Kinney, Joe Kane, Art Kleiner, Stephanie Mills, and Stewart Brand. "Wha' Happenin'?" *CoEvolution Quarterly* 33 (1982): 97. Web. 17 Jan. 2011. http://wholeearth.com/issue-electronic-edition.php?iss=2033.
Berg, Peter. "Bioregion and Human Location." 1983. Rpt. in *Envisioning Sustainability.* San Francisco: Subculture Books, 2009. 91–97. Print.
Berg, Peter, ed. *Reinhabiting a Separate Country: A Bioregional Anthology of Northern California.* San Francisco: Planet Drum Foundation, 1978. Print.
Berg, Peter, Beryl Magilavy, and Seth Zuckerman. *A Green City Program for San Francisco Bay Area Cities and Towns.* San Francisco: Planet Drum Books, 1989. Print.
Berg, Peter, and Raymond Dasmann. "Reinhabiting California." *The Ecologist* 7.10 (1977): 399–401. Rpt. in Andruss, et al., 35–38. Print.
Buell, Lawrence. *The Environmental Imagination: Thoreau, Nature Writing, and the Formation of American Culture.* Cambridge, Mass.: Belknap Press of Harvard University Press, 1995. Print.

————. *The Future of Environmental Criticism: Environmental Crisis and Literary Imagination*. Malden, Mass.: Blackwell, 2005. Print.

Charles, Leonard, Jim Dodge, Lynn Milliman, and Victoria Stockley. "Where You At?" *CoEvolution Quarterly* 32 (1981): 3. Rpt. Andruss, et al., 29–30. Web. 17 Jan. 2011. http://wholeearth.com/issue-electronic-edition.php?iss=2032.

Cheney, Jim. "Postmodern Environmental Ethics: Ethics as Bioregional Narrative." *Environmental Ethics* 11 (Summer 1989): 117–33. Print.

Dodge, Jim. "Living by Life: Some Bioregional Theory and Practice." *CoEvolution Quarterly* 32 (1981): 6–12. Rpt. in Andruss, et al., 5–12. Print.

Evanoff, Richard. *Bioregionalism and Global Ethics: A Transactional Approach to Achieving Ecological Sustainability, Social Justice, and Human Well-being*. New York: Routledge, 2011. Print.

Frenkel, S. "Old Theories in New Places? Environmental Determinism and Bioregionalism." *Professional Geographer* 46.3 (1994): 289–95. Print.

Garrard, Greg. *Ecocriticism*. London: Routledge, 2004. Print.

Glotfelty, Cheryll, and Harold Fromm, eds. *The Ecocriticism Reader: Landmarks in Literary Ecology*. Athens: University of Georgia Press, 1996. Print.

Heise, Ursula K. *Sense of Place and Sense of Planet: The Environmental Imagination of the Global*. London: Oxford University Press, 2008. Print.

House, Freeman. *Totem Salmon: Life Lessons from Another Species*. Boston: Beacon, 1999. Print.

Johnson, Josephine W. *The Inland Island*. Illus. Mel Klapholz. New York: Simon and Schuster, 1969. Print.

Kelly, Kevin. "The Big Here." *KK* Kevin Kelly*. Creative Commons, 2011. Web. 26 July 2011.

Kowalewski, Michael. "Bioregional Perspectives in American Literature." *Regionalism Reconsidered*. Ed. David Jordan. New York: Garland, 1994. 252–79. Print.

Li, Huey-Li. "Bioregionalism and Global Education: A Reexamination." *Educational Theory* 53.1 (Winter 2003): 55–73. Print.

Lindholdt, Paul. "Literary Activism and the Bioregional Agenda." *ISLE: Interdisciplinary Studies in Literature and Environment* 3.2 (Fall 1996): 121–37. Print.

Low, Setha M., and Denise Lawrence-Zúñiga, eds. *The Anthropology of Space and Place: Locating Culture*. Malden, Mass.: Blackwell, 2003. Print.

Lynch, Tom. *Xerophilia: Ecocritical Explorations in Southwestern Literature*. Lubbock: Texas Tech University Press, 2008. Print.

McGinnis, Michael Vincent, ed. *Bioregionalism*. London: Routledge, 1999. Print.

McKibben, Bill. *Eaarth: Making a Life on a Tough New Planet*. New York: Times Books, 2010. Print.

Murphy, Patrick. *Ecocritical Explorations in Literary and Cultural Studies: Fences, Boundaries, and Fields*. Lanham, Md.: Lexington, 2009. Print.

Nijhuis, Michelle. "Teaming Up with Thoreau." *Smithsonian* 38.7 (October 2007): 60–65. Print.

Robertson, David. "Bioregionalism in Nature Writing." *American Nature Writers* v. 2. Ed. John Elder. New York: Scribner's, 1996. 1013–24. Print.

Rueckert, William. "Literature and Ecology: An Experiment in Ecocriticism." *Iowa Review* 9.1 (Winter 1978). Rpt. in Glotfelty and Fromm, 105–24.

Sale, Kirkpatrick. *Dwellers in the Land: The Bioregional Vision.* 1985. Athens: University of Georgia Press, 2000. Print.

Silko, Leslie Marmon. *Ceremony.* 1977. New York: Penguin, 2006. Print.

Snyder, Gary. *Axe Handles.* New York: North Point, 1983. Print.

———. *Danger on Peaks.* Berkeley, Calif.: Counterpoint, 2003. Print.

———. *A Place in Space: Ethics, Aesthetics, and Watersheds.* Berkeley, Calif.: Counterpoint, 1995. Print.

———. *The Practice of the Wild: Essays.* Berkeley, Calif.: Counterpoint, 1990. Print.

Thayer, Robert L., Jr. *LifePlace: Bioregional Thought and Practice.* Berkeley: University of California Press, 2003. Print.

Thomashow, Mitchell. *Bringing the Biosphere Home: Learning to Perceive Global Environmental Change.* Cambridge, Mass.: MIT Press, 2002. Print.

———. "Toward a Cosmopolitan Bioregionalism." McGinnis 121–32.

Welch, Lew. "Step out onto the Planet." *Ring of Bone: Collected Poems 1950–1972.* Ed. Donald Allen. Bolinas, Calif.: Grey Fox Press, 1973. Print.

WiserEarth. WiserEarth, 2011. Web. 26 July 2011.

PART ONE

Reinhabiting

CHERYLL GLOTFELTY

Big Picture, Local Place

A Conversation with David Robertson and Robert L. Thayer Jr.

THE BUILDINGS OF THE UC Davis campus assert their verticality amid the flat, agricultural fields of California's Central Valley. Shrouded in bone-chilling, thick gray Tule fog for much of the winter, Davis is then baked by kilnlike heat in summer. With the sublime Sierra Nevada mountains ninety minutes to the east and the hip San Francisco Bay Area ninety minutes to the west, Davis appears as a podunk exit off of Interstate 80 on the way to somewhere else. Surprising, then, that in the 1990s Davis became a Camelot of place-based culture and bioregional thought, looked to as a model by other communities across the country. What happened and how? To find out, I conducted a joint interview in July 2008 with emeritus professors David Robertson and Robert L. Thayer Jr. Robertson, former chair of the UC Davis English Department, is cofounder and first director of UCD's innovative Nature and Culture Program and author of several books, including *West of Eden: A History of the Art and Literature of Yosemite* (1984) and *Real Matter* (1997), a personal inquiry into the meanings to be found in mountains, as illuminated by the works of Mary Austin, Jack Kerouac, and Gary Snyder. Thayer, a landscape architect, is the author of *Gray World, Green Heart: Technology, Nature, and Sustainable Landscape* (1994) and *LifePlace: Bioregional Thought and Practice* (2003), an important book that codifies major concepts of the bioregional movement and relates these ideas to the Putah-Cache watershed, of which Davis is a part. This article quotes highlights from our conversation as I review the lives and professional trajectories of Robertson and Thayer, focusing on how each found his way to a bioregional perspective. I then chart the evolution and activities of the Putah-Cache Bioregion Project (1993–2001), which Robertson and Thayer pioneered and regard as one of the most exciting endeavors of their careers. The article concludes by taking a philosophical turn as we discuss art, culture, and literary criticism in a local and global context.

David Robertson and his wife, Jeannette, kindly offered their home in Davis as a quiet place where we could meet to tape our conversation. They live in Village Homes, a 1970s ecofriendly subdivision that features passive solar homes, community parks and gardens, shared fruit and nut trees and vineyards, and frequent neighborhood potluck dinners on the commons. David and Jeannette had recently xeriscaped their fenced, front courtyard, and they showed me a small vegetable garden in their unfenced backyard, which borders a community walking path and, beyond it, a sprawling common lawn. A sprightly little pomegranate tree by the back patio, bearing exquisite fruit, seemed somehow symbolic. The neighborhood felt quiet,

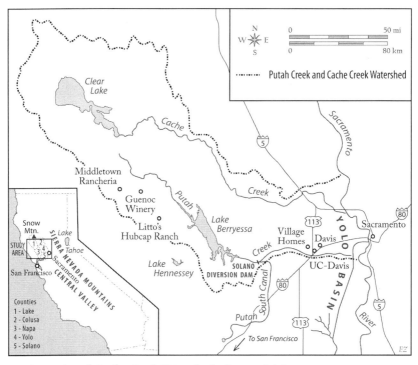

Putah Creek and Cache Creek Watersheds, Davis, California

Robert Thayer Jr. and David Robertson. Photograph by Stephanie Thayer, used with permission.

safe, and settled, graced with mature trees that almost entirely shade the intentionally narrow streets (reducing asphalt surface area), streets named for people or places in Tolkien's Middle Earth—Goldberry Lane, Oakenshield Road, Bombadil Lane, Bucklebury Road. Rob Thayer lives just down the street from the Robertsons. In front of his house was a "Free stuff" sign beside a pile of household appliances, old skis, books, and do-it-yourself gadgets. I spotted several kayaks suspended under the awning of Rob's covered driveway and an assortment of bicycles leaning against the walls. *An active family*, I observed, *and not too worried about theft*. When we convened around the Robertsons' coffee table and started the tape recorder, our talk meandered comfortably for nearly three hours, like the winding lanes in Village Homes itself.

TOWARD A BIOREGIONAL PERSPECTIVE: TWO TRAJECTORIES

In their educational histories and career paths, neither David nor Rob made a beeline for bioregionalism, to say the least. I asked them to recount the twists and turns of their careers that eventually drew them to a bioregional focus. David, who at seventy-one is inspiringly limber in mind and body, describes his professional life as "a good example of doing some creative stuff, followed by some panic because I didn't think I could pull it off, followed by some creative stuff, followed by 'oh, gotta retreat.'" In high school, Robertson decided to become a Methodist minister, so he went to Yale. About halfway through Yale he began to have doubts about "this Christianity stuff"; nevertheless, after graduating he made "a classic regressive move" and entered the Perkins School of Theology in Dallas, connected with Southern Methodist University (SMU). While there, Robertson became interested in the Bible and particularly in Hebrew. He was caught up in a kind of Holy Grail search for the key to unlock the ancient scriptures, thinking that if only one could learn Hebrew, one could decipher the truth of the sacred texts of long ago. After seminary, David earned an MA at the University of Toronto in Ancient Near Eastern Languages and returned to Yale for a PhD in the same field. His dissertation used linguistic evidence to date ancient texts written in Biblical Hebrew. Dr. David then made another "classic regression" and took a job at SMU, thinking that he wanted to work at a school where church was important. But, as he says, "It was a bad, bad decision." After three years at SMU, he recalls, "It was abundantly clear that not only was I not a liberal Christian, I wasn't a Christian at all." He remembers the precise moment, sitting in his study, when he said to himself, "You're not a Christian. This is some sort of charade you're going through. You don't believe this stuff."

So then David made what seems to him "an extremely logical switch. If you're interested in the Bible—and much of the Bible is *very* good literature—why not make the move to literature?" Which he did. He went to UC Irvine for a PhD in English and Comparative Studies, writing a dissertation that, he says, "can be summarized in one sentence: 'Wallace Stevens is Isaiah in the twentieth century who doesn't believe in God.'" A modernist, David was hired at UC Davis, in part because he could teach their "Bible as Literature" course. After writing *The Old Testament and the Literary Critic*, the book that earned him tenure in 1977, David decided to pay attention to literature about northern California. In the late 1970s, David heard Gary Snyder give a reading at a coffee house in Davis, and, intrigued, he began a correspondence with Snyder. Meanwhile, due to a serendipitous fluke, the Yosemite Natural History Association commissioned David to write a book on the art and literature of Yosemite. David knew that Gary Snyder had written some of his very earliest poetry in Yosemite while working on a trail crew there in 1955, so he interviewed Snyder for *West of Eden*. Hence, by the time Snyder joined the UC Davis faculty in 1986, the two of them had already formed a friendship, which deepened as they worked together to get the Nature and Culture Program off the ground. After the Yosemite book, David embarked on a similar type of research project to study the art and literature of the big places of California, such as Mount Shasta, Sequoia, and Tahoe. He worked on this book for several years before making a precipitous decision to abandon it. As David tells the story, sometime in 1991 or 1992 he was sitting up in his office when he suddenly said to himself, "This is a dead end! You're not *going* anywhere. You don't have *anything* to say other than what you've already said about these big places. I think the thing to do is turn to home."

Like David, Rob Thayer pays homage to Gary Snyder as having had a formative influence on his thinking. Sixty years old and athletic, Rob fizzes with such a surplus of physical and mental energy that he periodically bangs out impromptu drumrolls on the coffee table. An engineer by training, Rob started out as a product designer in the aerospace industry, designing zero-gravity space toilets and kitchens, tasked by his bosses at Grumman to devise ways of keeping people alive on a space flight to Mars. In designing systems for spacecraft, Rob "got this concept of closed-loop ecosystems—not spam in the can but ecosystems in the can. You are recycling everything." But, as he recalls, "I realized mid-way through '69 and '70 that I wanted out of the aerospace industry as soon as I could. I was going to work for the defense system by day and on the weekends I was going down and protesting the war in Washington D.C." As soon as he could swing it, Rob left industry for graduate school at Stanford, where he earned his MA in urban design, writing a thesis on an "ecosystemic house," a house designed to make visible how living systems are connected; anyone living in the house would become aware that "your shit turned into soil, which turned into food, which went into your mouth, which turned into shit." Soon after he received his degree in urban design, Rob made a lateral move to landscape architecture—"crashing the profession from the side door"—a field that allowed him to be the broadest thinker possible. Hired in 1973 at UC Davis, Rob drew on his background in physics to study technology. When windmills were installed at Altamont Pass, Tehachapi, and other places in California, Rob brought a landscape architect's perspective to the study of wind energy, "a regenerative, sustainable, highly *visible* technology, as opposed to the obscure, fossil-fuel, guilt-ridden, let's-put-it-way-over-in-the-corner" alternatives. Rob's first book, *Gray World, Green Heart: Technology, Nature and the Sustainable Landscape*, analyzes the conflict of three forces in our lives and in the landscape—love of nature (topophilia), love of and dependence on technology (technophilia), and fear of technology (technophobia)—pointing to sustainable design (years before "sustainability" became popular) as a promising future direction.

While Rob was writing *Gray World, Green Heart* two pivotal experiences moved him toward a bioregional framework for organizing his ideas about sustainable landscape planning. The first occurred in 1987, when Rob invited Gary Snyder to talk to his class about place issues. As Rob recalls with a chuckle, the class met "in this dumpy old room where people sewed and made dresses and things, and all the chairs were polyglot and were scattered everywhere. And one day I walked in there and they were all lined up, and there were these Klieg lights and a podium and somebody was fooling around, and I said, 'Excuse me, but this is my *class* meeting in here, and I have a guest speaker coming. What are you doing in my classroom?' He said, 'Oh, I'm Gary Snyder's archivist.' He had arranged everything, oh-so-sophisticated." Gary instructed Rob's class, "I want you to write your address using only bioregional nomenclature." At that time Rob was drafting his book on technology and sustainability, and Gary's talk about place, identification, and reinhabitation led Rob to the insight that "sustainability *had* to be bounded by a local space" or at least "approached in a relativistic sense of scale." For example, he explains, "It's easier to provide renewable energy for 200,000 people than for 200 million people just from a logistics standpoint. Two hundred thousand people is roughly downtown Sacramento. You could do that by putting PVs on everybody's roof and taking some of the rice hulls they ship down to the port and making them into some sort of biofuel. But when you do it for 200 million or on the scale of the country, the scale issues and pure physics of scale are such that it's just more difficult. Or, if you're trying to repair the Klamath River Basin, you can *only* do it by looking at the basin itself. And you've somehow got to VAT [value-added tax] how much are potatoes worth, and how much are salmon worth? Do you give free water to the people growing potatoes at a discount, or do you allow the water to flow down, and you have a fishing industry? Those kinds of naturally scaled issues, both in terms of energetics and in terms of managing multiple species and multiple resource regions, in addition to culturally asking people, 'what scale do you identify with most?'—I think all of those reasons point towards a localized view." "For a landscape architect to start thinking locally or bioregionally," Rob contends, "is very, very appropriate because whenever you're teaching landscape architecture at a university you're using the local region as a test laboratory. So it fits like a glove." Rob thinks of the bioregion as the best venue for conserving energy and growing food. To him a bioregional perspective toward land-use planning "is *so logical*."

While Snyder's talk pushed Rob intellectually toward a bioregional framework, other events were moving him personally in the same direction: "I had children. I lived here in Village Homes. I was rooting. I felt rooted. I had gotten involved in these nonprofit things." And, importantly, Rob found himself recreating near home: "I would head west. I would go paddle in Putah Creek. I'd ride my mountain bike up at Snow Mountain, and I'd go hiking up Snow Mountain. I started paddling Lake Hennessey, and I never wanted to ride across the traffic of Sacramento to go up to the Sierras." He believes that the subject of local recreation—"re-creation"— and the related idea of a "stay-cation," which scholars of leisure studies toyed with during the oil embargo of the 1970s, are fertile areas for renewed study as we enter an era of dwindling resources. Local recreation led to the second pivotal moment on Rob's path to a bioregional paradigm: "When my son Doug was eleven, which would have put it at 1992, we were mountain biking and he was saying, 'Dad, let's find the headwaters of Putah Creek.' I didn't find the headwaters of Putah Creek until 1992! We drove up there and found that it was a Douglas fir, ponderosa pine, and black oak forest with 4,000–5,000-foot mountains. I'm going, 'This is our watershed?!' It was astonishing."

THE PUTAH-CACHE BIOREGION PROJECT

In 1993, not long after Rob's epiphany at the headwaters of Putah Creek and David's major decision to turn to home in his work, they and a few others began meeting for lunch on a weekly basis. The lunch conversations were stunning. Rob exclaims, "I used to come out of there with the hair standing up on the back of my neck. I think it was the most exciting thing I've ever done." David nods in agreement. David Robertson was the leader and de facto chair of the group, its "godfather" or "kingpin" as Rob puts it. Other regular members included Dennis Pendleton, head of UC Davis's Public Service Research Program, aimed at "fostering environmental and civic engagement through university and community partnerships" (*Public Service Research Program*). Dennis had close ties to political leaders in Sacramento and to other biodiversity and watershed groups across the West. Joyce Gutstein, associate director of the Public Service Research Program, was chiefly interested in science education and in collaborating with public agencies to put a uniform message out to the public. Professor Peter Moyle, of uc Davis's Wildlife, Fish, and Conservation Biology Department, was a fish biologist who also wrote poetry. The group of five, then, brought a wide range of disciplinary perspectives to the table—art and literature, landscape architecture, environmental planning and politics, education, and biology. "From the word *go*," Rob explains, "the idea was to break barriers—disciplinary boundary dissolution. We wanted to break the barriers between the community and the academy. David used to say repeatedly, 'It would be a terrible mistake to assume that truth only lies within the academy.' On numerous occasions we had people from external to the university come in. We had two Lake Miwok guys from the Middletown Rancheria come down, and they were completely dumbfounded that professors would ask them to come down to talk about anything important. We had lots of that happen; we brought in lots of people from outside. We wanted to dissolve disciplinary boundaries between research and teaching and outreach, between nature, culture, planning, design, science, poetry, and art. We were trying to get the university to think more broadly disciplinarily-wise and more locally geographically-wise, which is the exact opposite of what the university does." David concurs, "The basic notion that knowledge, if it's knowledge, is universal means that in practice you tend to minimize the local." "Fortunately," he adds, "Davis, as a university campus, is rather more committed to its local area than many universities are."

A big break for the group came in 1997, when the uc chancellor awarded $450,000 to a joint proposal by David Robertson and Peter Moyle for the Putah-Cache Bioregion Project, recognizing their nature-and-culture type of proposal as an enterprising new direction in environmental studies. David and Peter divided the money among the five core members of the lunch group. Peter Moyle hired graduate students to inventory and monitor the fisheries resources in the Putah and Cache watersheds. Rob began doing a landscape assessment of the bioregion, hiring a graduate of the landscape architecture program to develop a gis database and draw "a whole bunch of maps" of the watershed—maps of topography, hydrology, watershed boundaries, land ownership, vegetation, natural diversity, land use, roads, farmlands, and traditional Native American territories.[1] Joyce Gutstein funded graduate students to work on education, starting an organization that still exists called the Putah Creek Discovery Corridor Cooperative. Dennis Pendleton used resources to further regional policy and planning and to strengthen contacts between the university and watershed stakeholders' groups such as the Blue Ridge-Berryessa Natural Area group. David funded and directed a Bioregional Artists-in-Residence program with the assumption that "if you want people to relate emotionally to something, get them to make art, get them to write about it. It's a bonding experience." An MA student in writing, María Meléndez, who became a participant in the Bioregion Project talks, got a grant to go to the Bodega Bay Marine Lab and work with a grasslands ecologist; the product of her grant was a series of poems, a perfect example, David says, of "a way in which we tried to get science and the humanities and the arts connected." Another graduate student, Jan Goggans, was funded to interview local farmers; her dissertation in English analyzed the photographs of Dorothea Lange. Another student, Dan Leroy, wrote a master's thesis on a project he called Restoria, focusing on the process of restoring a length of Putah Creek. One can get a more complete sense of the assorted activities, publications, artworks, and programs that the Putah-Cache Bioregion Project spawned by selecting "Bioregion" on the menu of UC Davis's Public Service Research Program website, which describes the Bioregion Project as "an integrated interdisciplinary suite of research and educational activities in the Putah and Cache Creek watersheds, the 'home region' of UC Davis. The overall goal is to develop foundations for community planning, resource management, and partnerships in the watershed. The project involves faculty, students, and staff from diverse departments and connects with community, organizational, and public groups in the region" (*Public*).

Amid this creative efflorescence of bioregional activity, two projects deserve special mention. While David champions writing and art as activities that bond a person to a place, Rob propounds a parallel view: "If you want somebody to understand where they're from, you've got to *take them to it*." Accordingly, Rob and David developed a 225-mile circumdrive of the Putah and Cache watersheds and for eight consecutive years led an annual all-day tour of the route, stopping frequently at designated sites to tell stories about the region from as many disciplinary perspectives as one can imagine, with stops and stories at the Solano Diversion Dam, the Putah Creek headwaters, Clear Lake, Guenoc Winery, Litto's Hubcap Ranch, and many others. Ritual chanting at certain stops tied the tour to the tradition of the ancient Yamabushi sect in Japan, who circumambulated their sacred mountains clockwise, stopping to chant at specific places. Rob produced a map and interpretive text (available online) that enables people to make the tour themselves, providing information keyed to each of the twenty-two stops. The guide concludes with the friendly injunction: "If you began at Davis and continued through each region, you have now toured our 'sibling' creeks, Putah and Cache, from source to outflow. Welcome to your bioregion, your 'life-place.' Learn about it, enjoy it, take care of it, and practice the best way to live here" (Thayer, "Yolo Basin").

Rob's circumdrive guide became the skeleton of a much larger, collaborative project, titled *Putah and Cache: A Thinking Mammal's Guide to the Watershed*, edited by Amy J. Boyar, Jan Goggans, Daniel Leroy, David Robertson, and Rob Thayer. This remarkable compilation, available free online, includes just over one hundred chapters, organized around the circumdrive and pursuing a wealth of intellectual tributaries, including natural history, historical documents, and creative writing tied to the region—with an appendix of haiku poetry about Tule fog! *Putah and Cache* provides an intellectual and artistic complement to the embodied experience of getting out into the region. The guide also constitutes a record of the activities and emphases of the Putah-Cache Bioregion Project itself, whose three years of funding ended in 2000. Since that time, David has combined his skills as an artist-photographer-writer to produce a series of self-published "See-Change" postcards, playing cards, calendars, and avant-garde guidebooks to particular places at home and abroad, such as his recent *On the Road Ecology: Memoirs of EcoHuman*. Rob has come full circle to his early work on energy flows and the "big physics" of sustainability, keen to undertake another collaborative, synergistic writing project.

BIG-PICTURE BIOREGIONALISM—ART, CULTURE, AND LITERARY CRITICISM

In the summer of 2008, when our conversation took place, oil prices had recently doubled, and the specters of peak oil and climate change were convincing Rob Thayer that, like it or not, people are going to be forced to re-localize, because the cost of moving people and things around will become prohibitively high.[2] Localism—which includes the local foods movement, remanufacturing, energy conservation, and alternative energy—raises one of the great puzzles of bioregionalism, and that is how to pay attention to the local and build a sustainable local culture without becoming narrowly provincial or exclusionary; in other words, how can we become place-based global thinkers? David tells a story about a trip he and Jeannette took to Alaska, which illustrates how a fruitful, local-global dialogue can happen—or fail to happen—in art: "If you go into the art galleries in Homer [Alaska], you find that it's clear that the artists are paying a great deal of attention to the local landscape and not any attention whatsoever to worldwide art movements. So the art is *way* behind the times in terms of technique and aesthetics. So then we went to an extraordinary exhibit in the City of Anchorage Museum, and they had an exhibit of native artists who had spent some time and had some training in New York, Paris, and London, but were *doing* indigenous, local kinds of stuff. The museum had the foresight to put together an exhibit of very traditional, half-a-century-to three-centuries-old indigenous art in one space. And in the other space were these guys who were looking at this, but were also looking at world-wide art. So my dream would be to get artists who are paying attention to the local area and landscape and issues but are cognizant of what's going on in the global art movement, so that you don't get what you get in Homer, which is a series of *very pretty* pictures of mountains and glaciers, of which you have seen maybe a hundred thousand already."

David thus espouses a very broad conception of bioregional engagement, which includes travel and information exchange via the World Wide Web. As he explains, "I think Gary [Snyder]'s got the right move here. He said, 'Well, my bioregion is Kitkitdizze. My bioregion is San Juan Ridge. My bioregion is northern California. My bioregion is where Doug fir grows. My bioregion is transpolar bear stories. It's the earth. And it's the solar system.' That's the nice thing about it—it's nested." In a brilliant essay on "Bio-regionalism in Nature Writing" for the Scribner's *American Nature Writers* reference work, David invokes the mandala to symbolize the ultimate oneness of nature and Nature, the specific and the universal, explaining during our conversation that such a view is, for him, a religious one: "One day in the past I decided I was no longer Christian. I no longer believed in any kind of afterlife. I no longer believed in any kind of God, in a Western sense, anyway. But it would be a *very* big mistake for anybody to conclude that I went from being religious to not being religious. I'm a *fundamentally* religious person. I would be willing to define what I mean by religion very, very loosely as someone who has this habit of paying attention to the big picture . . . to combine the specific with a very broad attempt to pay attention to the world and respond to it."

David's tendency to think of the big picture inflects his vision of how a bioregional approach to literary criticism might differ from other kinds of critical approaches. He points out that "almost all literary criticism is place-based. Look at *any* book on *any* writer. Faulkner could be Exhibit A. You can't write about Faulkner without paying attention to Mississippi. But the tendency is to reference Mississippi, or bears in Mississippi, or opossums in Mississippi, or white people–black people, or drugstore people, as kind of 'well they're there, but we're not going to pay a lot of attention to them.' What I think bioregional criticism can do is say, 'what we're going to do is pay attention to this broad context, *very* broad context that includes everything that's out there' and turn regionalism into a kind of bioregionalism, where, in this case, what you mean is *everything* that's in a place, including the author and the novel that the author writes. The emphasis of literary criticism is to say, 'You need to pay attention to Oxford if you're going to understand Faulkner. So we'll go to Oxford and try to learn something, but always the *referent* is Faulkner's novel.' I think bioregionalism would say, 'we'll pay attention to Faulkner's novel, but the *referent* is the total scene.'"

Rob Thayer, who up to this point had been dubious about the literary criticism currently in vogue, suddenly caught on: "That's a fundamental figure-ground issue! It's a landscape ecology issue! It's a matrix-patch issue, patch being the author, matrix being place. If you just looked at patches then you're really not looking ecologically. But if you look at a patch within a matrix then you are looking ecologically." My own doubts had more to do with the disciplinary placement of the kind of approach to literature that David was proposing, as I commented, "What some people might say, David, is that your notion of bioregional literary criticism more properly belongs in the discipline of human ecology than in an English department, because English departments look at the properties of literary works. And you're more interested in looking at a place. Granted, one of the elements of the place is this imaginative construction, but the *focus* becomes the place, which for you takes on a synecdotal relationship with the universe. By really getting to know this place, studying this place—including the role of authors and literary works in this place—you have this window onto the universe. But some people would say that your notion of bioregional literary study, where you're not studying Oxford to understand the novel, you're bringing the novel to an understanding of Oxford, would move the whole enterprise over into some other field like human ecology or cultural geography."

David, whose training in ancient religions affords him a long view, replied sanguinely, "Well that would be fine with me. Most people don't realize how short a time ago English departments came into existence. The study of English the way we do it is a century-and-a-half old if that. So things change. I've often said to people who ask about the English Department at Davis, 'The English Department at Davis doesn't exist.' They call it the English Department, but *nobody* does literary criticism the way in which it was done a hundred years ago, much less 125 to 150 years ago. And so, in fact, the whole English Department is turning into something in which literature is not necessarily the primary focus but is auxiliary to some other larger study of culture—cultural studies. And I think it's great." Catching on, I added, "And *we* would like to say, *bio*cultural studies, because we're not just interested in the human layer but in the whole fabric."

"Exactly," David agreed, and it was time for lunch. Jeannette had prepared a delicious dish from a recipe passed down from David's mother—chicken salad mixed with grapes and chopped celery, topped with a sauce made from curry powder and soy sauce, and sprinkled with locally grown roasted almonds.

NOTES

1. These maps are available online via links from the "The Putah-Cache Bioregion Project: Mapping & GIS" page on the *Public Service Research Program* website.

2. Thayer argues that the rising cost of transporting people and goods is creating for the first time in history an expanding world; see his essay "The Word Shrinks, The World Expands: Information, Energy and Relocalization."

WORKS CITED

Boyer, Amy J., Jan Goggans, Daniel Leroy, David Robertson, and Rob Thayer, eds. *Putah and Cache: A Thinking Mammal's Guide to the Watershed.* University of California, 2001. Web. 24 Mar. 2010.

Public Service Research Program. University of California, Davis, 2009. Web. 24 Mar. 2010.

Robertson, David. "Bioregionalism in Nature Writing." *American Nature Writers* v. 2. Ed. John Elder. New York: Scribner's, 1996. 1013–24. Print.

———. *The Old Testament and the Literary Critic*. Philadelphia: Fortress Press, 1977. Print.

———. *On the Road Ecology: Memoirs of EcoHuman*. Gorham Printing. David Robertson, 2008. Print.

———. *Real Matter*. Salt Lake City: University of Utah Press, 1997. Print.

———. *West of Eden: A History of the Art and Literature of Yosemite*. Yosemite Natural History Association. Berkeley: Wilderness Press, 1984. Print.

Robertson, David, and Robert L. Thayer Jr. Personal interview. Davis, California. 9 July 2008.

Thayer, Robert L., Jr. *Gray World, Green Heart: Technology, Nature, and Sustainable Landscape*. New York: Wiley, 1994. Print.

———. *LifePlace: Bioregional Thought and Practice*. Berkeley: University of California Press, 2003. Print.

———. "The Word Shrinks, The World Expands: Information, Energy and Relocalization." *Landscape Journal* 27.1 (2008): 9–22. Print.

———. [Robert Thayer] "Yolo Basin Wetlands and Putah Creek Outflow." *Putah and Cache: Circumdrive Stops*. University of California, 2001. Web. 24 Mar. 2010.

JOHN LANE

Still under the Influence

The Bioregional Origins of the Hub City Writers Project

I N THE LATE 1970S, I spent a year on the West Coast, and it was as close as I ever got to counterculture. During college, from 1973 until 1977, I stayed pretty close to the middle of the cultural road—short hair and plenty of beer but no pot or LSD. If the doors of my perception were cleansed, it was by poetry.

My friend John Featherston, certifiably one of Spartanburg's first hippies, says I really didn't miss much. There never really was a "counterculture" in upstate South Carolina. Instead, John calls what was afoot in Spartanburg in the 1970s a "subculture." There was an old lady at Sky City, a local department store, who would order albums with "wild swirling covers" only on request, and the local music hall, called The Sitar, had a "Tune in, Turn on, Drop out" poster on the wall, but the owners booked beach music bands because people still wanted to dance the shag.

John says the leather shop he ran sold rolling paper under the counter, but the ceramic pot pipes they made in the back room were for "export" to Columbia, Charlotte, and Charleston, not for the local retail market. There was a true cultural divide in the 1970s between the South and rest of the country. It was if there was an intellectual iron curtain at the Mason-Dixon line. Ideas like bioregionalism were probably stopped at the border.

Then in the summer of 1978 I left Spartanburg, South Carolina. I was a young southern poet just out of Wofford College. My head was full of the high modernists—Pound, Eliot, Williams, H.D.—and my heart full of hope for breaking into print. I went west.

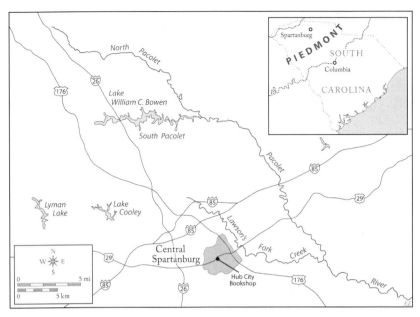

Spartanburg, South Carolina, and portions of the Carolina Piedmont Bioregion

I moved to Port Townsend, Washington, and the locals thought I was truly from another country. The morning I hitchhiked into town, I ordered breakfast on Water Street and the waitress returned with my plate of eggs and hash browns, considered my polite southern "Thank you, ma'am," then asked, "Are you from Australia?" For me the new pleasures of life in Port Townsend were sometimes too much for a conventional southerner to take. After I rented a room from a vegetarian poet, I tried meatless meals with him, but soon resorted to sneaking out once a week to the local A&W Root Beer stand for a cheeseburger.

I was searching for a literary scene, and I found one in Port Townsend. But the scene I found was not centered in publications so much as publishing, printing, and a type of emerging social West Coast activism I soon discovered was called "bioregionalism." I didn't realize it right away, but moving to Port Townsend had landed me in the middle of the intellectual and practical rethinking of the way we inhabit places, an intellectual project that would, years later, change the way I looked at my hometown of Spartanburg, and possibly even change the way it looked at itself. To be a part of that long-ago West Coast literary scene, I had to learn not only about poetry: I had to learn to make poetry books. I plunged in, and worked as an apprentice for Sam Hamill and Tree Swenson at Copper Canyon Press, working for almost a year learning letterpress. The practice of poetry in Port Townsend in 1978 was labor intensive rather than capital intensive. It operated outside traditional capitalist models. Sam Hamill referred to non-profit Copper Canyon as "life outside the mainstream capitalist economy, living mostly by the Buddhist begging bowl as it were." These were heady concepts for a southern Methodist.

What it meant was getting your hands dirty setting type, then cleaning your hands up for the printing. My first major publication was a letter-pressed pamphlet of a poem called *Thin Creek*, released in 1979. But what I remember most was working with some of the great poets writing in English—setting type for and helping print books, chapbooks, broadsides, and pamphlets by Thomas McGrath, Gary Snyder, Robert Hedin, Olga Bromas, and others. At the press I learned from Sam and Tree that if a culture is to have great poets, it needs not only great audiences (as Whitman said) but also great printers and publishers.

The ideas of bioregionalism were relatively new at that point. Sam and Tree got their bioregionalism from Gary Snyder and the Whole Earth movement in general, but the ideas had also drifted up from California where they'd originated in the early 1970s in the work of Peter Berg and others. The year before my arrival, Port Townsend's *Dalmoma*, edited by Michael Daley, became one of the first of a growing list of bioregional literary journals as the movement spread quickly across the continent.[1] The magazine reflected the interest of a group of Port Townsend writers, poets, artists, and intellectuals in "the visions and concerns of Pacific Rim communities, biological and cultural features of distinct regions, and in interdependence of all life along the Pacific Rim" (Daley).

Soon after I arrived in Port Townsend, I discovered the Imprint Bookstore. A place like Imprint was not part of my small-town southern literary DNA. It was the town's literary hub, a thriving book scene that included dozens of serious writers and two presses. It was a place where writers gathered, debated, flirted, and brooded. We never went to town for lunch without stopping in to see what was up at Imprint Bookstore. The book selections were serious. You knew that at Imprint you could find a new volume that could send your head and heart in a different direction.

At Imprint Bookstore I bought a copy of the second issue of *Dalmoma* and also Peter Berg's anthology *Reinhabiting a Separate Country: A Bio-regional Anthology of Northern California*. Berg's book was the first full-scale bioregionalism anthology, a collection of recorded stories, interviews, essays, drawings and photographs "exploring ideas for living in-place." Berg's brief introduction has embedded within it all the basics of the bioregional ethic: that there are countries that aren't found in the atlas and they have "soft borders" and that these natural countries are "populated by native plants and animals that have endured since the last Ice Age" (1). Berg ends his introduction by placing his natural countries in an anatomical metaphor suggesting the emerging Gaia hypothesis (that earth is one large organism) made popular by James Lovelock in the early 1970s: "Each [natural country] is a separate living part of the unified planetary biosphere; tissues and organs in the current manifestation of Earth's anatomy" (1).

Mentored by Sam Hamill and other Port Townsend poets, I soon bought and read books by Wendell Berry and Gary Snyder, and I began to rethink my own place in the natural order even though I was a continent away from my home ground. I pondered what Berg meant in the afterword to his anthology when he says that "living in-place means following the necessities and pleasures of life as they are uniquely presented by a particular site, and evolving ways to ensure long-term occupancy of that site" (217).

I see now, thirty years later, that the ideas of bioregionalism were central to the community process in Port Townsend: bioregions are areas that share similar topography, plant and animal life, and human culture; these regions are more often than not organized around watersheds and have nonrigid boundaries that differ from political borders like those around counties or nations. After only a few months in Port Townsend, I could have passed the midterm for bioregional studies 101. I knew that to be a bioregional thinker means to become aware of the ecology, economy, and culture of the place you live, and then to make choices to enhance that place.

But bioregionalism was not merely a set of ideas in Port Townsend. It was manifested in 1978–79 in the work to save Kai Tai Lagoon from a new Safeway grocery store. Kai Tai Lagoon is a brackish (saltwater and freshwater) marsh that fills with the tide. The Safeway Corporation wanted to close their downtown store, fill in a portion of the marsh, and construct a plaza on the edge of the lagoon, a place with large populations of nesting wading birds. An alliance formed to fight the construction. Sam Hamill was in the middle of the Kai Tai fight, and in 1979 Copper Canyon published

Gary Snyder's *Songs for Gaia* as a fund-raiser for the Kai Tai Alliance in an edition of 300 copies printed on Curtis Rag paper and bound in cloth over boards. In the end, Safeway won the battle and the plaza was constructed, but the fight raised consciousness in those who went through it.

In 1988 when I moved back to Spartanburg, I didn't intend to stay. I still had the same dreams of cultivating the life of the wandering bard that had taken me to Port Townsend in 1978. As I had moved around the country for ten years, bioregionalism had remained an interesting and engaging set of ideas, but each time I attempted to settle—to plant a garden, engage more deeply with the native wildflowers, sink my oar in the earth—I had found it impossible to commit to that sort of life. In 1988 I was working at Wofford College as an English instructor on one-year contracts and living in a small, one-bedroom apartment in a suburb of Spartanburg. I still imagined I'd soon live elsewhere when I got the big break most writers dream about.

That fall, talking briefly with the poet Gary Snyder unexpectedly headed me back toward earth. I was attending a conference in Wyoming in honor of the historian Alvin Josephy Jr., the author of *The Indian Heritage of America* and many other important books about Native Americans. Snyder was there and when he found out I was from South Carolina, he smiled and said that what he most wanted to see in the South was "the remaining first growth stands in the Smokies."

"Like Joyce Kilmer?" I said, referring to the grove of huge first growth poplars near Robbinsville, North Carolina.

"Yes, like Joyce Kilmer." Snyder tilted his head slightly back and smiled once more, this time, maybe considering the irony of the largest stand of big trees in the South named for Kilmer, the author of "I think that I shall never see / a poem lovely as a tree." But then Snyder explained an irony even more interesting to him: "You know, if I want to see what China looked like before they clear-cut it, I've someday got to go see that old growth stand in North Carolina."

During the conference, Snyder also sat on a panel concerned with the changing demographics of western communities. During his allotted time he articulated once again the same consistent position we are all so familiar with from *The Old Ways, Earth House Hold, The Real Work*, and most recently, *The Practice of the Wild*: the "poetics" of bioregionalism, of the human responsibility to mirror closely the natural communities of a watershed, a region. As always Snyder reconfirmed how for him values can be articulated by way of metaphors of landscape and earth science.

After our encounter and conversation in Wyoming, I reread one of Snyder's classic essays, "Poetry, Community & Climax," from *The Real Work*. It is there Snyder articulates one of his most compelling metaphors we can live by: communities tend toward diversity and climax. How does Snyder come to his conclusions? He looks, as always, toward the natural world. He defines climax much as an ecologist would: the communities of creatures in forests, ponds, oceans, or grasslands seem to tend toward a condition called climax, "'virgin forest'—many species, old bones, lots of rotten leaves, complex energy pathways, woodpeckers living in snags, and conies harvesting tiny piles of grass. This condition has considerable stability and holds much energy in its web—energy that in simpler systems (a field of weeds just after a bulldozer) is lost back into the sky or down the drain" (173).

Snyder continues with his metaphor, extending it to include not only natural systems but human culture as well: "as climax forest is to biome, and fungus is to the recycling of energy, so 'enlightened mind' is to daily ego mind, and art to the recycling of neglected inner potential. When we deepen or enrich ourselves, looking within, understanding ourselves, we come closer to being like a climax system" (173–74).

Human beings, Snyder would say, have a responsibility toward the "ecology" of a community: "Turning away from grazing on the 'immediate biomass' of perception, sensation, and thrill." Once this responsibility has been accomplished, humans must set about "re-viewing memory, internalized perception, blocks of inner energies, dreams, the leaf-fall of day-to-day consciousness." This activity "liberates the energy of our own sense-detritus" (174).

Snyder shows his real genius in metaphor by extending his forest metaphor not to the easy conclusion—that we must "flower" or "grow"—but to one much more complex. The "compost of feeling and thinking" appears to bloom "not as a flower, but—to complete the metaphor—as a mushroom: the fruiting body of the buried threads of mycelia that run widely through the soil, and are intricately married to the root hairs of all trees" (174).

"Fruiting" is what Snyder says we must accomplish as poets, artists or mystics; and then we must "reenter[] the cycle" and give what we have made as nourishment ("as spore or seed spreads the 'thought of enlightenment'") into "personal depths for nutrients hidden there, back to the community" (174). Rereading Snyder and considering my encounter with him has helped remind me that I, too, have always looked to ecology for values that matter: systems, when left alone, tend toward diversity and climax.

Soon after I came back from the Wyoming conference, I began to ask for the first time how our local community would change if we took Snyder's metaphor for values seriously. Maybe we could organize our aesthetic thinking in the twenty-first century around the idea that language in general is like the vegetable riot of the plant kingdom, and poetry in particular could be seen as a forest system that develops without disturbance in "stable" landscapes: a "climax" or first growth poetics, can be recognized as a fully developed and integrated poetics, such as an aboriginal people would have.

What I brought back from the West Coast was this sense of a language grounded in the metaphors of ecology, biology, and natural processes. Some of these ideas, such as landscapes tending toward what Snyder called "climax" have changed dramatically since the 1970s. Some would even say they have been discredited and now have little currency. As a poet I have always been aware that metaphors sometimes lose their meaning, but that has never for me distracted from Snyder's original essay.

I also brought back a deeply set urge to "fruit," to build a literary community in my hometown. I knew that no literary community develops without a press to anchor it, so I set about founding a press. I started Holocene, a small letterpress chapbook and broadside press in the basement of the Wofford College library. I quickly found that despite training by Sam and Tree, I didn't have the temperament for letterpress printing. I'm not detail oriented. Sometimes I'd leave the type unsorted in the trays and let the ink dry on the rollers. Books and broadsides would sit for months half-finished. For several years after that I experimented with offset, and then with the emerging digital printing, but after four or five years back in Spartanburg, Holocene lost steam.

A few years later, a Californian was driving through town. He opened a coffee house and roaster on the town square, and so Morgan Square Coffee was born. It was one of the first true coffee houses of upstate South Carolina. Within a few weeks hanging out there, I'd met Gary Henderson and Betsy Teter, both local journalists and writers. We began talking about our ideas of literary community. We proposed publishing a book of essays about Spartanburg. Gary was a decade older than Betsy and me, and he

John Lane

brought a depth of memory of "old Spartanburg" to the project. He clearly remembered the cotton mill town before it had collapsed into its post-industrial stupor. He'd also lived four years in Boulder, Colorado, a place ringed with 17,000 acres of green space, and so he had an appreciation for environmental issues. "I could walk out my back door," he once told me, "and pick up a trail and be in the mountains for an hour after dinner." Betsy had lived on Hilton Head Island and observed the development of Sea Pines Plantation as a resort community planned around its relationship to forest and sea. Betsy brought with her skills as a writer, editor, and her contacts with the "old money" of Spartanburg (her family has been in the Buick business in town for over 50 years). Both Gary and Betsy shared with me a sense that Spartanburg was ripe for a literary and environmental revolution—with a healthy population of writers and readers in its five colleges and universities and a rising interest in land use and green space among others.

Right there in Morgan Square Coffee the three of us founded our "writers' project," with the plan for the first book sketched out on a napkin. The name hearkens back to Roosevelt's Federal Writers Project because we felt Spartanburg was in a cultural depression in spite of the Chamber of Commerce's propaganda about the community and how one of its real strengths was its "pro-business environment."

We started much as Peter Berg had done in northern California with one book, an anthology, a collection of "personal essays," and photos of local art exploring Spartanburg experiences. Our book would be more polished than Berg's anthology. There would be no interviews, no idea pieces. We would ask for creative nonfiction written in the style of the emerging genre of the personal essay. The book would have an elegance of design and layout. We hoped that it would lift the literary spirits of the town and help triangulate an identity for the community. We held a meeting of potential writers and gave them a quick workshop in the art of the personal essay. When the pieces came in we were surprised by their variety. Some were about nature (including mine, about a hike in the old World War II camp near town) and others were about neighborhoods and old movie theaters. One writer remembered the musty smells of an old bookstore downtown in the 1950s when Spartanburg had its equivalent of Imprint Bookstore.

One African American wrote about hearing white clerks in a local department store break into applause at the moment John F. Kennedy's assassination was announced over the loudspeakers, so it wasn't all sweet nostalgia. The publication was a huge success. We paid for it by stealing an idea from Black Sparrow Press in California—raise $10,000 by selling one hundred $100 fine print hardbacks of the book, unavailable for retail. When the paperback came out in April of 1997, we sold 800 copies the first day at a book launch party down at the old burned-out train station.

That first *Hub City Anthology* led to *Hub City Music Makers* and *Hub City Christmas* the next year, and now, twelve years later, we have a list of subjects among our fifty-two titles as diverse as a local revolutionary war heroine, the story of two old army bases in town, two college histories, books of old photographs, a group-written local mystery novel, and collections of radio columns. There have also been a number of "nature" books, including a history of the peach farming culture of our county, a biography of a local community gardener, a coffee-table book of tree poems and photographs, and a photo-essay and series of sketches of a local trail.

During that time, the city flourished, too. Under the leadership of a progressive mayor and city council, a new cultural center was constructed downtown, the town square underwent a $3 million makeover, and even the old train depot was brought back to life, its parking lot now used on spring and summer Saturdays for the popular local farmers market. "Hub City" has now become the moniker for all things Spartanburg. Even the city's directional signs now call the community "Hub City."

A few years into the "project," we decided to focus on our local stream, the Lawson's Fork, but it was not the biodiversity issue or the desire to preserve a wild place that led the way. It was simply an attempt to "meet the creek." We wanted to reintroduce our community to its forgotten waterway. I had the initial idea, wrote some poems, and led the central narrative's author, David Taylor, down the creek in a kayak; Gary interviewed people along the waterway; and Betsy led the way in producing and publicizing our ambitious plans. She wanted local people to understand how Lawson's Fork was our community's "cultural main street," and how much of the important history of the area had taken place along its banks. So we published a book about the creek, held a five-day festival along its banks, and established a park and a paddling trail so that the stream would be more accessible.

The book, *Lawson's Fork: From Headwaters to Confluence*, turned out to be pure bioregionalism: a personal float narrative by David Taylor, drawings, poems, interviews, photographs, maps. It's a book that celebrates the very core of this place—our living, flowing stream. The festival Betsy pulled together had community elements that would have been recognizable on the streets of San Francisco in 1970—a local theater group performing amid garbage on the banks of the creek, a sacred jug made of local clay for transporting creek water from the headwaters all the way downstream to the confluence, a gospel choir singing "Shall We Gather at the River" on the last day, and a Cherokee medicine man blessing the creek at the conclusion alongside an Episcopal priest.

In many ways, the Hub City Writers Project (and bioregionalism) has been a catalyst for my life. Betsy and I married in 2002 and soon after, because of our love of the Lawson's Fork, we ended up buying land on the creek on the edge of a local suburb and building a "green" house. The Lawson's Fork festival and book was also a catalyst for my own nature writing. Much of my prose writing has grown out of that relationship to the creek, including my book *Circling Home*, a book-length narrative about exploring the mile around our new home. My five-year weekly newspaper column "Kudzu Telegraph" began with local observation, its target audience 30,000 locals, not some distant literary elite. I don't think I would now be focusing my attention on "nearby nature" if not for that period reading Peter Berg and working at Copper Canyon.

At times I've been frustrated that a true bioregional focus is so hard to hold in the South. Watching Hub City evolve over the years, I've been interested in the way ideas change forms in a community until they find a form that works—Gary Snyder's intricate metaphors of "community and climax" weren't going to work in Spartanburg. The single image that won over the legislative delegation for establishing the Lawson's Fork paddling trail was not one of climax forest trees along the shore or pristine waters within its banks but one of two kids "running the chute" in kayaks— recreation, pure and simple. Is this still "bioregional" or by this point has it migrated so far from the street theater and pamphleteering of Peter Berg that we can't even call it the same thing?

The metaphors that worked for Spartanburg were not the ones dealing with wildness, old growth forests, or the outdated idea of "climax" natural systems. Our metaphors were more often right out of our settlement history: trains, small towns, agriculture. If West Coast bioregionalism was "natural," then ours was clearly "cultural." Even the name "Hub City" was lifted right out of the nineteenth century, when this town prided itself as a hub for train travel, with eight trains departing daily.

In the past few years, the Hub City Writers Project has morphed and evolved in ways that may seem far from its original literary mission. The press now publishes five books a year, but we've also created a community-wide arts initiative called "Hubculture" that includes a performance space/ gallery downtown and four young artists-in-residence living in our building in a program called "Live Free and Create." The program is now five years old and involves participants from all over the country. Just recently we have opened a nonprofit bookstore, Hub City Bookshop, on the ground floor of a historic Masonic Temple near the square downtown. The capital for upfit, stock, and early operating expenses (nearly $300,000) was raised from donations from nearly 300 people in the community. A cadre of loyal volunteers performs much of the bookstore's work. Maybe what we're trying to do here is similar to what I saw in Port Townsend in the early 1970s. We're creating a labor-intensive book culture—including a regional press, active writers' community, and a nonprofit bookstore.

I see now that the bioregionalism I first encountered on my trips out West has somehow been transformed in Spartanburg into a sort of cultivar that has worked in my home territory. Thirty years after I first encountered bioregionalism in Port Townsend, the Hub City Writers Project has published nearly 400 writers in half a hundred books. Peter Berg would recognize many of the books as "place-based" accounts of the cultural and natural history of our community, but are these bioregional? Well, sort of. A case could clearly be made for the bioregional nature books, and I would argue that the others have helped return our town to one of Peter Berg's hallmarks of the bioregional movement, revealing a place to itself.

I was at an exit party last night for our current class of artists-in-residence. Jameelah Lang, a young fiction writer from Kansas, had invited her boyfriend Whit Bones down from Asheville. Whit is a furniture maker, and he moved to North Carolina "to ride Jameelah's coattails" and to be close to Asheville's formidable crafts scene. After a year of driving down the mountain, what did he think of Spartanburg? "Asheville's a cool town, but artists there think they're entitled to all that coolness. I think I prefer Spartanburg. There are plenty of cool artists here, but they really have to work at it."

In closing, I'd like to make another sort of case. I'd like to argue that Spartanburg and the Hub City Writers Project has pursued a successful fifteen-year experiment in what I might call "soft bioregionalism," the practice of place-based writing. Spartanburg isn't San Francisco or Marin County or Port Townsend, places with intact intellectual topsoil for growing bioregionalism in its pure form. Hub City has coaxed a "working-class" literary community from the depleted soils surrounding our postindustrial ruins. Spartanburg isn't even Asheville ("little Santa Fe"), our hypercool sister city to the north. As Hub City's mission statement says, we are "fostering a sense of community through the literary arts." Or, as Whit might say, we're working at it.

NOTES

1. For a little of the bioregional history of Poet Townsend's *Dalmo'ma*, see "Running on Empty" by Michael Daley.

WORKS CITED

Berg, Peter. *Reinhabiting a Separate Country: A Bioregional Anthology of Northern California*. San Francisco: Planet Drum Foundation, 1978. Print.
Copper Canyon Press. Copper Canyon Press, 2011. Web. 16 Jan. 2011.
Daley, Michael. "Running on Empty." *Pleasure Boat Studio: A Literary Press*. Pleasure Boat Studio: A Literary Press, n.d. Web. 16 Jan. 2011.
"Hub City Writers Project." *Hub City*. Hub City, 2011. Web. 16 Jan. 2011.
Planet Drum Foundation. Planet Drum Foundation, 11 July 2010. Web. 16 Jan. 2011.
Snyder, Gary. *The Real Work: Interviews & Talks, 1964–1979*. New York: New Directions, 1980. Print.

RINDA WEST

Representing Chicago Wilderness

IN DEFINING *BIOREGIONALISM*, Michael Vincent McGinnis writes, "Bioregionalists stress the importance of reinhabiting one's place and earthly home. A bioregion represents the intersection of vernacular culture, place-based behavior, and community" (3). Where do cities fit into this vision? How about the people who have come to the city through diaspora, migration, or economic opportunity? How are they to embrace vernacular culture or place-based behavior?

Many city dwellers have virtually no contact with wild nature or anything much beyond boxwoods and petunias—or weeds and vacant lots. To transform this alienation into a bioregional vision requires organizers to create the motive, means, and opportunity for people to expand their experiences and enlarge their values. But even in the Chicago metropolitan area, where people are lucky enough to have access to nature, changing practices, whether they are personal, professional, or commercial, is a slow and challenging process. In this paper, I explore some of the responses to that challenge by members of the Chicago Wilderness coalition as they work to inform and inspire a variety of audiences. I am particularly interested in the communication strategies of the consortium given the highly political nature of the work and the difficulty of making nature urgent in a city with no end to crises.

The roots of Chicago Wilderness go back to the late 1970s, when a small group of friends, inspired by the prairie restoration at Fermilab in Batavia, began to spend Sunday mornings in a few of the prairie remnants along

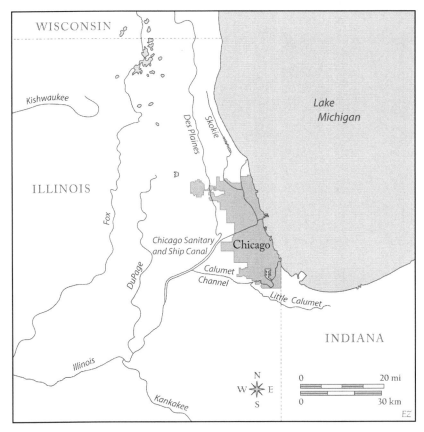

The Chicago Wilderness

the North Branch of the Chicago River. They found some of them surprisingly rich in rare native plant species, and they determined to restore small
plots to their presettlement condition. They worked closely with officials
of the Forest Preserve District to cut invasive European Buckthorn trees,
pull garlic mustard, collect and plant the seeds of local native plants, and
set prescribed burns, slowly opening up the canopy to make possible the
reblooming of the prairie. As more native plants returned, so did insects,
herps, small mammals, butterflies, and birds like the Cooper's hawk. As
volunteers spread word of their work, more and more people joined in what
became known as the North Branch Prairie Project. The work expanded
around the metropolitan area, and soon restoration was underway on many
other sites as well. Groups like the Sierra Club, Audubon, and others joined

in, and The Nature Conservancy developed an umbrella Volunteer Stewardship Network to coordinate communication and help volunteers.

In 1993, a group of people working across a spectrum of conservation organizations began a series of meetings to explore ways to coordinate their work. It was clear that their conservation missions could not be accomplished without cooperation across the region. Represented at the meeting, among others, were representatives of the U.S. Forest Service, the U.S. Fish and Wildlife Service, county forest preserve districts, the city of Chicago, the Illinois Department of Natural Resources, the Environmental Protection Agency, and nongovernmental organizations, including The Nature Conservancy, the Field Museum, Lincoln Park and Brookfield Zoos, the Chicago Botanic Garden, and Morton Arboretum. Many of these people had known each other and worked together for years. The intent of early meetings was to find synergies and efficiencies by coordinating some conservation activities, and to bring more resources to the region. The diverse agencies wanted to retain their autonomy, but they could see the benefits of collaboration, so they decided to share resources around common goals, engage in collaborative fund-raising, and work together to communicate a conservation mission. They chose to call themselves the Chicago Region Biodiversity Council, but "Chicago Wilderness" became the marketing name. Its simplicity, surprise, and suggestiveness made it stick. Thus "Chicago Wilderness," which has an oxymoronic ring, is a deliberate locution to underline the relationship between humans (in their urban guise) and wild nature. As John Rogner puts it in the Chicago Wilderness 2003 Annual Report,

> We have coined the term "Chicago Wilderness" to refer to the rich biodiversity that exists in and around this sprawling metropolitan area. This is a region that most people think of as anything but "untrammeled . . . where man is a visitor who does not remain" in the words of the Wilderness Act. . . . Although our wilderness is scattered throughout the region, in protected parcels that would be considered slivers by conventional standards, it totals more than 250,000 acres. We have called these lands and waters "wilderness" to emphasize the connections between formal wilderness in remote and inaccessible places and wild lands in the places where people live and work. The biotic connections exist on the land, and they ought to exist in people's minds as well. . . . The Chicago Wilderness consortium proposes to redefine wilderness to include local plant and animal communities which can only be sustained through direct, creative human intervention.

Formally launched in 1996, Chicago Wilderness now consists of more than 250 members from four states, including government bodies, museums, universities, local authorities, planning agencies, nongovernmental organizations, and a corporate council of 32 members. Its aim is "to create a metropolitan area in which nature thrives in harmony with people" (Crane 6).

Chicago Wilderness now designates the nearly 360,000 acres that are protected or managed by members. According to Ron Trigg, "The best definition for the Chicago Wilderness region—consistent with its role in United States History—may be that it's a meeting place, a nexus, a hub" (16). Trigg goes on to quote Floyd Swink and Gerould Wilhelm, authors of the definitive *Plants of the Chicago Region*, saying that this is the place where "the deciduous forests of the east meet the western prairies and savannas . . . northern bogs and swamp forests coexist with sand dunes and unique dolomitic limestone prairies." The lands of Chicago Wilderness extend from southwestern Wisconsin to the Michigan dunes. Thus the region defined by the consortium is not defined by a single watershed or ecosystem, but rather by the existence of protected and restored natural areas representative of the various ecosystems of the area.

The mission of Chicago Wilderness has three parts: to study, restore, protect, and manage the natural ecosystems of the region; to contribute to the preservation of global biodiversity; and to involve local residents and improve their quality of life. This third point has been crucial since the beginning. In 1996 the original participants released a statement that said, in part, "This effort has been described as having the elements of a new environmental ethic, one which recognizes human beings in a metropolitan area as important and necessary components of a thriving natural system. We envision the work in Chicago moving like a prairie fire, igniting the spirits of people in other places, and inviting people in other areas to take, like sacred fire, this idea home to their own communities" (qtd. in Ross 17).

One of the major tasks of Chicago Wilderness is to represent itself to its publics. It must communicate to parents and teachers, government officials, scientists, land managers, businesspeople, and the public that they have something priceless at their doorstep, that it is threatened, that they can help restore it to health, and that in the process they will enrich their own lives. Because the work of the consortium often requires the participation or at least the buy-in of elected officials, the language of its communications needs to avoid both academic jargon and the lyricism of the green faithful. Writers have to be careful to address the interests, concerns, and assumptions of zoning board and water district officials, of mayors and councilors. Officials have to believe that taxpayers support the often expensive priorities of conservation. The task became urgent when, in 1996, a newspaper columnist stirred up a backlash against restoration. Reactions against the use of controlled burning, objections to deer culling, and anxieties about herbicides resulted in a political furor that affected the work of Chicago Wilderness for several years. Still, the goal of the publications—to spread the mission of the consortium—remained the same. While leaders and volunteers of the restoration projects spent time testifying at county board meetings, writing letters to editors, and meeting with neighbors, the 1997 premier issue of *Chicago Wilderness* magazine provided a means to bring the Chicago Wilderness perspective to a wide audience.

A quarterly, *Chicago Wilderness* features the beauty, diversity, and rarity of the nature that comprises Chicago Wilderness. Gorgeous, seductive photography and articles on volunteers, feature species, activities for families, and calendars of activities reach out to the general public and speak passionately to the thousands of volunteers in restoration projects, focusing attention on the richness of the nature right around the corner and inviting people to befriend it. Attention to issues like prescribed burning and invasive species also helped the magazine explain restoration to people confused by the controversy.

In addition to the magazine, the consortium has published or collaborated on three significant one-off print publications. Their differences underline the communication strategies for different audiences. The publications are *Chicago Wilderness: An Atlas of Biodiversity* (1997), *Biodiversity Recovery Plan* (1999), and *Protecting Nature in Your Community* (2001, published in collaboration with the Northeast Illinois Planning Commission). The atlas of biodiversity speaks to a general reader and provides substantial information on the history, ecosystems and species of the region. Coming to print, as it did, while the political conflict over restoration was still potent, it provided a way to educate the public about the value of nature and the need for management of protected natural areas. Thus it became a significant tool in the process of changing public perceptions about, for example, the problems with letting nature take its course. *Biodiversity Recovery Plan* was written for internal audiences—staffers at the many agencies and organizations belonging to the consortium—so it speaks in more practical and scientific terms about the condition of the land and the steps needed to improve it. *Protecting Nature in Your Community* addresses local officials, in a language less technical and more practical; it has a different job of education and persuasion, directed at the interests and needs of politicians. At the time of its appearance, the controversy had simmered down, but the need to educate local officials about the value of protected and managed land and water was high.

Aimed at a general reader, with special value for classroom use, *Chicago Wilderness: An Atlas of Biodiversity* is the most visually and editorially appealing. *Biodiversity* was an unfamiliar word to most Chicagoans in 1997. The atlas set out to introduce the term, make it sexy, and enshrine it in the reader's affections. Early in the publication is a beautifully illustrated two-page spread that reads:

> Imagine a circle the size of a hula hoop. All 30 of the plants pictured on these two pages were found growing in just such a circle randomly placed at the Somme Prairie Nature Preserve in Northbrook, Illinois. Biodiversity is typical of tallgrass prairie . . . Several species of the tiny butterflies called skippers could reproduce in our hoop. Skipper caterpillars feed on grasses and sedges. On the violets we might find caterpillars that would grow into gaudy orange and black fritillaries. In healthy ecosystems, energy flows freely through the system. There are many pathways for it to follow. Plants of many species support a variety of insects. Snakes, salamanders, and meadowlarks eat the insects and northern harriers eat the insect eaters. Thanks to the biodiversity in our hoop, the flow of energy can support them all. (18–19)

The familiar image of a hula hoop engages the imagination of children and adults alike. The energy circuit flows through attractive species, and the plant images on the page are all in flower. Only if the publication could buzz and hum with the sounds of summer would the diversity of the prairie be more gorgeously represented. Written by Jerry Sullivan, who for years had written the "Field and Street" column for the free weekly *Chicago Reader*, the atlas of biodiversity makes Chicago's natural areas feel as familiar and as magical as the woods you played in as a child. The atlas was distributed free to schools and libraries, and the EPA put it on the Web. It has been widely taught, and the language and illustrations are well suited to classroom purposes.

Of all the publications of the alliance, the atlas of biodiversity has been the most useful.[1] The atlas teaches geology, ecology, biology, hydrology, and history. The story begins with ice. Glaciers "built the landscape of the Chicago Wilderness," creating the soils, landforms, and watersheds that define the area (6). But if ice got the work started, fire kept it going: the prairie fires renewed the grasslands and kept the system stable.

Readers learn about natural communities and native species. The atlas explains how the Illini confederation and the Potawatomi managed the land, farmed, traded, and used fire, and how European settlement brought changes, including intensive farming, tiling of wetlands, and increasing industry, development, and trade. The language of the atlas—for example, "The rivers of the Chicago region have been subjected to the same kinds of humiliations as other rivers in major industrial, population, and agricultural centers" (46)—makes the facts emotional. Most of the atlas, however, is devoted to species that can still be found in prairies, woodlands, and wetlands, as well as the ecology of still water and moving waters. The prairie section introduces fire, and an iconic graphic demonstrates the depth of roots of prairie plants. Prairie plants in bloom are followed by sections, complete with lush photographs, on birds, butterflies and moths, big grazers such as bison and elk, and herps, of the prairie. This last section contains language that exemplifies the teaching function of the atlas: "Herps can serve as guides to conditions on the land. Their limited mobility makes it difficult for them to travel in search of a better home, especially in a land of six-lane expressways. As a result, they are vulnerable to local extinction. If a small population dies out, new animals of the same species are unlikely to be able to colonize the vacated habitat" (23). Next to this passage is a photograph of a hand holding a tiny smooth green snake, "a lovely little serpent." This passage points to a significant threat to biodiversity and connects it to planning issues.

The atlas goes on to profile wooded communities—savannas, open woodlands, flatwoods, and forests—and the species that populate them. Distinguishing marshes, sedge meadows, fens, and bogs, the atlas makes wetlands appealing and teaches readers to see and understand the landscape. Although the atlas points wherever possible to improvements brought about by legislation, such as the Clean Water Act, it does not attempt to sweeten the consequences of neglect, poor planning, and rampant development. It concludes with the work of restoration and an emphasis on the central role of citizen volunteers.

John and Jane Balaban, who were among the original group of volunteers, have remarked that "one of the most significant obstacles to sound land management was a lack of familiarity with basic ecology and natural processes on the part of the public and elected officials" (242). The atlas, together with *Biodiversity Recovery Plan*, speaks to that basic need. Accessible to middle school students, it also educates adults about the history and the science relevant to local nature.

Biodiversity Recovery Plan (1999) is a series of working papers generated from background documents and workshops organized by Chicago Wilderness members, intended primarily for internal audiences to guide their work, set priorities, and direct resources. In tone and presentation, it is much more functional, with glossy photos only on the cover. It defines *biodiversity* on the second page: "Biodiversity is the totality of genes, species, and ecosystems in a region." This simple definition, followed by examples from the Chicago Wilderness region, is both large and precise enough for coalition members. The inclusion of ecosystems in this definition underlines the importance to the land managers who wrote the document of the regional nature of the enterprise. Whatever approach one organization might take, whether preserving habitat for an endangered species or monitoring non-point-source pollution, no one agency can achieve its goals alone: one fragmented habitat cannot protect a species; one township's water is vulnerable to runoff from the next.

The publication goes on to explain the importance of biodiversity. Although this might not have been necessary for alliance members, the document has, since its publication, been valuable in providing rationales for managers seeking funding for conservation; it offers the scientific basis for political choices. Thus, the language of the recovery plan addresses the values and concerns of decision makers who control resources needed for conservation, as can be seen in its opening discussion of biodiversity: "Around the world, people depend on biodiversity for the very sustenance of life. The living things with which we share the planet provide us with clean water and air, food, clothing, shelter, medicines, and aesthetic enjoyment, and they also embody our feelings of shared culture, history, and community. The nations of the world have signed a treaty calling biodiversity the common heritage of humankind and calling on all people to be custodians of the biodiversity found in their countries and regions" (6). This last sentence enlarges the scope of the mission, aligning the local with the global, while the substitution of "custodians" for the more familiar "stewards" simultaneously echoes Biblical injunctions and replaces the sense of dominion with an implication of interdependence. The idea that nature needs human assistance is thus given precedent and subtly modified.

The following paragraph explains the local value of biodiversity:

> In Chicago Wilderness, the value of biodiversity is not just at the global level, but most importantly for our own citizens. Natural communities and species are the basis of the region's environmental health. They provide ecological services in maintaining water quality, abating the impact of floods, supporting pollination of crops, and controlling outbreaks of pests. Equally important, biodiversity contributes immeasurably to the quality of life for the citizens of the region and to the region's long-term economic vitality. Recent polls and election results show that residents of the region strongly support protection of natural areas for the future. Only if we continue and expand upon the far-sighted conservation work of those who built the Chicago region, will we be able to pass these precious biodiversity values on to future generations. (6)

The practical and anthropocentric spin of this paragraph speaks to the political interests of local officials, as well as the values of staffers, scientists, and landowners. The plan that follows features analyses of the status of and threats to the various communities of the region as well as goals and checklists of actions that need to be taken to protect those areas. Although the language of the introductory remarks is emotive, what follows is largely scientific.

The publication *Protecting Nature in Your Community*, built on the working papers of *Biodiversity Recovery Plan*, was created by the North-eastern Illinois Planning Commission with funding from Chicago Wilderness.[2] It is directed primarily at local authorities. In *Biodiversity Recovery Plan*, the roles of and restrictions on these readers are analyzed, and these insights guided the composition of *Protecting Nature in Your Community*. For example, the recovery plan notes that reliance on property and sales taxes to fund municipal governments provides an incentive to expand development. This often conflicts with the goals of recovery, and the conflict needs to be addressed explicitly or implicitly. Whereas academic writers on biodiversity can be theoretical or analytical, the practical orientation of Chicago Wilderness requires political savvy.

It was also likely that most local officials would not understand the urgency of conservation, so the publication opens with this passage: "Imagine a region filled with life, where the evening air is rich with bird calls and the

scent of flowers, where children splash and play in clean creeks, and peer
below the surface of the water at fish and other aquatic creatures, where
people learn to gently and respectfully enter back into a positive relationship
with the nature that surrounds them, and where rare plants, animals, and
natural communities are nurtured back to health and offered a permanent
home next to our own—to the benefit of our health and our economy—in
preserves large enough to sustain them forever" (front matter).

Again, we see the appeal to imagination. From this lyrical beginning, the
publication goes on to spell out "A Critical Role for Local Governments"
and to answer questions such as "Why Preserve Nature?" (for "Quality of
Life, Recreation and Aesthetics," for "Public Support," "Economic Value,"
"Environmental Benefits," and "Spiritual Values.") It too addresses the central question of defining biodiversity early in the publication, and it offers
some different perspectives from the other two publications: "More than
200,000 acres of protected woodlands, wetlands, prairies, and streams in
the greater Chicago region provide refuge to thousands of plants and animal species, many of them rare, threatened, or endangered. Privately owned
lands, including our own backyards, provide additional habitat for wildlife,
such as migrating birds. This diversity of native plants and animals, or *biodiversity*, reflects the unique blend of landscapes that were formed around
the southern end of Lake Michigan by the forces of glaciers, wind, and
wildfires. The resultant ecosystems are so rare that they have been labeled
'globally significant' by ecologists" (1).

These opening sentences stress the regional nature of the project. Back
yards and privately owned land enter the conversation to appeal to voters
and increase the political will for conservation, but it's local planning and
zoning officers, elected officials, and managers whose attention the publication seeks. The closing sentence feeds local pride and magnifies the value
of the project.

The publication offers resources, suggested actions, rationales, and local examples of good practice. The writers, Jason Navota and Dennis W.
Dreher, strove to make it easy for local authorities to understand issues,
recommendations, and benefits. They recognize the practical concerns of
these readers, including of course funding and prioritizing.

All the publications underline the damage that has been done to these
precious natural communities by the pressures of development: altered
hydrology, introduction of invasive species, creation of small islands of
habitat, poor farming practices, dredging and filling of wetlands, fire sup-

pression, soil compaction from urban development, and on and on. These are all *regional* threats, which individual agencies or municipalities cannot deal with alone, but which can be addressed by coordination. In a conference paper, Sir Peter Crane and co-authors point out the need for "better communication about why seemingly 'natural' areas need to be managed" (15). *Protecting Nature in Your Community* recommends management of waterways with riparian buffers; it promotes landscaping with native plants on public properties; it urges preservation of open space; and it underlines the importance of volunteers in natural areas restoration. Conservation and biodiversity *recovery* require human engagement with the land, and *Protecting Nature in Your Community* provides rationales, benefits, resources, and examples that local officials can access.

All the publications underline the role of people in restoring biodiversity. To this end, the visual elements of Chicago Wilderness publications stress images of people in nature: we see pictures of schoolchildren oohing over butterflies or citizen monitors in waders collecting benthic macroinvertebrates, a Fish and Wildlife director hand-pollinating rare orchids, and African American schoolchildren examining goldenrods. The people pictured look like—and are—Chicagoans in all their own diversity. And they look happy. They are not only enjoying nature, they are contributing to the health of natural systems.

Chicago Wilderness has invested in research to understand the perceptions and interests of local residents. According to Crane and colleagues, "Attachment to place—and the desire for healthy open or green space—spans class, ethnic, and racial boundaries. Indeed residents in low-income communities which have often been deprived of access to green space have a long tradition of fighting for parks, forests, and open space as part of their efforts to make their communities more livable" (9). Chicago Wilderness has been careful to include communities of color and lower income areas in the work; the extensive project in the Calumet area brings together a region of considerable biodiversity, a population of displaced steelworkers, and a tradition of strong unions, uniting to restore the land and to educate the children.

Developing and facilitating the volunteer network has been one of the most important achievements of Chicago Wilderness. From its roots in volunteer restoration projects, the consortium has always recognized that bringing people to the land is necessary both for the land and for the people. Chicago Wilderness provides a kind of middle space between municipal authorities and agencies and individuals, making it possible to feel that one is genuinely helping nature heal. As Ted Bernard points out, today a person can identify volunteer projects from the Chicago Wilderness website and find an easy way to enter the community. The website also offers "communication tools on its website to help land stewards when using fire to manage land" (Crane et al. 11). (It's hard to imagine other municipal agencies explaining their work to neighbors; I have an image of the crews repairing the roads providing handouts on how the freeze-thaw cycle creates potholes.)

In *A Sand County Almanac*, Aldo Leopold argued, "An ethic to supplement and guide the economic relation to land presupposes the existence of some mental image of land as a biotic mechanism. We can be ethical only in relation to something we can see, feel, understand, love, or otherwise have faith in" (251).

The human goal of Chicago Wilderness is very close to Leopold's idea of giving people experiences of the land that will lead to loving it, treating it ethically, voting for it, and even working for it. Chicago Wilderness makes possible people's participation in the recovery of biodiversity, as restoration volunteers, citizen scientists, monitors of critical species, prairie gardeners, teachers, students, parents, and gardeners. It helps people to identify the local as lovable and in that way builds a genuine dialogue between humans and the land.

NOTES

1. In a recent internal survey, nearly half the members of Chicago Wilderness called the atlas "extremely valuable" as a communication tool, making it the favorite by far. (Email from Laurel M. Ross)

2. A few years later, a sister document was produced by the Northwest Indiana Planning Commission.

WORKS CITED

Bernard, Ted. *Hope and Hard Times: Communities, Collaboration and Sustainability*. Gabriola Island, B.C.: New Society, 2010. Print.

Chicago Wilderness. *2003 Annual Report*. Print.

————. *2007–2008 Annual Report*. *Chicago Wilderness*. Chicago Wilderness, 2010. Web. 16 Jan. 2011.

————. *Biodiversity Recovery Plan*. 1999. *Chicago Wilderness*. Chicago Wilderness, 2010. Web. 16 Jan. 2011.

Crane, Peter, Liam Heneghan, Francie Muraski-Stotz, Melinda Pruett-Jones, Laurel Ross, Alaka Wali, and Synne Westphal. "Chicago Wilderness: Integrating Biological and Social Diversity in the Urban Garden." Paper presented at The Social Life of Forests conference, University of Chicago, 2008.

Leopold, Aldo. *A Sand County Almanac*. 1949. San Francisco: Sierra Club/Ballantine, 1970. Print.

McGinnis, Michael Vincent, ed. *Bioregionalism*. London: Routledge, 1999. Print.

Northeastern Illinois Planning Commission. *Protecting Nature in Your Community: A Guidebook for Preserving and Enhancing Biodiversity*. 2000. *Northeastern Illinois Planning Commission*. Northeastern Illinois Planning Commission, 2001. Web. 16 Jan. 2011.

Ross, Laurel M. "The Chicago Wilderness: A Coalition for Urban Conservation." *Restoration and Management Notes* 15.1 (Summer 1997): 17–24. Print.

Sullivan, Jerry. *An Atlas of Biodiversity*. 1997. *Chicago Wilderness*. Chicago Wilderness, 2010. Web. 16 Jan. 2011.

Trigg, Ron. "Expanding Horizons." *Chicago Wilderness* 10.2 (Winter 2007): 16. Print.

NORAH BOWMAN-BROZ

"To Become Beavers of Sorts"

Eric Collier's Memoir of Creative Ecology at
Meldrum Creek

I N 1931, in the Chilcotin region of the British Columbia Interior, a
watershed was dying. Meldrum Creek, a narrow, weedy waterway, led
through "stagnant and smelly" meadows and past the "crumbling façade"
of abandoned beaver dams (Collier 5). Around the "sick" watershed were
"powder-dry grasses," and the forests and fields were unusually quiet of the
call of waterbirds (5). As described by Eric Collier, author of the memoir
Three against the Wilderness, the Meldrum Creek watershed was drying and
dying, and the birds and animals that relied on it were disappearing from
the creek and the surrounding forests. Collier's memoir, first published in
1959, translated into seven languages, and considered a classic account of
settler history in British Columbia, is the story of how the Collier family
moved to and restored the Meldrum Creek watershed and its dependent
ecology.

Three against the Wilderness narrates creative ecological practice grounded
in bioregional particulars. The Colliers' practice depends on intimate lived
knowledge of a dynamic ecosystem, and *Three against the Wilderness* follows the family as they develop and implement site-specific knowledge for
the benefit of multiple species. In the genre of colonial settler memoirs—
mostly episodic and monologic, and often racist and anthropocentric—
Three against the Wilderness is unique in that Eric Collier responds to intersecting social and animal interests. British Columbia settler memoirs
have received little critical attention; *Three against the Wilderness* has been
referred to three times in historic and sociological studies of the region,

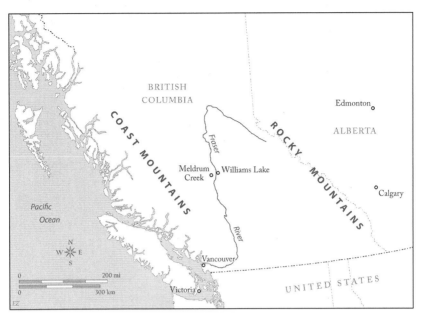

Meldrum Creek and the Fraser River Watershed

but has not been treated as a literary or ecological text. Settler memoirs, especially those set in British Columbia, are mostly read outside academia. Collier's *Three against the Wilderness*, now in the public domain, has been republished by three different publishers and maintains popularity across British Columbia.

Born in England in 1903 to a wealthy industrialist family, Eric Collier rejected urban living in favor of trapping, hunting, and homesteading in Canada. Neither the idea of "ecology" as a general study of the interactions between living organisms and their habitat or as a term describing a region within which organisms interact was known to Collier in the 1930s (Conley 117). Nor was "the environment," the notion of a surrounding natural space distinguished from humans, a subject of public discourse (117). Perhaps, then, it is even more remarkable that, from the earliest chapters of *Three against the Wilderness*, Collier exhibits an understanding that a successful ecological practice must recognize the influence of human culture and so-cial institutions (however arcane or hierarchical) as well as natural forces. The Colliers' ecorestorative success hinged on their ability to think laterally across human/animal, nature/culture divides. In *Three against the Wilderness*, the physical labor of moving logs and breeding beavers flows from minds open to interspecies epistemologies; the humans and animals are coproducers of an ecological artistry.

The creative epistemology in *Three against the Wilderness* charts the ground for a bioregional restoration narrative that speaks to artists, ecologists, environmentalists, and ecocritical theorists beyond the British Columbia interior. Collier narrates his family's creation of a site-specific ecosophy. Canadian philosopher Lorraine Code describes an *ecosophy* as a personalized environmental philosophy, one that maps "knowledge-enhancing and knowledge-impeding possibilities" (60), thus allowing for restorative ecological acts that might otherwise seem at best nonproductive and at worst downright odd. The Colliers' "becoming beaver" in the Meldrum Creek watershed is one such creative ecosophical act. Félix Guattari's environmental philosophy treatise *The Three Ecologies* proposes that global ecological restoration requires all humans to undertake a radical ecosophical shift in mental, social, and environmental registers. Philosopher Verena Conley writes that Guattari's ecologies demand that humans invent new ways of exchange between organisms, create "mutations in value," and learn to "think transversally" across "economic, scientific, [and] subjective" regimes (118). These transversal moves require creative courage, a mode of willed vulnerability to interspecies affect. As this essay demonstrates, *Three against the Wilderness*, despite a misleading title that is perhaps designed to position it in the settler-memoir market, is an exemplary case study of the kind of radical interspecies ecosophy that Guattari proposes.

Three against the Wilderness, set in a lodgepole pine forest without telephone, electricity or newspapers, generates an ecosophy specific to the Meldrum Creek watershed. But bioregional specificity can generate restorative practices beyond the scope of the innovator. The geopolitical and environmental challenges Collier faced in 1931 resonate with current conditions in the British Columbia Interior, an area described as "the front line of climate change" (CCBAC 2008). Due to an unprecedented Mountain Pine Beetle epidemic, biologists predict that by 2013, 80 percent of all pine forests in British Columbia will be dead (CCBAC 2009). Anthropogenic factors were, if Collier's record is correct, the sole contributors to the near-death of the Meldrum watershed. Like the dying Meldrum Creek watershed in 1931, the current Mountain Pine Beetle epidemic is a combination of (some) natural and (more) anthropogenic factors. Recent engineered responses to the pine beetle have proven ecologically disastrous; the worst was a secretive, government-funded project of injecting thousands of pine trees with MSMA, an arsenic-based pesticide. Obviously, even forty years after Rachel Carson's *Silent Spring*, a commitment to a locally sensitive, creative, restorative ecosophy is desperately needed.

This essay focuses on the beginning of the Colliers' project to repair the watershed and their early encounters with local water authorities, ranchers, and First Nations people. I read these encounters as ecological events creating the Colliers' inclusive, intuitive ecosophy that spans knowledge and practice regimes. The Colliers' success depends on their inclusive practice and their willingness to include diverse human and nonhuman needs as necessary to the watershed ecology. In "Coming into the Watershed: Biological and Cultural Diversity in the California Habitat," bioregional writer Gary Snyder describes how a "watershed gives us a home, and a place to go upstream, downstream, or across in" (82). The "familial branching" of plants, animals, and people in a watershed cross "subtly shifting" bioregional boundaries. Snyder writes that "only a grassroots engagement with long-term land issues" can succeed at long-term watershed preservation or restoration (83). The Colliers' bioregional citizenship, rooted in the ecocultural locus of the Meldrum Creek watershed, builds relationships between species, contributing to an emerging community ecosophy.

Small and flexible, communities of bioregional citizens often succeed at conservation where large organizations flounder. In *The Three Ecologies*, Félix Guattari describes why large organizations might fail to restore ecological damage: even when "political groupings" and "executive powers" recognize environmental change (the undeniability of climate change, melting icecaps, massive erosion, disappearing fish stocks), lest they appear foolish, their first and often only response is to "tackle industrial pollution" rather than seek deeper systemic fault (28). But restoring ecological damage, Guattari argues, is more a matter of human species subjectivity than industrial tweaking; although eliminating pollutants is laudable, only a significant change in the relations between humans and their environment can prevent long-term, large-scale environmental damage. Guattari points to the forces of the global market and the way these forces place a reifying market value on everything: "material assets, cultural assets, wildlife areas, etc." (29). Living and nonliving creatures are evaluated as potential assets, and their preservation depends on their relative value to the machine that Guattari calls Integrated World Capitalism (IWC); globalization and the ever-increasing differentiation of markets and products (bioproducts, green products, fair trade products) only increases the eco-ethical noise that swarms the earth. In conservation terms, this means that ecosystems are striated into discrete units, and that each unit is assessed for value to the proliferating markets. IWC conservation follows the needs of the market; in contrast, a Guattarian ecosophy follows a relational map of a populated ecosystem. Eric Collier's ecosophy, while responsive to the global fur market—Collier makes a living selling animal pelts—remains primarily vulnerable to, and therefore in relationship with, the seasonal needs of bioregional populations. I suggest that the Colliers, acting decades before the convolutions of globalized economics, model environmental practice that resembles Guattari's "three ecological registers (the environment, social relations and human subjectivity)" and that such a model is relevant for today's scientific, literary and artistic ecologists facing diverse global ecoharms (Guattari 28).

Collier comes to Meldrum Creek with an aim to return the watershed to health. He finds his "vision" in conversations with Lala, whom he describes as an "ancient unlettered" Chilcotin woman (16). Crediting Lala as a source of unquestionably authentic and reliable knowledge, Collier describes her further as "an ancient oak" whose "wise old mind" is "a veritable storehouse of knowledge concerning the land" as it was before colonialism (13–14). Collier creates a conservation epistemology around Lala and her "biological knowledge" from "the campus of the wilderness" (13). Collier writes at a time of intense racism in the Cariboo-Chilcotin, when violent confrontations between First Nations and settlers were common, and when children were being forcibly taken from their families to state-funded residential schools. The commonly held "idea of the frontier in the Cariboo Chilcotin" was based on a notion of the wilderness "offering an abundance of [available] resources" and on the "cultural, material" and "political" superiority of settlers to First Nations (Furniss 17). Aboriginal knowledge and independence was discouraged, even seen as "a hindrance to the advancement of the colonial economy" (Furniss 35). In this racist atmosphere, Collier's validation of Lala, while romantic and at times patronizing, is also an act of marked difference. Eric Collier welcomes Lala's knowledge as contemporaneous and creative, rather than (as indigenous knowledge in 2011 is still often framed) as antiquated, useless, or vanishing. Throughout the memoir, the Collier family defers to Lala's skills and knowledge. By building on Lala's bioregional knowledge, the Colliers create "neighborhood relations" and a connective "kinship" with an already fractured and colonized community; this is the kind of act that Guattari finds in the "social register" of a new ecosophy (Guattari 34–36). Lillian, Lala's granddaughter, meets and falls in love with Eric Collier. Equally smitten, Eric marries Lillian and vows to Lala that he and Lillian will repair the damaged watershed.

Eric Collier learns from Lala that, whereas gold panning, ranching, and trapping have damaged the watershed, the demise of the beavers was the loss from which the watershed could not recover. Without the beaver dams, the creek's flow was not slowed enough to fill ponds and lakes. Water birds lost a habitat, and predators lost water birds as prey. Fish disappeared from the creek, and birds and mammals that ate the fish starved.[1] Ranchers who had once drawn water from the ponds and lakes to irrigate hay fields looked further upstream to the large lakes that fed the creek. Drawing water from these lakes lowered the creek's waters even more, until the creek was but a narrow trickle, and the once-busy marshes, ponds, and lakes became muddy pits. Trees and grasses around the creek became tinder-dry, and the moose and deer lost watering holes and the cool shade and nourishment of willows and deciduous trees. Lala explains this chain of events as a direct result of colonial commerce: "'Until white man come,' she then went on to explain, 'Indian just kill beaver now an' then s'pose he want meat, or skin for blanket. And then, always the creek is full of beaver. But when white man come and give him tobacco, sugar, bad drink every tam' he fetch beaver skin from creek Indian go crazy and kill beaver all tam'.' Again her fingers clawed my arm. Harshly she asked, 'What's matter white man no tell Indian—some beaver you must leave so little one stop next year? What's matter white man no tell Indian—s'pose you take all beaver, bimeby all water gone too. And if water go, no trout, no fur, no grass, not'ing stop?'" (16). Lala confronts Eric with an ecopolitic: she asks him why the colonial settlers built a trade system so voracious that it destroyed the very resource it depended on. Lala implies that the violence is not accidental, that colonial powers withheld information that could have saved the watershed, just as they withheld warnings of alcoholism, disease, and social decay from native communities they wanted to manipulate. Grounded in social and ecological immediacy, Lala's ecopolitic is local, urgent, and, as Collier discovers, innovative: "After a few contemplative moments she suggested, 'Why you no go that creek and give it back the beavers? You young man, you like hunt and trap. S'pose once again the creek full of beavers, maybe trout come back. And ducks and geese come back too, and big marches be full of muskrats again all same when me little girl. And where muskrats stop, mink and otter stop too. Aiya! Why you no go that creek with

Lily, and live there all tam', and give it back the beavers?'" (16). Bypassing sublime rhetoric, Lala approaches the Meldrum Creek crisis at the level of bioregional particulars. Collier, a "young man," can "hunt and trap," and Lala reads his motivation correctly: he would wish the creek filled with beavers at least partly for his own benefit. Without suggesting *how* to restore the watershed, Lala decides that Eric Collier's task must be to move to the land with Lily, enter the Meldrum Creek time-space ("for all 'tam"), and repopulate the beavers.

Eric and Lillian marry, have a son, and move their new family to the Meldrum Creek watershed. For ten dollars and an agreement "to 'conserve and perpetuate all fur-bearing animals thereon,'" the Colliers gain legal trapping and habitation rights to over 150,000 acres of land around the watershed (17). From the outset, Collier follows the rules of the Fish and Wildlife authorities, even as he is aware that, until then, trapping "had been carried on upon a catch-as-can basis," with few registered traplines (16). The "conservation" the Colliers agree to is "not much more than a formality" since Eric and Lillian suspect that "the word 'conservation' [is] not to be found in the lexicon of the fur trade" (16). Their move to the watershed begins a new kind of conservation, one that responds to ecoharms in an immanent and local manner.

The Colliers' move to live in the watershed bioregion admits that human enterprise depends entirely on a location on the earth; their ecological practice reflects what environmental philosopher Val Plumwood writes is the essential ability "to see humans as ecological and embodied beings" (19). Embedded in their bioregional enterprise, the Colliers declare, "[h]ere we were and here we would stay" (29). They depend on the watershed for food, building materials, and trade goods, and they are vulnerable to the health of the ecosystem. Philosopher Patrick Hayden, recommending Gilles Deleuze and Félix Guattari's philosophies for environmentalism, writes that "for ecopolitical activism to compose itself effectively, it must steer clear of universalized abstractions and carefully study the specific needs and alternative possibilities within localized situations" (123). *Three against the Wilderness* does "steer clear" of religious, philanthropic, or romantic meditations on "nature"; indeed, the word *nature* is rarely used. *Three against the Wilderness* is unique among settler memoirs for this lack of pious abstraction; instead, Collier details specific animal, bird, fish, insect, and human populations in the Meldrum Creek watershed. He expresses intense joy at seeing the watershed populations thrive and anger when populations are threatened.

An attentive, behavior-based ecosophy works because, while grounded in location, it remains open enough to include "various members of the diverse yet interconnected milieux" (Hayden 122). Its "provisional, revisable" nature allows for organic and nonorganic entities' dynamic ethologies; beavers as well as ranchers influence the Colliers' restorative efforts (Hayden 122). Humans and the "social institutions" they create to manipulate the natural world can be assessed, equally, alongside the nonhuman: "no evaluation takes place in isolation from the ongoing processes of social composition in nature. Since these include human social institutions, it is vitally important to realize that ethical evaluation requires an examination of the practices of specific human social institutions as they relate to nonhuman social activity" (Hayden 122). The Colliers soon have an opportunity to examine official human practice in relation to the needs of the watershed. Eric writes a "lengthy letter" to the "Water Rights, Department of Lands and Forests," detailing the state of Meldrum Creek and proposing his "solution to the water problem" (Collier 57). He asks the Water Rights Branch for their "official blessing" and "some protection" for the Colliers' plan of "repairing the beaver dams scattered over the upper reaches of the watershed, and reflooding the marshes" (Collier 57). Eric wants assurance that the refilled beaver dams will not be "tapped of their water by the ranchers below" (Collier 57).

Eric and Lillian's intention of respecting and working with one of the region's powerful social institutions initially leads to disappointment. The Water Rights Branch responds, "We are of the opinion that your plan would be of no benefit whatsoever to the annual flow of Meldrum Creek," in a tone Collier describes as "polite, concise, chilly, the drab phraseology of officialdom wherever it might be encountered" (Collier 58). The register Collier recognizes is what Val Plumwood describes as the "sado-dispassionate rationalist model of personal objectivity" (41). This tone flourishes in an ecologically disastrous rationalist epistemology in which "emotional neutrality" is considered an "admirable trait" rather than, as Plumwood thinks of it, a "moral failing" (41). The rationalist epistemology derides subjective investment in an ecosystem, consequently ignoring rich bioregional knowledge; morality aside, "the drab phraseology of officialdom" misses much wisdom. Lorraine Code observes that bioregional narratives generate knowledge strengthened by "internal detail" and "situational sensitivity" (60–61). The Water Rights Branch letter writer has likely never seen the Meldrum Creek watershed; perhaps he or she has never seen a beaver, and certainly shows no understanding of the watershed's details.

The Colliers do not give up easily, and they next seek cooperation from a local authority figure who at least cannot disdain their plan from a "dispassionate" distance. Lillian suggests that Eric write a letter to Charles Moon, "the largest landowner in the valley" and a rancher with interest in a revivified watershed (Collier 58). Moon, downstream from the Colliers, has "first right on the creek for water" as well as social influence with other ranchers, and his committed conservation of any dammed ponds would be de facto protection for the Colliers' project (58). Moon's written response to the Colliers is sensitive to the watershed's dire condition: "Anything you do up there can't make matters much worse down here. I always have believed that the extermination of Meldrum Creek's beavers is largely responsible for the fix we are all in now. As far as I am concerned, go ahead with what you have in mind and let's see how it works" (58). These "vastly different results" to the Colliers' letter campaign show the practicality of a bioregional ecosophy. When the Colliers focus on making connections in their social register, they find cooperation for their work in the ecological register. Guattari would applaud the Colliers for strengthening "neighbourhood relations" as well as natural ecologies (Guattari 57–59).

The third register in Guattari's *Three Ecologies*, the mental (personal) ecological register, comes out of "focal points of creative subjectification" (57). Perhaps the most puzzling and provocative of the three registers, the mental register asks people to "pla[y] the game of the ecology of the imaginary" (57). Neither a return to bounded subjectivity nor a widening of already multiple postmodern subjectivities, Guattari's radicalized mental register requires an imaginative, flexible flow of both quotidian daily thinking and a limitless dream-state. From a reimagined mental register, creative ecosophies emerge, and any number of dreamed (and practical) restorative projects might take shape. Environmental historian and geographer William Cronon writes, "To protect the nature that is all around us, we must think long and hard about the nature we carry around inside our heads" (Cronon 20–21). Guattari would further ask that the "nature" in "our heads" must *be* the thinking we do; we must dream long, work imaginatively, and allow gracefully. We should allow creative relations and interspecies influences to inform our ecological practice. Guattari's ecosophers permit these influences and relations to run through their hearts, minds, and pocketbooks: a creative mapping of potential ecology.

Anticipating the kind of creative ecosophy that Guattari envisions, Eric Collier's narrative interludes of affective reflection, framing and introducing his narration of the restoration project, map the flow of his family's mental ecological register. As they approach the first physical labor of their restoration project, the game of "the ecology of the imaginary" becomes a joyful exercise: "And I'd have Lillian and Veasy, and a hundred and fifty thousand acres of wilderness, and as long as the three of us were together to share that wilderness, loneliness would never upset us. I was quite sure of that" (28). His optimism may be burnished by a memoirist's nostalgia, but I read this determination to happiness as a result of the Colliers' creative ecosophy. With their revisable ethic, the Colliers are free from restrictive notions of what a wilderness settler must do (usually, "carve" a hard-won niche, "discover" natural resources), how they must interact (usually, with suspicion and competition), or where they must position themselves on the species hierarchy (on the pinnacle). The Colliers behave openly and creatively, and their work becomes the language of bodies moving in a bioregion: the Western colonial image of man as subject moving relentlessly across an objectified landscape gives over to a reciprocal flow of human/nonhuman influences and intents. Happiness ushers the Colliers into this flow; later, they experience anger, sorrow, and fear, but the intensity of interspecies affect is constant.

Guattari's third register has a kinship with Gilles Deleuze and Félix Guattari's earlier notion of *becoming*, and especially *becoming-animal*. Philosopher Matthew Calarco writes that Deleuze and Guattari posit becoming-animal as "necessary" to the project of displacing "metaphysical humanism and anthropocentrism" (42). Like bioregionalism, Deleuze and Guattari's philosophy moves to dislodge anthropocentrism by "encountering and thinking from other-than-human perspectives" (Calarco 42). Deleuze and Guattari do not suggest that "becoming-animal entails actually *being* an animal" (42). Becoming is a transformative process, and is the result of "an encounter with nonhuman perspectives" (Calarco 42). But even the term *encounter* suggests a distinct human subjectivity under the influence of a nonhuman paradigm; Deleuze and Guattari describe becoming as a lateral movement, a process of creative evolution that "does not go from something less differentiated to something more differentiated" (ATP 238). Imagine a noncompetitive, creative, evolutionary exchange between spe-

cies; now imagine that this exchange moves rhizomatically, permeating species subjectivity as it moves. When this exchange flows between a human
and an animal (a pack or a single animal, or, in some cases, animal affect),
it is what Deleuze and Guattari call a becoming-animal.

In *Three against the Wilderness*, the Colliers know their bioregion as a
series of climatic and organic changes. Because they depend on the ecosystem for sustenance, they are vulnerable to these changes and receive them
affectively. They undertake their restoration project in this vulnerable state,
open to interspecies affective exchange. As Eric and Lillian begin repairing
the beaver dams, they move as a becoming-animal. With "the encourage-
ment of the rancher Moon," they decide, "In a few day's time, as soon as
the frost [is] gone from the ground, we too [are] to become beavers of sorts"
(95). The work they would do to repair the beaver dams at first seems "a
sheer impossibility," but by allowing an exchange of beaver-thinking to
influence their restoration, the task becomes a "grand design" (95). They
work to repair and maintain the beaver dams and to flood "every acre of
marsh upon the creek," all "without doing harm to anyone else" (95). Pro-
ceeding to "emplo[y] the tactics of a beaver itself," the pair study the materials and method the beavers used to build the dams (96). They gather the
same kinds of sticks, boughs, mud, and gravel, and apply them with "the
same principle" the beavers used, because, Eric says, "If it was good enough
for beavers it was good enough for us" (96). Through their mimetic labor,
the Colliers are affected *as* beavers *and* affect the wood and the water as
beavers. They profess to strive to harm "no-one," desiring a generative assemblage of animals and humans (96). The Colliers, at the moment when
their humanness would most limit their knowledge, become beaver. Following this becoming, relations between humans, animals, plants, and the
elements thrive in a regenerated and regenerative ecosystem.

Within weeks, with two dams repaired, the marshes become alive with
"crops of aquatic grasses and tubers" (97). The roots had been dormant,
needing beavers (or beaver-becoming humans) to reflood the marshes.
Within months, mallards, mink, and Canada geese return to the marshes.
Eventually beavers come back, ranchers' irrigation ditches fill, and the Colliers make a living hunting and trapping the Meldrum Creek watershed.

The Colliers, however, are trappers and hunters first, conservationists
second. Later in the narrative, Eric is enraged when wolves attack an "old
mother beaver" who would have "give[n] birth to four or five sturdy kits
each June for many a year to come" (207). He hates the wolves, their "san-

guinary lust for destruction," and in dramatic prose vows to hunt them (207). His animal-becoming flows with intense interspecies affect, and the limits of his ecosophy are the limits of his affective flow. The wolf who threatens Eric's beaver-lodge territory may demand a revised animal-human assemblage; Eric cannot extend his ecosophical community infinitely. His affective limit becomes an ecosophical limit, and he hunts the wolves with the same passion that he conserves the wetland.

Suffused as it is with the fears and desires of human subjectivity, motivated as much by the fur trade as by respect for ecology, the Colliers' project might be judged as a work of instrumental rationalism. However, I think that dismissing the ecosophical knowledge of this book because the Colliers continued to trap and hunt within the colonial fur economy would be shallow ecology, and that the inclusion of hunting, trapping, and ranching in the Colliers' bioregional ecosophy offers a contemporary environmental philosopher the ethical problem of the affective or instrumental limit. Surely the Colliers' ecosophical limits resonate with limits urban and rural people face today; while wolves and the colonial fur trade may not find direct parallels, trade, species hierarchies, and consumerism often limit the most sincere ecosophy. The bioregional particulars change while human limits recur. For this reason, studying ecology by observing interspecies affective exchange allows environmental thinkers to avoid moralizing or condemning humans as hopelessly anthropocentric; for a Deleuzian thinker, it is movements between and across species lines that allow for the most radical, the most startling ecological insight.

In the context of a bioregion, Deleuzian thinking proposes analysis of exchange, movement, and desire across ecological categories. The Colliers, in economic, social, and familial relations, as ecosophers and conservationists, are both affective organisms and bioregional citizens. Snyder recommends a bioregional citizenship based around the common cultural locus of a place; such a notion is compatible with Deleuze and Guattari's practice of following lines of connection and flight along a territory. Snyder offers the model of a watershed as a lateral, connective bioregion that needs intense interspecies cooperation: "Watershed consciousness and bioregionalism is not just environmentalism, not just a means toward resolution of social and economic problems, but a move toward a profound citizenship in both the natural and the social worlds. If the ground can be our common ground, we can begin to talk to each other (human and non-human) once again" (86). The Colliers' multiple intimacies with the Meldrum Creek watershed, along with a manifest goal to restore and maintain the diversity of the watershed ecosystem, provides them with accumulative, revisable, knowledge of how best to live in a bioregion.

NOTES

1. "Although Beavers are often considered destructive by anyone who happens to own property that these animals decide to log or flood, they perform a multitude of ecological services in a land of running water. In British Columbia's narrow, steep valleys, numerous small lakes and their inhabitants owe their existence to the stick and mud dams built by Beavers. In dry country, the pond behind the dam is an oasis, holding back the spring freshet and doling it out gradually through the summer. The Beavers' logging and flooding create sunny borders of sedge marsh and willow swamp, where Willow or Alder Flycatchers sally out after caddisflies; Common Yellowthroats, Northern Waterthrushes and Lincoln's Sparrows sing from the bushes; and Moose munch in the shallows. The flooded, dying trees that remain standing along the pond's edge become homes for woodpeckers, goldeneyes and Tree Swallows" (Cannings, *British Columbia* 290).

WORKS CITED

Barman, Jean. *The West beyond the West: A History of British Columbia.* 3rd ed. Toronto: University of Toronto Press, 2007. Print.

Braidotti, Rosi. "The Ethics of Becoming Imperceptible." *Deleuze and Philosophy.* Edinburgh: Edinburgh University Press, 2006. 133–59. Print.

Calarco, Matthew. *Zoographies: The Question of the Animal from Heidegger to Derrida."* New York: Columbia University Press, 2008. Print.

Cannings, Richard James, and Sydney Graham Cannings. *British Columbia: A Natural History.* Vancouver, B.C.: Greystone, 2000. Print.

Cariboo-Chilcotin Beetle Action Coalition. Web. <http://c-cbac.com/index.php>. July 2009.

Code, Lorraine. *Ecological Thinking: The Politics of Epistemic Location.* New York: Oxford University Press, 2006. Print.

Collier, Eric. *Three Against the Wilderness.* 1959. Surrey, B.C.: Touchwood, 2007. Print.

Conley, Verena Andermatt. "Artists or 'Little Soldiers?': Félix Guattari's Ecological Paradigms." *Deleuze/Guattari and Ecology.* Ed. Bernd Herzogenrath. N.Y.: Palgrave Macmillan, 2008. 116–27. Print.

Cronon, William, ed. "Foreword to the Paperback Edition." *Uncommon Ground: Toward Reinventing Nature.* New York: Norton, 1995. 19–22. Print.

Deleuze, Gilles, and Félix Guattari. *A Thousand Plateaus: Capitalism and Schizophrenia*. Trans. Brian Massumi. Minneapolis: University of Minnesota Press, 1987. Print.

Fenger, Mike, Todd Manning, John Cooper, Stewart Guy, and Peter Bradford. *Wildlife and Trees in British Columbia*. Edmonton: Lone Pine, 2006. Print.

Furniss, Elizabeth. *The Burden of History: Colonialism and the Frontier Myth in a Rural Canadian Community*. Vancouver: University of British Columbia Press, 1999. Print.

Guattari, Félix. *The Three Ecologies*. 1989. London: Athlone, 2000. Print.

Halsey, Mark. *Deleuze and Environmental Damage: Violence of the Text*. Hampshire, England: Ashgate, 2006. Print.

Hayden, Patrick. *Multiplicity and Becoming: The Pluralist Empiricism of Gilles Deleuze*. New York: Grove/Atlantic, 1998. Print.

Morice, A. G. *The History of the Northern Interior of British Columbia*. Cloverdale, B.C.: Interior Stationary, 1978. Print.

Nikiforuk, Andrew. "Pine Plague." *Canadian Geographic* 127.1 (January/February 2007): 68–76.

Plumwood, Val. *Environmental Culture: The Ecological Crisis of Reason*. New York: Routledge, 2002. Print.

Snyder, Gary. "Coming into the Watershed: Biological and Cultural Diversity in the California Habitat." *Chicago Review* 39.3/4 (1993): 75–86.

Turkel, William J. *The Archive of Place: Unearthing the Pasts of the Chilcotin Plateau*. Vancouver: University of British Columbia Press, 2007. Print.

Wynn, Graeme. "'Shall We Linger Along Unambitionless?': Environmental Perspectives on British Columbia." *BC Studies: On the Environment* 142,43 (2004): 5–68. Print.

CHAD WRIGLESWORTH

The Poetics of Water

Currents of Reclamation in the Columbia River Basin

SINCE 1902, western watersheds in the United States have been managed by the Bureau of Reclamation, an extension of the U.S. Department of Interior that was established to ensure the equitable distribution of water for purposes of settlement, irrigation, and hydroelectric production in seventeen arid and semiarid states. During the 1930s, federal engineers identified the Columbia River Basin as a latent powerhouse and planned to put it to work with hydroelectric dams made to serve regional and national interests. Franklin Delano Roosevelt's New Deal supported the Columbia Basin Project (1933), which was followed by the Reclamation Project Act (1939), and paved the way for nineteen hydroelectric dams on the main stems of the Columbia and Snake Rivers, forces of natural and human energy that transformed the free-flowing watershed into the largest producer of hydroelectricity in North America, or what Richard White rightly calls an "organic machine" (106).

The socioeconomic and ecological consequences of remaking the Columbia River Basin into a national seat of hydroelectric production are well documented by environmental historians, but changes to the watershed can also be traced through the work of bioregional poets who use turnings of verse to chart and enact changes to the river while also calling for more localized and sustainable methods of watershed inhabitation. William Stafford, Ed Edmo, Elizabeth Woody, and Sherman Alexie are among those who use the poetic line to communicate the fluid relationships between rhythms of language and watersheds by imagining the Columbia

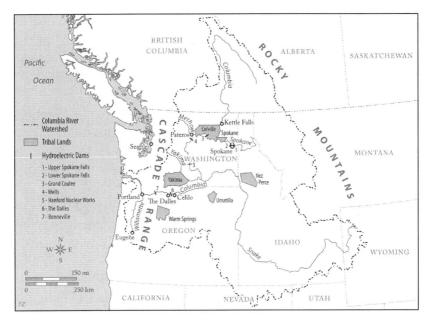

The Columbia River Watershed

River as a sort of poem, a force to be surveyed, measured, and even re-created through turnings of verse that are regulated and released by tools such as line breaks, dashes, commas, and periods. Robert L. Thayer Jr. claims that as local interest groups work to reclaim contested places, "a distinctly regional art, aesthetics, literature, poetics, and music can evolve from and support bioregional culture" (94). Although there are no indications that poetry will topple federally managed dams on the Columbia River Basin anytime soon, the transformation of place is currently under way along the Methow and Spokane Rivers, tributaries of the Columbia River, where bioregional poetry and public art are re-creating how the watersheds are understood and inhabited.

Contemporary poets of the Columbia River Basin are calling for more sustainable and localized methods of watershed inhabitation, but previous generations of national and regional artists actually supported the Bureau of Reclamation's vision of national progress. In 1941, Woody Guthrie was hired by the Bonneville Power Administration to write pro-hydroelectric folksongs like "Jackhammer Blues" and "Roll On, Columbia, Roll On" in support of Grand Coulee and Bonneville dams. At the same time, works of regional journalism such as Richard Neuberger's *Our Promised Land* (1938) and Murray Morgan's *The Columbia: Powerhouse of the West* (1949) linked local prosperity to hydroelectric dams, while Northwest novelists Margaret Thompson and Nard Jones made their own contributions to federal reclamation with novels such as *Space for Living: A Novel of the Grand Coulee and Columbia Basin* (1944) and *Still to the West* (1946).

Federal reclamation projects such as Bonneville, Grand Coulee, and The Dalles Dam provided inhabitants of the Columbia River Basin with numerous benefits, including thousands of jobs, affordable electricity, irrigation, flood control, and assurances of national security; however, the rapid and uneven development of the watershed also came with high social and environmental price tags, particularly for Native Americans, who depended on key salmon-fishing sites for biological sustenance, economic stability, and religious practices. When the intake gates of Bonneville Dam closed (1937), indigenous fisheries at Cascade Rapids were flooded; two years later, construction at Grand Coulee Dam (1939) blocked seventy percent of the Columbia's salmon spawning grounds, severing migrations to Kettle Falls and the Spokane River, primary salmon fisheries for the Confederated Tribes of the Colville Reservation and the Spokane Tribe of Indians. Celilo Falls, the last indigenous fishery on the mainline Columbia, was inundated by The Dalles Dam (1957). This ten-mile stretch of channels and rapids was the primary salmon fishery for Yakama, Warm Springs, Umatilla and Nez Perce Indians, and a place recognized as one of the oldest continuously inhabited communities in North America.

The inundation of Celilo Falls sparked local resistance against the federal reclamation of the Columbia River Basin, but signs of unrest were emerging at the close of World War II, when William Stafford began to question the controversial management and use of the river's power. In the wake of the bombing of Hiroshima and Nagasaki, the United States learned that Bonneville and Grand Coulee Dam enabled the production of plutonium at Hanford Engineer Works, the secret engineering plant that generated materials for "Fat Man," the atomic bomb detonated on Nagasaki in 1945. Stafford, a conscientious objector to the war, worked at pacifist labor camps in Illinois, California, and Arkansas before moving to Oregon to teach at Lewis and Clark College in 1948. An excerpt from his daily writing, dated 1951, recalls a trip made to Bonneville Dam Visitors' Center. While most citizens at the facility encountered the dam as a feat of human ingenuity, Stafford identified the dam as a "hemorrhage." He stood in line to tour the facility and was reminded of "an old forgotten sign" that told him to "be sure you are fighting the right enemy" ("Daily Writing").

Stafford's initial reflections evolved into "The Fish Counter at Bonneville" (c. 1951), a poem that articulates social and ecological anxieties that were beginning to circulate throughout the Columbia River Basin. From a comparative standpoint, the poem is a sharp critique of nationalist propaganda that was distributed by the Bonneville Power Administration during the 1940s. In a film called *Hydro* (1940), public viewers were promised that hydroelectric dams would provide jobs, create cheap electricity, and enhance salmon migration through the use of man-made fish ladders. In fact, the fish ladder at Bonneville, described by the narrator of *Hydro* as "the strangest channel ever made by man," was promised to be a much "easier" passageway for salmon to navigate than the "boiling Cascade Rapids" flooded by the dam. As evidence, the film shows footage of a laborer struggling to count an abundance of salmon migrating through the fish ladder. This image, joined by narration that optimistically announced "the salmon are going through," convinced citizens that the Columbia River was actually being improved by reclamation technologies. From Stafford's perspective, the Bonneville Dam was a dragonlike machine created to "spit its flame" of "power" across nations. Closer to home, energy produced by the dam was ironically beginning to shed "light" on the ecological problems embedded within the reclamation process. As Stafford surmised, the fish counter at Bonneville Dam, the salmon, and tourists shuttled through the visitors' center were all participants in a federally managed "game" that "killed a river" and now herded "dumb shapes" and voiceless "Chinook souls" through man-made chambers of power (*The Way It Is* 68).

Stafford's suspicion that hydroelectric dams were killing the Columbia River peaked with the completion of The Dalles Dam (1957), an event that caused the "Death of Celilo Falls" and sparked more literary resistance against the federal process than any other event in the watershed's complex history. Ed Edmo, a Shoshone-Bannock poet and storyteller, grew up at Celilo Falls from 1946–1957 and was twelve when the falls and salmon fishery were inundated by The Dalles Dam. Edmo was accustomed to meeting white visitors, tourists, and photographers at Celilo Falls, but on one occasion he met a U.S. government official whose appearance and mannerisms enacted the mechanistic vision of hydroelectric progress that arrived to flood his home and the ancient fishery. He describes the memory in "Celilo Blues" (1985), a poem that begins with a staggered current of unpunctuated lines—that *fall* down the page—in a series of gravitational steps, like the ten-mile flow of rapids that defined the pre-inundated site. As Edmo explains:

> he arrived
> automation-atomic-government-man
> with briefcase in hand
>
> wire rimmed glasses
> that hung from his nose
>   his whining voice
>   came out in a
>   never ending drone. (13)

The multihyphenated title of the nameless government man suggests he was welded together and operated by a series of cogs and wheels that cranked out the "whining voice" and "never ending drone" that came from his mechanized body. Edmo's use of the word "drone" and repetition of long vowels cast the man as a sort of worker bee, a laborer who hums the turbine-tune of The Dalles Dam and a litany of "promising / promises" rehearsed to browbeat Columbia River Indians into federal compliance. From Edmo's perspective, this industrialized laborer was programmed with "deafened / ears" separated from his body, via the poetic line, and "paid / not to hear."

As "Celilo Blues" continues, the visual structure of the poem moves from a current of cascading descent into a linear channel of funneled oppression that ends on the word *drowned*. More than a word, it is a visual marker that enacts the burden of the federal government's version of progress that weighs heavily on Columbia River Indians. As Edmo remembers, when the agent was finished

> mouthing
> words of pre-recorded
> briefing sessions
> behind armed guards
>
> again
> we drowned (13)

The phrase "we drowned" is buried at the bottom of a linear current that enacts the repercussions of The Dalles Dam. Moreover, it is offset by *again*, a word that calls readers to consider deeper patterns of injustice within a tradition of treaty making and the legislation of unjust land and water rights. These patterns are evident in *Hydro* (1940), a film that promised viewers that Columbia River Indians, whose salmon "means their very existence," would "go on spearing the royal Chinook in the tumultuous roar of Celilo Falls," when in reality the Army Corps of Engineers and Bureau of Reclamation had already proposed the construction of a hydroelectric dam at The Dalles in 1932 (Billington and Jackson 153). From this perspective, Edmo's use of the word "again" illustrates how the inundation of Celilo Falls was a horrific event, but actually "shockingly unremarkable and predictable" in the longer history of U.S. and Columbia River Indian relations (Barber 184).

Elizabeth Woody was born in 1959, two years after the inundation of Celilo Falls. As an enrolled member of the Confederated Tribes of Warm Springs, she has spent much of her life hearing stories about the death of Celilo Falls "as an orphan lives hearing of the kindness and greatness of his or her mother" ("Recalling" 10). This sense of personal and communal loss is documented in "The Markers of Absence," a poem from *Luminaries of the Humble* (1994) that strives "to give voice to" the "many people who struggle to make small gains of renewal" after the loss of Celilo Falls (xiv–xv). Throughout the poem, Woody uses personification to document and enact inscriptions on the land and waterway that are ongoing reminders of the socioeconomic and ecological repercussions of The Dalles Dam. She writes:

> The leaves denote by their pitch
> the endurance of drought.
> The clouds are sallow exhaustion.
> Tumbleweeds roll a weak case
> for the heart of shadows.
> Flowers known to no one are tiny
> with tough hides, sigh the color of sienna. (21)

Like an actual book, the "leaves" of this sparsely treed landscape "denote" a physical and acoustic "pitch" that is socioeconomic as well as ecological. In the wake of The Dalles Dam, the indigenous community at Celilo Falls has become an unpopulated landscape of "sallow exhaustion," a place that bears people with tough hides the "color of sienna," but who are seemingly "known to no one." The tumbleweeds, like their voices of resistance, continue to speak of federal injustice, but "roll a weak" legislative "case / for the heart of shadows" (21).

Looking to the river, the largest markers of absence are etched by Lake Celilo, a place of slack water behind The Dalles Dam that covers history in need of excavation. While surveying and literally measuring—via the poetic line—what has been lost to the reclamation process, Woody uses a set of restrictive commas to enact and bind the condition of the waterway, thus, slowing the current of the river as well as her poem. She writes:

> The river turns, leveling, from the white
> demarcation on the bank.
> Reminder of stains that tears have left
> as collected, by increments gained and as lost
> as Salmon. No one grows or laughs. (21)

Until this point, the lines of the poem moved with minimal syntactical restraint, but here the lyrical current, like the waterway being described, is restricted by two damlike commas, slowing and regulating a stretch of words that describes the "leveling" consequences of federal reclamation. The word *turns* is equally provocative, for despite the appearance of stagnation, the inundated falls continue to turn below the surface. Through the fluidity of language, the word *turns* also shifts and evokes a tone of betrayal when joined with the word *white*. Moving this direction, suggests the silenced river has turned away from "white" laborers of progress who survey and mark the watershed according to "increments" of economic gain and loss. Their measurements are indicated by a "white" line of brine on the water's edge, a point of "demarcation" that continues to rewrite the river according to principles of federal reclamation. From Woody's perspective, this process has turned Celilo Falls into a place of human *tears*, a word that also testifies how The Dalles Dam creates "tears" in the watershed's complex social and ecological fabric. This reality is enacted in the closing lines of the poem, when Woody breaks the poetic line between "lost" and "Salmon," literally separating the fish from the larger current of her site-based poem.

Poetry by Ed Edmo and Elizabeth Woody illustrate ways that currents of poetry can document the historical and geographical transformation of the Columbia River Basin, which leads one to wonder if poetry might transform this watershed in the future. There are signs of this taking place through locally initiated projects on the Methow River and Spokane River, tributaries within the watershed that are being re-created through the presence of bioregional poetry and public art.

In 1993, Sheela McLean and Curtis Edwards, two Forest Service rangers, were stationed along the Northern Cascades Highway in Winthrop, Washington. They were responsible for designing natural-history signs along the Methow River, a vibrant stretch of water that originates in the 8,000-foot peaks of the Northern Cascades, before it weaves through the Methow Valley and joins the Columbia River at the town of Pateros. As natural-history writers, the rangers wanted to offer "hundreds of thousands of tourists" who visit the area each year something more than consumable and encyclopedic facts about the river. A thought came to mind: it might be possible to help visitors feel or remember something about the Methow Valley by merging poetry with natural-history writing. They wrote William Stafford a letter and explained their situation in the following way: "We are tired of our own mediocre natural-history writing. We need someone who can relate feelings as well as facts with only a few words. Poetry, actually, is what we need" (McLean and Edwards, 20 April 1993). They invited Stafford to write site-specific poetry for seven porcelain enamel signs that would be joined with artwork and natural-history writing and mounted at predetermined locations along a fifty-mile stretch of the Methow River.

The project evolved into *The Methow River Poems* (1994), an innovative confluence of poetry and place that invites readers to consider the interdependent relationships that humans share with place. The first poem in the sequence is located at Pateros, Washington, a small town that marks where the Methow River merges with the Columbia just above Wells Dam (1967). At this place, where the water runs smooth and wide, readers encounter "Time for Serenity, Anyone?" a poem that explores the permeable relationship between language, the body, and nature. Stafford begins the poem by telling readers,

> I like to live in the sound of water,
> in the feel of mountain air.

The repetition of the preposition *in* collapses the body into the river's surroundings, as sound and breath are enveloped into air and water—elements that sustain the entire poem—as well as human existence. As the current of the poem continues to move with the river, Stafford reminds visitors that this slow-moving stretch of backwater is "still alive," using the word *still* to document apparent stasis, as well as the resilience of the river. Stafford writes,

> . . . A sharp
> reminder hits me: this world is still alive;
> it stretches out there shivering toward its own
> creation, and I'm part of it. Even my breathing
> enters into this elaborate give-and-take,
> this bowing to sun and moon, day or night,
> winter, summer, storm, still—this tranquil
> chaos that seems to be going somewhere.
> This wilderness with a great peacefulness in it.
> This motionless turmoil, this everything dance. (*Even* 95)

By describing water as "shivering" over a more predictable "shimmering," Stafford steers readers away from encountering an inanimate reflection. Instead, the river is alive, comingling with the reader's body as it "stretches" and is "shivering" along the bank. When the traveler stops to read this poem out loud, even "breathing / enters into this elaborate give-and-take," as the essence of the body is released into language—given back to the earth's wind-breath—and then renewed by line break and inhalation. Stafford offers readers new possibilities for inhabiting place, but will not offer visitors clean categories, souvenirs, or consumable facts about the river. Instead, they are confronted with paradoxes like "tranquil / chaos" and "motionless turmoil," phrases that are not reconciled, but left to stand as an "everything dance," a holistic and manifold presence that resists measurement and human possession.

To gain further insight on ways bioregional poetry and public art can transform place and environmental policies, we need only to follow the Columbia River to the confluence of the Spokane River, and travel upriver to downtown Spokane, Washington, where a public installation of Sherman Alexie's poem "That Place Where the Ghosts of Salmon Jump" has contributed to the rewriting of water policy at Spokane Falls. The process began in 1990, when the citizens of Spokane, Washington, approved a 28.8-million-dollar bond measure for the construction of a new library facility in downtown Spokane. In an effort to integrate the history and aesthetic appeal of the falls into the architectural design of the new building, the Spokane Public Library Board of Trustees allocated one percent of funds to support public art projects to integrate aspects of the river into the downtown library. In the process, they reclaimed and developed Overlook Park, a one-time 600-square-foot parking lot across the street from the library that is now home to Alexie's poem.

"That Place Where the Ghosts of Salmon Jump" begins by turning to a Salish Indian story about the creation of Spokane Falls. The story tells of a meeting with Coyote, the hero-trickster-buffoon who appears in Native American stories all throughout the West. Throughout the Columbia River Basin, Coyote was particularly tuned to the rhythms of salmon, and as a character with an appetite for beautiful wives, was known to offer or restrict the migration of fish depending on tribes' willingness to accommodate his voracious appetites. According to indigenous accounts of the falls, a dispute between Coyote and Salish leaders led to the creation of Spokane Falls. Coyote was traveling up the Spokane River and arrived at the place where Spokane Falls now exist. He was determined to take a young Salishan wife for his partner, but was denied and mocked by tribal elders. Enraged and lonely, Coyote punished the Salishan tribes by creating Spokane Falls so that salmon could no longer pass up the river.[1]

"That Place Where Salmon Jump" speaks directly into the Salishan story, but also reshapes the past through modern developments on the Spokane River. Alexie tells readers that

> Coyote was alone and angry because he could not find love.
> Coyote was alone and angry because he demanded a wife
> from the Spokane, the Coeur d'Alene, the Palouse, all of those tribes
> camped on the edge of the Spokane River. (19)

After being rejected and mocked by leaders and those gathered to fish, Alexie also explains how the unrequited lover smashed his paw across the water—splitting open the river bottom—so that salmon could not travel beyond the falls. The tone of the poem shifts when Alexie tells Coyote that the loss of salmon above Spokane Falls has nothing to do with mythical powers, but the presence of white men who have poured a "graveyard" of "concrete" over the river. After calling Coyote a "liar" and someone not to be trusted, Alexie points to the work of white engineers who installed a network of dams, penstocks, and turbines—creating a place of extinction—where only the "ghosts of salmon jump." As evidence, the young poet challenges the old trickster, as well as readers at the installation, to look over the falls and try to

> see beyond all of the concrete
> the white man has built here. (19)

This allusion references a series of seven dams on the Spokane River that were constructed between 1890 and 1922 and managed by the Washington Water and Power Company. The dams were not designed with fish ladders or passageways for salmon, the most important source of biological and spiritual health for Spokane and Colville tribes. Anthropologists estimate that in years preceding the rapid transformation of the Spokane River, Spokane Indians harvested roughly 500 pounds of salmon per person each year, accounting for approximately five-eighths of each individual's annual consumption of food (Fahey 122). The completion of Little Falls Dam ended salmon migration on the upper Spokane River, but for the next twenty years, salmon continued spawning near the Spokane Reservation, below Little Falls Dam. These migrations ended when the Bureau of Reclamation closed the intake gates of the Grand Coulee Dam (1939) and severed all salmon spawning grounds in the watershed's upper interior.

In *The Summer of Black Widows* (1996), "That Place Where the Ghosts of Salmon Jump" reads as a sequence of couplets, but at the publically installed version of Alexie's poem, the structure of the verse moves as a single line of current that spirals through a line etched in granite and concrete. To read the poem, readers must "step into" the current of concrete and ascend a textual version of the Spokane River. As readers step into the poem as metaphorical salmon, they migrate toward the falls—the poem's center—and are spun and turned by a series of textual currents. When they reach the last phrase of the poem, they are left "alone and angry" inside a constricted space of concrete. Originally, Alexie was not sure if he liked the design of the poem, but one day, while lurking in the distance, he saw "a man and woman walking the spiral to read the poem." At that point, he was hooked. He explains, "Their movement was a dance. The design forces people to dance. The true power of it is watching people read it in that way" (Petitt 57). The image of a "man and woman" dancing through a current of watery words is provocative and potentially regenerative, for it evokes a permeable relationship between humans and salmon, the latter of which can no longer migrate past Grand Coulee Dam to perform their spawning "dance" of regeneration.[2]

Recently, the public presence of "That Place Where the Ghosts of Salmon Jump" has made significant contributions to the flow of water on the Spokane River. A major controversy of the dams operated by the Washington Water and Power Company, now Avista Corporation, has been the seasonal diversion of water by the Upper Falls Dam (1922) for purposes of hydroelectric production. For decades, the company diverted all of the river's water through a series of penstocks and left Lower Spokane Falls completely dry for much of the summer. Alexie alludes to the ongoing nature of this problem by telling Coyote and readers of the public installation that since completion of the dams the falls have "fallen further" and now "sit dry and quiet as a graveyard" (19).

The Upper Falls Dam operational license was up for fifty-year renewal in 2009. In an attempt to make a once-in-a-lifetime change to public water policy on the Spokane River, regional activists penned letters to the Washington State Department of Ecology, posted letters and alerts on websites, and spoke on behalf of the falls at hearings with the Federal Energy Regulatory Commission, repeatedly citing Alexie's lamentation about concrete barriers, dry falls, and ghosts of salmon as a witness to environmental injustice. During the campaign, John Osborne, webmaster and board member for the Center for Environmental Law and Policy, states that Alexie's poem was distributed to thousands of activists and played an integral role in the campaign. Through the efforts of the Spokane-based organization, the Sierra Club, and the Berman Environmental Law Clinic at University of Washington, a court settlement was reached with Avista Corporation that will revise the management of Lower Spokane Falls, guaranteeing a year-round flow.

Using poetry and public art to re-create the Columbia River Basin may not seem like normative practice, but accounts of the Methow River and Spokane Falls are indicative of ways that site-based literature contributes to the ongoing reinscription and reclamation of place. Gary Snyder alludes to this phenomenon in *The Practice of the Wild* (1990), when he describes land and waterways as archival texts that carry histories of human interactions with place. He explains, "A place will have been half riverbed, it will have been scratched and plowed by ice. And then it will be cultivated, paved, sprayed, dammed, graded, built up. But each is only for a while, and that will be just another set of lines on the palimpsest. The whole earth is a great tablet holding the multiple overlaid new and ancient traces of the swirl of forces" (29). From this bioregional perspective of time and place, literary criticism can excavate "the swirl of forces" that transformed specific watersheds; but more importantly, the arts can undermine and contest environmental injustices in ways that call for the reconstruction of human relationships with place. Although the future of the Columbia River Basin sometimes appears to be murky, there are good reasons to believe that bioregional poetry and public art will contribute to the ongoing re-creation of this long-contested watershed.

NOTES

This research was assisted by a Recent Doctoral Recipients Fellowship, which is part of the Andrew W. Mellon/American Council of Learned Societies Early Career Fellowship Program.

  1. For Native American accounts of Coyote and the creation of Spokane Falls see: Thompson and Egesdal 191–192; and Judson.

  2. Salmon migration and spawning is often referred to as a "dance." For examples of this see: Woody, "Voice of the Land" 155; Duncan 113, 124–125; and Lang and Lang 55–56.

WORKS CITED

Abbott, Carl. *Greater Portland: Urban Life and Landscape in the Pacific Northwest.* Philadelphia: University of Pennsylvania Press, 2001. Print.

Alexie, Sherman. *The Summer of Black Widows.* New York: Hanging Loose Press, 1996. Print.

Barber, Katrine. *Death of Celilo Falls.* Seattle: University of Washington Press, 2005. Print.

Billington, David P., and Donald C. Jackson. *Big Dams of the New Deal Era.* Norman: University of Oklahoma Press, 2006. Print.

Duncan, David James. *My Story as Told by Water.* San Francisco: Sierra Club, 2002. Print.

Edmo, Ed. *These Few Words of Mine.* Marvin, S.Dak.: Blue Cloud Quarterly Press, 1985. Print.

Fahey, John. "Power Plays: The Enigma of Little Falls." *Pacific Northwest Quarterly* 82.4 (October 1991): 122–131. Print.

Guthrie, Woody. *Columbia River Collection.* CD. Cambridge, Mass.: Rounder Records, 1987.

Hydro: The Story of Columbia River Power. Video Cassette. Portland, Ore.: Bonneville Power Administration, 1940.

Jones, Nard. *Still to the West.* New York: Dodd and Mead, 1946. Print.

Judson, Katharine Berry. *Myths and Legends of the Pacific Northwest.* Lincoln: University of Nebraska Press, 1997. Print.

Lang, Fraser, and Alison Lang. "The Salmon Circle." *Home! A Bioregional Reader.* Ed. Van Andruss, Christopher Plant, Judith Plant, and Eleanor Wright. Philadelphia: New Society, 1990. Print.

McLean, Sheela, and Curtis Edwards. "Letter to William Stafford: April 20, 1993." William Stafford Archives, Lewis and Clark College, Portland, Oregon. Print.

Morgan, Murray. *The Columbia: Powerhouse of the West.* Seattle: Superior, 1949. Print.

Neuberger, Richard L. *Our Promised Land.* New York: Macmillan, 1938. Print.

Pettit, Stephanie. "Spiral of Alexie Poem a Visual Monument." *The Spokesman-Review.* 7 February 2008: 57. Print.

Snyder, Gary. *The Practice of the Wild.* San Francisco: North Point, 1990. Print.

Stafford, William. "Daily Writing, September 7, 1951." *William Stafford Archives.* Lewis and Clark College, n.d. Web. 16 Jan. 2011. http://williamstaffordarchives.org/poem/23/.

———. *Even in Quiet Places.* Ed. Kim Stafford and Jim Hepworth. Lewiston, Idaho: Confluence Press, 1996. Print.

———. *The Way It Is.* Minneapolis: Gray Wolf Press, 1999. Print.

Thayer, Robert, Jr. *LifePlace: Bioregional Thought and Practice.* Berkeley: University of California Press, 2003. Print.

Thompson, Margaret. *Space for Living: A Novel of the Grand Coulee and Columbia Basin.* Portland: Binfords and Mort, 1944. Print.

Thompson, Terry, and Steven M. Egesdal, eds. *Salish Myths and Legends: One People's Stories.* Lincoln: University of Nebraska Press, 2008. Print.

White, Richard. *The Organic Machine.* New York: Hill and Wang, 1995. Print.

Woody, Elizabeth. *Luminaries of the Humble.* Tucson: University of Arizona Press, 1994. Print.

———. "Recalling Celilo." *Salmon Nation: People, Fish, and Our Common Home.* Ed. Edward C. Wolf and Seth Zuckerman. Portland, Ore.: Ecotrust, 1999. 9–16. Print.

———. "Voice of the Land: Giving the Good Word." *Speaking for the Generations: Native Writers on Writing.* Ed. Simon Ortiz. Tucson: University of Arizona Press, 1998. Print.

SERENELLA IOVINO

Restoring the Imagination of Place

Narrative Reinhabitation and the Po Valley

For Cheryll

W HEN YOU TRAVEL along the countryside of the Po Valley, it is hard not to feel like a stranger." The speaker of these lines is a native writer, Gianni Celati, who was born in Sondrio, Lombardy, and grew up in Ferrara, near the river's mouth. In such a rich and culturally specific bioregion, one in which territorial stances based on place identity led an autonomist party in the government coalition called the Northern League, a native feels like a stranger. Why might this be so? Maybe because a profound crisis, both cultural and ecological, is fatally affecting these places, a crisis stunningly visible in the landscape's decline: once the heart of a fertile country and of potentially harmonious comingling of nature and urbanization, the Po River Valley is now one of Europe's most polluted fluvial areas.

How to respond to this crisis? The autonomist proposals have so far proven inadequate. They have, in fact, little to do with the protection of an endangered heritage, serving rather an ideology of territorialism, industrial development, local privilege, and xenophobia. But if a cultural survival strategy is required, bioregionalism might, in turn, become a valuable tool. Bioregional narratives, in particular, can be used as tools to "restore the imagination" of place, namely, to understand and to orient the evolutionary dynamics connected to the life of place, involving an open and more inclusive reflection on identity, history, and ecology.

100

THE PO VALLEY: BIOREGION OR NECROREGION?

The Po River Valley (*Valle padana* or *Pianura padana*) is a vast bioregion of the Italian territory: extending along 46,584 square miles, it covers nearly one-fourth of the country's entire area. The Po (Latin: *Padus*) is the longest Italian river: from its sources on Mount Monviso (Cozie Alps), in Piedmont, to its six-fold mouth in the Adriatic Sea, it flows along 405 miles, crossing four of the major Italian regions: Piedmont, Lombardy, Veneto, and Emilia-Romagna. The Valley is densely populated (fifteen million inhabitants) and its human alteration can be dated back to the Cenozoic Era. The river's course has been constantly modified by human activities. The mouth, in particular, has experienced large and continuous alterations, especially due to the massive deforestation in the inland zones. Some areas have been declared protected with the institution of the Po Fluvial Park (35.689 hectares).[1] Since the early 1990s, the Po Valley and Northern Italy in general are often referred to as "Padania," a polemic denomination introduced by the Northern League against the centralized state.

The ecology of the Po and its valley is, like many other Italian bio-

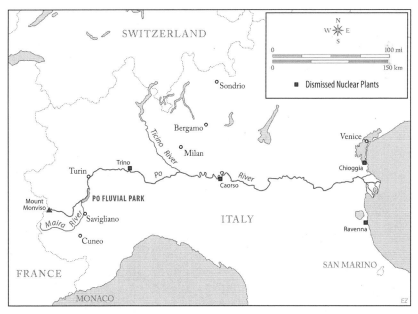

Italy's Po River Watershed

regions, long and deeply compromised. After decades of uncontrolled industrial development and urban sprawl, made recently even more serious
by the criminal business of the so-called ecomafia,[2] the Po Valley is slowly
dying. A dying region is literally at odds with the very idea of a *bio*region. A
detectable state of cultural and ecological abandon indicates that it would
be more realistic to speak, here, of a *necro*region. In a landscape of suburban countryside made of houses, industrial sites, electric power plants,
and decommissioned nuclear reactors, the "stories" and "wisdom" of places
seem on the verge of extinction. Once the familiar bond that connected
people and their landscape has been worn out, a growing sense of alienation takes over. Gianni Celati, quoted at the beginning, describes this
feeling of estrangement as a transitive state, affecting both the self and the
land: "When you travel along the countryside of the Po Valley, it is hard
not to feel like a stranger. More than the Po's pollution, more than the sick
trees, more than the industrial stench, more than the state of abandon in
which lays everything not involved in the making of profit, even more than
a building development made for interchangeable residents, with no country nor destination—more than all that, what is surprising is this new kind
of countryside, where all you can breathe is an air of urban solitude" (9).[3]

The problem of the Po Valley, Celati suggests, is the material crisis of
its landscape as a life place. A living landscape, with its built environment,
is an attempt "to make place out of raw space" (Thayer 103). A place is a
space where one can imagine living, a home to which values, in ethical and
aesthetic terms, are attached. What happened to the Po Valley is exactly
the reverse. From a place, this country has been turned back to a mere
space—a space for real estate, for intensive farming and agriculture, for
energy production, for industrial development: a space for "growth." In
the Po Valley space has become more valuable than place. If sense of place
is lost, it is because this place—in Celati's picture a depressed countryside
disguised as urban outskirts—makes no sense anymore.

ET IN PADANIA EGO; OR, HOW I BECAME A NATIVE

I am not a native of this place. I saw the Po for the first time some thirteen
years ago, following a native, Maurizio, who subsequently became my husband. We spent four years wandering across Italy and Germany, naively be-
lieving that philosophy students should feel at home where good libraries

are. In 2000, Maurizio got his professorship at Turin University. One year later, I obtained mine. We moved here, deciding to settle down in Savigliano, a little baroque town, deep in Padania's productive countryside.

It was not easy for me to get used to this place. Not easy, as a person accustomed to feel the Mediterranean wind mounting on a calm, maternal sea which nobody would ever call "the ocean." And not easy, as a southern Italian, to be transplanted into a land where, for decades, southerners have been seen as inconvenient strangers, up to the point that when, in the early 1990s, a protest party arose, it chose to name itself the *Northern* League.

But, little by little, I started to appreciate this country. I started to value these agricultural plains, the wetlands where Thomas Jefferson once came to buy rice, which in the spring are home to herons and cranes; these precious vineyards that novelist Cesare Pavese described as waves within the plains; the precarious terracotta belfries where storks nest. I learned to see this wounded landscape, with its polluted soils and waterways, its ambivalent residents, its ancient beauty replaced by ugly factories and anonymous condos. Little by little, this place was growing into me. It was rising in my imagination, and my imagination was out there. This place was making sense to me.

My dawning awareness was reflected in my everyday life: in the small choices, such as the purchasing of food directly from the local farmers at the weekly market.[4] And in choices not so small, such as that to campaign against the decision of the town's administration to "secure"—by means of reinforced concrete cages—the banks of the Maira river, a minor tributary of the Po, alleged to endanger the population in case of heavy rain. (To my sadness, and to the sadness of many fellow citizens, the campaign was a complete failure. The "securing" of the river banks ended up with the destruction of an entire ecosystem, resulting in an ecological and aesthetic disaster.)

It was inevitable that living here would affect my work. In my early Padanian years, seconding a physiological metamorphosis, I was converting from German philosophy and literature to environmental ethics and ecocriticism. This made me particularly sensitive to the landscape of values and stories that intersected with the landscape of people and places. As I came to realize, values and stories were people and places, indeed. They were people and places declined over time, stories being an imaginary or real vision of the past, and values (both social and natural) being the condition to extend the present into a project of permanence or of sustainable transformation. My research and classes reflected this new awareness: understanding, interpreting, and teaching about place-based stories and values was becoming an instrument of social pedagogy, something that could be helpful to restore the imagination of this place. I did not know it clearly yet, but if to imagine a place is the first step to reinhabiting it, this was becoming my personal contribution to my new home.

FROM PRACTICE TO THEORY: UNDERSTANDING A PLACE'S MIND

Reading bioregional texts can be very useful to conceptualize this experience. Berg and Dasmann's idea of reinhabitation, in particular, offers a very interesting theoretical framework. In fact, it reflects a situation's critical condition, revealing at the same time the possible keys for a survival strategy: "*Reinhabitation* means learning to live-in-place in an area that has been disrupted and injured through past exploitation. It involves becoming native to a place through becoming aware of the particular ecological relationships that operate within and around it. It means understanding activities and evolving social behavior that will enrich the life of that place, restore its life-supporting systems, and establish an ecologically and socially sustainable pattern of existence within it. Simply stated, it involves becoming fully active in and with a place" (399).

As here outlined, reinhabitation is not only a mode of ecological restoration and planning, but—and primarily—an ethical-educational practice. In areas that have been "disrupted and injured," like the Po Valley, reinhabitation means *learning* to *live*-in-place. Since we normally live in our places without a prior education to live-in-place, this task entails both awareness and commitment. For this reason, Berg and Dasmann aver that reinhabitation involves activities and behaviors based on the *understanding* of the "life of that place," a life that results from the *coevolution* of society and natural environment.

But here a further question occurs: What does it mean to understand the life of a place, and what are the "particular ecological relationships that operate within and around it"? As epistemologist Gregory Bateson maintained, within and around the ecology of living forms an ecology of ideas, or of mind, exists, which strictly interacts with the former one. In this framework, *mind* is not synonymous with human *self* nor *brain*—it is in turn an ecological function, mirroring the concrete, ineludible interrelatedness between the self and the environment. To say that our ideas are "out there" means that they come from (and are part of) that complex circuit of information that constitutes the world.[5] American ecophenomenologist David Abram has lyrically expressed this thought in a recent volume: "Mind . . . is very much like a medium in which we're situated, and from which we are simply unable to extricate ourselves without ceasing to exist. Everything we know or sense of ourselves is conditioned by this atmosphere. We are intimately acquainted with its character, ceaselessly transformed by its influence upon us and within us. . . . We are composed of this curious element, permeated by it, and hence can take no distance from it" (*Becoming Animal* 125–26).

If mind is a "medium"—a middle place where the inside and the outside meet—then there is nothing merely subjective in place imagination, and to imagine a place is never an abstract activity, nor a monological one. To imagine a place is always to imagine *with* a place, in the same way to dream of something is to dream *with* something, as philosopher Gaston Bachelard insisted.[6] Being that mind is the "subtle intelligence of a place" (Abram 139), place imagination is an ecology of mind. And each place, with its biospheric as well as its cultural elements, is "a unique *state* of mind" (133).[7]

This has its practical repercussions. If a society becomes alienated from the land, it is because its imagination of the land has become disconnected from its natural referent, resulting in a worldless dimension and in potential self-destruction. In the perspective of the ecology of mind, this cultural and perceptual separation between self and nature is a form of schizophrenia and, more generally considered, it can be seen as the very root of the ecological crisis. In fact, given his conception of a healthy mind as a complex "survival unity" of environment and self, Bateson refers to the ecological crisis as a breakdown of the mind.[8]

In the terms of our discourse, to understand the life of a place means to understand all the levels of this place's ecology: the cultural as well as the biological. The ecological crisis of place is not limited therefore to its being "disrupted and injured" in its organic balances. It is a crisis that involves a place's ecology of mind, namely, its imagination.

AN ETHIC OF STORIES AND PLACES: NARRATIVE REINHABITATION

Place imagination entails ethical and aesthetic values; it entails memory and identity. Being parts of this imagination, the stories of a place belong to this place's ecology of mind; and as such they are part of the "survival unity" that includes ourselves and the world in which we live. What I call "narrative reinhabitation" is a cultural-educational practice that consists of restoring the ecological imagination of place by working with place-based stories. Visualizing the ecological connection of people and place through place-based stories is a way to remember a dismembered unity, to enliven our cultural and ecological potentialities—to reanimate the world.[9]

A significant ethical dimension is here elicited. By conveying the imagination of the coevolution of environment and society in a specific place through its stories, narrative reinhabitation is a way to understand the life of that place in its multiple levels (above all, in terms of time, of space, of acting figures). Narrative reinhabitation stirs up awareness about values and responsibilities connected to the life-in-place (the "sense of the story") and allows the envisioning of suitable strategies of change in the form of possible narrative "endings." From an ethical perspective, the epilogue of a story is a task rather than an already accomplished reality. By telling a story, narrations not only confer a *shape* (namely, a sense) to the events that happen in a given context, making them understandable; they also creatively enable a *project* that takes on society and its values. In other words, by inspiring awareness, narrations can be a *creative* form of ethical responsibility, and the object of the story can be turned into a (moral and therefore political) project.[10] Narrative reinhabitation means to plan ways of learning to live-in-place using place-based stories as "moral instructions": "[i]f value is implicit in our descriptions of the world and our place in it, then the narratives we construct will embody value and orient us" (Cheney 132).[11]

A way to overcome the feeling of alienation described by Celati consists thus in retrieving the stories of places, but above all in imagining, through these stories, new "endings" for places and their inhabitants. The framework of such stories will be an open and nondeterministic vision of reality: namely, an ethical vision. This is the gist of an ethic of narration: to transform words into actions or—quoting French philosopher Paul Ricoeur—to move "from text to action." An ethic of narration, Ricoeur suggests, is based on the idea that "[t]he past must be reopened, and the unaccomplished, thwarted, even massacred potentialities rekindled" (221). And this is also the gist of reinhabitation as a dynamic process: to transform life-in-place from a fact into an act, into an "ecologically and socially sustainable" practice, whose players are multiple and ever evolving. In this process, we can truly "reopen the past," reinventing ourselves as "native" and becoming "fully active in and with a place" (Berg and Dasmann 399). To tell stories of people and places is a way to reactivate their "unaccomplished potentialities," and to restore ecological imagination as our fundamental "survival unity."

FROM THEORY TO PRACTICE: REQUIREMENTS AND KEYWORDS

A practice of narrative reinhabitation (for class teaching, or for a critical analysis) will start with selecting the stories. As regards the Po Valley, this is not an easy task: works on these lands are countless, in Italian literature and culture. Some have attained the status of classics, like Riccardo Bacchelli's peasant epos *The Mill on the Po* (1938–40).[12] Nevertheless, in the framework of our project, I believe that stories should be privileged that suggest an "open vision" of this complex bioregion—"open," in terms of critical perspectives, of acting figures, of values, of imagination. The most suitable narrative dimension is that of a genre that could be called an "anti-epos": whereas the epos is a basically immobile representation, crystallized in an unchangeable destiny, our approach requires mobility, plasticity, "open-endedness."

This "being open" of the stories is here essential. In fact, it is the condition for both shaping the vision of place and involving a multiplicity of subjects within the narrative framework. On the social level, this means to redefine in evolutionary terms the concept of place identity, understanding it as a process (a "route") rather than as an essence (a "root"), and therefore transforming it into an instrument of social inclusion that is decisively in contrast with the exclusionary rhetorics of place such as those upheld by autonomist parties.[13] On the environmental-ethical level, "being open" means to enlarge the scope of morally valuable subjects, highlighting the role of natural agency: landscape and nonhuman subjects have to be integrated in the narrative framework as essential components of the place's "material imagination." *Awareness* (about values and critical issues), *projectuality* (vision of the future), and *empathy* (as a mutually enhancing dialectic amid different subjects) are here the keywords.

REINHABITING PADANIA: GIANNI CELATI AND ERMANNO REA

I would like to provide two examples of narrative reinhabitation: *Verso la foce* (*Toward the River's Mouth*, 1989) by Gianni Celati[14] (b. 1936) and *Il Po si racconta* (*The Po River Tells Its Stories*, 1990–1996), by Neapolitan Ermanno Rea[15] (b. 1927). Enthusiastically praised by literary critics and very appreciated by the educated audience, Celati and Rea are not best-selling authors. Nonetheless, framed into a discourse of bioregional narrative, their two works may have a strong educational impact and would be very interesting to teach together. In fact, although not overtly aimed at restoration, they share a sense of ecological and cultural loss, and suggest two complementary pathways of reinhabitation, equally "open" to an evolutionary view of the Po Valley's life.

Verso la foce and *Il Po si racconta* are diaries of a trip along the river's banks. It is intriguing and fruitful to read a native vis-à-vis an "alien" (Rea 222), a postmodern writer whose style evokes Walter Benjamin's "oral storyteller" vis-à-vis a social novelist and journalist. These differences reverberate in their styles as well as in their traveling: Gianni Celati takes his journey downstream, partly driving and partly walking, sometimes silently accompanied by a photographer friend of his. Rea travels upstream, alone in his old Citroën, his camera always at hand. Their narrative perspectives are divergent, too. In order to record places and stories in an apparently vanishing landscape, Celati uses a phenomenological technique, in which the verbal and visual dimensions are unified.[16] He seems almost to wait for those places and stories to reveal themselves, in spite of the residents' apparent aphasia. This gives a distinctly lyrical and antisubjective character to his prose, which truly appears "grounded in geography rather than in a linear essentialized self" (Cheney 126). On the other hand, Rea, a committed intellectual, adopts the approach of the environmental pragmatist. By shedding light on the concrete aspects of the river's life, he stirs up in the reader a sense of urgency about the issues at stake with its decline. With his direct, journalistic style, he supplies an enormous amount of information about ecology, economy, and society.

It is fascinating to compare the ways both authors portray the "transfiguration" of the river basin through its uses, above all those connected to energy production. The fact that both works were published shortly after Chernobyl's disaster is not a minor detail here. By that time, four nuclear reactors were active in Italy (two of which are located in the Po Valley), but a referendum held in 1987 decreed their complete decommissioning by 1990.[17] Rea and Celati witness this situation, describing a landscape irremediably compromised by industrial exploitation.[18]

Rea in particular links environmental abuse to a profound crisis of citizenship. A case in point is that of the numerous power stations that, even after the nuclear phase-out, are tied to the political hopelessness of the nearby communities: "[The electric plants] rise from the green country like monstrous overlapping buildings, suburban lumps glued upon a mildly bucolic background. Still, . . . nobody protests. And to the visitor's eye this is even more amazing because, the damage being unquestionable, if nobody complains, it means that the devil must have bought the soul of an entire community" (131). In another stop, Rea points at a power plant inside a natural reservation in Lombardy, presenting it as a sign of the hypocrisy and incoherence typical of Italian environmental policies.[19]

The same "toxic landscape" is depicted by Celati as surrounded by an ill-omened and spectral aura. In the sites of Italy's early industrialization, abandoned factories appear like deserted shrines for the "place deities" of the "eras when everything was blackening" (80). The heritage of those eras is, he suggests, overall disorientation. The narration echoes Celati's own bewilderment: "I went down the river's bank, and collected plants that must have survived from the eras when everything was blackening. Their leaves were deformed; they had no bilateral symmetry . . . . In the country, . . . the sky dense with steam, a little sheep flock was now grazing around those old tanks. The shepherd was an old man wearing a yellow raincoat. Sitting on a metal pipe, he was listening to his transistor radio" (80). As in Rea's description, a reassuring bucolic landscape has here turned into Celati's antipastoral version.[20] The dying places have almost become monstrous: necroregionalism has metamorphosed into terato-regionalism. But, while Rea highlights the social and political effects of this mutation, Celati prepares the "objective" groundwork to a place ethic rising from the places themselves, from their tangible agony. Regardless of human consideration and presence, places do have an intrinsic value and an independent life.

Like their visions of landscape, Rea and Celati's visions of people also act as perfect counterpoints to one another. Rea collects numerous "stories of men and women" (20), "of places, stones, landscapes, social and economic events, collective expectations, collective disenchantments" (11). Celati in turn experiences the Po Valley mostly as a land of silence. He is constantly confronted with the inhabitants' estrangement from their places—places "where nobody wants to live anymore, because 'nothing happens' there" (67). A striking example is a man who, in spite of his fame as a "local expert," declares to have "no interest whatsoever for places and landscapes," having understood that "there is nothing to see, and that one place is worth any other" (24). This reflects a sense of deep cultural loss. Indeed, if folklore may remain, the ancient "river's wisdom"—"knowledge of herbs and trees, of lands and waters, ways to forecast the weather and forms of popular medicine" (119)—seems to have been repudiated by the old people, now nearly "ashamed" of their skills (119). Still, this dismissive attitude reveals the inhabitants' unease and ambivalence toward the fate of their land. At odds with the "local expert," Celati introduces a very poetic figure: "the penitence hero," an old man whose "penitence" (almost a symbolic fee for a collective responsibility), consists of cleaning up abandoned houses along the river. Pointing at the toxic dumping of power plants, he deprecates that "everybody treats the river as an inanimate object." The consequence of this behavior is that the Po is "slowly becoming insane and its moves [are] no longer understandable" (73). The agony of the river is here the agony of a disappearing, age-old culture of interdependence between people and places.

Nevertheless, it is from the encounter with these stories of both struggles and disorientation that Rea and Celati envision their strategies of reinhabitation. Coming from the "variously native" people he meets during his journey (many of them are immigrants), Rea's stories mirror the multifaceted and compound identity of the Po plains and their inhabitants: an environmental and human richness endowed with enormous potentialities to preserve the "local" in a globalizing society.[21] This very richness leads him to see a partial territorial autonomy (both ecologically aware and culturally "permeable") as the only viable solution. Reshaped as a new Italian macroregion, "Padania" could indeed evolve from a controversial political flag into an avant-garde example of sustainability:

> Padania . . . has to be created now: in order to grant protection and planning to our agricultural and food industry, but not only for that. Above all, in order to ensure protection to the river. . . . How could one deny that a regional institution denominated "Padania," capable of taking the responsibilities related to the life, reclamation, health and even re-evaluation of the Po would be a fundamental progress . . . ? . . . [T]his—and only this—is the vision of Padania which fascinates us . . . : a complex of values, projects, and aspirations, that are worth a small institutional reform—one not intended to divide Italy, but to make it more cohesive. (219–22)

Explicitly responding to autonomist claims, Rea suggests that neither to turn this territory into an independent geopolitical entity, nor to secure its borders against potential immigrants would enhance its life. The true way to "free" Padania, we might paraphrase, is to reinhabit it. Namely, to develop within it "social behaviors" that could "enrich [its] life . . . , restore its life-supporting systems, and establish an ecologically and socially sustainable pattern of existence" (Berg and Dasmann 399). This task is impossible, though, without appreciating the "stories of men and women," of "places, stones, and landscapes," being all equally involved in the life of the land. Without having Aldo Leopold in mind, Rea is formulating a cultural land ethic, one that expands the borders of citizenship and views the land as a shared place for action, memory (as a form of biocultural conservation), and social evolution. Probably without having heard a word about bioregionalism, Rea is envisioning a bioregional future for the Po Valley.

The stories of Padanian people suggest to Rea a political blueprint. Correspondingly, it is the encounter with a river "slowly becoming insane" (73) that proves to Celati that a dying region can be reinhabited only by recovering its imagination. As Bateson would also say, the "insanity" of the river is a "crisis" in this place's ecology of mind. The alienation experienced by Celati comes from the forcible separation within the "survival unity" of human mind and the mind of place. But, he observes, we have to comprehend that the human mind *is* the mind of place; and imagination represents both this unity, and its condition. Imagination is something that "puts us in a state of love for something out there" (103). Surprisingly resonating with Bateson's ideas, Celati considers imagination "part of the landscape" (103). To restore imagination means to restore the intimate osmosis of inside and outside, of human mind and the mind of place. More profoundly, he writes that "the intimacy that we carry with us is part of the landscape; its tone is given by the space that opens out there, at every glance; and thoughts as well, they're outer phenomena into which one bumps, like a light cut on a wall or the shadow of clouds" (93).[22]

At odds with the sooty totems of industrialism, imagination is the "indispensable goddess leading every look—a figure of horizon" (103).[23] Beyond land-abusing instrumentalism, this "goddess" makes a place out of raw space, bequeathing it a sense that transcends its being usable or economically valuable. In other words, imagination takes back the "transcendence" of place and, putting us "in a state of love for something out there," makes a place "sacred" again.

THE PARTS, THE WHOLE, THE EVOLVING MIND

In almost the same period that Celati and Rea were narrating their journey, Ermanno Olmi, a native of Bergamo (Lombardy) and one of the most praised Italian directors, shot *Lungo il fiume* (*Along the River*, 1991), an intensely lyrical documentary on the Po. The river (here a metaphor of nature) is depicted as an *imago Christi*: its ecological misery, visually followed along the course of its waters, is spoken through the words of the Passion. But the meaning of this symbolic representation is above all a nonreligious appeal to human responsibility toward nature—a *moral* subject which is more than human, in the sense that nature is necessarily "more" than merely human. Without involving a "spiritual" awe, this responsibility expresses the realization that the whole may depend on one of its parts to continue existing.

This is the meaning of the "sacredness" that imagination bestows to the place: *awareness* about the multiplicity of the interconnections which constitute the life of a place, and awareness of their vulnerability; *empathy* within the different subjects of this interconnection—something that we humans can cultivate as an extended and conscious biophilia, on the organic as well as on the social level; and *vision* of the future, meant as the implementation of responsible behaviors through which humans can watch over this whole complexity, taking care of a more-than-human reality on which they also depend. To restore the imagination of place means therefore to restore the sense of this complexity, and orient our survival toward its basic unity. In this framework, narrative reinhabitation—as a cultural and educational strategy—aims to "activate" the ethical function of the stories produced by this imagination; namely, to envision ways to transform necroregions into evolutionary landscapes. Accordingly, place identity has to be seen as a complex notion: flexible, built over time, and above all ethically in progress. If being native is a fact, becoming native can be a moral commitment.

For a "native-in-progress" such as I am, writing this essay has been a chance to reflect on the many ways our identity can interact with the identity of places, and on the necessity of stories not only for our lives, but also for the lives of places. As David Robertson suggests in his interview with Cheryll Glotfelty in this volume, a bioregion *is* a story—an open, permeable story. Such a story thrives with the biodiversity of ideas and subjects, experiences and visions through which imagination enables the future of a place. In this future, all citizens—human and nonhuman—will be story-tellers, able to keep the memory of places by keeping the boundaries of their identity open, and always negotiable.

Yesterday, returning from Milan, I drove along a portion of land where the Po is joined by the Ticino, another big river crossing these plains. It was a purple and blue sunset. The air was thin after a glorious, sunny November day. The river was large and low, its banks dark with poplars and grasses. I felt that I really owe something to this mistreated country, my life place. Certainly, these pages will not be enough. But still, every thought, every word, is part of a story that can reopen the experience of this place. Everything comprising what I am, here and now, is an elemental fragment, minimal and yet necessary, of its evolving imagination.

NOTES

1. <www.parks.it/parco.po.cn>. See also: *Parchi e aree naturali protette d'Italia*.

2. *Ecomafia* is a nationwide phenomenon in Italy. The term was introduced by Legambiente (the country's most relevant environmental NGO) in 1997, and it describes a large number of environmental crimes (illegal recycling of waste, unauthorized building, animal racketeering, illegal trade of archaeological pieces, illegal trade of endangered plant and animal species, etc.). An updated report on *Ecomafia* in Italy is yearly released by Legambiente.

3. Where not otherwise indicated, all the translations of Italian texts supplied in this article are mine.

4. Said incidentally, more than elsewhere in Italy, healthy and sustainable eating is almost a philosophy here: it is not a coincidence that the now-worldwide Slow Food movement was founded in Bra, a town ten miles from Savigliano. See Petrini, *Slow Food Nation*.

5. See, for example, *Steps to an Ecology of Mind* (1972); *Mind and Nature: A Necessary Unity* (1979); *A Sacred Unity* (1991).

6. A reference to the role of "material imagination" in Bachelard's works cannot be omitted. See, for example, *Water and Dreams: An Essay on the Imagination of Matter* (1942) and *The Poetics of Space* (1958).

7. See also Abram, *Spell*.

8. "[A]s you arrogate all mind to yourself, you will see the world around you as mindless and therefore not entitled to moral or ethical consideration. The environ-

ment will seem to be yours to exploit. . . . If this is your estimate of your relation to nature and you have an advanced technology, your likelihood of survival will be that of a snowball in hell" (*Steps* 468). The survival unity is described by Bateson in holistic terms as "ecological mind." See also Mathews, *The Ecological Self.*

9. I owe this ethical reflection on the narrator's commitment to "remember the dismembered" to Chickasaw writer Linda Hogan (personal communication).

10. See Nussbaum and Cavarero. The discourse I am proposing here finds interesting correspondences in Hubert Zapf's theory of "literature as cultural ecology," namely, the function that literature has to renew and restore cultural dynamics by shedding light on ideological blind spots and mechanisms of social exclusion (see Zapf, *Literatur als kulturelle Ökologie* and "State of Ecocriticism").

11. "Bioregional narratives are normative, and they are subject of social negotiation" (Cheney 134).

12. Even Alessandro Manzoni's *The Betrothed* (*I Promessi sposi*, 1827), the archetype of Italian historical novel, is set in the Po Valley, more precisely between the Lake of Como and Milan.

13. Cf. Clifford. As rightly observed by Mike Carr, the concept of bioregion "transcends a strictly local definition of place." For this reason, a bioregional identity can be said to be a "wider" one, meaning that "the terrain of consciousness extends beyond the local ecosystem scale" (77). Speaking of the ideology of place identity upheld by the Northern League, the philosopher and novelist Umberto Eco, himself a Northern Italian, has depicted it as "pre-modern" expressions of a "qualitative populism" (65–88).

14. The recipient of many prestigious literary prizes (Bagutta, Viareggio, Grinzane Cavour, etc.), Gianni Celati is one of the major contemporary Italian writers. He has authored books in different genres, including fiction, critical essays, travel diaries, and translations. As a professor of Anglo-American literature, he has taught at Cornell and at Bologna University. The Po is a constant in Celati's work, and a significant collection of tales of his, *Narratori delle pianure* (1985), has been translated into English, titled *Voices from the Plains* (London: Serpent's Tail, 1990). His production encompasses not only writings but also several documentaries on the Po River Valley, among them *Mondonuovo* (directed by Davide Ferrario) and *Strada provinciale delle anime*, defined by Rebecca West "a silent movie about nothing" (129, 137).

15. As a journalist, Ermanno Rea has worked for several of the foremost Italian newspapers. His narrative works result often from a very interesting combination of biographical experiences and social inquiries. His novel *La dismissione* (*The Decommissioning*, 2002), for example, discusses Naples's failed industrialization through the story of the dismantling of the ILVA metallurgic factory. Like Celati,

Rea has also been awarded important literary prizes (Viareggio and Campiello). He currently lives in Milan.

16. "Celati . . . has long accompanied the pair—visual and verbal—on his own journey in the country of stories, and the role of the 'eye,' more than the role of the 'I,' has been of fundamental concern to him" (West 93).

17. Nuclear energy is an extremely controversial issue in Italy. In 2008, the right-wing government decided to reverse the referendum of 1987 and to restart production, but another referendum, that took place in 2011 right after the Fukushima disaster, reaffirmed the popular decision of 1987. The issue of nuclear waste in Italy is very problematic as well. Once again, the Po Valley is a threatened territory. In fact, the decommissioned plant of Saluggia (Piedmont), where 1500 cubic meters of highly radioactive material are disposed, is situated on the banks of the Dora Baltea, very near the point at which this river merges into the Po. Furthermore, the plant is located directly on the Piedmontese aquifer faults, on a high-alluvial-risk zone.

18. Starting his travelogue in 1983, Celati in particular testifies the transition to the phase-out.

19. "[O]n this biotope raised to the privileges of a 'protected area,' the huge chimneys of the power plant impend . . . . Boschina Island lies there, at their feet, like the kneeling body of a humiliated person, . . . an allegory of the tragic conflict about the Big River's banks, everywhere suspended between enchantment and plunder, (actual) abuse and (dreamt) preservation" (Rea 141).

20. On antipastoral, see Gifford 116–145.

21. Rea's book was written in 1990. A revised edition, documenting a second journey taken by the author in order to update his work, was published in 1996. Rea seems to be extremely aware about the issues of globalization and the potentialities of local resources to confront it.

22. "I am here by the Po's mouth . . . . All of a sudden you can hear seagulls calling each other, one calls, and others reply. Words too are calls, they do not define anything, they just call something, so that this something could remain with us. All we can do is to call things, to evoke them, so that they could come to us with their stories: to call them, so that they wouldn't become so much a stranger as to go away, each one by itself in a different direction of the cosmos, leaving us here, unable to recognize a trace to orient us" (134).

23. Imagination is said to be a "goddess" mostly because the Italian word *immaginazione* is feminine. But I believe that Celati, a writer with an extremely solid background in English literature and culture, might also refer here to the generative power of imagination as a universal "sexual" force as theorized, for example, by British natural philosopher and physician Erasmus Darwin (Charles' illustrious

grandfather) in his works *The Loves of the Plants* (1789) and *Zoönomia* (1794–96). On Darwin's doctrine of love and imagination, see Valsania.

WORKS CITED

Abram, David. *Becoming Animal: An Earthly Cosmology*. New York: Pantheon Books, 2010. Print.

———. *The Spell of the Sensuous: Perception and Language in a More-Than-Human World*. New York: Vintage, 1997. Print.

Bateson, Gregory. *Mind and Nature: A Necessary Unity*. New York: Bantam, 1979. Print.

———. *A Sacred Unity: Further Steps to an Ecology of Mind*. New York: Harper-Collins, 1991. Print.

———. *Steps to an Ecology of Mind*. 1972. Chicago: University of Chicago Press, 2000. Print.

Berg, Peter, and Raymond Dasmann. "Reinhabiting California." *The Ecologist* 7.10 (1977): 399–401. Print.

Carr, Mike. *Bioregionalism and the Civil Society: Democratic Challenges to Corporate Globalism*. Vancouver: University of British Columbia Press, 2004. Print.

Cavarero, Adriana. *Relating Narratives*. London: Routledge, 2000. Print.

Celati, Gianni. *Verso la foce*. Milan: Feltrinelli, 1989. Print.

Cheney, Jim. "Postmodern Environmental Ethics: Ethics as Bioregional Narrative." *Environmental Ethics* 11 (Summer 1989): 117–134. Print.

Clifford, Jim. *Routes: Travel and Translation in Late Twentieth Century*. Cambridge, Mass.: Harvard University Press, 1997. Print.

Eco, Umberto. *Five Moral Pieces*. Orlando: Harcourt, 2001. Print.

Gifford, Terry. *Pastoral*. London: Routledge, 1999. Print.

Mathews, Freya. *The Ecological Self*. London: Routledge, 2003. Print.

Nussbaum, Martha C. *Cultivating Humanity: A Classical Defense of Reform in Liberal Education*. Cambridge, Mass.: Harvard University Press, 1997. Print.

Parchi e aree naturali protette d'Italia. Milano: Touring Club Italiano, 1999. Print

Petrini, Carlo. *Slow Food Nation: Why Our Food Should Be Good, Clean, and Fair*. Milan: Rizzoli Ex Libris, 2007. Print.

Rea, Ermanno. *Il Po si racconta: Uomini e donne, paesi e città, lungo le rive di un fiume sconosciuto*. Milan: Net, 2004. Print.

Ricoeur, Paul. *From Text to Action: Essays in Hermeneutics II*. Evanston, Ill.: Northwestern University Press, 1991. Print.

Thayer, Robert L. Jr. *LifePlace: Bioregional Thought and Practice*. Berkeley: University of California Press, 2003. Print.

Valsania, Maurizio. "Another and the Same: Nature and Human Beings in Erasmus

Darwin's Doctrines of Love and Imagination." *The Genius of Erasmus Darwin.* Ed. C.U.M. Smith and Robert Arnott. London: Ashgate, 2005. 337–56. Print.

West, Rebecca. *Gianni Celati: The Craft of Everyday Storytelling.* Toronto: University of Toronto Press, 2000. Print.

Zapf, Hubert. *Literatur als kulturelle Ökologie: Zur kulturellen Funktion imaginativer Texte am Beispiel des Amerikanischen Romans.* Tübingen: Niemeyer, 2002. Print.

———. "The State of Ecocriticism and the Function of Literature as Cultural Ecology." *Nature in Literature and Cultural Studies: Transatlantic Conversations on Ecocriticism.* Ed. C. Gersdord and S. Mayer. Amsterdam: Rodopi, 2006. 49–70. Print.

BART WELLING

"This Is What Matters"

Reinhabitory Discourse and the "Poetics of
Responsibility" in the Work of Janisse Ray

J

UST AS BIOREGIONS ARE more than purely physiographical entities, *reinhabitation*, one of bioregionalism's core concepts, has always been about more than planting trees and building sustainable homes
from recycled materials in degraded and abandoned places. Acknowledging the centrality of *cultural* transformation to reinhabitory projects of
every kind, founding bioregionalists Peter Berg and Raymond Dasmann
defined *bioregion* in their 1977 essay "Reinhabiting California" as both a
"geographical terrain" and a "terrain of consciousness," both "a place and
the ideas that have developed about how to live in that place" (218). As vital
as their overtly physical engagements with place have been, bioregionalists
have never lost sight of the powerful contributions that literature and other
arts can make in helping transform the terrains of consciousness that have,
in turn, shaped and been shaped by the physical landscapes they occupy.
Bioregional writers and artists have participated in the work of reinhabitation by (among many other things) memorializing built-over landscapes
and exterminated species that would otherwise be forgotten; by finding
creative ways to overcome consumerist apathy and misinformation-driven
hostility; by raising "watershed consciousness" and related forms of ecological awareness on the part of the public; by providing the current residents
of a place with new and long-forgotten narratives, dramas, and rituals of
local-place attachment; by imagining futures defined by human and nonhuman coflourishing instead of exploitation and destruction; and even by
popularizing evocative place names that can be used to generate political

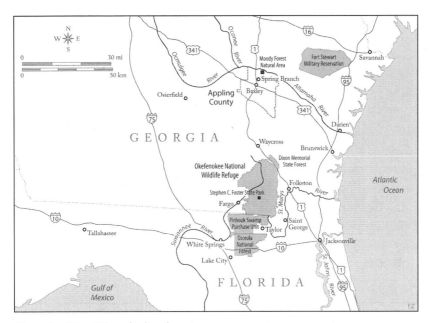

Altamaha River Watershed and environs

support for bioregional efforts. In his recent study *LifePlace: Bioregional Thought and Practice*, Robert L. Thayer Jr. examines all of these cultural possibilities and more, advancing an "Artistic Hypothesis" that holds that a *"distinctly regional art, aesthetics, literature, poetics, and music can evolve from and support bioregional culture"* (94; italics in original). Thayer does not explain fully what he means by *poetics*, but his use of the term is provocative, given all that the study of poetics has taught us about the deep interrelatedness of structure and meaning in literature—and, by extension, linguistic representations and their extratextual referents. In treating form and theme, poetry and its extrapoetic materials, as dialogically entangled elements of literature, poetics can offer a less dualistic vision of things than the theories that have guided other branches of literary studies. And as a growing body of work on environmental poetics attests, this vision can have a bearing on ecological matters as well as literary questions. A bioregional poetics would not just involve writing *about* a place but would be concerned from the start with questions relating to what we might think of as the coimbrication of literature and bioregion.

Bioregional literature is especially interesting from an ecocritical perspective because of the ways in which the poetics of reinhabitation can inform ecocriticism's approach to the connections between literary texts and the larger world—an approach which, it must be acknowledged, can be quite dualistic. Cheryll Glotfelty's 1996 definition of *ecocriticism* as "the study of the *relationship* between literature and the physical environment" (xviii; emphasis added) appeared to open the door to a methodology that would explore and explain the literal and imaginative entanglements of place and literature in a way that no other branch of literary scholarship had done. However, a good deal of ecocriticism produced so far—responding to the world-marginalizing excesses of postmodernism and poststructuralism, and under the influence of a wilderness ideology that privileges direct contact with untrammeled nature over the manifestly messy and nonideal conditions in which we tend to "make a home in nature" (see Cronon 89) day by day—has depended on an underdeveloped and strangely abstract theory of textuality, in which texts *represent* environments on a symbolic level but do not materially participate in the life cycles and human practices that they document. In contrast, a bioregional poetics would define the text as a thoroughly *emplaced* phenomenon. Such a theory would help us see more clearly how all texts are embedded in various physical, economic, and intellectual networks of production, distribution, and readerly consumption, and how texts are indebted to the actual places that supply trees for paper, coal for electricity to power the computers and printing presses, oil for the trucks that carry books to bookstores, and so on. Likewise, a literary theory attuned to bioregional concerns would have to attend to the situatedness of authors and readers in a more-than-metaphorical way, that is, in a way that does not just address authors' and readers' respective "places" in terms of race, class, gender and sexual orientation, religion, and other categories that mainstream literary theory tends to detach from physical bioregions. Rather, such a literary theory would take bioregional "whereness" seriously as a significant (if always complicated, and never wholly determinative) shaper of, and index to, the aesthetic standards that guide authors' depictions of places and readers' responses to these depictions.

In short, bioregional literary theory might resemble Donna Haraway's recent work in its concentration on "material-semiotic" encounters in which "trope and flesh" are "always cohabiting, always co-constituting" (383n11) instead of constantly battling for primacy or maintaining only shadowy and distant relations with each other. This sort of theory would undoubtedly help ecocriticism take the "materialist turn" that Greg Garrard and Cate Mortimer-Sandilands identified in their joint keynote address at the

2009 conference of the Association for the Study of Literature and Environment as a transition that the movement needs to make if it is to realize its full potential, moving from what Garrard has elsewhere characterized as a scientifically, historically, and politically suspect "poetics of authenticity" toward a "poetics of responsibility." In this new poetics, the focus shifts from how humans can *be* more "natural, primal or authentic" to how we can *create* "a more effective rhetoric of transformation and assuagement" (*Ecocriticism* 71–72). This commitment to rhetorical and political transformation is closely aligned with an acknowledgment of humanity's ability, for good as well as bad, to transform every bioregion we have inhabited, including areas that many of us now consider the most "pristine" wildernesses. So the idea of *taking* responsibility is crucial. But it can't end there. A bioregional poetics would also require us to broaden our understanding of community and political agency, viewing responsibility not simply as a one-way expression and acting out of accountability—whether we're thinking of the responsibility that ecocritics might have to help change the larger public's views of nature, or of the role that people in general have played in transforming the earth—but as something closer to what Haraway means by "response-ability." This entails recognizing every encounter with our "significant others" as a mutually transformative exchange in which "all the actors become who they are *in the dance of relating*, not from scratch, not ex nihilo, but full of the patterns of their sometimes-joined, sometimes-separate heritages both before and lateral to *this* encounter" (25). The "significant others" Haraway is describing in this passage happen to be baboons, but, as I hope to show, it makes good sense to explore response-ability's bioregional potential with respect to human interactions with family members, neighbors, and other bioregional stakeholders, as well as with the plants and animals that may have begun reinhabiting a place long before bioregionalists have gotten around to doing so. Unlike Robert Frost's speaker in "The Gift Outright" (1942), bioregional authors never assume that the lands in which they dwell and write are "unstoried [and] artless" (15), blank slates open to environmental reinvention, no matter how badly humans may have exploited them in the past. Likewise, the poetics of responsibility demands that we engage seriously with the cultures that we find inhabiting bioregions we would wish to restore, even when these cultures may bear primary responsibility for the damage we want to repair.

My purpose in this essay is to help lay the foundation for bioregional literary theory by analyzing the potential strengths and limitations of one form of material-semiotic engagement, which I will be calling *reinhabitory discourse*, as exemplified by the bioregional work of someone who has displayed a particularly keen grasp of it: the Baxley, Georgia–raised writer and activist Janisse Ray. Ray is an unlikely environmentalist,[1] given her upbringing in a fundamentalist Christian home located in the middle of her father's junkyard, surrounded not by "virgin wilderness" but by wrecked cars and trashed longleaf pine forests that had almost all been clear-cut decades before she was born. But she has emerged as a powerful spokesperson for the kinds of unloved and nonpicturesque—but nonetheless diverse and potentially restorable—bioregions in which huge numbers of people around the world actually live. Ray's home bioregion is part of a larger ecologically fragmented and politically conservative biocultural region: the U.S. South, where mainstream environmentalism has made less headway than in other regions thanks to its uneasy relationship with Christianity, its biocentric ethics, its reliance on enhanced governmental oversight in environmental matters, and, one suspects, its sublime aesthetics, which originated in and still tend to focus on vast and rugged landscapes very different from the pine flatwoods in which Ray's ancestral Cracker culture took root. Ray, however, has managed to reach remarkably substantial and diverse audiences in the region, and I would credit her success in large part to her skillful use of reinhabitory discourse.[2]

Reinhabitory discourse refers, first of all, to representations of a bioregionalist's efforts to reinhabit what Gary Snyder calls a "zone of ecological recovery" (278), including relatively wild landscapes, the built environment, and the human cultures associated with the place. So, simply stated, it is a type of discourse in which reinhabitation is the major theme. But the term also gestures towards a deeply, if complexly, related *process* in which the bioregionalist, as an acknowledged creature of language as well as of the world of trees and roads, finds new reinhabitory uses for more traditional discourses. These include discourses that outsiders may consider outmoded as well as ecologically, ethically, or politically dangerous, but which nonetheless reflect and condition the terrain of consciousness occupied by the majority of the human inhabitants of the bioregion and thus must be engaged with if bioregionalism's democratic potential in that area is to be realized. Working in this second mode, the bioregional author-activist essentially reinhabits discourse itself. This is about more than bioregionalism with a southern accent; the process involves bioregionalists in complicated and often risky forms of rhetorical literalization, transgression, and expansion as they attempt to create new shared languages for bioregional stakeholders in places where discursive conflicts may have thwarted environmentalist or bioregional projects in the past. As with bioregionalist practice in general (see Garrard 120), it would be wrong to treat reinhabitory discourse as a panacea either for what ails ecocriticism or for popular apathy or antipathy regarding bioregional causes, not least of all because of the ways in which it could conceivably fail, backfire, or be mimicked, co-opted, or otherwise exploited for *anti*bioregional purposes. However, Ray's work demonstrates how the careful and conscientious use of this discourse could reinvigorate bioregionalism, which Garrard defines as a politics of reinhabitation (118), helping it realize its potential to change how everyday people as well as ecocritics think and live in place.

By *work*, of course, I mean a set of activities including the rhetorical and the textual in addition to the more exclusively physical. And my defini-tion of reinhabitory work is based largely on Ray's. She makes it clear in the introduction to her second memoir, *Wild Card Quilt: The Ecology of Home* (2003), that she views words and deeds, the tangible and less tangible forms of bioregional practice, as shifting, overlapping, and coconstituting points on a material-semiotic continuum rather than the stable, discrete, or even antithetical phenomena posited by so many Western thinkers over the past several centuries. Although Ray's introduction begins conventionally enough, discussing her decision to return to Baxley in hopes of "find[ing] there a home" she had been looking for since leaving the town behind as a teenager, her writing quickly takes a more active, and indeed a more performative, turn. After noting that "*In this book I rejoin* with place, land, kin, history, and neighbors in an attempt to gather the pieces of my life," Ray shifts effortlessly from a poetics of textual embodiment to one of em-bodied textuality: "I wanted to live in a less fragmented, less broken, more meaningful way, to have more of what I loved around me, *to say with my body, 'This is what matters'*" (xi, emphasis added). Writing *matters* on mul-tiple levels here: ethically, politically, ecologically, bibliographically. Light years away from Emerson's famous "transparent eyeball" passage, Ray's narrator rejects what Haraway frequently calls "god tricks," choosing the limitations as well as the possibilities inherent in embodiment and bio-regional situatedness over the ultimately illusory pleasures of objectivity and transcendence. Writing becomes a meaningful activity not because of the intellectual coherence it imposes on a previously meaningless life or on chaotic nature, but because it is a fully integrated part of an unfinished wider search for meaning, and because it is one form of embodied and emplaced bioregional work among many others.

To be sure, it is also one that has the distinction of both representing and animating the rest, and Ray ends her introduction to *Wild Card Quilt* with a passage in which literature takes on an unusually large share of responsibility for the vitality of a place. However, it does so in a genuinely response-able way, eschewing the righteous outsider's perspective and overconfident narratives of management, salvation, and apocalypse to which much environmentalist rhetoric has been prone in favor of a non-teleological rhetoric of immersion, collaboration, and uncertainty. Shortly after speculating that "Perhaps stories keep us as a people in place glued together," Ray goes on to write, "I am clinging to a shaking cobweb strung between a leaky house and a wind-torn barn. I am spinning like crazy to reconstruct it, conversing with the ghosts of the pine flatwoods to weave their old stories in with the new ones. Here and there across the web, others are working hard, laying thread on top of sticky thread, to catch and bind us anew. People are spinning night and day, adding the bright colors of their dreams. We may make a beautiful net yet" (xii). Ray's poetics of responsibility manifests itself here as an awareness that her account is taking place, and making place, in the midst of many other stories to which it is not superior but rather intertextually related and historically indebted. Moreover, despite the striking physicality of her language, the passage stresses that there is no guarantee that her efforts will succeed, given the hardships involved in renovating her grandmother's long-vacant farmhouse and in attempting to reinhabit and restore a terrain of consciousness that has historically been bound up with what she describes in her first memoir, *Ecology of a Cracker Childhood* (1999), as a "legacy [of] ruination" (87). Living responsibly, as Haraway demonstrates throughout *When Species Meet*, requires opening ourselves to the ethical demands placed on us by others, including species that science has historically regarded as incapable of making ethical demands in the first place; in Ray's case this sense of openness leads her to acknowledge that her bioregional projects may be overwhelmed by the modern forces that are tearing local communities and ecosystems apart, if not by the legacies of poverty, racism, sexism, and religious intolerance that drove her out of Baxley as a teenager. Crucially, Ray's sense of responsibility to her native culture expresses itself in the context of a response-able attitude towards the "more-than-human world" (Abram) on which it depends for its survival. In both of her memoirs, nonhuman "ghosts of the pine flatwoods" (in the form of extinct and endangered species) feature as prominently as the spirits of her ancestors. And Ray's use of a hybrid spider-storyteller persona in this passage goes even further than her reference to these ghosts to complicate tidy distinctions between human culture and nonhuman nature.

Not coincidentally, in the course of framing her reinhabitory work as a process related in a more-than-symbolic way to the work carried out by spiders in repairing their damaged webs, Ray simultaneously reinhabits at least two discourses pertaining not just to work, but to women's work in particular. One of these acts of discursive reinhabitation is, perhaps, to be expected. In taking on the voice of the spider-woman, Ray joins a distinguished genealogy of female authors who have compared or aligned their work with the habits of spiders in order to challenge patriarchal origin stories, phallocentric narrative techniques, masculinist assumptions about women's literary abilities, and male-dominated ways of thinking about the relationships between literature and the extratextual world and between women and nonhuman beings. For instance, it is worth reading the introduction to *Wild Card Quilt* alongside the first poem incorporated in Leslie Marmon Silko's 1977 novel *Ceremony*; Silko's poem comprises a feminist retelling of the Laguna Pueblo creation story in which Ts'its'tsi'nako ("Thought-Woman, the spider"), in marked contrast to the Judeo-Christian God, doesn't just create the physical universe (consisting of the "four worlds below" in addition to "this world") but also invents the story that the narrator promises to relay to the reader via thought-acts that unfold cyclically in a kind of continuous present rather than in the long-finished and immutable past signaled, in Genesis, with the words "In the beginning . . ." (*Ceremony* 1). Ray's invocation of the spider-narrator anticipates (in *Wild Card Quilt*) and recalls (in *Ecology of a Cracker Childhood*) experimental narratives through which she, like Silko, rejects the andro- and anthropocentric aspects of Euro-American culture that would consign her to silence, powerlessness, and separation from nonhuman life.

More surprisingly, however, Ray does this while reinhabiting a discourse, and a place, to which this first discourse may seem directly opposed. In moving into her grandmother Beulah's house and consciously taking up the role of the southern homemaker, Ray may appear to surrender her hard-won physical and literary independence to the patriarchal regional and religious culture that defined her childhood—during which, she writes in *Ecology*, "the chance to be simply a young mammal roaming the woods did not exist" (121). But in accepting limitations that may seem intolerable from some feminist standpoints, she nonetheless manages to expand the boundaries both of the home and of the discourse she wants to reinhabit. She does this by emphasizing her involvement in traditionally masculine restoration activities along with chores that her female ancestors would have been expected to do ("Daddy and I got the hot water heater working again. Mama and I swept and mopped" [18]), but also, in essence, by redefining the old clichés about southern hospitality. In the *Wild Card Quilt* chapter "In This House We Are Not Separate," Ray catalogs the holes in her grandmother's house and the many creatures that take advantage of these openings, from field mice and "cotillions of ladybugs" (211) to chimney swifts, rat snakes, anoles, tree frogs, and cockroaches. At first lamenting, "The house was abominably open to the world," Ray proceeds to confess by the end of the chapter, "Although I declared these things, the truth was that I loved living with only a permeable screen between us and outdoors. In the openness of our house, I didn't feel separated from the rest of life. It was a fine habitat" (214). Although Ray ultimately chooses to evict her more troublesome nonhuman visitors, just as her grandmother would have done, it is significant that her narrative does treat animals and insects less like faceless invaders than like known guests (however unwelcome) in a shared "habitat." Simply by acknowledging that her grandmother's house has many nonhuman visitors, and that these creatures are just as eager to reinhabit it as she is, Ray models a form of hospitality in which both home and homemaker are redefined in bioregionally productive ways. She also subtly challenges a form of anthropocentrism latent in the term *reinhabitation* itself, which depends on the assumption that humans are the beings actively working to reinhabit a place, while the place—including its nonhuman occupants—passively allows itself to be reinhabited.[3] Just as she situates her discursive work within a matrix of other human stories, Ray takes the conscious reinhabitory efforts and modes of communication of other beings seriously, including fire ants "[f]ollowing a message trail laid by one of their outriders" and a Carolina wren that flies into the dining room, apparently in search of a "secluded nesting spot" (211). Response-ability does not preclude competition with these other beings, but it does call for a certain openness, an awareness of the ways in which human habitats are fundamentally and irrevocably connected to the life places of other species.[4]

As Ray's use of the word *habitat* to describe her grandmother's house indicates, her willingness to rethink the boundaries of home can dovetail neatly with her efforts to redraw the boundaries of the human body, specifically the female body. One of the most important examples of this occurs in the final chapter of *Ecology of a Cracker Childhood*, in which Ray envisions rising from her grave "with the hunger of wildcat, wings of kestrel," her heart transformed into a "cistern brimming with rainwater" (273); in death she has become both animal and place, forcefully rejecting the patriarchal religious discourses and practices that had denied her the right as a girl "to be simply a young mammal roaming the woods" (121). However, this reincarnation story is preceded by a "creation story" (7) at the beginning of the book in which these discourses are not rejected but, for a time, *reinhabited* in a way that reveals the bioregional potential of narratives that would be easy to dismiss as antienvironmental and misogynistic nonsense. The chapter "Child of Pine" begins with a scene, set on a bitterly cold night in February, 1962—Candlemas, Ray notes, referring to an obscure holiday commemorating events from the infancy of Jesus—in which Ray's parents have gone out into the junkyard in search of a lost pregnant sheep. Hearing a "bleating cry . . . coming from a clump of palmettos beneath a pine," Ray's father reaches into the palmettos (without her mother's assistance) to discover not a lamb but baby Janisse, "cradled" in pine needles with a piney "duff" of dark hair. Before puncturing the mysterious tone of the story with a humorous admission that it originated with her parents, who used it to avoid providing her and her siblings with a biologically valid explanation of sex, Ray observes that "I came into their lives easy as finding a dark-faced merino with legs yet too wobbly to stand" (6). With its echoes of changeling legends but also of the Christian nativity story,[5] this straight-faced retelling of a virgin birth narrative that many would regard as silly, if not dangerous, manages simultaneously to honor Ray's parents, to interrogate their beliefs, and to invest their story with a bioregional significance that they had never seen in it. If she was, in fact, literally a "Child of Pine," barely distinguishable at birth from the lambs being born around her, then perhaps the boundaries between her body, the animals, and the mother-land that, from an ecological perspective, *had* actually birthed her needed to be reimagined. But it is important to note that Ray's version of the story, while it resists certain Christian ideas of male control over female sexuality and human dominion over nature, does not add up to a parodic dismissal of Christianity. Indeed, it highlights the unexpected bioregional value not just of Ray's parents' story but of a religion centering on a "Lamb of God" who is thought to have taken the place of an animal both at birth, in a manger, and—in expiating the sins of humankind, like the scapegoat and other creatures used in ancient Jewish sacrifices—in death.

Ray's reinhabitation of Judeo-Christian discourse, including the language of prophecy, achieves some of its most powerful effects in the *Ecology* chapter "Clearcut," in which she appeals directly to loggers who would describe themselves as believers, warning them that "God doesn't like a clearcut," and that "it's fairly certain he's going to question your motives, want to know if your children are hungry and your oldest boy needs asthma medicine—whether you deserve forgiveness or if you're being greedy and heartless" (123–24). The chapter certainly constitutes a jeremiad, but an unusual one in that it combines the jargon typically employed by the addressees ("dozer," "cruising timber," "manning the saw head" [123]) with sympathy for their precarious economic circumstances, as well as with a decidedly anthropomorphic vision of a limited and fallible God who "likes to prop himself against a tree in a forest and study the plants and animals," but who, when he sees forests being wiped out, gets into "a quarrelsome mood, wondering where he went wrong" (125–26). Instead of being framed as irredeemable ecovillains, as they often have in the jeremiads produced under the sign of an environmentalist "poetics of authenticity," Ray's loggers—who also happen to be positioned as her readers—are treated as fellow bioregional stakeholders with everyday jobs, ordinary kids, and very difficult decisions to make about how to make a living in forests that they see both as resources and as God's creation.

As I acknowledged earlier, using reinhabitory discourse can be a risky proposition. It wouldn't be hard to imagine some environmentalists faulting Ray for her willingness to engage with what they see as hopelessly anthropocentric (or theocentric) Christian discourses, just as some evangelical Christians may find her handling of a God in whom she does not literally believe to be insincere, manipulative, or even blasphemous. (On religious matters, she notes sadly in *Wild Card Quilt*, "[M]y father and I have no common language" [76]). Outsiders who use reinhabitory discourse to appeal to local groups may come across as patronizing, while local bioregionalists who depend too heavily on certain traditional discourses may alienate stakeholders who have much to offer to bioregional projects: women, the young, people of color, gays and lesbians, and members of minority religious communities. Reinhabitory discourse as a poetics of responsibility could conceivably ossify into a new poetics of authenticity, in which newcomers to a place would be shut out of bioregional conversations because of their perceived lack of local knowledge. And then there are many unresolved questions concerning the links, or gaps, between the more physical and more linguistic acts of reinhabitation. Corporations and advocacy groups have long been using elements of local culture to promote products and practices that actually destroy local cultures and ecosystems, and, by the same token, there is nothing in the nature of reinhabitory discourse to prevent someone from writing about his or her reinhabitory activities in a literarily satisfying, but factually false, way. All of these potential problems deserve the attention of ecocritics. But then so do the potential benefits. One of the biggest of these is the possibility of genuine dialogue that opens up in surprising places when we deal with traditional discourses response-ably instead of rejecting them out of hand. "The requirements of our place in a community may land us in the middle of odd, funny stories we never schemed for ourselves," writes Ray. "What we are asked to contribute may lie outside the lines of what we imagine" (*Wild Card Quilt* 273). When it works, as Ray suggests it does in her relationship with her mother—as epitomized by their work on the quilt that supplies the title for her second memoir—reinhabitory discourse may allow us to be "woven into beauty" (159). Or, as she says at the beginning of the book, we may make a beautiful net yet.

NOTES

1. It is as an environmentalist, not a bioregionalist, that Ray tends to define herself, but I hope it will become clear by the end of the essay why it makes good sense to approach her books as bioregionalist texts.

2. Two of Ray's texts, *Ecology of a Cracker Childhood* (1999) and *Pinhook: Finding Wholeness in a Fragmented Land* (2005), have been included in the lists of "25 Books All Georgians Should Read" put out by the Georgia Center for the Book (in 2002 and 2008, respectively). As part of the Center for the Book's outreach efforts, Ray traveled to public libraries around the state, where (as can be seen in a video of her appearances graciously supplied to me by Tom McHaney of Georgia State University) she drew unusually large and enthusiastic audiences, including Georgians young and old—many of whom, as Ray told one of my classes during a visit to the University of North Florida in 2005, would probably never turn out to listen to an author billed strictly as an environmental activist.

3. I should stress that this kind of anthropocentrism, while subtextually present in the term *reinhabitation*, is something that bioregionalists have generally worked hard to avoid in *practice*.

4. David Abram's account of how people in Bali have learned to maintain viable boundaries with ants without resorting to pesticides or other forms of interspecies violence (see *Spell* 11–16) suggests that what Thayer calls a "seasoned life-place culture" (67) can find ways to coexist even with species that most people in the U.S. would consider pests, although invasive species like fire ants obviously present difficult bioethical (as well as practical) challenges to would-be reinhabitants.

5. On biblical allusions in *Ecology of a Cracker Childhood*, and particularly in "Child of Pine," see McHaney 104.

WORKS CITED

Abram, David. *The Spell of the Sensuous: Perception and Language in a More-Than-Human World.* New York: Pantheon, 1996. Print.

Berg, Peter, and Raymond Dasmann. "Reinhabiting California." *Reinhabiting a Separate Country: A Bioregional Anthology of Northern California.* Ed. Berg. San Francisco: Planet Drum, 1978. 217–20. Print.

Cronon, William. "The Trouble with Wilderness: Or, Getting Back to the Wrong Nature." *Uncommon Ground: Rethinking the Human Place in Nature.* Ed. Cronon. New York: Norton, 1996. 69–90. Print.

Frost, Robert. "The Gift Outright." *The Poetry of Robert Frost.* Ed. Edward Connery Lathem. New York: Holt, 1979. 348. Print.

Garrard, Greg. *Ecocriticism.* The New Critical Idiom. London: Routledge, 2004. Print.

Garrard, Greg, and Catriona Mortimer-Sandilands. "Our Critical Challenges: What's Next for Ecocriticism?" Association for the Study of Literature and Environment (ASLE) Conference. Victoria, B.C., 4 June 2009. Address.

Glotfelty, Cheryll. "Introduction: Literary Studies in an Age of Environmental Crisis." *The Ecocriticism Reader: Landmarks in Literary Ecology.* Ed. Glotfelty and Harold Fromm. Athens: University of Georgia Press, 1996. xv–xxxvii. Print.

Haraway, Donna. *When Species Meet.* Posthumanities 3. Minneapolis: University of Minnesota Press, 2008. Print.

McHaney, Thomas L. "The Ecology of Uncle Ike: Teaching *Go Down, Moses* with Janisse Ray's *Ecology of a Cracker Childhood.*" *Faulkner and the Ecology of the South.* Ed. Joseph R. Urgo and Ann J. Abadie. Proc. of the 2003 Faulkner and Yoknapatawpha Conference, University of Mississippi. Jackson: University Press of Mississippi, 2005. 98–114. Print.

Ray, Janisse. *Ecology of a Cracker Childhood.* Minneapolis: Milkweed, 1999. Print.

———. *Wild Card Quilt: The Ecology of Home.* Minneapolis: Milkweed, 2003. Print.

Silko, Leslie Marmon. *Ceremony.* 1977; New York: Penguin, 1986. Print.

Snyder, Gary. "Kitkitdizze: A Node in the Net." *The Gary Snyder Reader: Prose, Poetry, and Translations, 1952–1998.* Washington, D.C.: Counterpoint, 1999. 277–83. Print.

Thayer, Robert L., Jr. *LifePlace: Bioregional Thought and Practice.* Berkeley: University of California Press, 2003. Print.

PART TWO

Rereading

CHRISTINE CUSICK

Mapping Placelore

Tim Robinson's Ambulation and Articulation of Connemara as Bioregion

> *The bog is not for me an emblem of memory, but a network*
> *of precarious traverses, of lives swallowed up and forgotten.*
> *I plan to revisit every part of it and rescue all its stories and*
> *write them into this book.*
> Tim Robinson, *Connemara: Listening to the Wind*

THE STORIES OF IRELAND'S Connemara bogland bear a formidable and sometimes inchoate legacy for how humans dwell in place. Tim Robinson's ambition reveals an authentic desire to honor the complexities of these histories, finding their depth in both the human and nonhuman layers of a place that is too often held hostage to narratives of colonial conquest and rebellion. Born in Yorkshire, England, trained at Cambridge as a mathematician, experienced in the London art scene as a visual artist, Tim Robinson, along with his partner, moved to the Aran Islands in 1972 in an effort to find the sustenance that a cosmopolitan art community failed to provide. His intentions, though, were not to seek a muse in the rugged and desolate Inishmore. Rather, his desire to understand his surroundings, what Peter Berg might describe as his "life-place," led him to cartography and nonfiction prose as tools that would make such knowledge possible (qtd. in Thayer xvii). Through both process and product, Robinson's work offers us an enactment of how humans might more purposefully dwell in the places that sustain them.

In "Timescape with Signpost" from *Stones of Aran: Pilgrimage*, Robinson

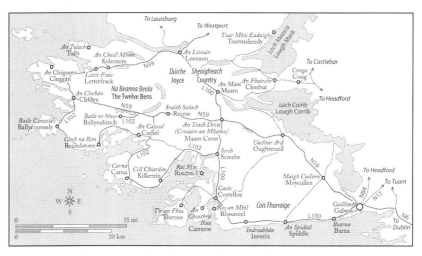

Connemara; adapted from *Iar-Chonnacht / West Galway* by Tim Robinson,
Folding Landscapes, with permission

notes that it was a postmistress from Cill Mhuirbhigh who suggested that
he make use of his good ear for the Irish language and his agility on the
rugged limestone terrain to create a map of the Aran Islands (11). The conversation inspired Robinson to begin his sketches that very day, and since
that time his mapping project and a specialty press, Folding Landscapes,
have evolved to national acclaim, earning Ireland's winning entry for the
Ford European Conservation awards in 1987. A rich subject for study in
their own right, Robinson's maps are the result of meticulous ambulation
of every corner of the island and are literary in their attention to nuance
and contour, their reliance on placelore and local knowledge. Robinson's
maps have earned him the respect of local inhabitants, perhaps the most
important testimony to his investment, as well as the admiration of scholars such as geologist J. H. Andrews, expert on the Ordinance Survey of the
nineteenth century, who remarks that Robinson expresses "a poetic appreciation of landscape all too rare among geographical communicators in any
country" (203). With similar admiration, Irish poet and scholar Eamonn
Wall writes: "Robinson's 'deep map' of Inishmore is a prose narrative composed from disparate parts—a kind of bricolage—and, moreover, one that
looks toward literary, rather than cartographic, models for its form" (68).

Even in their intricacy, however, the processes of map making revealed to
Robinson a need for language; the land called for more than the systematic
marking of line and scale:

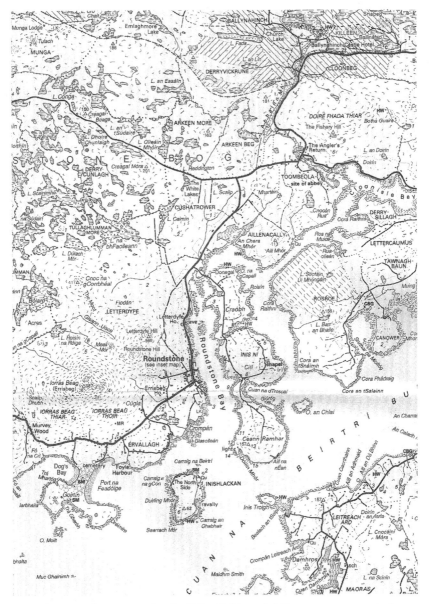

Roundstone and environs, detail of Tim Robinson's "Connemara: a one-inch
map." Used with permission from Tim Robinson, Folding Landscapes.

> I have walked the islands in companionship with . . . visiting experts as
> well as with the custodians of local lore whom I sought out in every village,
> and have tried to see Aran through variously informed eyes—and then,
> alone again, I have gone hunting for those rare places and times, the nodes
> at which the layers of experience touch and may be fused together. But I
> find that in a map such points and the energy that accomplishes such fu-
> sions can, at the most, be invisible guides. . . . I now regard the Aran maps
> as preliminary storings and sorting of material for another art, the world
> hungry art of words. (*Stones of Aran* 11)

In this way, we see in Robinson's work an example of how our engagement with place relies on linguistic navigation, one that allows room for
both scientific acuity *and* cultural connotation and that articulates the
often-neglected intersections of the two.

There is yet another layer of place that Robinson's work successfully honors, and that is a history of colonization. As Eamonn Wall asks, "how could
an outsider—an Englishman, no less—find a way to penetrate Inishmore's
oral culture, where its maps are written deepest?" (69). As an Englishman,
making a home amid the most isolated of Irish communities, those that
live vigorously to preserve not only a sustainable coexistence with some
of the roughest coastal lines but also the language and folklore that define
them, Robinson has earned a valued trust among the native communities
of his home. He describes his own map making as a sort of "post-colonial
reparation," a gesture that has historical resonance as the British Crown's
Ordinance Surveys of the nineteenth century marked the overt erasure and
Anglicization of Irish place names (Robinson, "An Interview" 38). When in
a more recent interview I asked Robinson about his anomalous position of
being an Englishman living in and writing about Ireland, he responded, "I
try to draw both fangs of this snaky consideration: one, by saying that I live
in Aran, the Burren and Connemara rather than in Ireland; the other by
regarding nationality as a set of limitations to be jumped over or wriggled
through" ("Mindful Paths" 209). Robinson's conscious articulation of place
as defined by location rather than allegiance is a political gesture, yes, but it
is also an ecological statement. His concern in mapping and writing about
his place is to understand the specificity of his locale as it is governed not
by the human constructed boundaries of nation but as it is designed by
the ecological principles of natural science and by the cultural contexts
that respond to this science. It is, in short, an expression of a bioregional

imagination, and it indicates how such an imagination might respond to the complexities of place identity in a postcolonial context.

In Robinson's most recent works, his narrative engagement calls on common stories, charts understandings of local habitat and built environments, and maps walking paths of the Connemara region and its subregions. Connemara's place name is derived from its medieval inhabitants, _Conmaicne Mara_, "the Conmaicne of the Sea," an etymological beginning that, like many place names in Ireland, articulates the intersection of story and terrain (_Connemara_ 301). There are no marked or legal boundaries that separate the Connemara region from the rest of County Galway. Connemara's most distinctive borders come from its peninsular position, a geographical fate that historically made it less desirable for settlement but that has simultaneously preserved a distinct, though not undisturbed, connection to cultural heritage. Similarly, its remote sea-bound geography has resulted in vestiges of preserved natural habitat. John Feehan, for example, observes that the "neglected old fields of Connemara" are among the few places in Ireland where one can find the species-rich grasslands of the Middle Ages (21). Connected to these distinctions, the Irish language endures in the Gaeltacht (Irish-speaking) regions of Connemara, as do farming practices that negotiate the tenuous line between land and sea. Robinson's maps, both visual image and written word, pay attention to these nuances and bring them in alignment with contemporary change and threats to these anomalies. In so doing, he engages in a cultural dialogue that effectively offers us a paradigm of bioregionalism that also enacts the textured intersection of cultural and natural histories. Paul Lindholdt writes that "bioregionalism is more than mere philosophy or pedantry, more than some theory nice to contemplate. It truly gets us where we live. It teaches us the means by which we can reinvestigate our living regions and reinvest ourselves" (136). A fitting example of such reinvestment, Robinson's narrative is propelled by his physical ambulation of his subject, is sustained by his interactions with the stories of nonhuman and human life processes, and is made possible through memory.

In a recent book of narrative scholarship, Scott Slovic writes that as ecocritics "We must not reduce our scholarship to an arid hyperintellectual game, devoid of smells and tastes, devoid of actual experience. . . . [We must] analyze and explain literature through storytelling" (28). The nonfiction writing of Tim Robinson is not "scholarship" in the traditional sense, but it is a trenchant body of inquiry, both learned and visceral, into how humans dwell amid their physical place, an expression of what we might consider a bioregional phenomenology. The depth of his product is an extension of his process, one that seems to enact the very narrative engagement that Slovic envisions.

Within moments of encountering Robinson's work, readers quickly realize that his experience of his subject is intensely sensory and physical. His words are attached to the movement of his body, a kinetic process that becomes a stylistic expedient for understanding both the cultural and natural textures of place. In "Scailp," his first chapter of *Connemara: Listening to the Wind*, for example, he traces his various routes to this destination, a sheltering cliff on a hillside surrounded by bogland, immediately transcribing his physical encounter with the land in a manner that suggests both the agency of that land and his own accommodations to that agency: "Bogland is an obstructive, argumentative, quibbling, contentious terrain; it demands step-by-step negotiations" (5). These negotiations define much of Robinson's writing, the reader accompanying his balancing act between the physical and the intellectual perceptions of his subject. At the same time, the reader learns through his intensely personal encounter: "I catch myself admiring my ability to move fast over such a tricky surface, and have to remind myself that this is a loan from fortune and will soon be withdrawn" (5). Jettisoned against his own reflections on mortality, Robinson positions his theory of approach: "Ideally, I feel, a walk should be undertaken with the respect for its own timescale and structures and ceremonies of mood one brings to the hearing of a piece of music. Conversation, except on what's to hand or underfoot, is redundant, inopportune. . . . I aspire to a compensating gift of walking, not in a way that overcomes the land but in one that commends every accident and essence of it to my bodily balance and my understanding" (5). Such intellectual mindfulness, however, does not preclude the possibility that his ambulations are often purposefully physical encounters: "Sometimes, though, after one of these almost ceremonial or ritual walks I am disappointed to find very little in my mental knapsack; I have taken the distance only in my stride and not in my mind. But perhaps that is for the best in the case of a walk with a goal like Scailp, where there is . . . almost nothing; I go out there to wrestle with emptiness, and success would be to bring exactly nothing home with me" (5).

Robinson's ambulation, much like his writing, is not exclusively a quest for destinations. It is more often a mode of discovery. By putting foot to sod, he is not merely finding answers but discovering the questions. In "Walking the Skyline," from *Connemara*, he explains his decision not to follow the popular Gleann Chóchan circuit across the Connemara hills: "my favoured mode of walking being not a single-minded goal-bound linear advance but a cross-questioning of an area, or even a deliberate seeking out of the *fóidín mearaí*, the 'stray sod' that is said to put anyone who treads on it wandering" (364). Much of Robinson's writing relies on such a purposeful abandonment to his terrain, an attempt to mindfully surrender to the immediacy of his surroundings. Such engagement demands an attentiveness to detail, an openness to intimacy with his immediate environment. This is the same call and risk of bioregional thought. Michael Vincent McGinnis writes, "Bioregionalists believe that as members of distinct communities, human beings cannot avoid interacting with and being affected by their specific location" (1). Through Robinson's method of ambulatory writing, he is not only accepting this inevitability, he is allowing his work to rely on it. Within the harsh contours of the Connemara region, a limestone-strewn bogland that resists agrarian use, Robinson's experience is but one life amid a long tradition of natives' negotiation of a region that determines its own fate. In this way, both his step and his words honor the materiality of his subject. It is such attention to geographical nuance that leads narrative scholars such as John Elder to commend Robinson's zealotry: "Even when compared with a writer like John McPhee, who shares his fascination with the lore of plate tectonics, mineralogy, and weathering, Robinson's geological investigations are extraordinarily tenacious and sustained" (x). Elder's observations, therefore, speak to the ways that Robinson's insistent record of the local has crept into the imaginative and intellectual space of his larger context of contemporary traditions and philosophers of place.

Robinson's maps and nonfiction are largely the result of ambling with an obsession for detail, but they are also the result of seeking, with a propensity for hearing, the fading words that shape the land. Integral to his achievements has been his investment in learning the Irish spoken in the Gaeltachts, regions in Ireland where Irish is the first spoken community language. While these areas are currently protected by formal cultural heritage efforts, historically, the endurance of the Irish language in these regions has in many ways been made possible by their geological resistance to agrarian use, colonial enterprise, and outside commercial development. Generational commitment to the Irish language is an inherent part of a conservation ethic in these areas and reminds us that a bioregion must be read through a cultural lens as well as a scientific one. Robinson understands this, and his sincere respect for the Irish language of the Gaeltacht regions has earned him the trust of their inhabitants because his investment invites and honors these layers of history. And while these stories are not limited to natural history, implicit in the regions' concern with the preservation of the Irish language are ways of knowing the natural world, ways that are often closely attuned to local knowledge but that have been lost through a forcibly removed language. In this way, the Gaeltachts are implicitly attuned to bioregions and the communities that sustain them, privileging local village over political boundaries.

Robinson's physical engagement and observation has taught him what questions to ask about the local histories. In effect, Robinson has given value to what Chet Bowers calls "low-status knowledge" which "encompasses the knowledge accumulated over generations of communal experience with the cycles and patterns of life, forms that make up the environment" (197). Robinson's attentiveness to these forms of knowledge, and his commitment to their transcription, is evidenced in the way he carefully weaves local lore with natural history, cultural artifact with sensory perception, granting to these different forms of knowing an epistemological equivalence.

This knowledge, however, relies on Robinson's engagement with his local community. In Barry Lopez's essay "Landscape and Narrative," he writes of storytelling that "intimacy is indispensable—a feeling that derives from the listener's trust and a storyteller's certain knowledge of his subject and regard for his audience" (63–64). Robinson's record of story reverently enacts such intimacy. When I asked Robinson how he nurtures such relationships with native inhabitants and local experts, he responded emphatically:

> They nurture me! . . . But when people realise that I really do want to know something—a scrap of an old song, a decayed placename, a half-forgotten anecdote—they respond by taking the item seriously, perhaps for the first time, having been persuaded by modernity that it is obsolete nonsense. And this revalidates their own experiences and memories. And then to one degree or another all these contributors can eventually see what they have given me treasured-up in the white of a printed page. The map or book becomes to a certain degree a communal property. ("Mindful Paths" 207)

And so by simply asking questions, expressing interest, and listening to answers, we both realize and actualize the value and memory of human place experience. Such attunement to locale, both its nonhuman nature and its human nature, is where the hope of bioregionalism lies. Mitchell Thomashow writes, "Before people can become citizens, they must see themselves as neighbors. It is their attachment to a place, the fact that they all live there and care about it, that brings them into relationship with one another, making them neighbors" (97). Storytelling reveals to Robinson, and to the neighbors that he walks beside, that despite different national and political origins they are bound in relation to the human and non-human life forms of their common region.

This relationship is perhaps most evident in shared stories about the place names of Connemara. In a talk given at Ireland House, New York, in 1994, titled "Listening to the Landscape," Robinson says, "Enquiring out placenames . . . has become for me . . . a mode of dwelling in a place. In composing each of the placename instances I have given you into a brief epiphany, a showing forth of the nature of a place. I am suggesting that what is hidden from us is not something rare and occult, or even augustly sacred, but, too often, the Earth we stand on" (164). At the same time, Robinson's knowledge of and attention to *dinnseanchas*, the lore of places, suggests not just an attention to natural history, but also to how human interaction infuses this history. As John Wilson Foster notes in "Encountering Traditions," "Named places, sometimes defined and identified by a natural feature (a mountain, a bog, a strand, a river, a natural well, etc.), did not generate simply local lore, but also a topography intimately bound up with families, ownership, genealogy" (43). Robinson's companion booklet to his map of the Aran Islands dedicates most of its pages to these etymologies, and his nonfiction—from the *Stones of Aran* to his more recent *Connemara* series—all express his vow to recall and record the lore that captures and defines the collective memory of his bioregion. Because of this promise, his community has granted him an earned place within this living memory: "One of my functions in the village is to be a perambulating historical litter basket; anyone who comes across an old account book or remembers a placename their grandparents used to use may rely on me to receive it into my care" (*Connemara* 157). Robinson is acutely aware of his dependence on local knowledge for his understanding of this land: "A few hundred yards further south is the village of Troscaí, the inlet that almost divides the island's middle portion from its southern one. (These placenames are nowhere officially recorded—I have them only from my Inis Ní acquaintances of that immediate vicinity" (253). And while Robinson's recording of seemingly anecdotal knowledge about this region is sometimes tempered by wit and jovial exchange, there is a pervasive sense of concern for the dying ways of rural life that he witnesses: "What will become of the land as the farming families die out? Will Ceann Ramhar be so treasured by the summer visitors that it will be cleared of fences and preserved in its fierce proximity to heaven? Who is to care for the island's holy places and workaday shores, remember the names of its fields?" (262). In "Interpreting Bioregionalism: A Story from Many Voices," Doug Aberley traces the history of bioregionalism, remarking that it is "a story best learned by listening over a very long period of time to many voices" (14). As if with this prescriptive in mind, Robinson's walking work enacts this gesture with both faith and result, collecting the voices of a place for posterity and preservation.

Robinson's account of these voices, however, does not nostalgically fix them in their historic moment; rather, he carefully positions them against a changing and contemporary reality, one that allows him to carry a cell phone on his rambles, write his books on an iMac, and tell his own story to a global audience. He is careful not to romanticize the traditional ways of subsistence but rather offers the past as a lens through which to understand the sometimes-disinterested development associated with economic growth, most recently that of the boom period of the 1990s famously known as the Celtic Tiger. Robinson records the stories that often get lost in the business of change and most importantly, is vigilant to remind his readers that the present as well as its textured origins are part and particle of the mud on his boots.

While Robinson turns to story and the written word as a tool of this preservation, he bears no false sense of grandeur. He is consistently indebted to his community: "Hundreds of Connemara people have helped me in my explorations over the last third of the century," he acknowledges in his author's note to *Connemara*, and he is acutely aware of the limitations of language: "How can writing, writing about a place, hope to recuperate its centuries of lost speech? . . . I am aware of the selectivity of my written response to living in Connemara. I concentrate on just three factors whose influences permeate the structure of everyday life here: the sound of the past, the language we breathe, and our frontage onto the natural world" (3). With humility and these "organizing principles" in mind, Robinson uncovers the depths of regional empathy; he charts the place of Connemara, records its histories, identifies its flora, and embeds his own story into the record. His story, rooted in the physical and philosophical engagement of experience, becomes our lens through which we can more fully understand the brimming contradictions of Connemara.

At the same time, Robinson is modest enough to nod to the primacy of place stories, some of which he deems himself unworthy to carry. In writing about the deserted village of Aill na Caillí, for example, he recalls,

> A man who used to live there tells me that the old folk of the village used to believe that when the heron shrieks on a moonlit night, it is because it has been frightened by its shadow on the water; somehow this scrap of lore seems to me to speak obscure but eloquent volumes about the place. There are perhaps two more recent stories to be told about Aill na Caillí . . . but for various reasons these are not mine to tell. So I will leave the place to the heron, and return northwards by a winding grassy way across the bogs. (*Connemara* 265)

Even in its subtlety, this surrendering of place to story, to a narrative that exceeds his footsteps and his time, suggests a mindful recognition that local knowledge, much like natural habitat, is not his to own, and that however much he learns about his place (and he has learned a prodigious amount), he will never exhaust its riches.

Writers who map nonhuman nature are inevitably bound by their own processes of perception, by the inadequacy of language, and possibly by a desire to give meaning to their onerous treks. Responsible environmental writers, however, are aware of these entrapments, and seek always to remember themselves as only one piece of a vast natural history. Eamonn Wall observes of Robinson, "He is involved in his work while maintaining his detachment; this stance assures the focus remains on the place rather than on its recorder. What he encounters is as constantly changing as the ground under his feet is undulating. Throughout, Robinson is always the student and never the master of the island" (77). Such humble engagement leads to a keen sense of the ecological interactions of the region and results in a fuller sense of human place amid them. Robinson's attention to the interface between the histories of both human and nonhuman nature incur an obligation to their subject, but as Aldo Leopold reminds us, "Obligations have no meaning without conscience" (387). For Robinson, the conscience comes from the intellectual approach of a cultural anthropologist and the curious intent of a writer, the result of which reminds us that such engagement is not limited to the remote spaces of Europe's western borders: it is also possible in our own backyards.

While this sense of an environmental ethic is partially imposed on Robinson's subject, it is also, in part, realized because of it. In the chapter titled "Catchment" he writes,

> A catchment area is a naturally defined and functionally integral facet of the world's surface, unlike a parish or electoral division or county whose boundaries may or may not be given by landscape features; as such, a catchment can be taken as a microcosm of the whole. It is an open, self-renewing, dynamic system supporting and supported by a vast number of life-forms and all their interrelations. Even its basic topography . . . is profoundly suggestive of a way of looking at the world and caring for it. (*Connemara* 273)

In these words we see that such physical engagement with the local reveals inherent models for human stewardship of the natural world, models found in the implicit rhythms of a watershed that is in itself a kind of bioregion. In this same chapter, Robinson recognizes these systems of connection in a more direct manner:

> This captures the ethics of a catchment. Through its ramified watershed it scrupulously delivers rainwater . . . and through the conjugate ramifications of the watercourses receives the salmon (and all the forms of life of the food chain headed by the salmon). The balance is precarious and precious, and becomes a matter of ethics since we, humankind, by the weight of our numbers and demands, are forced to become the managers and conservators of the process. . . . A river's ills may be discarded into the sea, but, the way things are, we keepers of the world-catchment cannot be exonerated of our responsibility. (*Connemara* 274–75)

Through careful attention to the processes that sustain this ecological exchange, Robinson articulates what Gary Snyder names "watershed consciousness . . . a move toward resolving both nature and society with the practice of a profound citizenship in both the natural and the social worlds" (235). The power of Robinson's bioregional sensibility is that while it may begin with his own predilections and human biases, he permits it to evolve in concurrence with the logic of the nonhuman systems that surround him. At the same time, he understands these systems as embedded within the social history and present era of this region called Connemara.

The ambulatory and corporeal qualities of Robinson's prose style in *Connemara* reap a rich and unwaveringly honest uncovering of the layers and textures of the place it honors. In this honesty, there is a keen awareness of "fading and soon to be forgotten ways and words," of a land "in crisis," and of an "entropic shaming of the land." And yet, though clearly aware of the threats and abuses of the natural world in these regions, Robinson's attention to regional knowledge and to a bioregional epistemology of place ultimately enables him to rest, and perhaps continue on, in a deeply rooted hope in human nature's capacity for recovery. Robinson closes *Connemara* amid such a moment. In the book's final chapter, "Curse and Blessing," he draws hope from the ancient site and stories of Mám Éan (Pass of Birds): "And among the messages wrapped into this bundle of old tales is the assurance that as a species of all the talents, as warriors, cup-bearers, poets, and chess-champions, we can countermand the curses we have laid upon the earth" (411). When asked how he would receive a reading of his work as an instrument of hope, Robinson responds, "I permit it to myself, so I can hardly deny it to the reader. Maybe hope is a stylistic device of the universe to keep us reading on, and I borrow it for the same reason" ("Mindful Paths" 211). This impulse of "borrowing from the universe" is a recurring thread in the product and processes of Robinson's work. A reader witnesses these recursive acts in the way Robinson honors the histories of his walking paths and generously offers his encounters to local neighbors and curious academics. We witness this munificence even through the living space of Nimmo, the home he and his partner, "M," share, which they open to writers and teachers for conversations on "Place and Story" and have willed to the National University of Ireland, Galway, for future studies of place and community (*Connemara* 150). Such purposeful gestures of community sculpt Robinson's relationship with his own place: "We feel relieved of the burden of ownership, as if we were now just the temporary caretakers of the house, and we revel in the freshening wind of futurity blowing through it" (150). Perhaps this is the humility that humans must bring to bioregional action, an understanding that even in the seeming smallness of our regions, we are still merely passing through.

Daniel Kemmis writes that bioregionalism "is an utterly organic phenomenon. It is never possible to tell a place that it is a region; either it is a region inherently, by its own internal logic, or it is not a region at all" (xvi). Understanding of such inherent patterns is inexorably earned through time and trial. In his chapter "Tales to Lengthen the Road," Robinson writes,

"'You can't eat the view' is an almost traditional retort of the embittered Connemara native to the visitor enthusing over the beauty of the place" (287). This refrain is more than a witty comeback to the romantic outsider's naïveté; it is testimony that for the inhabitants of the Connemara landscape the internal logic of their region is a part of daily routine, a part of the nuances of language, a part of all the layers of memory and story that map the workings of a day. The shores of the Aran Islands and the fields of Connemara are among the most daunting exchanges of land and water that exist in Europe, and those who dwell amid this ebb and flow bear daily reminders of its force. And so what Robinson observes and describes in his nonfiction is a telling of endangered stories, a telling of what has largely been unheard and of what is perhaps needed now more than ever. His words and maps remind an international audience that what sustains us has very little to do with a shared allegiance to state and much to do with a willingness to hear the stories that give meaning to our sensory trek on this shared planet. Without this investment there will be no tender care for the "precarious traverses" of place that Robinson's work calls us to witness.

WORKS CITED

Aberley, Doug. "Interpreting Bioregionalism: A Story from Many Voices." McGinnis 13–42.
Andrews, J. H. "Paper Landscapes: Mapping Ireland's Physical Geography." Foster, *Nature in Ireland* 199–218.
Bowers, Chet A. "The Role of Education and Ideology in the Transition from a Modern to a More Bioregionally-oriented Culture." McGinnis 191–204.
Elder, John. "Introduction." *Stones of Aran: Labyrinth*. New York: New York Review of Books, 2009. Print.
Feehan, John. "The Heritage of the Rocks." Foster, *Nature in Ireland* 3–22.
Foster, John Wilson. "Encountering Traditions." Foster, *Nature in Ireland* 23–70.
———, ed. *Nature in Ireland: A Scientific and Cultural History*. Dublin: Lilliput, 1997. Print.
Kemmis, Daniel. Foreword. McGinnis xv–xvii.
Leopold, Aldo. "From *A Sand County Almanac*." *Nature Writing: The Tradition in English*. Ed. Robert Finch and John Elder. New York: Norton, 2002. 376–97. Print.
Lindholdt, Paul. "Literary Activism and the Bioregional Agenda." *ISLE: Interdisciplinary Studies in Literature and Environment* 3.2 (1996): 121–37. Print.

Lopez, Barry. "Landscape and Narrative." *Crossing Open Ground*. New York: Vintage, 1989. 61–72. Print.

McGinnis, Michael Vincent, ed. *Bioregionalism*. London: Routledge, 1999. Print.

Robinson, Tim. *Connemara: Listening to the Wind*. Dublin: Penguin, 2007. Print.

———. "An Interview with Tim Robinson." Brian Dillon. *Field Day Review* 3 (2007): 33–41. Print.

———. "Listening to the Landscape." *Setting Foot on the Shores of Connemara & Other Writings*. Dublin: Lilliput, 1996. Print.

———. "Mindful Paths: An Interview with Tim Robinson." Christine Cusick. *Out of the Earth: Ecocritical Readings of Irish Texts*. Cork: Cork University Press, 2010. Print.

———. *Stones of Aran: Pilgrimage*. London: Penguin, 1986. Print.

Slovic, Scott. *Going Away to Think: Engagement, Retreat, and Ecocritical Responsibility*. Reno: University of Nevada Press, 2008. Print.

Snyder, Gary. *A Place in Space: Ethics, Aesthetics, and Watersheds*. Washington, D.C.: Counterpoint, 1995. Print.

Thayer, Robert L., Jr. *LifePlace: Bioregional Thought and Practice*. Berkeley: University of California Press, 2003. Print.

Thomashow, Mitchell. *Ecological Identity: Becoming a Reflective Environmentalist*. Cambridge, Mass.: MIT Press, 1995. Print.

Wall, Eammon. "Walking: Tim Robinson's Stones of Aran." *New Hibernia Review/ Iris Éireannach Nua* 12.3 (Autumn / fómhar 2008). 66–79. Print.

HARRY VANDERVLIST

The Challenge of Writing Bioregionally

Performing the Bow River in Jon Whyte's *Minisniwapta: Voices of the River*

> Minisniwapta *is a poem about the Bow River, the gentle green river which has always flowed—flowed longer than the Rockies have stood as the sentinels we believe them to be; always on the western edge of the small green world I have always called home. If the river seem [sic] to flow through you as you perceive this poem, consider that we are the landscape life flows through, the mind the mountains myth flows from, time the river whispering by.*

WITH THESE WORDS, Jon Whyte introduces a poem he never completed, but one that raises intriguing questions about what it might mean to write from a bioregional perspective, especially for a poet like Whyte, for whom place meant literally everything. The following discussion first explores those aspects of Whyte's idea of place that make him a candidate for the title "bioregional poet" and then examines the poetic strategies of his river poem, strategies that develop directly from this conception of place. First, however, it might be helpful to locate Whyte's subject, Alberta's Bow River, and then to place his poem within the context of his poetic career, since Whyte is far less widely known than some of his contemporaries such as Margaret Atwood (born two years earlier than Whyte, in 1939).

Canada's Bow River begins as drops of meltwater from the Bow Glacier, forty kilometers north of Lake Louise in the Canadian Rockies. Over the course of about two weeks, this trickle, augmented by nearly fifty tributary

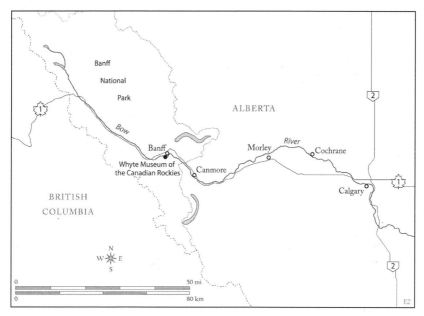

Upper reaches of the Bow River Valley, Alberta, Canada

creeks and rivers, flows past the towns of Banff and Canmore, and through Morley, the largest town on the Nakoda (Stoney) Nation reserve east of the Rockies. (Whyte takes his poem's title from the Nakoda name for the river.) After flowing through the city of Calgary, the Bow River ends, 587 kilometers from its source, at its confluence with Oldman River. Here the two streams join to form the South Saskatchewan, which then carries those drops of glacial meltwater to Lake Winnipeg, and later into Hudson's Bay. The upper reaches of this river define the Rocky Mountain valley, which Banff poet Jon Whyte always considered his home.

From 1941 to 1956, Whyte grew up a few feet from the river, in the home of his aunt and uncle, Catherine and Peter Whyte. Both were painters and passionate cultural historians of life in the Rockies. Together they founded Banff's Archive of the Canadian Rockies in 1965. By 1968 the archives had developed into the Whyte Museum of the Canadian Rockies, where Jon Whyte's papers are now held, along with thousands of other documents, artifacts, and photographs crucial to understanding the region's human history. For Jon Whyte, those early years in Banff created deep roots. After completing master's degrees in English (at the University of Alberta in Edmonton) and communications (at Stanford) he made a very deliberate decision to pursue his adult life and work in Banff: he even precisely notes the date, describing himself as "reborn, Banff, June 23, 1968" (Anson). Rather than following his friends and contemporaries to larger centers such as Toronto or London, Whyte remained in the small town of Banff until his death from cancer in 1992.

Throughout these years, he documented the Bow Valley by writing and editing ten works on local history and Rocky Mountain artists; by contributing weekly columns to the Banff newspaper, *The Crag and Canyon*; and by working as a curator for the Whyte Museum. The Canadian critic W.H. New sums up this eclectic activity when he describes Whyte as not only a poet, but also "a journalist, regional historian, museum curator, and specialist in the topography and representation of the Banff area." From 1970 on, Whyte advocated protection of the valley's environment, first as an executive member of the Bow Valley Naturalists (a group founded in 1967) and later as a trustee of the National Parks and Wilderness Association of Canada (McIvor). However, his activist and interpreter roles were never entirely separable from his work as a poet. Through most of his adult life, Whyte worked on an epic, encyclopedic poem, whose projected five volumes would present a comprehensive imaginative vision of Whyte's part of the Canadian Rockies. The first two volumes, *The fells of brightness [first volume]: some fittes and starts* and *The fells of brightness: second volume: Wenkchemna*, were published in 1983 and 1985. By the 1980s, Whyte had established himself as a noteworthy, if not a leading poet in Canada. In 1982, Robert Kroetsch describes an early section of *The fells of brightness [first volume]*, published in Whyte's 1981 collection, *Gallimaufry*, as "proof positive that that poem is on its way to greatness." In 1984, poet and critic Eli Mandel calls Whyte "one of the two outstanding radical innovators in Canadian poetry" (Mandel). (The other innovator is Christopher Dewdney.) Following Whyte's death in 1992, Robert Fulford's *Globe and Mail* obituary describes him as "a very important figure" for Alberta's literature, "a man who combined strong international cultural interests with a deeply rooted sense of belonging to Banff" (Fulford).

The third volume of Whyte's epic, *Minisniwapta: Voices of the River*, never appeared in published form. Whyte's papers hold three typescript versions of the poem (from 1987, 1990, and 1991), plus a spoken-word recording for four voices, broadcast in 1987 by the Canadian Broadcasting Corporation. (Part of this recording can be heard on the Whyte Museum website, at http://www.whyte.org/jonwhyte/soundriver.html.) The poem's text—

printed in landscape format on a long ribbon of accordion-fold computer paper—was also displayed at the Whyte Museum of the Canadian Rockies. Seen this way, the text would have appeared as a concrete poem, long but shallow like the Bow itself, broadening, narrowing, meandering, braiding, and gathering tributaries in the form of quotations from "the world's literature of rivers," as it wound around all four walls of an exhibition room. As Whyte told a radio interviewer, *Minisniwapta* is "a long shallow poem, about 150 ft long and 11 inches deep" (Whyte, CBC Radio interview). Presented this way, the text shows why Whyte could describe it as part poem and part "musical score, words on horizontals on a scroll moving forward." The poem is indeed "shallow," leaving large white spaces on each page as four enormously long lines of verse progress: Whyte's way of printing the poem means the lines can overflow the page breaks and space themselves according to phrase breaks instead. In some places, the lines echo one another; in others they seem to move with their own individual rhythms, enacting the river's multiple voices on the page. The poem's opening lines employ fragments of Nakoda, as if the river is searching for its voice, while at the same time the words mimic the single drops of meltwater, which will gather to form its first trickling strands:

> Wap nis ni Minisni wapta mi Minisniwapta wapta Minisni quiet
> river moving silently
>
> mi ta ni mi Minisni waptata wapta Minisniwapta wapta river the
> river
>
> ni wap nis wap nis wapta wapta Minisniwapta wapta Minisniwapta
>
> nis mi ta ta wap ni wap Minisni wapta Minsiniwapta: ice cold
> river broad and deep. (*Minisniwapta*)

Whyte's river poem offers one example of what a bioregional poem might look like in the hands of a poet who thinks big. Whyte's published work and archived papers suggest he was thinking in terms that might now be labeled "bioregional," just at the time that term was being invented, and certainly before the word itself came into general use. His project for a Rocky Mountain epic, which would take a different approach from earlier poems about Canada's mountains, came into being in the early 1970s: he was corresponding about it with Canadian poet Earle Birney as early as 1969 (Whyte, Letters). In an undated essay, Whyte says, "Place matters, and what could matter more than the relationship of place and mind?"

(Whyte M88/125). This attitude informs all of his work and echoes the terms Peter Berg and Raymond Dasmann use when they describe a bioregion as "both . . . geographical terrain and a terrain of consciousness" (qtd. in Cresswell 134). It is Whyte's imaginative vision of place, then, and the poetic strategies he develops to realize this vision, that connect him most plausibly with the concept of a "bioregional imagination."

Whyte's sense of place always includes the idea that place is not given: every place needs to be imagined, and reimagined, by and for those who experience it. In the mid-1970s, as he begins to elaborate his epic project, he undertakes this responsibility for the Bow Valley, essentially nominating himself as the bard of Banff:

> I've lived in Banff for twenty-five of my thirty-five years and the family has roots that go back to the arrival of the railroad on my father's side, to the second wave of exploration (1890 on) on my mother's. So as far as "place" is concerned, there is no area in Canada of greater importance to our sense of being somewhere than in the Rockies. Given my sense of place, my eclecticism (broad knowledge of literature, the visual arts, natural sciences history, folklore, private and public memory) I am uniquely equipped to explore and invent anew the structure of this place. (Whyte M88/124)

Whyte also recognizes that there is much more to "place" than location and terrain—although the first two volumes of his epic certainly devote more detailed attention to "terrain," in the form of geology, than perhaps any other Canadian poet before or since. He writes, in the preface to his 1981 poetry collection *Gallimaufry*, "My Rockies are, I hope, an archetype of anywhere, a complex of folk tale and anecdote, personal experience and Earth, a geography of climate, passions, and place" (10). Here he speaks partly as a poet influenced by the modernist quest for the universal in the particular. Whyte acknowledges modernist models for his mountain epic, including Joyce's "Anna Livia Plurabella," William Carlos Williams's *Paterson,* and David Jones's *The Anathemata*. He favors Jones's approach as a model "to stray from, not adhere to" (M88/124). (His preference for David Jones may well have to do with Jones's emphasis on the "mythy" or archetypal style of modernist approach to epic descended from T.S. Eliot and Robert Graves and influentially explicated by Canadian critic Northrop Frye.) Yet Whyte's terms here also overlap with those of David Robertson, paraphrased by Cheryll Glotfelty elsewhere in this book, which describe an approach to human ecology in which "the focus becomes the place, which [for Robertson] takes on a synecdotal relationship with the universe. By really getting to know this place, studying this place—including the role of authors and literary works in this place—you have this window onto the universe" (this volume, 44). Blending works of the imagination together with the study of human ecology this way might blur the boundaries of what we now call "literary study," as Glotfelty points out. For Jon Whyte, the boundaries between poetically imagining a place, studying the natural and human history of a place, and defending the environmental integrity of a place, never really existed. All of these activities formed interdependent facets of his life and work. His choice of the Bow Valley as his subject reflects his roots there—but he seems to have subscribed to the belief that a writer could start from any particular place and arrive, as he did, at "an archetype of anywhere."

At the same time, it is important to understand how Canadian literature in the 1960s and 1970s experienced a strong regional emphasis, one with which Whyte affiliates himself when he writes, "By going back to Banff, as Al Purdy went back to Ameliasburg, as our French Canadian writers go back to their parishes, as Sheila Watson got to know the Cariboo country of British Columbia, I feel I am doing the country and its readers more of a service than I could possible perform staying in Edmonton, Vancouver, Toronto or Montreal" (Whyte m88/125). Interestingly, Whyte's emphasis here is not on political regions so much as on towns, parishes, and a small subregion of British Columbia's interior. These are all candidates for "home places," and Whyte's reference to them, placed together with his highly distinctive emphasis on the natural history of his home valley, help support the idea that Whyte's thinking was perhaps moving beyond Canadian literature's political regionalism. The fact that he lived in one of the few Canadian towns located in a national park and was already a committed environmental activist helps to demonstrate that he had already begun to put the "bio" element into what can now be called a "bioregional" sense of his territory. The title of one undated essay in his collected papers, "Geo-poetics," sums up the close connections Whyte felt between the natural and the imaginative worlds.

For Whyte's river poem, one consequence of this inclusive view of place was that the poem would have to do much more than present the Bow as an element in a landscape, or as Tim Cresswell defines that term, "a thing to be outside of" (10). Yet neither does the river, as poetic subject, easily fit Cresswell's definition of place as "a thing to be inside of." (It can be a thing to fall into, however, and Whyte's poem includes an anecdote from outfitter Tom Wilson, in which railway engineer Albert Rogers, for whom Rogers' Pass is named, tumbles into the river while making a joke about "the clever Greek" who quipped, "You can't fall in the same river once.") More obviously than other places, a river both defines and exceeds a sense of "where." In what sense is one ever "at" a river, exactly? Whyte and the local guides, painters, and mountaineers he conversed with could, and did, visit the source of the Bow within a couple of days' ride from home— extending, perhaps, Thoreau's sense of "the limits of an afternoon's walk" (qtd. in Thomashow 126) to include a significant part of the river's upper reach. Yet, by extension, the river links Whyte's home valley to the entire Hudson's Bay drainage. Whyte's imaginative representation of the Bow River would need to develop implications of the way he had previously represented place as an interplay between observer and observed, past and present. In *The fells of brightness [first volume]*, Whyte's depiction of Lake Louise as shaping his own consciousness is captured by Cresswell's description of place as "as a way of understanding" (12). *Minisniwapta* would try to develop this approach even further.

Whyte recognizes this when he asks, in his proposal for the 1987 audio recording of the poem, "Is this the bloodstream, stream of consciousness, (roman fleuve), Anna Livia's river or Marilyn Monroe's *River of No Return*, the ancient, older-than-the mountains or pre-orogenic Bow, River of Time? Well, those rivers yes, but that river outside my door too, the particular, powerfully free-flowing Bow" (Whyte, proposal to CBC, "State of the Arts"). Whyte's approach to his river poem certainly offers what Jim Cheney calls "contextualized discourse of place" (Cheney 126–27), and perhaps the river as subject renders unachievable any totalizing impulse Whyte may have inherited from his modernist predecessors. In any case, the poem's unfinished state and Whyte's early death make it impossible to know whether later versions might have aimed for, or realized, any kind of artistic closure. Still, the existing drafts work toward a poem that truly is more a "way of understanding" than a record of something understood. It will be a poem with multiple entrances, as Whyte seems to recognize that his concept of place requires an approach that offers readers access to a sort of poetic collation of many elements of "the mindscape/landscape which emerges from our narrative and mythical embedment in some place" (Cheney 130).

Although the notion of "mindscape" was always especially vivid for Whyte, in *Minisniwapta*, it is the multiplicity or polyvalence of this mindscape that becomes especially important. Unlike Canadian poet E.J. Pratt (1882–1964), whose 1952 poem *Towards the Last Spike* narrated the building of the Canadian Pacific Railroad, Whyte could not write the Bow River from a single commanding epic viewpoint. Whyte is attracted to epic because of its inclusive and cosmological aspects, rather than the qualities of single-pointed perspective that led Bakhtin to use epic as a counterpoint to the novel's dialogic quality. In the 1986 essay "Cosmos: Order and Turning," Whyte defines epic as "something akin to 'the narrative that defines the universe at the time'" (269). Thus Whyte's version of a Rocky Mountain epic seeks "to integrate ecological and cultural affiliations" making Whyte the kind of cosmopolitan bioregionalist described by Mitchell Thomashow, one who points out that "a bioregional sensibility requires multiple voices and interpretations" (121, 130).

Whyte's embrace of this many-voiced approach can be seen everywhere in the poem, starting with the subtitle, *Voices of the River*. In *Minisniwapta* Whyte raises new challenges for himself by attempting to give voice to the Bow River in a way that would add even more dimensions to his already multidimensional representations of the Rockies. Whyte's previously published poems on the Rockies had already included elements of concrete poetry, using audacious page design and shaped blocks of type. In *The fells of brightness [first volume]*, as Canadian critic W.H. New describes it, Whyte's words "construct mountainous towers on the page, and cumulative lexical towers that snap, slip, skid, sink, fall, chip, rift, rent, gash, split, cleft, crack, break, slump, cleave, tremor, topple, as tribes scatter, tongues disperse, and form fails to last." To such concrete-poetry strategies, Whyte had already added multiple entwined narratives, as in *The fells of brightness: second volume: Wenkchemna*, in which a historical narrative from 1894 and a first-person account from 1983 sidle down the pages together, linking past, present, and place.

Yet in *Minisniwapta* Whyte would try to take such strategies even further. While continuing to write a poem with strong visual elements, including science and history, past and present, he would also try to add a strong element of sound, while also incorporating a literal anthology of literary voices, whispering about rivers around the world. In the 1990 typescript, this anthology element is represented by detached quotations that supplement the flow of the poem's main text, like the glosses in *The Shepheardes Calender* perhaps. In *Minisniwapta*, he quotes from Ann Zwinger: "The river becomes a way of thinking, ingrained, a way of looking at the

```
tion Green River                                  whee-oo-ee-ah

      the Cold River


          River Where Bow Willow Grows

                              Askow          the river changing
```

A "page" from the 1990 draft of Jon Whyte's *Minisniwapta*: "a long shallow poem, about 150 ft long and 11 inches deep" (Part IV, Flow and Flux: 2–3). Whyte Museum of the Canadian Rockies (M88/35–1990, Jon Whyte fonds).

world." He includes Peter Steinhart's observation that "to spend childhood days along creeks is to be drawn into the wider world." From a review of Wayne Fields's *What the River Knows: An Angler in Midstream*, Whyte cites a phrase he might well have written himself: "Even the most disciplined observer cannot enter a stream without also entering a metaphor, and it is helpful to know when the currents pressing against him are those of memory and emotion." Other quotations cite Barry Lopez, Norman McLean, and the literature of Canadian mountain exploration (including William Spotswood Green's *Among the Selkirk Glaciers* and Charles S. Thompson's 1896 essay "At the Headwaters of the Bow.")

In the 1991 typescript, which by then occupied 346 pages of sparsely filled accordion-fold printer paper, the strategy of accompanying "glosses" yields to an attempt to incorporate quotations directly into the poem text.

a face changing nature as character flows through it

as language char

the land changing character as the river flows through it

character as it flows through the land   ah-ee-i-

"There has been since the eighteenth century some kind of dream that
science was missing the evolution of shape in space and the evolution
of shape in time. If you think of a flow, you can think of a flow in
many ways, flow in economics or a flow in history. First it may be
laminar, then bifurcating to a more complicated state, perhaps with
oscillations. Then it may be chaotic."
        Albert Libchaber, quoted in Chaos, Making a New Science
        James Gleick, p. 195.

The overall structure of *Minisniwapta*, however, remains consistent from 1987 to 1991. Twelve sections take their names from stages in the river's own progression, beginning with its "prehistory as glacial melt," i, Primordial; ii, Glacier; iii, Crevasse; iv, Flow and Flux; v, Fall; vi, Lake; vii, Muskeag; viii, Braid; ix, Confluence; x, Stream; xi, Meander; and xii, Rapids. The scope of the poem's ambition shows itself clearly in this attempt to, in a sense, start from two poles at once—from the literal, observable river at one "end," with the "plink plink plink" of water drops on a glacier, and, from the other "end," with the human archive of imagined and narrated rivers. Using the visual strategies he had developed with the concrete-poetry elements in earlier work, and adding the aural aspect of the sound recording for which *Minisniwapta* is the score, Whyte attempts to bring all of these elements into relation with one another as simultaneously as possible. At the same time, the narrative element that the river itself presents, as it meanders from mountain glacier to the prairies, would bring in the elements of time and distance for which rivers so often serve as metaphor. It is difficult to resist seeing the poem as an instance of poetry straining toward the condition of cinema—and who knows whether Whyte might not have eventually returned to the medium he used for his Stanford master's project, *Jimmy Simpson: Mountain Man*, a 1973 film about a Banff neighbor and guide.

Does it matter whether Whyte's poem would ever have succeeded in integrating all of these elements had he lived to finish it? In a sense, it is not fair to Whyte to discuss *Minisniwapta* in such terms, since even those readers who visit the Whyte Museum Archive do not have access to a poem, but to the record of an unfinished process of composition. Had Whyte lived longer, he might have taken the project in completely different directions. Compared to the first two volumes of his Rockies epic, the *Minisniwapta* typescript shows less of Whyte's distinctive mingling of details from science and both local and personal history, for example. (These elements are present, but in *Minisniwapta* they do not appear with the same density of reference and detail.) Nevertheless, this record of a work in progress can still suggest the kinds of questions raised by the idea of bioregional writing and the potential strategies a poet might use to address these questions. Taken as an example of such writing, what can Whyte's unfinished poem tell us about the distinctiveness of writing bioregionally?

Tim Cresswell writes, "Bioregionalists argue that our present system of places is arbitrary and too much the product of human artifice" (134). Whyte might agree with "arbitrary" and would likely affirm the bioregionalist argument for rooting oneself in a place defined more clearly by an ecology and a mode of life. He might not agree that places are "too much" the product of human artifice, as he was a strong proponent of the concept that place and mind cocreate each other. A bioregionalist approach, of the sort Whyte's poem adumbrates, underlines this aspect of cocreation, which tends to be erased by the "givenness" of place that is common in so many everyday ways of thinking about it—place as nation, for example, or city, both with preexisting, seemingly solidified histories. (It is interesting to see how well this cocreation approach works when used to guide a historical rather than a poetic approach to representing the Bow River: see, for example, Armstrong, Evenden, and Nelles's recent study *The River Returns: An Environmental History of the Bow*.)

By defining "place" along different lines, bioregionalism resituates human stories and aligns authors with new points of departure. Whyte certainly aimed to do something like what Gary Snyder describes in his phrase "showing solidarity with a region" (41). As I have already mentioned, one poem that Jon Whyte saw as both inspiration and counterexample, when it came to writing his Rocky Mountain epic, was a poem usually discussed in Canadian nationalist terms, E. J. Pratt's *Towards the Last Spike*. Whyte explicitly positions his early work in relation to Pratt's when he asserts in the introduction to *The fells of brightness [first volume]*: that "if Pratt could write a poem as long as the CPR, I would write a poem as big as a mountain." In a period when Canadian literature was conscripted for purposes of cultural nationalism, Whyte does not explicitly describe nationalism as an "impostor" or see in it the "grinning ghost of lost community" (Snyder 43). However, he does aim to speak for a place, which he thought of not in nationalist terms, but instead in terms of the combination of the land he saw outside his door and the human history and understanding attached to it. A bioregionalist literature speaking in this way would offer affiliations more immediate than national literature. Such a bioregional literature would also play a cosmological role, in a sense, by explaining the human relation to the world as a relation of cocreation, requiring deep understanding and care.

Unfinished though it remains, Whyte's poem anticipates more current work redefining "place," such as that of Mike Pearson, in whose presentation of Lincolnshire, England, "performance becomes a topographic phenomenon of both natural and local history" (3). Whyte also shows how far "personal biographies, social identities and a biography of place are intimately connected" (Tilley, cited in Pearson 12). As Whyte wrote *Minisniwapta* between 1987 and 1991, he appears to have moved quite far toward writing bioregionally—a process that required him to cultivate new resources as a poet, and to craft strategies that continue to be explored by writers in the present.

NOTE

The author would like to express his gratitude to Harold Whyte for permission to quote from unpublished material, and to the staff at the archives of the Whyte Museum of the Canadian Rockies for their invaluable help and expertise.

WORKS CITED

Anson, Peter, ed. Biographical note on Jon Whyte. *Canada First: a mare usque ad Edmonton; New Canadian Poets*. Toronto: Anansi, 1969. Print.

Armstrong, Christopher, Matthew D. Evenden, and H. V. Nelles. *The River Returns: An Environmental History of the Bow*. Montreal: McGill-Queen's University Press, 2009. Print.

Cheney, Jim. "Postmodern Environmental Ethics: Ethics as Bioregional Narrative." *Environmental Ethics* 11 (Summer 1989): 117–34. Print.

Cresswell, Tim. *Place: A Short Introduction*. London, Blackwell, 2004. Print.

Fulford, Robert. *Globe and Mail*, 1 September 1992: A9. Print.

Kroetsch, Robert. "From Magpies to Booby Coots." *Books in Canada*, July 1982: 9. Print.

Mandel, Eli. "The Post Structural Scene in Contemporary Canadian Poetry: A Note." *Poetry Canada Review* 5.5 (Summer 1984): 10. Print.

McIvor, Mike. "Former CPAWS Trustee Dies in Banff." *Borealis* 3.3 (Fall 1992): 51. Print.

New, W. H. "Tops and Tales: Mountain Anecdote and Mountain Metaphor." *Canadian Poetry* 55 (Fall/Winter 2004): n. pag. Web. 14 March 2010.

Pearson, Mike. *"In Comes I": Performance, Memory and Landscape*. Exeter: University of Exeter Press, 2006. Print.

Schreiber, Le Anne. Rev. of *What the River Knows: An Angler in Midstream* by Wayne Fields. *New York Times Review of Books*, 7 Oct. 1990: 9. Print.

Snyder, Gary. *The Practice of the Wild: Essays*. New York: North Point Press, 1990. Print.

Steinhart, Peter. "The Meaning of Creeks." *Audubon Magazine* (May 1989): 22–24. Print.

Thomashow, Mitchell. "Towards a Cosmopolitan Bioregionalism." *Bioregionalism*. Ed. Michael Vincent McGinnis. London: Routledge, 1999. 121–32. Print.

Thompson, Charles S. "At the Headwaters of the Bow." *Appalachia* 8 (1896–98): 320–27. Print.

Tilley, Christopher. *A Phenomenology of Landscape: Places, Paths and Monuments*. Providence: Berg, 1994. Print.

Whyte, Jon. CBC Radio interview with Vicki Gabereau. Audio recording. S28/40.

———. "Cosmos: Order and Turning." *Trace: Prairie Writers on Writing*. Ed. Birk Sproxton. Winnipeg: Turnstone Press, 1986. 269–74. Print.

———. *The fells of brightness [first volume]: some fittes and starts*. Edmonton: Longspoon Press, 1983. Print.

———. *The fells of brightness: second volume: Wenkchemna*. Edmonton: Longspoon Press, 1985. Print.

———. *Gallimaufry*. Edmonton: Longspoon Press, 1981. Print.

———. Jon Whyte Fonds, ts M88/123.

———. Jon Whyte Fonds, undated ts M88/124. (An internal reference to Whyte's "thirty five years" suggests this dates from 1976.)

———. Jon Whyte Fonds, undated ts M88/125.

———. Letters from Earle Birney, 7 February 1969, 28 February 1971. Jon Whyte Fonds, M88/246. M88/249.

———. *Minisniwapta: Voices of the River.* s28/1 to 39. Broadcast on "State of the Arts," Canadian Broadcasting Corporation, 1987. Audio recording. Jon Whyte Fonds, Whyte Museum of the Canadian Rockies, Banff, Alberta, Canada.

———. *Minisniwapta: Voices of the River.* Ts, M88/34,35,36. Jon Whyte Fonds, Whyte Museum of the Canadian Rockies, Banff, Alberta, Canada.

———. ts proposal to CBC "State of the Arts," M88/E Disk 9.

Zwinger, Ann. *Run, River, Run: A Naturalist's Journey Down One of the Great Rivers of the West.* New York: HarperCollins, 1975. Print.

RUTH BLAIR

Figures of Life

Beverley Farmer's *The Seal Woman* as an Australian Bioregional Novel

THE BIOREGION

THE OTWAY PLAIN BIOREGION, in the southwest of the state of Victoria, Australia, is bordered on one side by the Otway ranges and on another by the western shore of the vast Port Phillip Bay, with the town of Queenscliff sitting on its furthest point.[1] On one side of this outpost town is Bass Strait, a major shipping lane that separates the mainland from Tasmania (Antarctica is the next landmass to the south); on the other, formed by the small peninsula on which Queenscliff sits, is Swan Bay. Close by is the township of Point Lonsdale. Between them, Queenscliff and Point Lonsdale have three magnificent lighthouses, all still in operation.

BIOREGIONALISM AND SENSE OF PLACE

A sense of place is strong in contemporary Australian writing. I have seized the opportunity offered by this collection of essays to discuss the work of Beverley Farmer who, to my mind, is Australia's most "bioregional" writer. Since her first novel, *Alone* (1980), Farmer has written across a number of genres—short stories, essays, poetry, mixed genre works, and the novel— always with a strong sense of place, whether of her home place or other places in which she has sojourned. As the scope of this essay does not permit an overview of Farmer's work, I have chosen to focus on her novel *The Seal Woman* (1992), which offers a meticulous exploration of a cherished

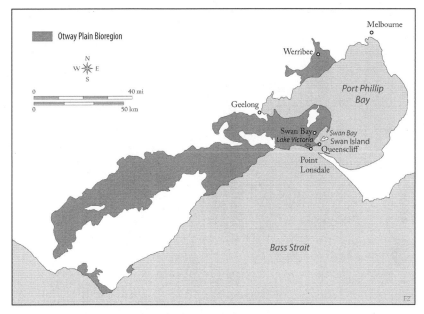

Queenscliff and the Otway Plain Bioregion, Victoria, Australia

locality. It also gives us ways to think about what a "bioregional novel" might be, as one of the vehicles through which the creative imagination and language form our relationships with place.

For the greater part of her writing life, Beverley Farmer has lived in Point Lonsdale, in the shadow of its lighthouse and amid its typical coastal vegetation of indigenous banksias and tea trees. Much of her writing and photography gathers within the folds of this landscape. In his essay "Landscape and Narrative," Barry Lopez describes a "pervasive sense of congruence" that the reader will feel upon reading a narrative whose integrity derives from respect for the "exterior landscape" in which it is conceived (66). This challenging point is borne out by Farmer's writing that seems deeply to derive from a sense of place, not in any decorative sense but as its sine qua non. More than this, however, the inflection of Farmer's attention is bioregional in the sense that the lives she describes are stitched into the physical environment. It is not their "setting" and they are not its "inhabitants." Rather, life, as represented in Farmer's writing, is a constant process of relationship and negotiation among phenomena.

Farmer's writing is highly considered in Australia, yet there remains something elusive about her work.[2] I suggest that reading for the bioregion (as opposed to "reading for the plot") makes *The Seal Woman* "readable." It is the deep foundation that Lopez describes. The very idea of the bioregion, with its sense of locality as the way to begin to understand how we humans live on the earth, gives me a way into the core of Farmer's work that I believe is not available when critical scholarship cleaves to human-centered approaches, seeing her environmental interests as yet another theme (with, for example, feminism) and not the groundwork of it all.

I must at this point establish a position in relation to the somewhat contested ground of the bioregion. I have invoked the concept of the local and have done so in cognizance of Ursula Heise's and others' strong dissection and questioning of the term.[3] In Australia, *bioregion* is well bedded down as a working term in a range of areas and government agencies, from science to agriculture to environmental activism.[4] It is a term that relates to the land itself, encouraging the consideration of where one lives in terms of its "geology, landform patterns, climate, ecological features and plant and animal communities" (Australian Government, Department of Environment, Water, Heritage and the Arts). Reflecting on this phenomenon has led me to ask if it might be possible to rethink the persistent idea of the local in nonbinary terms. I see the idea of the local implied in the term *bioregion* not so much as what is divided off from or in opposition to something larger, or other, and thus freighted with particular sets of social and political agendas (which we must not lose sight of), but rather as naming a kind of attention. I have a strong sense that we shouldn't throw the baby out with the bathwater, but rather stress, in our range of interpretations of the term, the sense of context—the inflection bestowed on it by the many organizations like the Common Ground movement in the United Kingdom that go about the business of teaching us to pay attention to how we live within (and with) whatever locality we find ourselves in or are drawn to.[5] *The Seal Woman* is set in Beverley Farmer's own home place, but her central character is a sojourner.

Ursula K. Heise describes bioregionalism as a "resilient" discourse (44). It is also old. The concept has not sprung newly out of contemporary environmentalism. It is present in the sense of biophysical distinctiveness evident in Heine's poem about the pine tree yearning for the palm tree;[6] scientifically it is there in Wallace's Line[7] (but not Mason and Dixon's); it is in Gilbert White's Selborne; and it resides in ancient local wisdoms. With its newish, scientific-sounding name, it is useful to ecologists and to a range of scientific studies. Doug Aberley's essay, "Interpreting Bioregionalism: A Story from Many Voices," traces the recent history of the term, explaining the conjunction of environmental/scientific and social justice concerns that led activists and writers like Peter Berg and Raymond Dasmann (1978) and Gary Snyder (1990) to champion the concept as promoting a better awareness of community as a community of people and environment. In a sense, then, storytelling, quite as much as the descriptive tradition of place-based writing, is suited to the expression of bioregional concerns.

In what follows, I first try to develop an understanding of ways in which *The Seal Woman* exemplifies not only the sense of human embeddedness in particular physical contexts, but also some of the preoccupations that have become associated with the term *bioregionalism*. I then use Farmer's text as a basis for exploring the role of the novel in the development of bioregional awareness.

READING BEVERLEY FARMER

PAYING ATTENTION

The Seal Woman is a paean to the coastal area of Queenscliff and Point Lonsdale as bioregion in the sense developed by Snyder and others of a "wholeheartedly lived-in landscape" (Tall 10). In the novel, the Queenscliff area is given a fictional name, "Swanhaven," echoing the real "Swan Bay" (named for its black swans), and physically corresponding with the coastal extremity of the Otway bioregion. From its rock pools and dunes to its wetlands, the bay, an old settler-planted banyan tree, and more recent house gardens, the area is minutely and lovingly connected with through all the senses as it touches the lives of characters in the novel.

A story of movement between the two hemispheres, the novel links local environmental issues with global ones. Dagmar, the central character and narrator, is a Danish woman, returned to stay at Swanhaven as she goes through the long process of grieving for her sailor husband, Finn, lost in a shipwreck in the northern seas. Finn had once worked on a Danish ice-breaker, the *Nella Dan* (a real and famous ship that ferried expeditioners between Australia and Antarctica), and Dagmar had lived in Swanhaven while he did so. At the invitation of old friends, she returns to live out some of her grief in this seaside place of formerly more hopeful waiting. But other deaths than Finn's haunt the novel: Dagmar and her Australian

Swan Bay fog lifting. Photograph by Beverley Farmer, used with permission.

Swan Bay swans. Photograph by Beverley Farmer, used with permission.

friends read accounts of the bodies of thousands of seals washed up on the
Swedish coast, believed to have been killed by the level of toxic chemicals—PCBs, dioxins, mercury—in the ocean.

The Seal Woman is a story of healing through the land (and sea), not
unlike Leslie Marmon Silko's *Ceremony* (1977), which also links the global
with the local—for Silko, through nuclear energy and its powers of destruction. Farmer's novel begins in the place to which her writings frequently return: the shore and a rock shelf on the point.

> White worms with lips are grazing in midair, nuzzling their way over
> the mounds, the boulders. The tide is out. Their white fins drift, veils and
> webs, gossamer, as if in water. They feed on the corruption. Shore sand,
> bull kelp, boulders of grey flesh, and nowhere a crab, a fly or a wasp, only
> the filmy-finned floaters. Over the whole shore, layer on layer of white
> veiling lifts and bells, flattens and hangs drifting. The boulders are great
> animals, diminishing slowly, torpid, already porous on the grey sand where
> soon not even bones will be left. (1)

From the first lines of this novel, we enter an ecology—a world heady with
connections. The "gossamer" of the third sentence is a web. Dagmar makes
the connection with the Danish *gås-ame* and finds in the dictionary that
the core meaning of the English word is "a fine filmy substance, a kind of
delicate cobweb, floating in the air in calm clear weather . . . formed by
a small species of spiders" (18). Webs, as in Silko's novel, are a dominant
motif in the narrative, as the reader is drawn into a world of living and
nonliving things that are equally alive through textures, sights, sounds,
and smells: "A honey box of old Baltic pine, [the house] has high planked
ceilings with no attic, no roof windows. . . . Cobwebs swing in the draught
as you open doors and walk past. Beards of web hang in corners. Bees
surge through an open window or bang on the glass walls at the back. . . .
The sun glitters in on a long dining table as rough and warm as bread. A
dresser to match it stands where the sun falls through a window over the
sink; a jug of chrysanthemums as sharp as apples" (5). We see here, as in
the first paragraph of the novel, how metaphor contributes to the sense of
interconnection. In the earlier, dreamy depiction of the coastal landscape,
rocks are "animals," "grey flesh." A little further on, human animals in a
bathtub are like sea creatures: "Finn and I, a white octopus overflowing
and groping, knees in the air, for this soap like a goldfish" (6). The world
of the novel is predicated on a constant process of metamorphosis, where

language facilitates correspondence and connection. But also pertinent to the bioregional aspects of the novel are the kinds of attention paid. Here is a passage that looks a little like nature writing:

> This stretch of the shore I knew well, this jungle of berry bushes, creepers and ivy, webbed branches, bottles and bird carcases in a hollow, low scrub on the slope to the railway line and beyond it the saltmarsh flats and the sandbanks. Salty, pearly air of the late winter's day, rose-stained even at noon through the clouds, a far spill of mercury turned off like a tap. Ibises and a grey heron were hunched at the water's edge, swans a long way out in a current, shags on posts, pairs of finning swallows. A couple of children ambled past on horseback without seeing me. The air condensed into a dew, large drops, a slick of rain brushing the surface and tailing off. Pale ink in shades of blue-grey, streaks that could be islands or hills or water shadows, dots of swans and their reflections, the crawling bubbles that were crabs. (37–38)

This is a world in which everything is going about its separate business yet is connected, not in some kind of central harmony—more like the concurrent melodies of the gamelan. It is also bioregional (in the sense of Snyder and others) in that people are part of their environment. Even the narrator is a participant. She (and we through her) sees, tastes, and touches the scene around her, thoroughly alive in its moment. There is an echo of Thoreau here in the sense of immersion in an environment, as there is in the distant sound of a train in an earlier description of the tidal lagoon: "You hear a ripple and hiss of windy water, peep-peeps and coos and honks, a fly-sizzle. Only the old steam train intrudes, and then only on Sundays, pluming out smoke as it barges along the shoreline sending a wave of swans over the water with its roar and hoot" (9).[8]

However, the darker side of the human presence in Farmer's novel is not, as it is for Thoreau, about alienation of the human connection with nature by the mechanical but about degradation of the environment by human activity.[9] Further on in this description, a hint of darkness builds to a crescendo: "Lengths of the shore at low tide have a rime of froth, a scattering of shell and bottle shards, green and tawny, crystalline or clouding like a poached egg; rags of sea lettuce, shells that birds have left hinged open. . . . Rubbish lies in the same place for days: polystyrene cups, plastic bags, papers, a car tyre, rusty cans; and everywhere the ringed plastic six-pack holders that in the water clench in a ruff of lace on the necks of diving birds" (9). What appears at first to be an aestheticizing of detritus is undercut by the image, shocking in its irony, of the six-pack holder as a "ruff of lace" around a dead bird's neck.

Environmental degradation is a significant thread in the narrative. The northern hemisphere dead seals become a motif, recalled intermittently through newspaper accounts, built on through Dagmar's quest to find out more about seals and related sea creatures, and culminating in her diving among the seals of Port Phillip Bay. The novel ends with a version of the legend of the Seal Wife or *Sælfruen*—an ancient tale of a female seal who casts off her skin to become a woman, marries a human, and finally returns to the sea. This story retrospectively casts another kind of light on the seals, which I shall discuss further on. Through this web of connections, the novel forges a link between close attention to the place one inhabits and a wider concern for the earth and the human place in it.

The entwining of local and global perceptions bears out Mitchell Thomashow's belief that "learning to perceive global environmental change requires a daily practice of natural history observation" (73). But what I find particularly affecting about Farmer's work is that she strives to reduce the dominance of the visual—unusual for a writer who is also a passionate and accomplished photographer, as the photographs accompanying this essay show. In Farmer's writing "the eyes, the skin, the tongue, ears, nostrils—all are gates where [the] body receives the nourishment of otherness" (Abram ix). In the descriptions of landscape quoted above, we smell and taste the salt air, hear the train, feel the slick of rain. Not surprisingly to readers of Farmer's earlier and later works, the sense of taste is particularly important, often expressed through the preparation and eating of food. Dagmar prepares local fish—grass whiting, one "daubed with a tropical blue so intense that around the red eye it throbbed and made the fawn lacework along the skull seem an after-image" (51). She stuffs them with herbs to bake them, puts "half-moons of pumpkin" and potatoes in salted skins in the oven, salts slices of "mirror-bright eggplant." She dishes out the meal: "a pale fish each for them and the blue one for me, and all the rich vegetables" (52).[10]

Descriptions involving food and eating in *The Seal Woman* have an aura of the sacramental. Everything to do with food, here and in Farmer's other writing, forms, through a vocabulary of cherishing, a kind of counterweight to death and destruction—an iconic gesture of the "comedy of survival," as Joseph Meeker deemed it. In *The True Story of the Novel*, Margaret Doody analyzes the "hermeneutic demands" (428) of food in fiction, concluding that food "has the job of standing up for being" and that "references to food, however slight or comic, pay homage to biological life as real life" (431).

There is a great deal about the body and about women's bodies in particular in this text, and through these explorations of the body come very clear messages. A central one is the capacity for healing that lies within humanity and the capacity for life itself to heal. There is no easy answer to humanity's capacity to destroy, no easy answer for the seals. But there is hope. In the story, healing takes the form of hitherto (she believes) sterile and now (she also believes) menopausal Dagmar conceiving a child. The freight of that trajectory carries a sense of hope—not quite optimism, but nevertheless a daring thing to promise in this time of pessimism and in what is in many ways a novel of dystopic vision. The novel moves outward from its particular setting and preoccupations to larger concerns that include sense of agency, which is an important (yet rarely discussed) tool we develop through attention to our bioregions.

SEDIMENTATION

Interconnections in *The Seal Woman* are temporal as well as geographical, invoking both what we in the West call historical time and the amorphous time of myth. Farmer spent several years in Greece, and this experience, I believe, has had a profound influence on the way she has come to understand what Maurice Merleau-Ponty describes as "the presence of all presents in our own" (*Signs* 96). Farmer's early stories set in Greece (in the collections *Milk* [1983] and *Home Time* [1985]) are full of the sense of a community deeply embedded in a landscape where plants and people have an age-old symbiotic relationship entwined within pre-Christian and Christian mythologies. Here, belief and tradition knit together human and nonhuman activity to make meaning out of life. Similarly in *The Seal Woman*, the legend of the Seal Woman or Seal Wife is the presiding story that helps to make sense of life and death, of women's lives, of love, of birth, and of seals and of humans' relationships with them.

Merleau-Ponty's term (after Husserl), *sedimentation*, graphically describes the process of laying down temporal connections, but also, in his hands, expresses the complexity of our human relationships with the past. I like *sedimentation* for its sense of the physical world, for its sense of layers of meaning and for Merleau-Ponty's (dialectical) insight that "sedimentation is not only the accumulation of one creation upon another but also an integration" (*The Prose of the World* 100). It offers rich insights into how we might connect historical issues with current ecological concerns in thinking about the bioregion—a process explored in *The Seal Woman*. It also provides a stepping-stone on the path towards understanding the importance of storytelling, which is predicated on temporality and connection.

For Dagmar there is already a personal past in Swanhaven, associated with her life before her husband's death. And the fact of this central death reminds us that sedimentation necessarily involves death as one of its processes. Unsurprisingly, what the grieving Dagmar finds herself fascinated with, in the present moment, is the deaths of the seals, but also with ancient deaths. Farmer herself comments in an interview that Dagmar's "landscape" is "a vast graveyard full of relics and ghosts" (qtd. in Jacobs 101). Her Scandinavian roots invoke the image of the bog man, "that [body] taken from the bog where it had lain two thousand years" (Farmer 158). On an excursion to observe whales in the Great Australian Bight, which involves also a visit to ancient caves, Dagmar comes close up to relics of the deep cultural history of Australian Aborigines.[11]

The legend of the *Sælfruen* connects the narrative with mythic time. In its various manifestations through ages and places, this legend has woven a tragic love story out of the idea of the metamorphosis of a seal into a woman through the shedding of its skin. The version that ends Farmer's novel connects with the text that precedes it in many ways. Broadly speaking, in the way it has traditionally told the story of people and place we see its ancient understanding of passing and renewal; but perhaps most importantly, in the story of a seal who sheds and restores her skin, moving in and out of "animal" and "human," it challenges the reader to question the meaning of those boundaries. They are, in a sense, ineluctably there (the tragedy of loss that the legend presents), but also not (the ability of the seal to become a woman). Without denying difference, this old, many-versioned story reminds us of shared qualities.

A BIOREGIONAL NOVEL?

At times, this section speaks of the environmental novel in broader terms, because I see the bioregional novel, with its focus on close attention to locality, as a subgenre of this larger concept. Jim Cheney argues that "bioregionalism is a natural extension of the line of thought being developed by those advocating a view of ethics as contextualist narrative" (33). From this point of view, the novel becomes an appropriate and adaptable vehicle, though at first glance it is far from being the obvious form to carry environmental or bioregional awareness. With its modern origins in early Western industrial culture and in social interaction, it remains a character-centered genre, and, concomitantly, "description" has remained something of a kid-glove area in narrative theory. Lawrence Buell describes the ability of narrative to dramatize experience within an environment (240–41). Buell's book *Writing for an Endangered World* identifies traditional *topoi*, genres and rhetorical gestures that have been employed to dramatize contemporary environmental discourse. Following Buell's line of argument, *The Seal Woman* is a bildungsroman and also an example of mixing genres and discourses. But I am more interested in what I see as a key feature and a key problem in writing environmental fiction, and especially bioregional fiction: the relationship between story and description—and more broadly between the genres of nature writing and storytelling. Terry Tempest Williams's pioneering autobiographical narrative, *Refuge* (1991), interlaces the two genres. But the novel is another matter. Longish passages describing the physical environment, like Thomas Hardy's evocation of Egdon Heath at the beginning of *The Return of the Native* (1878), stand out as a bit odd. The ancient rhetorical term *ekphrasis* has been invoked to account for them.[12] While I can't attempt a theory of the environmental novel here, I would like to take a closer look at some of the processes in Farmer's text.

The distinction in narrative theory between "story" (simply put, what is told) and "discourse" (the telling) provides a useful way of seeing what is at work in Farmer's manipulations of the elastic (Henry James's term) form of the novel. There is the clear story of Dagmar's journey of healing, which involves a relationship with a local man, Martin. There are the backstory of her marriage, and accompanying stories, both literal (seal deaths) and mythical (the *Sælfruen*). The level of the telling intricately and innovatively supports these stories. Take the description of the house quoted above, for example. It signals much more than "setting" or "the real."[13] Rather, there is another level of signification at work in the metaphors of the house like a bee box or the table warm as bread, or the rocks of gray flesh. The very discourse of this novel is announcing an ecological worldview in which everything, including human beings, and indeed language itself, exists within an intricate web of relationships.[14] Dagmar's healing involves close attention to the place where she is—a way of being totally within the present moment, in all its complexity. This process becomes at times a hymn to this place, mingled with anxiety (at moments elegiac) for a lack of steward-ship, which is mirrored on a global scale in anxiety about the seals.

The discourse can be seen as ecological in other ways, ones we are now familiar with in the contemporary novel: stitching disparate fragments of time together and including uncharacteristic narrative modes such as ver-batim pieces of other kinds of text—here often the "prosaic" discourses of newspaper reporting or encyclopedias or magazines. So, of course, does what many see as *the* great environmental novel, *Moby-Dick* (1851).[15] And in fact, *The Seal Woman* mirrors Melville's text in a number of ways. It moves easily and persistently between microcosm and macrocosm. *Moby-Dick*, too, is a book about an animal and industry (though coming from a dif-ferent set of cultural perceptions). Melville's text becomes a great scripture, the book of the world. *The Seal Woman* is a book about a loved place in all its detail that becomes a book about the world and how human beings inhabit it in our time. Both books have a presiding myth and both call on a range of mythologies to frame understanding. Both see language as a fun-damental part of the process of being human in the world and gladly get hung up on etymologies. Both books were ahead of their time, Melville's by a good half-century, and Farmer's by fifteen or so years where an Australian audience is concerned. Both books thrive on excess. They also share, along with Silko's *Ceremony*, an intensely symbolistic cast to their presentation that intensifies the reader's sense that there are indeed "tongues in trees, books in the running brooks,/Sermons in stones" (Shakespeare, *As You Like It* 2.1.16–17).

We are all learning or trying to learn to live with awareness in our bio-regions. But we need to write our bioregions as well or have them written for us. Human language is the magical tool we possess, and anciently, to forge connections. "Perhaps it is not surprising," Richard Mabey writes, "that our working relationships with the natural world are like nothing so much as the business of using language" (54). Language, as David Abram argues, is what enables us to live in a meaningful world (179 and passim). In *The Seal Woman*, the ancient story of the *Sælfruen* guides the process of making sense of the world of the novel. Myths "*locate* us in a *moral* space which is at the same time the space we live in physically" (Cheney 34; em-phasis in the original). They tell of the power of language and imagination. Beverley Farmer demonstrates in *The Seal Woman* that storytelling can be an important vehicle for the elaboration of multiple issues surrounding a contemporary sense of place. She has also shown the vital capacity of the novel to represent ways of belonging in the world.

NOTES

1. A description of this bioregion can be found on the website of the Victorian Government Department of Primary Industries, downloadable as a PDF file ("Bellarine Landscape Zone Plan December 2003"). <http://search.dpi.vic.gov.au/search/search.cgi?query=Queenscliff+bioregion&submit.x=0&submit.y=0&collection=dpi>.

2. Lyn Jacobs's book *Against the Grain* has a substantial bibliography of works by and about Farmer. See also *Southerly*.

3. Heise gives a succinct summary of critical approaches to the idea of the bioregion in *Sense of Place and Sense of Planet*, 45–48.

4. On governments' adoption of the term see, for example, the entry "Australia's Bioregions" on the website of the Australian Government's Department of Environment, Water, Heritage and the Arts <http://www.environment.gov.au/parks/nrs/science/bioregion-framework/index.html> and "What is a Bioregion?" by the New South Wales Department of Environment, Climate Change and Water <http://www.environment.nsw.gov.au/bioregions/BioregionsExplained.htm>. See also note 1 of this essay.

5. For information on Common Ground (U.K.) see: <http://www.commonground. org.uk/>.

6. Heinrich Heine, "Der Fichtenbaum und die Palme" (The Pine Tree and the Palm; 1823) Web. <poemhttp://www.autodidactproject.org/other/heinepoem.html>.

7. The British naturalist and evolutionary theorist, Alfred Russel Wallace (1823–1913) observed in the islands of what is now Indonesia a dividing line between Asiatic and Australasian fauna. This became known as Wallace's Line.

8. The steam train in this description is a special tourist train that runs on an otherwise disused track along the Queenscliff peninsula. One of the photographs of Swan Bay accompanying this essay shows the smoke from this train.

9. See Leo Marx's now iconic work *The Machine in the Garden*.

10. In her article, "Rethinking Dichotomies in Terry Tempest Williams's *Refuge*," Cassandra Kircher takes issue with a perceived contradiction between Williams's sense of stewardship for birds and her seemingly unthinking eating of the Thanksgiving turkey. I see no such contradiction in Farmer's work. Even beyond the respect shown for the fish that are to be eaten (and the vegetables, one might add!), Farmer has an interest in the role of food in the processes of life that is

simply not a topic for Williams. Margaret Doody's comments on food in fiction (to follow) help us understand Farmer's position.

11. It is important to note that Farmer isn't, here, locking (or freezing) Australian Aborigines into some ancient past. Dagmar encounters in Swanhaven a group of Aborigines picnicking in a park, and while the book does not explore Aboriginal disposession at length, the recognition is there, and in a heartfelt way. See *The Seal Woman* 203–4, 244–56.

12. *Ekphrasis* literally means "description," but the term has come down to us in its sense (from rhetoric) of the description of works of art within a verbal text. As Timothy Morton and others show, it is increasingly being applied to any long description where "the time of narration is held in stasis" (Morton 44) and is therefore a potentially useful term in ecocriticism for texts incorporating lengthy descriptions of the natural world. For a sustained account, see Murray Kreiger, *Ekphrasis*. See also Margaret Doody, *The True Story of the Novel*.

13. I am thinking here of Roland Barthes' identification of the role of much description in narrative texts as "reality effect" in his essay of that name. See also Barthes' *The Rustle of Language*.

14. I am aware of arguments for metaphor as appropriation, especially in relation to writing about animals, but it is also the strongest linguistic strategy we have for establishing connections through shared qualities, related, in this context, to the idea of metamorphosis.

15. After Annie Dillard's famous comment that it is "the best book ever written about nature" (Dillard 316). Buell discusses *Moby-Dick* at length in *Writing for an Endangered World*.

WORKS CITED

Aberley, Doug. "Interpreting Bioregionalism: A Story from Many Voices." *Bioregionalism*. Ed. Michael Vincent McGinnis. New York: Routledge, 1999. 13–42. Print.

Abram, David. *The Spell of the Sensuous: Perception and Language in a More-than-Human World*. New York: Vintage, 1996. Print.

Australian Government, Department of Environment, Water, Heritage and the Arts. "Australia's Bioregions." Web. <http://www.environment.gov.au/parks/nrs/science/bioregion-framework/index.html>.

Barthes, Roland. "The Reality Effect." *French Literary Theory Today: A Reader*. Ed. Tzvetan Todorov. Trans. R. Carter. Cambridge: Cambridge University Press, 1982. 11–17. Print.

———. *The Rustle of Language*. Trans. Richard Howard. Oxford: Blackwell, 1986. Print.

Berg, Peter, and Raymond Dasmann. "Reinhabiting California." *Reinhabiting a Separate Country: A Bioregional Anthology of Northern California*. San Francisco: Planet Drum, 1978. 217–20. Print.

Buell, Lawrence. *Writing for an Endangered World: Literature, Culture and Environment in the U.S. and Beyond*. Cambridge, Mass.: Harvard University Press, 2001. Print.

Cheney, Jim. "Postmodern Environmental Ethics: Ethics as Bioregional Narrative." *Postmodern Environmental Ethics*. Ed. Max Oelschlaeger. Albany: State University of New York Press, 1995. 23–42. Print.

Dillard, Annie. "Natural History: An Annotated Booklist." *The Nature Reader*. Ed. Daniel Halpern and Dan Frank. Hopewell, N.J.: Ecco, 1996. 315–21. Print.

Doody, Margaret. *The True Story of the Novel*. New Brunswick, N.J.: Rutgers University Press, 1996. Print.

Farmer, Beverley. *Alone*. Carlton, Victoria: Sisters Publishing, 1980.

———. *Home Time*. Ringwood, Victoria: McPhee Gribble/Penguin, 1985. Print.

———. *Milk*. Ringwood, Victoria: Penguin, 1983. Print.

———. *The Seal Woman*. St Lucia, Queensland: University of Queensland Press, 1992. Print.

Hardy, Thomas. *The Return of the Native*. London: Macmillan, 1958. Print.

Heine, Heinrich, "Der Fichtenbaum und die Palme." Web. <poemhttp://www.autodidactproject.org/other/heinepoem.html>.

Heise, Ursula K. *Sense of Place and Sense of the Planet: The Environmental Imagination of the Global*. Oxford: Oxford University Press, 2008. Print.

Jacobs, Lyn. *Against the Grain: Beverley Farmer's Writing*. St Lucia: University of Queensland Press, 2001. Print.

Kircher, Cassandra. "Rethinking Dichotomies in Terry Tempest Williams's *Refuge*." *ISLE: Interdisciplinary Studies in Literature and Environment* 3.1 (1996): 97–113. Print.

Kreiger, Murray. *Ekphrasis: The Illusion of the Natural Sign*. Baltimore: Johns Hopkins University Press, 1992. Print.

Lopez, Barry. *Crossing Open Ground*. New York: Vintage, 1989. Print.

Mabey, Richard. *Our Common Ground: A Place for Nature in Britain's Future?* London: Arrow Books, 1981. Print.

Meeker, Joseph. *The Comedy of Survival*. Los Angeles: Guild of Tutors Press, 1980. Print.

Melville, Herman. *Moby-Dick*. Harmondsworth: Penguin, 1972. Print.

Merleau-Ponty, Maurice. *The Prose of the World*. Ed. Claude Lefort. Trans. John O'Neill. Evanston, Ill.: Northwestern University Press, 1973. Print.

———. *Signs*. Trans. Richard C. McLeary. Evanston, Ill.: Northwestern University Press, 1964. Print.

Morton, Timothy. *Ecology without Nature: Rethinking Environmental Aesthetics.* Cambridge, Mass.: Harvard University Press, 2007. Print.

New South Wales Department of Environment, Climate Change and Water. "What is a Bioregion?" Web. <http://www.environment.nsw.gov.au/bioregions/ BioregionsExplained.htm>.

Silko, Leslie Marmon. *Ceremony.* New York: Penguin, 1977. Print.

Snyder, Gary. *The Practice of the Wild.* New York: North Point Press/Farrar, Straus and Giroux, 1990. Print.

Southerly 58.3 (1998) (Special issue: *Reading Beverley Farmer*). Print.

Tall, Deborah. *From Where We Stand: Recovering a Sense of Place.* Baltimore: Johns Hopkins University Press, 1993. Print.

Thomashow, Mitchell. *Bringing the Biosphere Home: Learning to Perceive Global Environmental Change.* Cambridge, Mass.: MIT Press, 2002. Print.

Thoreau, Henry David. *Walden and Resistance to Civil Government.* Ed. William Rossi. 2nd ed. New York: Norton, 1992. Print.

Victorian Government Department of Primary Industries. "Bellarine Landscape Zone Plan December 2003." Web. <http://search.dpi.vic.gov.au/search/search .cgi?query=Queenscliff+bioregion&submit.x=0&submit.y=0&collection=dpi>.

Williams, Terry Tempest. *Refuge: An Unnatural History of Family and Place.* 1991. New York: Vintage, 1992. Print.

HEATHER KERR

Melancholy Botany

Charlotte Smith's Bioregional Poetic Imaginary

*Charlotte Turner Smith (1749–1806) was one of England's
most popular writers in a period when literary tastes mirrored
the revolutionary changes taking place in the political and
economic spheres of life in the western world. Her four
volumes of poetry, ten novels, translations, and moralistic
children's books made her one of the most prolific writers of the
last years of the eighteenth century, and readers of the day were
usually quite ready to support both critically and financially
this woman who dared on the one hand to question the
social structures under which she lived while on the other
she challenged the already crumbling literary standards of a
rationally prejudiced age.*

Paul and June Schlueter, *An Encyclopedia of British Women Writers*

BIOREGIONAL LITERARY CRITICISM is demonstrably productive for readings of modern and contemporary authors, but can it
be fruitfully applied to authors from earlier periods? My essay explores the
poetry of a major pre-Romantic author, Charlotte Turner Smith, whose
collection of *Elegiac Sonnets* (first published in 1784 and revised in multiple
editions to 1800) revived the sonnet form for the first generation of English
Romantic poets. Together with her loco-descriptive and politically radical poems such as *The Emigrants* (1793) and the posthumously published
blank verse topographical experiment *Beachy Head* (1807), her poetry is

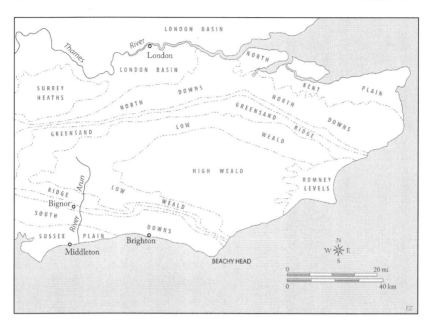

South-East Down and Weald, England

the subject of sustained critical attention.[1] Many commentators remark on
Charlotte Smith's interest in concepts that are pertinent to a bioregionalist
literary criticism: for example, the relations between local and global economics, geography, and biodiversity; tensions between arbitrary political
and ecosystem boundaries; histories of place; natural right and questions
of morality; imaginative and physical belongings; and territories of the
mind. As yet, Smith's work has not been read with explicit reference to
bioregionalist thought. My focus is on Smith's poetics of place, a sustained
local attentiveness to the bioregion of the English southeast that contrasts
strikingly with her novelistic cosmopolitanism. In considering the effects of
this poetic localism, I propose to bring together two lively but apparently
separate critical trends: the investigation of Smith's investment in literary
subjectivities, defined in part by a "melancholy poetics" (Pratt), and the
investigation of her literary investments in natural history. I aim to sketch
her bioregionalist poetic imaginary, first with reference to the *Elegiac Sonnets*, in which "picturesque" locations spatially formalize Smith's sense of
"biographical alienation," social marginalization, and personal loss (Sodeman 135); and second, with reference to *The Emigrants* and *Beachy Head*,

in which Smith lays out a "metaphorical map that offers an alternative to dominant geographical [social and political] configurations of England and France" in the eighteenth century (Wiley 55).

To attend to particular local natural histories is to attend to the ways in which particular bioregions offer ethically preferable alternatives to generally institutionalized injustices, whether interpersonal or international. In Michael Wiley's assessment, "the natural on this [metaphorical] map does not oppose the social; rather, the natural has . . . a socially radical, reformist purpose" (56). What is the relationship between Smith's compassion for French émigrés of the 1790s and her poetic attention to the biota of the commons? As Donna Landry's ecocritical analysis points out, Smith "demonstrated that poetry could also be natural history, and that natural history could lead to ethical statements and social comment" (489). My essay pursues some bioregionalist possibilities of this observation, using examples from Smith's poetry.

I conclude with an assessment of the "scalar" effects achieved by Smith's deployment of Fancy, an eighteenth-century understanding of the sympathetic imagination (cf. Pappas). How does Smith's poetry use Fancy to "scale up" from particular to general phenomena? And how do Charlotte Smith's pervasive sense of exile and persistent demands for readers' sympathy relate to her interest in local natural history? What, in other words, is the relationship between Fancy (or sensibility) and Linnaean botanical taxonomy (or science) in the eighteenth century? Throughout this essay I assume that the bioregional setting of Smith's poetry is no mere background but the very condition of possibility for an unswerving attentiveness to the effects of systemic injustice in the period following the French Revolution. I argue that in her poetic exploration of multiple forms of interrelatedness, Smith represents an early instance of "parochial cosmopolitanism" (cf. Menely).

Charlotte Smith's bioregional poetic imaginary is a dynamic terrain of consciousness, a memory map of sites saturated with particular emotions and characterized by multiple, sympathetic affiliations (Meredith 90, 93). This atlas of affect has its correlative formal bioregion (Meredith 89) in England's South-East Down and Weald, especially the county of Sussex (J. T. White, "South-East" fig. 2, 18). Rather than assume this formal bioregion is a realist portrait of Charlotte Smith's places of lived belonging, I propose we attend to the slide between literal and figurative functions (Mikulak 47) performed by three interconnected microregions in her bioregional poetic imaginary. First is Arundel, the Sussex microregion of the River Arun, together with Bignor Park, the Turner family seat and Smith's childhood home (Stanton 686); second is the Sussex coast and South Downs; and third is Beachy Head and the Sussex Weald (J. T. White, "South-East" fig. 29, 117). These three microregions are nested, overlapping terrains of consciousness, a mosaic of concurrently available sites with complicated, multiple affiliations—past, present, and future. Her poetry performs a paradoxical outsider-belonging, self-consciously mapping the precarious conditions of nonproprietorial relationships to place, relationships often occasioned by systemic injustice. As a married woman unable to own property or enjoy the income from publications in her own right, and unable to participate independently in the dominant masculine literary culture of her day, Smith's "precarious relation to the literary marketplace and estrangement from Britain's . . . intellectual circles" is "thematize[d]" as "exile" and "wandering" (Sodeman 133). Smith's speakers voice their apparently transitory belonging from an emotional and physical "outside," never settling in comfort. Her poetry is criss-crossed by transients, migrants, and exiles, and is always alert to the possibilities of others "who might arrive" (Meredith 84).

Charlotte Smith's bioregionalist poetic imaginary is produced by a cast of speakers in their favorite positions, frequently "on the edge" (of the River Arun, of the South Downs, of the Weald, of the seashore, of cliffs, of despair, of abjection), and often on the high moral ground. Her vision is sometimes nocturnal, storm wracked, alienated, and uncanny (Stokes). At its most extreme, as in Sonnet 44, the potential for a reassuring version of bioregionalist "being there" (Simpson) is all but cancelled out by the un-homeliness of a scene "written in the church-yard at Middleton in Sussex":

> Press'd by the Moon, mute arbitress of tides,
>   While the loud equinox its powers combines,
>   The sea no more its swelling surge confines,
> But o'er the shrinking land sublimely rides.
> The wild blast, rising from the Western cave,
>   Drives the huge billows from their heaving bed;
>   Tears from their grassy tombs the village dead,
> And breaks the silent Sabbath of the grave!
> With shells and sea-weed mingled, on the shore

> Lo! Their bones whiten in the frequent wave;
>> But vain to them the winds and water rave;
> They hear the warring elements no more:
> While I am doom'd—by life's long storm opprest,
> To gaze with envy on their gloomy rest.

Smith's endnote, printed as a footnote in Curran's edition, tells her readers: "Middleton is a village on the margin of the sea, in Sussex, containing only two or three houses. There were formerly several acres of ground between its small church and the sea, which now, by its continual encroachments, approaches within a few feet of this half-ruined and humble edifice. The wall, which once surrounded the church-yard, is entirely swept away, many of the graves broken up, and the remains of the bodies interred washed into the sea; whence human bones are found among the sand and shingles on the shore" (Curran 42). In the sonnet form, which she regards as "no improper vehicle for a single Sentiment" (Curran 3), Smith maps an eroding microregion of despair. The sequence of *Elegiac Sonnets*, developed over many years in multiple editions, is an analogue for the dynamic, overlapping clusters of sites that add up to a complex bioregional terrain of consciousness.

Nested in and complicating Smith's bioregional poetic imaginary is Bignor Park, the Turner family home: its loss confirms her sense of "interiorized exile" (Curran xxv). Her first authorial self-definition as "Charlotte Smith of Bignor Park, in Sussex" was a genteel cover for the lived experience of child marriage to the possibly violent and certainly profligate Benjamin Smith, her profound unhappiness and twelve pregnancies before legal separation from him in 1787 (Wolfson). The late Sonnet 92, "Written at Bignor Park in Sussex, in August, 1799," rehearses the valedictory effect of all the sonnets about her childhood home (Stanton 686):

> Low murmurs creep along the woody vale,
>> The tremulous Aspens shudder in the breeze,
> Slow o'er the downs the leaden vapours sail,
>> While I, beneath these old paternal trees,
> Mark the dark shadows of the threaten'd storm,
> . . . My fate
>> Nor hope nor joy illumines—Nor for me
>> Return those rosy hours which here I used to see! (Curran 78)

This persistent site of memory is a subset of the larger microregion of Arundel, an earlier jurisdictional area defined by invaders and the river that flows through it (J. T. White, "South-East" 30, 100).[2]

The banks of the River Arun are haunted with regret for lost childhood innocence and happiness. The Arun is also a wellspring of homegrown poetry:

> laurels grow luxuriant on thy side,
> And letters live along thy classic meads. (Curran 35, lines 7–9)

The speaker acknowledges "British bards," "native" to Arundel, and frequently apostrophizes Melancholy in terms that acknowledge its generative potential for poetry. For example, Sonnet 32, "To melancholy. Written on the banks of the Arun, October 1785":

> O Melancholy!—such thy magic power,
> That to the soul these dreams are often sweet,
> And soothe the pensive visionary mind! (Curran 35, lines 12–14)

Just as Bignor Park and the River Arun are nested in the larger bioregional poetic imaginary of Sussex and the South Downs, so Smith's Melancholy imagination depends on poetic Fancy, a capacious category of the eighteenth-century imagination. Melancholy, conceived as tenacious emotional connection (Kerr, "Fictocritical Empathy"), is sister to the brighter, nomadic agency of Fancy. Melancholy and Fancy are interdependent (Robinson; Carlson). In other words, Melancholy "connectedness" is the cognitive partner of "mobile" poetic Fancy in the *Elegiac Sonnets*. More generally, Smith's poetic career harnessed their imaginative interdependence. Sonnet 79, "To the Goddess of Botany," demonstrates what might happen when melancholy connection meets fanciful parataxis (Robinson 13):

> Of Folly weary, shrinking from the view
>   Of violence and Fraud, allow'd to take
>   All peace from humble life; I would forsake
> *Their* haunts for ever, and, sweet Nymph! With you
>   Find shelter; where my tired, and tear-swoln eyes,
> Among your silent shades of soothing hue,
>   Your "bells and florets of unnumber'd dyes"
>   Might rest—And learn the bright varieties
> That from your lovely hands are fed with dew;

> And every veined leaf, that trembling sighs
> In mead or woodland; or in wilds remote,
>   Or lurk with mosses in the humid caves,
> Mantle the cliffs, on dimpling rivers float,
>   Or stream from coral rocks beneath the Ocean waves. (Curran 68)

The speaker trails off into a luxurious, potentially endless listing of subjective possibilities. The poem slides between literal and figurative immersion in microregional botanical habitats (Robinson 66, 67). Botanical study, Smith's long note explains, can be therapeutic for the "stagnant [melancholy] imagination" (Curran 69; George). Charlotte Smith's fashionable interest in Linnaean botanical taxonomical techniques is well known (Pascoe). Fancy's ability to find out similarities and differences, to sort and name, to move between special and general phenomena, indicates a cognitive affinity with taxonomic methods (Porter 41), a point to which I return in the conclusion to this essay. Smith's bioregionalist poetic imaginary enacts a "fanciful" interdependence between the activities of poetry, botanizing and "ceaseless grief" or melancholy, almost "vegetative" stasis: "It is literally vegetating, for I have very little locomotive powers beyond those that appertain to a cauliflower" (Stanton 609; Kautz 37).[3]

In this historical period it is acceptable for the woman writer to perform "maternal grief," variants of "the needy woman," the "moral guardian," and the "didactic mentor" of children: Smith performs all these literary subjectivities and more.[4] We find a spectrum between two extremes: the apparently "feminized" posture of connected, microregional immersion in nature's particularity, and the "masculinized" posture of alienated, exilic wandering (Sodeman; Labbe, "On the Edge"). For example, Sonnet 31, "Written in Farm Wood, South Downs, in May 1784," renews connection. The sonnet is "occasioned," as Curran's note explains, "by Smith's returning to her Sussex environs for a short visit after having spent the previous several months sequestered with her husband and children in the King's Bench prison" (34).

> Spring's dewy hand on this fair summit weaves
>   The downy grass with tufts of Alpine flowers;
> And shades the beechen slopes with tender leaves,
>   And leads the shepherd to his upland bowers,
> Strewn with wild thyme; while slow-descending showers
>   Feed the green ear, and nurse the future sheaves! (lines 1–6)

The speaker alternates between close-up observation of botanical particulars and a telescopic view from the woodland across pasture and cultivated fields. Smith's endnote remarks of "Alpine flowers," "An infinite variety of plants are found on these hills, particularly about this spot: many sorts of Orchis and Cistus of singular beauty, with several others" (Curran 34). Smith's bioregional localism is a function of her very sense of exclusion from it: "Ah! what to me can those dear days restore, / When scenes could charm that now I taste no more!" (lines 13–14). The Sussex environs of the *Elegiac Sonnets* are at once literal and literary. They offer a sequence of personal narratives of "residence," as if exemplifying Rolston's idea of multiple and overlapping "stories" (Meredith 90). Smith's bioregional poetic imaginary gathers stories that "accumulate and move through 'particular regions and tracks of nature so as to make a [poetic] career'" (Meredith 90). Her poetic career is acutely attuned to the fact that "identities, attachments, and affiliations are multiple and are spread throughout space and time. Location is never the singular determinant of identity" (Meredith 90). Indeed, despite her preferred "residence" in named locales, Smith is dismissive of naive localism: "Well! Local attachments are very foolish" (Stanton 686). A longer study would draw out the often stark contrasts between her imaginary and lived experience of place. The disparity is evident from her letters. By October 1803, for example, increasing debility meant that Smith required help "even to move from one room to the other" (Stanton 593). In January 1804, she writes from Elsted, near Godalming, in Surrey: "I have never moved for ten months, & above eight of those months I have not been even round my little garden" (Stanton 603). The vigorous mobility of her various poetic speakers, their ability to move freely within apparently accessible landscapes across her poetic career, is an imagined rather than lived experience of particular regions and tracks of nature.

If her Sussex environs provide microregional memory-sites of attachment, they are also terrains of consciousness from which the speaker imagines a drastically exilic fate. For example, the speaker of Sonnet 12, "Written on the sea shore.——October, 1784" looks out to sea from the

> rude fragment of the rocky shore,
> Where on the fractured cliff the billows break (Curran 21, lines 1–2)

and in an uncanny reversal of the poetic gaze, imagines "Like the poor mariner, methinks I stand,

> Cast on a rock; who sees the distant land
> From whence no succour comes—or comes too late.
> Faint and more faint are heard his feeble cries,
> 'Till in the rising tide the exhausted sufferer dies. (10–14)

The figures of wanderers, migrants, and exiles are fellow sufferers who perform a crucial "cosmopolitan" function in the larger bioregionalist imaginary, an analysis of which must remain outside the scope of this essay. Smith's cosmopolitan novels in particular are concerned with Europe devastated by wars, colonial and imperialist politics and trade, and the utopian prospect of America. In the "intensely xenophobic 1790s Britain" (Craciun, "Citizens" 176), to essay cosmopolitan fellow-feeling in the interests of social justice is politically contentious, whether in poetry or prose (Craciun, "Empire" 47).

The Emigrants is a 440-line amplification of the *Elegiac Sonnets'* experiments with radical affiliation and setting. It is set in a politically charged conjunction of space and time: "Book I, Scene, on the Cliffs to the Eastward of the Town of Brightelmstone in Sussex. Time, a morning in November, 1792" (Curran 135). Curran's note reminds us that the setting is "modern Brighton, located across the English Channel from France. On September 22nd, two weeks after the Massacres, France had declared itself a Republic. By November Robespierre had gained complete control over the French Convention, which on the 19th of that month affirmed its support for the revolutionary movements in Europe, posing a threat of insurrection to the British Government" (135). The second book of *The Emigrants* opens "on an Eminence on one of those Downs, which afford to the South a View of the Sea; to the North of the Weald of Sussex. Time, an Afternoon in April, 1793" (149). Noting that on 21 January 1793 Louis XVI was guillotined and that war was declared between England and France in February of that year, Curran underlines the politically charged context of this work. More broadly, this political moment is defined by government measures such as the Alien Act of 1793, of particular relevance to Smith's French émigré son-in-law (cf. Garnai). As Michael Wiley has argued in an important recent essay, *The Emigrants* performs a "complex critique of the dominant geographies of nations and national identity" and proposes an alternative, "immanent in nature itself" (57). The "natural-political geography" that emerges "replaces" the literally and figuratively stranded geopolitics of the French emigrants and is facilitated by Smith's strategically cosmopolitan sympathy for them (Wiley 57). Among the dejected French aristocrats on the shoreline is a "mother, lost in melancholy thought" (book 1, line 213), her children

> around her run,
> On the rough shingles, or the chalky bourn,
> . . . Who pick the fretted stone, or glossy shell,
> Or crimson plant marine. (lines 202–6)

A pitiful figure, perhaps even a projection of Charlotte Smith, "too long a victim of distress" (line 212), the woman invites our fellow-feeling in the interests of a virtual cosmopolitan affective community. As the emigrants wait by the sea, Smith's speaker observes and integrates the elements of the scene from a height that affords a "prospect" of Sussex, a synecdoche for England, ideally demilitarized and socially reformed.

In *The Emigrants*, Smith's bioregionalist poetic imaginary is drawn to "wide-extended" regions of fellow-feeling:

> Poor wand'ring wretches! whosoe'er ye are,
> That hopeless, houseless, friendless, travel wide
> O'er these bleak russet downs. (book 1, lines 296–98)

> Poor vagrant wretches! outcasts of the world!
> Whom no abode receives, no parish owns;
> Roving, like Nature's commoners, the land
> That boasts such general plenty: if the sight
> Of wide-extended misery softens yours
> Awhile, suspend your murmurs!—— (lines 303–8)

The Emigrants closes with a prayer,

> In unison with murmuring waves that now
> Swell with dark tempests (book 2, lines 402–3),

for the "reign of Reason, Liberty, and Peace" (book 2, line 444), made

> [t]o him who hears even silence; not in domes
> of human architecture, filled with crowds,
> But on these hills, where boundless, yet distinct,
> Even as a map, beneath are spread the fields
> His bounty cloaths; divided here by woods,
> And there by commons rude, or winding brooks. (book 2, lines 390–95)

Wiley argues that "on this map, naturalized lines formed by 'woods,' 'winding brooks,' and the 'commons rude' circumscribe the space owned by humans: 'the fields.' In other words, this map replaces standard cartographic dividing lines, which demonstrate institutional power over humans and over nature" (55). The poem's metaphoric map represents what Wiley calls a "leveling nature that promotes those lacking power over those who normally wield it" (56). And Smith "resists" the cartographic perspective of the "lines of a militarized nation state," attending to the functional bioregion rather than, for example, the lines on the contemporaneous ordinance survey of Sussex (1792/3) (56). Apparently, Smith's ambition to map the border zone between private experience and our common natures across troubled national boundaries was not entirely successful; in the words of one contemporary reviewer, she "herself . . . fills the foreground" (Andrews).

Whereas the *Elegiac Sonnets* demand reader sympathy by using "the language of wounded nature" (Andrews 26) and *The Emigrants* attempts channel-crossing transnational empathy, the 731-line experimental blank verse poem *Beachy Head* offers yet further prospects and differently tangled nature cultures. *The Emigrants'* radical remapping of the Sussex Down and Weald is recapitulated with variations. One example of a frequently represented scene must suffice.

Beachy Head revisits a maternal group, and all but immerses them in nature's commons. In contrast to the falsity of

> the poet's fabling dreams
> Describing Arcady (lines 209–10)

this version of pastoral includes a subsistence economy. The shepherd's

> industrious mate
> Shares in his labour. (lines 212–13)

> . . . Where the brook is traced
> By crouching osiers, and the black coot hides
> Among the plashy reeds, her diving brood,
> The matron wades; . . . (lines 213–16)

> . . . Otherwhile
> She leads her infant group where charlock grows
> 'Unprofitably gay,' or to the fields,
> Where congregate the linnet and the finch,

> That on the thistles, so profusely spread,
> Feast in the desert; . . . . (lines 219–24)

As if herself a bird with her brood, the woman frequents the fields that are

> Stony and cold, and hostile to the plough,
> Where clamouring loud, the evening curlew runs
> And drops her spotted eggs among the flints:
> The mother and the children pile the stones
> In rugged pyramids; . . . . (lines 231–35)

Smith's botanical and ornithological notes particularize a scene of rural penury starkly juxtaposed with the wealthy, apparently indifferent traveler, a "child of Luxury" (line 245), whose *per diem*

> Would cheer [the laborer] for long months, when to his toil
> The frozen earth closes her marble breast (lines 253–54).

Beachy Head does not idealize nature cultures.

Smith's avowedly "local poem" (Stanton 705) draws explicit attention to smuggling and poaching that accompanied subsistence in the region of Beachy Head (McGavran). More broadly, Lily Gurton-Wachter points out that "the cliff figured prominently in the national imagination at the time as a border space rife with questions of immigration, commerce, smuggling, fishery, shipwrecks, war, and perhaps primarily, anxieties about French invasion" (200). *Beachy Head*'s critique of the prevailing contemporary idea of France as a "natural enemy" is in part effected by particular attention to nature's "minimal" signs (203)—for example,

> the sea-snipe's cry
> Just tells that something living is abroad (lines 113–14).

In this view, Smith's poem is concerned with "the mediation of foreignness itself" and proposes an ethical attentiveness. The snipe's cry is merely the sound of creaturely flourishing "that the rhetoric of the natural enemy forecloses" (203); *Beachy Head* is a topographical poem with a potentially cosmopolitan bioregionalist ethical agenda (Cheney 126).

> On thy stupendous summit, rock sublime!
> . . . I would recline: while Fancy should go forth. (Curran 217, lines 1, 4)

Fancy, a faculty of the eighteenth-century imagination, is audaciously free to roam the fields, commons, wastes, and walkways of the South-East Down and Weald. This nonproprietorial, outsider-belonging owes much to vestigial forest law and to honoring commons' rights and obligations (Manwood 77–87; Landry 486). Charlotte Smith's bioregional poetic imaginary does not seek vantage points that pretend to the imagined pleasures of ownership. Smith's commitment to "natural rights" discourse sets her at odds with the British preference for "positive law" which privileges land ownership (R. S. White, *Natural Rights*; Johnson). For this reason, I reject Labbe's suggestion that Smith makes Beachy Head her imaginary private property ("Locating the Poet" 162; Kerr, "Sympathetic" 118, 119). Fancy's lines of sight seek prospects of sympathy for the victims of systemic injustice.

Fancy's other capacities include the poetic power to telescope space and time in contemplation of exemplary details, such as "picturesque" fossils, theories of "sublime" geology, and perspectives on Biblical cosmogony (Wallace; Heringman, *Science*; *Rocks*). In the microregion of Beachy Head, Charlotte Smith maps a many-storied synecdoche of the "green peopled world" (Curran 294, line 130), "this suffering globe" (163, line 422). Clearly this raises the related problems of scale and interconnection that beset bioregionalism and, by implication, Charlotte Smith's poetic imaginary. Her poetry negotiates these problems through the deployment of two discursive sets familiar to bioregionalism: sensibility and science (Alexander). I have noted that the *Elegiac Sonnets* cultivate reader sympathy for the author and her avatars "from the soil of despair" (Andrews 26). Readers of *The Emigrants* must "scale up" the exercise of sympathetic recognition in the service of a politically radical affective community, ideally capable of contesting arbitrary borders in the aftermath of the French Revolution. *Beachy Head* experiments with a proliferation of literary subjectivities, performing a relay of pitiful figures in a landscape, and "introducing new speakers on the heels of old ones" (Labbe, "Locating" 159). But does this potential chain of sympathizers join to create something approaching "affective community"? According to Gurton-Wachter, *Beachy Head* refuses to "embrace the alternative to antipathy: sympathy" (201). The poem's open-ended form is perhaps an analogue of sympathy's tendentiousness as a remediating force (Rogers 129). Sequential sympathy, nonetheless, is an affective correlative of Fancy's associative mobility and parataxis: sympathy moves on, and on, but these fragmentary links of feeling fail to assemble.

Deploying this paratactic poetics, *Beachy Head* traces a functional bio-regional itinerary that marks attempted shifts in scale, in particular the complex interrelationship between micro- to macro-levels of individual emotional attentiveness and broader social comment. Kari Lokke remarks that "Charlotte Smith's *Beachy Head* (1807) moves quite spectacularly from a sweeping and panoramic cosmological, geographical and historical vision, to a regional portrait of the Sussex Downs, to a series of village vignettes, before concluding with the single and isolated figure of the lone Hermit in the final lines of the poem" (45). The poem's audacious movement, from Beachy Head's "stupendous summit, rock sublime!" to

> Just beneath the rock
> Where Beachy overpeers the channel wave
> Within a cavern mined by wintry tides (lines 671–73)

is counterpointed by a remarkable attentiveness to natural historical detail, "observing objects more minute" (line 372) and rehearsing "a poetics of the botanically exact" (Pascoe 201; Porter 41). Theresa Kelley suggests that *Beachy Head*'s botanizing tests the late eighteenth-century cultural tensions around questions of taxonomy, in this case, between "local" plant names and "cosmopolitan," Linnaean, Latin terms ("Exemplarity" 234). For example,

> the short turf is gay with tormentil,
> And birdsfoot trefoil, and the lesser tribes
> Of hawkweed

is glossed in Smith's notes: "*Tormentilla reptans*," "*Trifolium ornithopoides*," and "*Hieracium*, many sorts" (lines 353–55; cf. lines 439–55). Charlotte Smith's bioregional poetic imaginary evidences an increasingly particularized and authoritative botanical (and ornithological) localism, but it is not simply a display of imaginative parochial attachment.

Taxonomic discourses are concerned with the relationships between potentially incommensurate "parts and wholes" (Kelley, "Exemplarity" 232). This characterizes not just Romantic thought about species and genus, but also the problem of the relationship between micro-narratives of local, particular times and places, and what might be thought of as "scaled up" macro-historical narratives, "where different levels of generality and abstraction pull away from the micro-event or detail" ("Exemplarity" 224). In Kelley's view, "Romantic attention to taxonomy, including poetic attention,

registers . . . the problem of relating parts to whole or even finding wholes
for those parts, whether the inquiry is aesthetics, politics, philosophy, or
natural history" ("Exemplarity" 225; cf. Kelley, "Histories"). *Beachy Head*'s
paradoxical status as a fragmentary epic, simultaneously essaying the narrowly parochial stories of local habitations and the vast scope of deep geological time, enacts a phenomenology of "intimate immensity" (Bachelard
183). Like Romantic historiography, late eighteenth-century taxonomy, and
the Romantic urge for "organic relations between parts and wholes," Charlotte Smith's bioregionalist poetic imaginary makes a "familiar gesture"
(Kelley, "Exemplarity" 225; cf. Legg 222). Less grandly, her bioregionalist
poetic use of botanical nativism, with reassuringly loyalist overtones in a
time of war, neutralizes some of the politically dangerous sympathy for
the "insulted rights of man" that defines her politics ("Exemplarity" 235;
cf. George).[5] The sympathetic imagination and cognitive techniques of
Fancy do the work of moving between and attempting to "scale up" the
"discordant levels" of special and general phenomena in two discourses
that have tended to be treated separately in the critical literature: (melancholy) sensibility and (botanical) science. Charlotte Smith's poetry invites
us, in Thomashow's words, to "have compassion for the chasms of despair"
(131). In the politically fraught context of 1790s xenophobic Britain, poetic gestures of prospective fellow-feeling across cultural—and physical—
geographical "borders" are apparently a "catalyst for . . . recommitment to
the local" (Heise 391): in this case, the bioregion of the imagination and its
reassuring signs that "something living is abroad" in the nature cultures of
poetry's commons. Poised on the edge of Romanticism, Charlotte Smith's
outsider-belonging in the poetic imaginary of the South-East Down and
Weald rehearses some of the prospects and limits of "parochial cosmopolitanism" (cf. Menely), a paradoxical formation emerging in the eighteenth
century and familiar to contemporary ecocritical and bioregionalist discourses alike.

NOTES

Thanks to Catherine Wait for her excellent research assistance and to the Faculty
of Humanities and Social Sciences, University of Adelaide; the award of the Dean's
Prize for Teaching (Supervision) provided funds for this research during 2009.

   1. Throughout, I refer to Stuart Curran's edition of *The Collected Poems of Charlotte Smith* (1993) and Judith Phillips Stanton's edition of *The Collected Letters*

of Charlotte Smith (2003), major contributions to the growing scholarship about Smith's vigorous and generically varied publishing career. For recent examples, see Jacqueline Labbe's collection *Charlotte Smith in British Romanticism* (2008) and the Special Issue of *Women's Writing* (19.1:2009) devoted to Smith.

2. There are six "Sussex Rapes"—see J. T. White fig. 29, 117; river systems, 30; cf. 100 "The Wealden edge was not just a physical frontier, it was a legal divide."

3. Women are to plants as men are to animals, an analogy that opens onto a crowded field of sexual politics: see Bewell, "'Jacobin Plants.'" Smith's melancholy is particularly focused on the loss of her daughter, Anna Augusta, who married a French émigré and died in childbirth: see Dolan, Hawley.

4. See *Rural Walks* (1795) and *Rambles Farther* (1796), *Minor Morals* (1798) and *Conversations Introducing Poetry* (1804); see Stanton, *Collected Letters*, "Chronology," xxxix–xlv.

5. This is, in effect, a historically and culturally specific variant of the schema developed in Heise's discussion of the relationship between ecopolitical radicalism and the cosmopolitan family romance in some contemporary American fictions. See Heise, "Ecocriticism and the Transnational Turn."

WORKS CITED

Alexander, Donald. "Bioregionalism: Science or Sensibility?" *Environmental Ethics* 12.2 (Summer 1990): 161–73. Print.

Andrews, Kerri. "'Herself [. . .] Fills the Foreground': Negotiating Autobiography in the *Elegiac Sonnets* and *The Emigrants*." *Charlotte Smith in British Romanticism*. Ed. Jacqueline M. Labbe. London: Pickering and Chatto, 2008. 13–27. Print.

Bachelard, Gaston. *The Poetics of Space.* Trans. Marie Jolas. Boston: Beacon Press, 1969. Print.

Bewell, Alan. "'Jacobin Plants': Botany as Social Theory in the 1790s." *Wordsworth Circle* 20.3 (Summer 1989): 132–39. Print.

Carlson, Julie. "Fancy's History." *European Romantic Review* 14.2 (2003): 163–76. Print.

Cheney, Jim. "Postmodern Environmental Ethics: Ethics as Bioregional Narrative." *Memory, Identity, Community: The Idea of Narrative in the Human Sciences*. Ed. Lewis P. Hinchman and Sandra K. Hinchman. New York: State University of New York Press, 1997. 328–49. Print.

Craciun, Adriana. "Citizens of the World: Émigrés, Romantic Cosmopolitanism, and Charlotte Smith." *Nineteenth-Century Contexts* 29.2/3 (June 2007): 169–85. Print.

———. "'Empire without End': Charlotte Smith at the Limits of Cosmopolitanism." *Women's Writing* 16.1 (May 2009): 39–59. Print.

Curran, Stuart, ed. *The Collected Poems of Charlotte Smith*. Oxford: Oxford University Press, 1993. Print.

Dolan, Elizabeth A. "British Romantic Melancholia: Charlotte Smith's *Elegiac Sonnets*, Medical Discourse and the Problem of Sensibility." *Journal of European Studies* 33.3/4 (Dec 2003): 237–53. Print.

Garnai, Amy. "The Alien Act and Negative Cosmopolitanism in *The Letters of a Solitary Wanderer*." *Charlotte Smith in British Romanticism*. Ed. Jacqueline M. Labbe. London: Pickering and Chatto, 2008. 101–12. Print.

George, Sam. *Botany, Sexuality and Women's Writing 1760–1830: From Modest Shoot to Forward Plant*. Manchester: Manchester University Press, 2007. Print.

Gurton-Wachter, Lily. "'An Enemy, I suppose, that Nature has made': Charlotte Smith and the Natural Enemy." *European Romantic Review* 20.2 (April 2009): 197–205. Print.

Hawley, Judith. "Charlotte Smith's *Elegiac Sonnets*: Losses and Gains." *Women's Poetry in the Enlightenment: The Making of a Canon, 1730–1820*. Ed. Isobel Armstrong and Virginia Blain. New York: St. Martin's, in association with the Centre for English Studies, School of Advanced Study, University of London, 1999. 184–98. Print.

Heise, Ursula K. "Ecocriticism and the Transnational Turn in American Studies." *American Literary History* 20.1/2 (2008): 381–404. Print.

Heringman, Noah. *Romantic Rocks, Aesthetic Geology*. Ithaca, N.Y.: Cornell University Press, 2004. Print.

———, ed. *Romantic Science: The Literary Forms of Natural History*. Albany: State University of New York Press, 2003. Print.

Johnson, Nancy E. *The English Jacobin Novel on Rights, Property and the Law: Critiquing the Contract*. New York: Palgrave Macmillan, 2004. Print.

Kautz, Beth Dolan. "Mary Wollstonecraft's Salutary Picturesque: Curing Melancholia in the Landscape." *European Romantic Review* 13.1 (2002): 35–48. Print.

Kelley, Theresa M. "Romantic Exemplarity: Botany and 'Material' Culture." *Romantic Science: The Literary Forms of Natural History*. Ed. Noah Heringman. Albany: State University of New York Press, 2003. 223–54. Print.

———. "Romantic Histories: Charlotte Smith and *Beachy Head*." *Nineteenth-Century Literature* 59.3 (December 2004): 281–314. Print.

Kerr, Heather. "Fictocritical Empathy and the Work of Mourning." *Cultural Studies Review* 19.1 (2003): 180–200. Print.

———. "Sympathetic Topographies." *Parallax* 7.2 (2001): 107–26. Print.

Labbe, Jacqueline M., ed. *Charlotte Smith in British Romanticism*. London: Pickering and Chatto, 2008. Print.

———. *Charlotte Smith: Romanticism, Poetry and the Culture of Gender*. Manchester, U.K.: Manchester University Press, 2003. Print.

———. "Locating the Poet in *Beachy Head*." *Charlotte Smith: Romanticism, Poetry and the Culture of Gender*. Ed. Jacqueline M. Labbe. Manchester, U.K.: Manchester University Press, 2003. 142–65. Print.

———. "On the Edge: Politics and the Strictures of Subjectivities in *The Emigrants*." *Charlotte Smith: Romanticism, Poetry and the Culture of Gender*. Ed. Jacqueline M. Labbe. Manchester, U.K.: Manchester University Press, 2003. 116–41. Print

Landry, Donna. "Green Languages? Women Poets as Naturalists in 1653 and 1807." *The Huntington Library Quarterly* 63.4 (2000): 467–89. Print.

Legg, Stephen. "An 'Indispensible Hypodermis'? The Role of Scale in The Birth of Biopolitics." *Journal of Cultural Economy* 2.1 (2009): 219–25. Print.

Lokke, Kari. "The Figure of the Hermit in Charlotte Smith's *Beachy Head*." *Charlotte Smith in British Romanticism*. Ed. Jacqueline M. Labbe. London: Pickering and Chatto, 2008. 45–56. Print.

Manwood, John. *A Treatise and Discourse of the Lawes of the Forrest*. 1598. New York: Garland, 1978. Print.

McGavran, James Holt, Jr. "Smuggling, Poaching and the Revulsion against Kinship in *The Old Manor House*." *Women's Writing* 16.1 (May 2009): 20–38. Print.

Menely, Tobias. "Traveling in Place: Gilbert White's Cosmopolitan Parochialism." *Eighteenth-Century Life* 28.3 (Fall 2004): 46–65. Print.

Meredith, Dianne. "The Bioregion as a Communitarian Micro-region (and Its Limitations)." *Ethics, Place and Environment* 8.1 (March 2005): 83–94. Print.

Mikulak, Michael. "The Nature of Solidarity and Nature's Solidarity: Bioregionalism, Situated Knowledge, and Unity in Diversity within Biocultural Systems." *Atenea* 27.2 (December 2007): 33–53. Print.

Pappas, Nickolas. "Fancy Justice: Martha Nussbaum on the Political Value of the Novel." *Pacific Philosophical Quarterly* 78 (1997): 278–96.

Pascoe, Judith. "Female Botanists and the Poetry of Charlotte Smith." *Re-visioning Romanticism: British Women Writers, 1776–1837*. Ed. Carol Shiner Wilson and Joel Haefner. Philadelphia: University of Pennsylvania Press, 1994. 193–209. Print.

Porter, Dahlia. "From Nosegay to Specimen Cabinet: Charlotte Smith and the Labour of Collecting." *Charlotte Smith in British Romanticism*. Ed. Jacqueline Labbe. London: Pickering and Chatto, 2008. 29–44. Print.

Pratt, Kathryn. "Charlotte Smith's Melancholia on the Page and Stage." *Studies in English Literature, 1500–1900* 41.3 (Summer 2001): 563–81. Print.

Robinson, Jeffrey C. *Unfettering Poetry: Fancy in British Romanticism*. New York: Palgrave Macmillan, 2006. Print.

Rogers, Kathleen Béres. "Permeability and Its Uses: Affect and Audience in Charlotte Smith's *Elegiac Sonnets*." *Women's Writing* 16.1 (May 2009): 126–42. Print.

Rolston, Holmes, III. *Environmental Ethics*. Philadelphia: Temple University Press, 1988. Print.

Schlueter, Paul, and June Schlueter, eds. *An Encyclopedia of British Women Writers*. New Brunswick, N.J.: Rutgers University Press, 1998. Print.

Simpson, David. "Being There? Literary Criticism, Localism, and Local Knowledge." *Critical Quarterly* 35.3 (1993): 3–17. Print.

Sodeman, Melissa. "Charlotte Smith's Literary Exile." *ELH* 76 (2009): 131–52. Print.

Stanton, Judith Phillips, ed. *The Collected Letters of Charlotte Smith*. Bloomington: Indiana University Press, 2003. Print.

Stokes, Christopher. "Lorn Subjects: Haunting, Fracture and Ascesis in Charlotte Smith's *Elegiac Sonnets*." *Women's Writing* 16.1 (May 2009): 143–60. Print.

Thomashow, Mitchell. "Toward a Cosmopolitan Bioregionalism." *Bioregionalism*. Ed. Michael Vincent McGinnis. New York: Routledge, 1998. 121–32. Print.

Wallace, Anne D. "Picturesque Fossils, Sublime Geology?: The Crisis of Authority in Charlotte Smith's *Beachy Head*." *European Romantic Review* 13.1 (2002): 77–93. Print.

White, John Talbot. *The South-East Down and Weald: Kent, Surrey and Sussex*. London: Eyre Methuen, 1977. Print.

White, R. S. *Natural Rights and the Birth of Romanticism in the 1790s*. New York: Palgrave Macmillan, 2005. Print.

Wiley, Michael. "The Geography of Displacement and Replacement in Charlotte Smith's *The Emigrants*." *European Romantic Review* 17.1 (January 2006): 55–68. Print.

Wolfson, Susan J. "Charlotte Smith: 'to live only to write & write only to live.'" *The Huntington Library Quarterly* 70.4 (October 2007): 633–59. Print.

KENT C. RYDEN

The Nature of Region

Russell Banks, New England, and New York

T HE LINE BETWEEN THE IDEA of cultural region, generally delineated according to human criteria, and ecological region and
bioregion, defined by natural factors, would seem to be fairly sharp and
clear. Sometimes, though, that line becomes blurred in ways that force
closer examination of these spatial concepts and the ways that they relate
to each other. For example, northern New England can be seen as a distinct literary subregion distinguished by the differences that writers more
or less self-consciously draw between dominant tropes of New England
regional identity as a whole and the ways of life that they feel characterize
rural and small-town Maine, New Hampshire, and Vermont in particular
(Ryden). Russell Banks is an important contributor to this literary thread.
His novel *Affliction* and his short-story collection *Trailerpark*, both set in
New Hampshire, coincide closely in setting, theme, and characterization
with other works of contemporary northern New England fiction and poetry. But then again, so does his novel *The Sweet Hereafter*, which is set in
the Adirondack Park area of upstate New York, a region that lacks New
England's cultural cachet within the United States. This geographical out-
lier suggests that perhaps the literature in question is not simply that of
the cultural region of northern New England but rather an ecoregional
literature attached to the larger Northern Forest in general, a circumstance
that only emphasizes the constructed, sometimes geographically arbitrary
nature of cultural regions. It also suggests that we can't truly understand

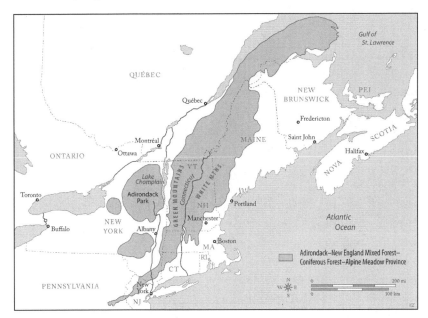

Northern New England, upstate New York, and the Northern Forest Bioregion

northern New England as a literary region without taking into account how its *natural* identity helps shape its *cultural* identity.

For Banks, that natural identity exists most meaningfully on the level of the ecological region rather than the bioregion. Three spatial concepts are important to reading Banks's New England and New York books: the cultural region, a large-scale unit defined according to human perceptual criteria (e.g., New England, the South, the West); the ecological region, also a large-scale unit determined in this case by the distribution of like physical features, particularly vegetation, climate, and soils; and the bioregion, a much smaller-scale space than the ecological region—a spatial subset of that larger region, such as an individual watershed—that also implies a particular shared ethical, communal, and political awareness among the people who live within it. As I argue, the similarities among Banks's New England and New York books arise from the common economic constraints imposed on characters who live within the Northern Forest ecological region. Within these constraints, Banks's characters exhibit little by way of a bioregional consciousness. The seeds for such an awareness are not altogether absent, but its relative lack suggests that perhaps bioregionalism as a sociocultural phenomenon depends on a certain level of educational, class, or economic attainment. The people in Banks's Northern Forest fiction have a limited range of choices in their lives and have to scramble hard simply to get by on a daily basis. For these characters, it seems, thinking politically, communally, and ethically within a bioregional context is not a priority.

First, some brief context. For the past thirty years or so, a group of what I call northern New England neorealists have written against the familiar popular images that characterize the region in American culture, images that carry with them an air of historical weightiness and touristic attractiveness and that define New England as a land of neat white villages populated by Anglo-Saxon-descended Yankee farmers. Novelist Ernest Hebert, who has set six novels in the fictional town of Darby, New Hampshire, summarizes the group's cultural politics: "When I started the Darby series I wasn't interested in maintaining the stereotypes of frugal Yankees and cracker barrel philosophers who said, 'Pahk the cah' and 'Ayup.' I strived to portray the townspeople as I believed them truly to be. I also deliberately put the emphasis on the neglected classes, what today would be called rural underclass and rural working class" ("People" 11). That is, Hebert tries to redress the cultural balance in New England, writing those who do not fit the popular image back into the literary record, restoring them to full regional citizenship.

Thus, Howard Elman, the main character of Hebert's first and best Darby novel, *The Dogs of March*, is an uneducated laid-off mill worker who lives in decidedly nonscenic surroundings that suit him just fine: "Birches, a score of junk cars, a swing on the limb of a giant maple, a bathtub in the garden, a gray barn, a house sided with fading purple asphalt shingles, a washing machine riddled with bullet holes—to Howard, these things were all equal in beauty. He saw no ugliness on his property" (1–2). Howard's landscape aesthetic is about as far from the idealized New England image as you can get. His nemesis in the book, however, a rich New Yorker named Zoe Cutter who buys into the image completely, purchases the property next to his intending to refurbish not only her house but the entire town, making it fit the classic New England template of her imagination. Howard Elman's place, of course, is the chief blot on her vision, and she spends most of the book trying to remove him from his property so she can remove that property from her line of sight. In the conflict between Howard and Zoe, Hebert enacts what he sees as the cultural politics of the dominant tropes of regional identity, the way they erase certain people and places from the imagination.

Along with Hebert, other northern New England neorealists—good examples include Carolyn Chute, Cathie Pelletier, Howard Frank Mosher, David Budbill, and Annie Proulx when she writes about Vermont—fill their books with scenes of poverty, economic failure, spiritual despair, violence (domestic and otherwise), alcoholism, and the occasional suicide. These are not the kinds of things that make it into *Yankee* magazine. And yet, by virtue of the contrast they draw with the kinds of ideas about New England that many readers bring to their books, these writers too mount a sharp critique of regional identity, replacing romantic idealizations with what they see as the harsh realities of life in a geographically, economically, socially, and culturally marginal place.

Russell Banks's two New Hampshire–based books resemble other works of northern New England neorealism in their stark geographical settings, their marginal working-class characters, and the failed lives that those characters pursue. Most of *Affliction* takes place during a cold and snowy winter in the economically downtrodden town of Lawford, New Hampshire, a place "where unemployment from December till March was close to forty percent" (81) and which the book's narrator describes as "one of those towns that people leave, not one that people come back to" (5). Its main character, Wade Whitehouse, was routinely beaten as a child by his alcoholic father. Once a star high school athlete, in his early forties Wade is a divorced part-time policeman, part-time well digger, and part-time snowplow driver whose young daughter is increasingly estranged from him and whose ex-wife despises him. He lives in a trailer and drinks heavily. Over the course of the novel, Wade's life and mind unravel as he pursues his obsessive belief that a friend of his killed a Massachusetts man whom he had been working for as a hunting guide; in the end, he clubs his hated father to death, sets fire to the body and his father's barn, and vanishes for good, whereabouts unknown.

As for *Trailerpark*, that very setting, a clutch of shabby single-wides outside the equally shabby mill town of Catamount, New Hampshire, contrasts implicitly with the expected white-clapboarded New England village; the park is, in fact, a collection of "an even dozen trailers, pastel colored blocks, some with slightly canted rooves, some with low eaves, but most of them simply rectangular cubes sitting on cinderblocks, with dirt or gravel driveways beside them, usually an old car or pickup truck parked there,

with some pathetic, feeble attempt at a lawn or garden evident, but evident mainly in a failure to succeed as such" (36). The stories in *Trailerpark*
feature an unbalanced woman who raises hundreds of guinea pigs in her
trailer, a murder in the wake of a drug deal gone bad, promiscuous marital
infidelity, childhood illness and death, the by-now-expected divorce and
alcoholism, and other assorted lurid episodes that add up to an unrelenting
portrayal of hopelessness. One could argue perhaps that Banks's portrayal
of northern New England life is just as negative as the dominant image is
positive, and therefore just as partial and unrealistic and unrepresentative,
but it is that very negativity and opposition that give his and others' books
a sharply critical charge when read in a regional context.

And then there's *The Sweet Hereafter*. This novel is set in the Adirondack
town of Sam Dent, New York, but that name could easily be changed
to Lawford or Catamount, New Hampshire, without having to change
anything else about the book. The setting is similar: cold, snowy, bleak,
and in the middle of nowhere; as local garage owner Billy Ansel says about
northern New York in early March, "I don't care how much you think
you like the snow and ice and darkness of upstate New York; after four
or five months of it, nobody in this region manages to keep from being
depressed that late in the winter. And unless you drive a snowplow or run
a ski lift, you're not making any money here anyhow" (44). The town
is familiar: ugly and economically moribund. We've seen these characters
before: uneducated, poor, trapped, living dead-end lives. And the book's
plot is, once again, dark: the action of the novel, narrated consecutively
by four characters, including Billy Ansel, centers on a school bus accident
that kills fourteen children, the giving-up on life of some of their parents,
and the possibility of a lawsuit instigated by a visiting high-powered New
York City lawyer. The lawsuit falls apart, though, when one character, a
teenaged girl who survived the accident but has been left in a wheelchair,
tells a deliberate, suit-exploding lie in her deposition as a means both of
drawing the community back together (or so she hopes) and of getting
revenge on her father, who has been sexually abusing her for years; because
the lawsuit dissolves, he won't get the settlement money that he has been
counting on. So, be it in setting, characterization, or dramatic trajectory,
we remain firmly within the fictional territory of *Affliction*, *Trailerpark*, and
other works by other northern New England writers, and yet that territory
has been moved out of New England. In upstate New York, this tragedy

carries no regional resonances, implies no regional critiques; it is simply a tragedy.

The difficult lives of Banks's characters can be accounted for in part by the physical place in which they live. According to the U.S. Forest Service's widely used classification of ecosystem provinces in the United States, a discontinuous ecological region called the Adirondack–New England Mixed Forest–Coniferous Forest–Alpine Meadow Province unites Maine's northwestern mountains, the White Mountains of New Hampshire, the Green Mountains of Vermont, and the Berkshires of Massachusetts, jumps over the Lake Champlain and Housatonic River valleys, and takes in the Adirondacks as well (Bailey). As the name of the province implies, the common factor that defines it, and distinguishes it from other areas, is its characteristic vegetation, which indicates similarities in climate, elevation, and substrate as well. And common landscapes suggest common economic ways of life—although, it must be added, not in any kind of environmentally deterministic sense; given the realities of geography, weather, available resources, transportation infrastructure, distance from markets, the positive or negative values and qualities that outside visitors ascribe to places, and other such factors, certain economic and entrepreneurial choices have made more sense than others over time, and this in turn has conditioned the lives that residents (and literary characters) live.

In 1988, the U.S. Forest Service and the Governors' Task Force on Northern Lands jointly commissioned a Northern Forest Land Study to gauge the effect of changing land use on the forest and the human communities within it. The territory officially designated as the Northern Forest "comprises over 26 million acres of essentially forested land stretching for over 450 miles from the northern tip of Maine to the Tug Hill region in upstate New York" (Trombulak 12). (American governments, scientists, writers, and activists often tend to ignore the contiguous forested areas of Canada when discussing the Northern Forest, suggesting the power of political boundaries in shaping human perceptions of naturally defined regions.) This area corresponds closely to the Forest Service ecosystem province described above, and is characterized by particular patterns of economic activity. As Middlebury College economist Thomas Carr summarizes, "The economy of the Northern Forest region is intricately linked to the natural resource base. The timber resources are a primary input in the production of paper and allied products and a variety of wood products. . . . Numerous recreational opportunities are available in the region, including hunting, fishing, skiing, hiking, camping, canoeing, and horseback riding. These activities are the basis of a substantial regional tourism industry. Increasingly, many people are finding the special attributes of recreation opportunities, open space, and aesthetic landscapes excellent incentives to invest in a vacation home" (52). A 1995 report on the economic importance of the Northern Forest found that forest-based recreation and manufacturing provided employment for 226,630 people, with 140,580 of those jobs in forest-based recreation and 86,050 associated with the wood-based forest economy, including manufacturing (NE Forest All. 2). Accordingly, these related natural and economic qualities play a large part in how Banks and other northern New England neorealists characterize their region, not only in terms of physical setting but in terms of how characters interact with that setting. As mentioned earlier, for instance, the process of Wade Whitehouse's unraveling in *Affliction* is set in motion by a hunting accident involving a wealthy Boston union official who has a vacation home in the area; the largest employer in *Trailerpark's* Catamount is a tanning mill that "kept between seventy and eighty families in the area of the marginally poor" (23), and tanning is a process that traditionally uses a lot of tree bark; two of the bereaved parents in *The Sweet Hereafter* run a motel that, during the novel's wintry setting, sits empty except for the visiting lawyer.

This last detail suggests something else that is important about the Northern Forest economy: historically, it has been both uneven and seasonal, qualities that affect the well-being of residents be they actual or fictional. As a 1991 U.S. Department of Agriculture study on resident attitudes and resource use in the Northern Forest summarizes the situation, "The relatively low population totals and densities which characterize these northern New England counties may contribute to economic problems as much as they do to the quality of life. In particular, employment, unemployment, and underemployment, as well as changes in job quality, are of concern" (3). During the 1970s and 1980s, lumber prices largely remained stagnant. Thirty percent of U.S. lumber consumption was supplied by imports from Canada. The South became the primary region in the country for plantation forestry. Technological developments meant fewer workers were employed (Klyza 37–39). Working in the timber industry, or in any job in the Northern Forest for that matter, was not particularly lucrative anyway: in the mid-1990s, Northern Forest per capita income was eighty percent that of statewide figures (that is, per capita income for Vermont, New Hampshire, and Maine as a whole) (Carr 53). And as for tourism, not only are some places more touristically attractive than others (one character in *The Sweet Hereafter* describes the town of Sam Dent as "one of those towns that's on the way to somewhere else, and people get this far, they usually keep going" [21]), some touristic activities—hunting and skiing, for instance—are more seasonally appropriate than others, leading to regular, periodic hard times for locals.

These economic factors have contributed to a deteriorating quality of life in the region over the past two decades. A 2008 Northern Forest Center report on *A Strategy for Regional Economic Resurgence* finds one important challenge to be the fact that "in places where opportunities for living-wage jobs have declined, many Northern Forest communities are struggling to maintain their civic structure and community and social infrastructure (housing, water and sewer, education, health care, main streets, arts and culture). Many indicators of personal well-being—e.g. education and health—are stagnant or lag [sic] the southern tiers of the Northern Forest states" (16). Speaking specifically about the Adirondacks, historian Philip Terrie notes that "while some towns, like Keene Valley or Lake Placid, attract swarms of tourists and their dollars, others, off the main tourist corridors"—like the fictional Sam Dent—"appear dilapidated and unkempt" (182).

The qualities of the ecological region, then, can be a crucial factor in northern New England and upstate New York life and landscape; Banks acknowledges this when he says, regarding northern New Hampshire, that "those who have lived [there] have reflected in their daily lives the astringency, the sheer malignity and the dull extreme of the climate there" (*Affliction* 61). This astringency seems particularly obvious to characters who are outsiders to the area, people who have the objectivity to critically contemplate local life rather than simply and doggedly live it. Attorney Mitchell Stephens, for example, the New York City lawyer attempting to interest bereaved Sam Dent parents in a lawsuit, describes the town in a way that captures the region's physical appeal as well as the economic hardships that can attend living there for the rural working class, adding his own perspective to the physical evidence of the lives that he sees around him:

> They have these huge trees everywhere, on the mountains, of course,
> but down in the valleys and in town, too, and surrounding the houses,

even outside my motel room; they've got white pine and spruce and
hemlock and birches thick as a man, and the wind blows through them
constantly. . . . [M]ost of the people who live there year round are scattered in little villages in the valleys, living on food stamps and collecting
unemployment, huddling close to their fires and waiting out the winter,
until they can go back outdoors and repair the damage the winter caused.
It's a hard place, hard to live in, hard to romanticize. But, surprisingly, not
hard to love—because that's what I have to call the feeling it evokes, this
strange combination of fear and awe I'm talking about, even in someone
like me. (93–94)

Stephens, of course, is an out-of-town visitor from the big city, much
more able than local residents to experience and assess landscapes in aesthetic rather than economic terms. And yet, these places are not irredeemable, nor are their residents merely hapless victims of economic and ecological circumstance; we should not assume that Banks's characters are so
downtrodden that, unlike Stephens, they are unaware of or insensible to
the beauty and value of their surroundings. This becomes clear when we
consider the experiential rather than the economic context of characters'
lives. Banks's characters live in and experience their worlds on a small,
bioregional-level scale: Wade Whitehouse's identity and sense of belonging in the world, for instance, is located most meaningfully in the river
valley that encloses Lawford, not in some larger and more abstract space
such as New England or the Northern Forest. While Banks focuses mainly
on the ecological region and the economic and emotional strains that it
puts on people, then, he is also aware of the human, imaginative aspect of
bioregion that can make it a sustaining locus of contemplation and attachment, no matter how complexly those positive features are tied up with the
many other factors that help constitute a particular bioregion—or, at least,
he recognizes the possibility of such a relationship.

Wade Whitehouse may not know that he lives in a particular ecological
province or even what the word "bioregion" means, but his relation to his
piece of northern New Hampshire demonstrates what we might think of
as a sort of proto-bioregional sensibility. While driving down a river valley
one day, for instance,

Wade liked the way the river looked in the new snow and milky early
morning light. That is a tourist's idea of New Hampshire, he thought,
with pine trees drooping over the water and snarls of icicle-laden birches

clumped at the edge of eddies and pools, with large snow-covered boulders in the middle of the stream and dark-green water churning, swirling and splashing past and over them, raising a thick white crust of ice at the crest marks. At moments like this, Wade felt something like pride of place, a rare and deeply pleasurable feeling that started with delight in the sight of the country, passed through a desire to share that delight with someone else and abruptly ended in a fantasy in which he stands before the scene and spreads his arms wide as if to embrace it whole, then steps aside and reveals it to . . . to whom? (59; ellipsis in original)

True, the passage brings us back to a reminder of Wade's deep and essential loneliness, another outgrowth of Northern Forest residence in Banks's view, but while much inside of Wade has died, his sense of his region's beauty and potential for community remains alive and ready to be awakened. The main reason that Wade has remained in Lawford, depressed and alcoholic and violent, is not simply that he would likely be depressed and alcoholic and violent anywhere but because of a simple truth that he once admitted to his brother Rolfe, the novel's narrator: "he said it with a wince, a slight ironic twist on his face: he loved the town, and he could not imagine loving any other" (84).

And yet, economic reality can twist incipient place-love into something ugly, an anger fueled not by a healthy partnership with the landscape but by a jealous possessiveness in the face of tourists and vacationers, a group of people with whom natives are all too often forced into a master-servant relationship; the landscape becomes a field for class conflict and resentment, not a seeding ground for bioregional comity. Jack Hewitt, for instance, the young hunting guide in *Affliction* whom Wade Whitehouse suspects of murder, rues the economic inequity of his life as he contemplates his out-of-state client's brand-new and expensive hobby: "Ah, sweet Jesus, these rich old guys and their toys! . . . Men like Twombley, over-the-hill fat cats, cannot ever truly appreciate the beauty of things that they can afford to buy. And the men who can appreciate a gun like Twombley's, guys like Jack Hewitt, say, who can remember the feel of a particular gun in their hands for years afterwards, as if it were a marvelous woman they slept with once, will never be able to own it" (65). While bioregionalism is usually presented by its practitioners and advocates as a more or less utopian movement, life on the bioregional level in Russell Banks's Northern Forest is more dystopian than anything else, a matter of circumscription and frustration rather than possibility and hope.

Contemporary Northern Forest writers, then, be they writing about New England or New York, tend to define their region in both physically shabby and sociologically grim terms, a function of the limited and limiting economic relationship that their working-class characters have with the ecological province in which they live. While the possibility of an emotionally sustaining bioregional consciousness exists, however dim that consciousness may be, characters are rarely if ever able to step back and use that awareness as a basis for organization or action; it is hard enough for them just to stay alive, physically and spiritually. And yet, those books' *specific* location on the ecological map ultimately matters importantly. *Affliction* means something different from *The Sweet Hereafter* because it takes place in New England, not New York; its separate meaning springs from its position within a larger literary framework that sees the popular image of New England as a whitewash as far as its marginal people and places are concerned, that acknowledges the fact that northern New England has long had a sort of colonial relationship to the rest of the region in which the colonized contribute to the colonial center while not always getting much in return, and that seeks to counteract regional romanticism with an admittedly often exaggerated realism. *Affliction* joins a chorus comprising many other recent works that both critically examine and culturally advocate for the particular *places* in New Hampshire, Maine, and Vermont where the rural working class, the people whom their characters represent, get their livings and spend their days; when produced and read in that literary framework, a book like *Affliction* inevitably gets caught up in its cultural politics. So, while understanding northern New England as a cultural region necessarily involves understanding it as part of a larger ecological region, those specifically northern New England resonances that divide *The Sweet Hereafter* from *Affliction* and *Trailerpark* demonstrate that regionalism, in the cultural sense, retains a great deal of power as a framework for literary interpretation and can in fact trump environmental considerations, in New England or anywhere else.

WORKS CITED

Bailey, Robert G. "Ecosystem Provinces." *Description of the Ecoregions of the United States*. U.S. Forest Service, March 1995. Web. 23 July 2009.

Banks, Russell. *Affliction*. 1989. New York: HarperPerennial, 1990. Print.

———. *The Sweet Hereafter*. 1991. New York: HarperPerennial, 1992. Print.

———. *Trailerpark*. 1981. New York: HarperPerennial, 1996. Print.

Carr, Thomas. "The Northern Forest Economy." Klyza and Trombulak 52–70. Print.

Hebert, Ernest. *The Dogs of March*. 1979. Hanover: University Press of New England, 1995. Print.

———. "People of the Kinship." Afterword. *The Kinship: Two Novels from the Darby Series*. By Hebert. Hanover: University Press of New England, 1993. 1–22. Print.

Klyza, Christopher McGrory. "The Northern Forest: Problems, Politics, and Alternatives." Klyza and Trombulak 36–51. Print.

Klyza, Christopher McGrory, and Stephen C. Trombulak, eds. *The Future of the Northern Forest*. Hanover: University Press of New England, 1994. Print.

Northeastern Forest Alliance. *The Economic Importance of the Northern Forest*. Saranac Lake, N.Y.: NE Forest All., 1993. Print.

Northern Forest Center and North Country Council. *A Strategy for Regional Economic Resurgence: Recommendations of the Northern Forest Sustainable Economy Initiative*. Bethlehem, N.H.: N. Forest Cent. and N. Country Coun., 2008. Print.

Ryden, Kent C. "Region, Place, and Resistance in Northern New England Writing." *Colby Quarterly* 39.1 (2003): 109–20. Print.

Terrie, Philip G. *Contested Terrain: A New History of Nature and People in the Adirondacks*. Syracuse: Syracuse University Press, 1997. Print.

Trombulak, Stephen C. "A Natural History of the Northern Forest." Klyza and Trombulak 11–26. Print.

United States. Dept. of Agriculture. *Northern Forest Lands: Resident Attitudes and Resource Use*. Washington: U.S. Forest Service, 1991. Print.

DAVID LANDIS BARNHILL

Critical Utopianism and Bioregional Ecocriticism

We can . . . consider a bioregion as a unit of space where,
by locating ourselves there, we place ourselves in a physical,
mental, and spiritual relationship with the whole.
David Robertson, "Bioregionalism in American Nature Writing"

IN HIS IMPORTANT STUDY of bioregional literary criticism, David Robertson discusses some of the key components of bioregionalism: a delineation of place in terms of a bioregion, which reflects properties of the natural world rather than human artifice; a holistic integration of the individual person with that bioregion; and the interconnectedness of physical world, human psychology, and spirituality. Bioregional literary criticism, Robertson continues, is characterized by the drive "to identify and understand the niche of writers in their bioregional habitat" (1017).

Although Robertson deftly articulates several components of bioregionalism, much more is involved. As a concept and as an ecosocial movement, bioregionalism is compelling in part because it is highly inclusive. It assumes an interweaving of humans and nature, emphasizing the value of nature while also emphasizing human life within nature, making use of nature as one of its parts rather than merely contemplating it from the outside. It has a profound psychological and spiritual dimension (as Robertson highlights), while at the same time it is has social, political, and economic dimensions. It also works on the personal level as well as the social structural level. And it has on the one hand a pragmatic and reformist aspect of micro-level work being done now on the ground (such as farmers markets

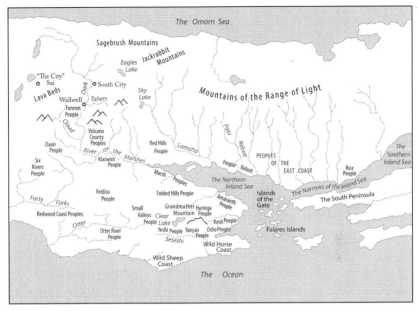

Adapted from "Some of the Places and Peoples Known to the Kesh" by Ursula K. Le Guin from *Always Coming Home*, with permission

or cohousing), and on the other a radical, transformist, and utopian aspect, imagining and working toward an ideal society in harmony with the community of life.

A fully developed bioregional literary criticism needs to draw on all of these aspects. Robertson says we place ourselves in a physical, mental, and spiritual relationship with the whole; I would add that we also place ourselves in a social, political, and economic relationship with the whole, a whole that includes human society in all its complexities, problems, and utopian potentials. The bioregional habitat we identify with, then, involves not merely physical space but also social structures, economic systems, and political power. Somehow those elements need to be part of bioregional literary criticism. When they are, the importance of the utopian dimension of bioregionalism becomes more evident. It is a conceptualization and application of utopian bioregional literary criticism that I articulate in this chapter.

CRITICAL UTOPIANISM AND BIOREGIONAL LITERARY CRITICISM

Utopianism as a social philosophy has suffered from bad press. It has been accused of being an irrelevant dreaming that fails to analyze society's problems and a compensatory fantasy that keeps one from responding to those problems. In addition, critics argue that utopia consists of an ideal of perfection that is either impossible or at the least unachievable from where we are. And even if we could achieve it, utopias may turn out to have profoundly dystopian characteristics, in some cases a totalitarian imposition of happiness.

But utopian thinkers, including literary critics, claim that utopian imagination is essential. If we have any hope of really discerning the outrages of today's society and moving toward a better one, we must cultivate the ability to imagine something else.[1] Antonio Gramsci has argued that one of the chief goals of those in power is precisely to suppress that ability. Thus we have conservative British Prime Minister Margaret Thatcher's oft-repeated slogan about the global dominance of neoliberalism: "There is no alternative." Utopianism asserts that there are alternatives. To use Lyman Tower Sargent's term, utopianism is a form of "social dreaming" that enables us to imagine radically different positive alternatives (3). And bioregionalism in its utopian dimension does just that.

Recent developments in utopian thought have revealed some of the significance of this social dreaming and have responded to critics of utopianism. One of the most important is the idea of "critical utopia" (Moylan, *Demand*). Unlike traditional utopias, critical utopias are imperfect and in process. They head toward rather than achieve the ideal, and they are contingent and vulnerable. Instead of presenting a blueprint for the ideal society, they offer a rich blending of creative fantasy, critical thinking, and oppositional activism. And instead of offering a unitary perspective, such texts may be self-reflexive, multivocal, and fragmented. This notion of critical utopianism helps counter the narrow understanding of utopianism that has made it easy to reject. In doing so it better enables bioregionalism to articulate and defend its utopian project.

The notion of critical utopia leads to a crucial revision in the definition of utopia. It is no longer limited to a perfectly realized ideal society, and Sargent offers this more relativistic definition: a utopia is a society that is "considerably better than the society in which that reader lived" (9). Darko

Suvin uses the term "more perfect": a utopia designates a society "where sociopolitical institutions, norms, and individual relationships are organized according to a more perfect principle than in the author's community" (Suvin, *Metamorphoses* 49). Tom Moylan, focusing on the utopian impulse rather than a utopian text, speaks not of final achievement but of "moving beyond" contemporary society: "Utopia, therefore, names the sociopolitical drive that moves the human project for emancipation and fulfillment beyond the limits of the current system" (*Scraps* 65).

Another crucial development in contemporary utopian thought is *novum*. Derived from the works of Ernst Bloch, *novum* refers to something fundamentally new in comparison with current society. Suvin has applied this term to analyze science fiction novels that present not only new technologies but also alternatives to the existing social order and political hegemony. For the Marxist Bloch, to be a true novum the new society must differ fundamentally from the current socioeconomic system. Moylan summarizes how Suvin continued this political stance: "through the textual novum, toward the potential for radically new directions in the latencies of that moment, Suvin's claims for sf [science fiction] brought it to a level of sociopolitical value that many sensed but never fully theorized," adding that "extreme care must be taken to distinguish between the novum of opposition and the pseudo-novum of commodification that has come to dominate the terrain of the 'new.'" A true novum is a "critical and subversive form of knowledge" (*Scraps* 45, 47, 287).

Novum has become a key idea in science fiction studies,[2] and it is in science fiction that many current explorations of utopia are being imagined. It is interesting to consider nature writing—and particularly bioregional writing—in a similar way, which leads us to make some important distinctions. Most nature-writing texts celebrate the earth in some way. Others include a painful portrait of the degradation of nature. Others go beyond these to offer a sweeping critique of culture. And still others articulate an ecosocially positive alternative to contemporary culture, thus becoming a critical and subversive form of knowledge. Many nature writers, particularly since the 1960s, present such a critique and ideal, and in doing so engage the utopian dimension.

But the term *novum* is not always appropriate in nature writing. "Newness" is not what is essential, and in fact some ecosocial ideals are strongly influenced by what is "old," with Wendell Berry and Gary Snyder as but two examples. Their works may not involve novums in Bloch's or Suvin's sense of "new." Is there an appropriate parallel, one that emphasizes nature, natural, and native, and the possibility of giving birth to a more ecological culture?

The etymological root of the words *nature, natural,* and *native*—as well as *nascent*—is the Latin *natus,* meaning "birth," with *natum* meaning "born." We can say that any nature writing that presents both an ecosocial critique of contemporary culture and an ecological alternative involves a "natum."[3] The term *natum* is, in one sense, very simple: it points to the presence of an ecosocial critique and ideal. But in doing so it helps us identify and highlight the presence of these elements in a work of nature writing. As such, the term helps us distinguish ecosocially ambitious nature writing from other kinds more narrowly focused on, say, the personal experience of nature in solitude. It also directs bioregional and utopian literary analysis: Is there a natum in a text, and if so what is it and how fully is it developed? How important is the natum to the work being analyzed? Does an author's natum change over time? How does that natum compare with those of other texts? How should that natum be evaluated: in what ways is it compelling and what limitations does it suffer from? A natum, then, becomes a key focus for interpreting the utopian dimension of bioregional texts, and it can refine our critiques of texts that lack such an ecosocial vision. And it opens a door for a cross-fertilization of science fiction and utopian literary theories with bioregional ecocriticism.

But is a bioregional natum translatable to social reality? Utopianism in general is haunted by what we can call the "radical paradox." If things are *really* bad now and the ideal is *fundamentally* different, it would seem that efforts to achieve it will almost inevitably fail. Or if we focus on what is achievable, our efforts will be superficial and we won't be able to effect the necessary change. Worse still, if we work on achievable reforms, we may actually help sustain what is a fundamentally toxic society.

Critical utopian theories offer a response to this paradox by emphasizing inevitable imperfection and a never-ending pursuit of the good. Critical utopias are part of a *process* of imagining a better alternative, what Phillip E. Wegner calls "a *mapping,* or an ongoing totalization rather than [a] picture, a map, an imaginary mimesis, or a completed totality" (68). Suvin distinguishes conventional and critical utopias by arguing that the former proposes an "Ultimum," an omega point of final fulfillment and teleological arrival. By contrast, in critical utopias, perfection is a receding horizon that we can work toward but never achieve (Moylan, *Scraps* 49). Suvin speaks of three points: the locus of the present, the ever-receding horizon of the ultimate ideal, and *"orientation*, a vector that conjoins locus and horizon" (Suvin, "Locus" 131). It is the utopian orientation rather than the Ultimum that is most important in critical utopias.

If utopia is seen as an ongoing orientation toward a receding horizon, the paralysis of the radical paradox of achievement can be broken. The challenge is to pursue pragmatic reform initiatives (such bioregional projects as community-supported agriculture) but treat them as dimensions of working toward the ideal rather than as ends in themselves. Community-supported agriculture does little to impact the enormous inertia of our destructive society, nor does it by itself challenge the power structure that consumes the earth and people. But it can, along with other pragmatic reform initiatives, effect substantial gains at a micro level, and we must not slight the good work we may be able to do in the short term to reverse the ever-present ecological and social devastations. And if such initiatives are conceived of not as end goals but as *means* toward the utopian horizon, they may be able to work on both the reform and the radical levels.

UTOPIAN BIOREGIONALISM AND TWO WORKS BY URSULA K. LE GUIN

Utopian bioregional literary criticism is particularly relevant to the study of science fiction novelist Ursula K. Le Guin. Le Guin has become known for her feminism, anarchism, and deep sensitivity to nature, and is considered one of the key figures in the resurgence of utopian writing starting in the 1970s.[4] Two books, *The Dispossessed: An Ambiguous Utopia* (1974) and *Always Coming Home* (1985), are both utopian and environmentally oriented. Analyzing them in terms of utopian bioregional literary criticism helps illuminate Le Guin's writing in new ways, including how the bioregional quality of her writing developed over time.

The Dispossessed takes place on two planets, Urras and Anarres, each the moon of the other. Urras is a planet much like Earth and is home to the country of A-Io, an affluent capitalist society. Anarres, on the other hand, is a desolate planet, with a dry and harsh environment. Until recently, Anarres had been used only for an exploitive mining operation for Urras. But some 150 years before the narrative present, an anarchist movement gathered force, led by Laia Odo. She died the day before the Odonians initiated a partially successful uprising,[5] strong enough to challenge the rulers of A-Io, but not strong enough to overthrow their authoritarian regime. The result was that the Odonians were allowed to move to Anarres to set up their anarchist society. A-Io was allowed to continue mining operations on Anarres in exchange for certain manufactured goods, but that operation and all contact with A-Io was literally and figuratively walled off from Anarresti Society.

Le Guin's presentation of utopian anarchism in *The Dispossessed* developed out of her reading of Petr Kropotkin, Emma Goldman, and Paul Goodman, among others. Anarresti society is strongly pacifist and communitarian, with no property and no laws. It is a classless society with equality of the sexes. Daily life is frugal, but with full communism of production and distribution. Personal liberty is balanced with social pressure to avoid "egoizing" and with admonishments against being "propertarian."

The Dispossessed is a *critical* utopia in detailing serious imperfections in Anarresti society. In the generations since its establishment, revolutionary idealism started to ossify, with metaphorical walls blocking a realization of personal fulfillment and social harmony. The young physicist Shevek attempts to break the walls both within his society and between Anarres and Urras, and he makes an unprecedented visit to A-Io, where he pursues his groundbreaking research, which was stifled in a society that had come to resist individual brilliance. At the end of the novel, Shevek succeeds in developing a new understanding of temporal physics that results in the creation of an ansible, a machine that enables instant communication across vast distances. He returns to Anarres with various walls having been shattered, but with the future of his flawed utopia uncertain.

Although *The Dispossessed* is primarily focused on the articulation of the potentials and problems of Anarresti anarchism, nature plays a significant role, and the novel exemplifies some important features of bioregionalism:

> Decentralization had been an essential element in Odo's plan for the society. . . . She had no intention of trying to de-urbanize civilization. Though she suggested that the natural limit to the size of a community lay in its dependence on its own immediate region for essential food and power, she intended that all communities be connected by communication and transportation networks. . . . There was to be no controlling center, no capital, no establishment for the self-perpetuating machinery of bureaucracy and the dominance drive of individuals seeking to become captains, bosses, chiefs of state. (95)

With a decentralized society, a strong focus on the local, and dependence on the bioregion's potentials and limits, Odo's ideals resonate with some aspects of the bioregional movement that was just beginning to take shape as Le Guin was writing the book.[6]

Odo's descendents exemplify some of her social vision. Anarresti society integrates local, self-organized worker groups within in regional syndicates (254). The Anarresti also seek to integrate society and its environment: "Man fitted himself with care and risk into this narrow ecology. If he fished, but not too greedily, and if he cultivated, using mainly organic wastes for fertilizer, he could fit in" (186). In addition, there are passages that present a biocentric consciousness. When Shevek for the first time looks into the eyes of a donkey on Urras, he thinks of his lover Takver, who has not only scientific knowledge of nature (she is a marine biologist) but also a deep intuitive connection to the natural world. "He wondered what [the donkey's] deep, dry, dark gaze out of the darkness would have meant to Takver. She had always known that all lives are in common, rejoicing in her kinship to the fish in the tanks of her laboratories, seeking the experience of existences outside the human boundary" (22). Later, reflecting again on Takver, Shevek concludes that there are souls "whose umbilicus has never been cut. They never got weaned from the universe. . . . It was strange to see Takver take a leaf into her hand, or even a rock. She became an extension of it, it of her" (185).

One of the principal functions of a utopia is to critique contemporary society, which *The Dispossessed* does in three different ways. Shevek's first reaction to A-Io (with its strong parallels to contemporary American society) is amazement at its apparent affluence, but slowly the curtain is pulled aside to reveal the oppression and suffering that this wealth is based on. On the other hand, A-Io is a largely sustainable society that has transcended the self-plundering excesses of an earlier historical era (82, 94), suggesting that our own exploitive economy is something even A-Io has transcended. And then at the end of the novel, Le Guin depicts a possible future for our planet if we continue in our voracious and belligerent ways. Shevek talks with a diplomat from Terra (Earth), who informs Shevek that Earth is a "planet spoiled by the human species" (348). The only way Terrans have survived on a ruined planet is through totalitarianism.

The Dispossessed, however, falls short of some bioregional ideals. The passage summarizing Odo's original vision mentions social and economic decentralization of largely self-reliant communities, yet there is no suggestion of an ecological consciousness of local bioregions nor of anything we could call reinhabitation. These absences are even stronger in Anarresti society, in part because of the severe environmental conditions. Odo's plans, we are told, "had been based on the generous ground of Urras. On arid Anarres, the communities had to scatter widely in search of resources, and few of them could be self-supporting, no matter how they cut back their notions of what is needed for support" (95). The narrator then comments on why frugality was insufficient: "They cut back very hard indeed, but to a minimum beneath which they would not go; they would not regress to pre-urban, pre-technological tribalism" (95).

Some in the contemporary bioregional movement uphold a posturban and posttechnological society as the ideal. In addition, in order to maintain the "minimum" standard of living in a harsh environment, a central computer matches an individual's skills with the needs of different regions of the planet and determines the best posting for that individual. Because it is an anarchist society, an individual may refuse a posting, but a sense of social responsibility usually leads him or her to accept it. The result is that Anarresti society is far more transient than the American society that Wendell Berry castigates in *The Unsettling of America*. (Imagine Berry receiving a posting from a computer!)

What of cultural diversity? In one passage, the narrator claims that Anarresti anarchism "was the product of a complex diversified culture" (95), but we get little sense in the novel of the kind of locally adapted cultural multiplicity bioregionalists call for or the cultural heterogeneity that postcolonial thinkers highlight.[7] The Anarresti exhibit a planetary rather than a bioregional culture. This planetary focus dovetails with a call from some contemporary thinkers for a more global perspective than bioregionalism conventionally provides. Mitchell Thomashow, for instance, has argued for a "cosmopolitan bioregionalism" and a biospheric consciousness in addition to a bioregional one (*Bringing* and "Cosmopolitan Bioregionalism"). Ursula K. Heise, in *Sense of Place and Sense of Planet*, has argued that in an age of globalization, writers and ecocritics need to develop a nuanced understanding of globality and the mobility that characterizes much of human life, with a sense of *planet* more crucial than a sense of place. However, Heise emphasizes the necessity of cultural heterogeneity, while on Anarres there is but one global culture.

When we turn to *Always Coming Home*, published a decade later, we find a robustly bioregional work. This story[8] takes place not far away (California) but rather in a far-distant future. Large nation-states and industrial economies are long gone, replaced by social decentralization that resonates with bioregional ideals: "the very loose, light, soft network of the human cultures, which in their small-scale, great number, and endless diversity, manufactured and traded more or less actively, but never centralized their industry, did not ship goods and parts far, did not maintain roads well, and were not engaged in enterprises requiring heroic sacrifice, at least on the material plane" (380). The book centers on the Kesh, a community that exhibits many of the anarchist philosophy and values seen in *The Dispossessed*, such as communism of production and distribution, absence of social hierarchy, and communitarianism. Unlike the Anarresti, however, the Kesh display a deep sense of place and bioregional consciousness. The protagonist, Stone Telling, recalls that as she left her home valley of Na, "I began to feel the Valley behind me like a body, my own body. My feet were the sea-channels of the River, the organs and passages of my body were the places and streams and my bones the rocks and my head was the Mountain" (189). Animals are considered part of one's family, and there is a type of communion, even communication, with rivers and rocks (e.g., 33, 22, 19).

Reality is characterized by dynamic interrelatedness: "It was the network, field, and lines of the energies of all the beings, stars and galaxies of stars, worlds, animals, minds, nerves, dust, the lace and foam of vibration that is being itself, all interconnected" (290–91). Le Guin conveys an ecological holarchy in which things are both a system with subsystems as well as a subsystem of larger systems: ". . . every part part of another part and the whole part of each part, so comprehensible to itself only as a whole, boundless and unclosed" (291).[9] The interconnection of humans and the more-than-human world is repeatedly emphasized: "Thinking human people and other animals, the plants, the rocks and stars, all the beings that think or are thought, that are seen or see, that hold or are held, all of us are beings of the Nine Houses of Being, dancing the same dance" (307).

The utopian critique of contemporary society found in *Always Coming Home* takes two forms. In the narrative context of a distant future looking back at our time, we are told of the Kesh's bewilderment at what our historical era produced: "the permanent desolation of vast regions through release of radioactive or poisonous substances, the permanent genetic impairment from which they suffered most directly in the form of sterility, stillbirth, and congenital disease" (159). In their attempt to understand such evils, the Kesh concluded that we had our "heads on wrong" (159) and lived "outside of the world" (153).

The second critique concerns the Condor, a patriarchal, militaristic culture that treats women as property and seeks to conquer others. An extrapolation of some of the sinister tendencies of our own culture, the Condor follow a rigidly hierarchical religion centered on the One: "True Condor warriors were to be one thing only, reflections of One, setting themselves apart from all the rest of existence, washing it from their minds and souls, killing the world, so that they could remain perfectly pure" (201). They too live "outside the world" (367).

The Condor are finally defeated, victims of their ideological blindness to nature's limits, and Kesh society continues with its bioregional anarchism. But *Always Coming Home* is a critical utopia. Some of the Kesh, including Stone Telling and her mother, are drawn to the way of the Condor. At the beginning of the narrative, Stone Telling leaves behind the Kesh to follow her Condor father, only to quickly find how oppressive that society is. In addition, among the Kesh there are dissension and pettiness. As Stone Telling says in concluding her narrative, "I have come to think that the sickness of Man is like the mutating viruses and the toxins: there will always be some form of it about" (386). Le Guin repeats this perspective in an interview that occurred while she was writing *Always Coming Home*: "As soon as you get real people involved in something, no matter how idealistically motivated they are, everything is eventually going to get mucked up. With people, nothing pure ever works quiet right. We're awful monkeys" (McCaffrey 170). Still, for Le Guin, Kesh society is a utopia: "my book that is a pure utopia, my utopia, my dream world. . . . I tried working out in [*Always Coming Home*] the world that I think I would like best to live in. Although this one will do" (Walsh 90–91).

NATUM AND THE QUESTION OF PROCESS

The Dispossessed and *Always Coming Home* clearly present a novum, a fundamentally different and, for Le Guin and many of her readers, positive alternative to contemporary society. But do they articulate a bioregional natum, an ecologically harmonious alternative that reflects the basic characteristics of bioregionalism? Anarresti society's anarchism displays bioregional ideals of decentralization, egalitarianism, and communitarianism. But the Anarresti are attuned to nature primarily in the sense of living sustainably in an austere environment. From a bioregional perspective, Anarresti society fails to suggest a robust bioregional natum. However, a decade later, in *Always Coming Home*, there is a full-bodied bioregional natum. In fact, this latter work could be considered a paradigmatic bioregional text. It is worth noting, however, that Kesh bioregionalism is clearly localist, lacking the cosmopolitan bioregionalism and biospheric consciousness espoused by Thomashow and open to criticism by Heise for its narrow localism.

In both cases, the question of process toward the ideal is problematic. The critique and the ideal are clearly articulated, but the two books do not suggest how we might move toward either ideal. The radical paradox seems to be in full force. The books present utopian horizons, and it is up to us, as part of what Daniel Anderson calls critical bioregionalism,[10] to discern what actions today might orient us toward those ideals or others like them. As such, the books return us to contemporary bioregional thought and practice for insights into how we might work toward a better future. Utopian bioregional literary criticism has much to offer that effort.[11]

NOTES

1. One of the most prominent voices of this view is Fredric Jameson. See, for example, *Archaeologies of the Future*.

2. Istvan Csicsery-Ronay Jr. has claimed that "[f]ew critical concepts have had greater influence on sf theory than the *novum*" (47).

3. Csicsery-Ronay Jr. (56–57) distinguishes between material and ethical/social novums in science fiction (e.g., a time machine and the society of Eloi and Morlocks). Natums, on the other hand, except for speculative fiction of Le Guin and others, rarely involve a material novum, as they usually assume the phenomenal world as we know it. Instead, they concern a culture, society, and ethics that are radically different from and superior to those of the present. That radical difference may have never existed historically, or it could derive from a culture in the historical past (and thus such texts are not properly called novums). Bioregional writings often present natums, including Wendell Berry's historical fiction of rural Kentucky.

4. Critic Carl Freedman has claimed that *The Dispossessed* "is not only the central text in the post-war American revival of the positive utopia, but, arguably, the most vital and politically acute instance of the positive utopia yet produced, at least in the English-speaking tradition" (114).

5. Her last day is narrated in "The Day Before the Revolution," a short story Le Guin wrote after the publication of *The Dispossessed*.

6. The (as we will see, limited) bioregional nature of *The Dispossessed* resulted in part from the many resonances between anarchism (in its communitarian and pacifist form) and bioregionalism, with the theories of Kropotkin particularly relevant.

7. See, for instance, Ursula Heise's *Sense of Place and Sense of Planet*, where she criticizes those who promote a sense of place for failure to recognize cultural heterogeneity.

8. The structure of *Always Coming Home* is highly unusual. There is a novel-like narrative, but it is scattered within other types of texts, such as anthropological analyses, poetry, histories, dramatic works, and biographies, as well as musings by the cryptic Pandora. The book thus exhibits the self-reflexive, multivocal, and fragmented character associated with some critical utopias.

9. This statement is echoed by Gary Snyder in his *Practice of the Wild*: "To know the spirit of a place is to realize you are a part of a part and the whole is made of parts, each of which is whole. You start with the part you are whole in" (38).

10. See his "Critical Bioregionalist Method in *Dune*: A Position Paper" in this book, in which he calls for "critical bioregionalism as a philosophy of praxis."

11. For introductions to utopian thought in general, Moylan's *Demand* and *Scraps* are excellent. For a study that is more directly relevant to bioregional utopianism, see de Geus, *Ecological Utopias*. For an anthology of utopian science fiction that is particularly relevant, see Robinson's *Future Primitive*.

WORKS CITED

Berg, Peter, ed. *Reinhabiting a Separate Country: A Bioregional Anthology of Northern California*. San Francisco: Planet Drum, 1978. Print.

Berg, Peter, Beryl Magilavy, and Seth Zuckerman. *A Green City Program for San Francisco Bay Area Cities and Towns*. San Francisco: Planet Drum, 1989. Print.

Berry, Wendell. *The Unsettling of America: Culture and Agriculture*. New York: Avon, 1977. Print.

Bloch, Ernst. *The Principle of Hope*. 3 vols. Cambridge: MIT, 1986. Print.

Csiscery-Ronay, Istvan, Jr. "Fictive Novums." *The Seven Beauties of Science Fiction*. Middletown, Conn.: Wesleyan University Press, 2008. 47–75. Print.

de Geus, Marius. *Ecological Utopias: Envisioning the Sustainable Society*. Utretcht: International, 1999. Print.

Freedman, Carl Howard. *Critical Theory and Science Fiction*. Middletown, Conn.: Wesleyan University Press, 2000. Print.

Gramsci, Antonio. *Selections from the Prison Notebooks of Antonio Gramsci*. New York, International, 1971. Print.

Heise, Ursula K. *Sense of Place and Sense of Planet: The Environmental Imagination of the Global*. New York: Oxford University Press, 2008. Print.

Jameson, Fredric. *Archaeologies of the Future: The Desire Called Utopia and Other Science Fictions*. New York: Verso, 2005. Print.

Le Guin, Ursula K. *Always Coming Home*. New York: Harper, 1985. Print.

———. "The Day Before the Revolution." *The Wind's Twelve Quarters*. New York: Harper & Row, 1975. 260–77. Print.

———. *The Dispossessed: An Ambiguous Utopia*. New York: Harper and Row, 1974. Print.

McCaffery, Larry. *Across the Wounded Galaxies: Interviews with Contemporary American Science Fiction Writers*. Urbana: University of Illinois Press, 1990. Print.

Moylan, Tom. *Demand the Impossible: Science Fiction and the Utopian Imagination*. New York: Methuen, 1986. Print.

———. *Scraps of the Untainted Sky: Science Fiction, Utopia, Dystopia*. Boulder, Colo.: Westview, 2000. Print.

Robertson, David. "Bioregionalism in American Nature Writing." *American Nature Writing*. Ed. John A. Murray. San Francisco: Sierra Club. 1996. Print.

Robinson, Kim Stanley, ed. *Future Primitive: The New Ecotopias*. New York: Tom Doherty Associates, 1994. Print.

Sargent, Lyman Tower. "The Three Faces of Utopianism Revisited." *Utopian Studies* 5.1 (1994): 1–37. Print.

Snyder, Gary. *The Practice of the Wild*. San Francisco: North Point, 1990. Print.

Suvin, Darko. "Locus, Horizon, and Orientation: The Concept of Possible Worlds as a Key to Utopian Studies." *Not Yet: Reconsidering Ernst Bloch*. Ed. Jamie Owen Daniel and Tom Moylan. London & New York: Verso, 1997. 122–37. Print.

———. *Metamorphoses of Science Fiction: On the Poetics and History of a Literary Genre*. New Haven: Yale University Press, 1979. Print.

Thomashow, Mitchell. *Bringing the Biosphere Home: Learning to Perceive Global Environmental Change*. Cambridge, Mass.: MIT, 2002. Print.

———. "Toward a Cosmopolitan Bioregionalism." *Bioregionalism*. Ed. Michael Vincent McGinnis. New York: Routledge, 1999. 121–32. Print.

Walsh, W. "I Am a Woman Writer, I Am a Western Writer: An Interview with Ursula Le Guin." *Conversations with Ursula K. Le Guin*. Ed. Carl Freedman. Jackson: University Press of Mississippi, 2008. 77–91. Print.

Wegner, Phillip E. "Horizons, Figures, and Machines: The Dialectic of Utopia in the Work of Fredric Jameson." *Utopian Studies* 9.2 (1998): 58–73. Print.

White, Jonathan. *Talking on the Water: Conversations About Nature and Creativity*. San Francisco: Sierra Club, 1994. Print.

DANIEL GUSTAV ANDERSON

Critical Bioregionalist Method in Dune

A Position Paper

A DISCLOSURE: IN PROPOSING "critical bioregionalism," I assume that diverse bioregions are *functionally homogenous*. In other words, claims about the cultural life of bioregion X must be significant and meaningful to those who live in bioregion Y. As Pavel Cenkl observes in his essay in this collection, productive labor is one such function common to all bioregions; he argues that the qualities of that labor make the North both distinct from and comparable to any other bioregion. Absent the assumption of functional commonalities, one could only speak responsibly of a bioregional culture by celebrating its cultural artifacts and practices without reference to any other, which amounts to *yay-for-us* jingoism—an ethically repellent approach.[1]

Some justification for making this assumption can be found in Gary Snyder's claim that "every region has its wilderness" (28) and is characterized by a distinct field of forces Snyder refers to as the "spirit of the place" (38). Bioregions are celebrated for their subtle distinctions from each other, their specificities, which add up to this spirit of place, and yet each has its unique version of this spirit; all bioregions share something in common in their difference. So I ask: What is it about the cultural lives of contemporary bioregions that makes regions X and Y legible to each other as different and significant, but not incomprehensibly *alien* to each other?

One plausible answer has to do with how human lives are presently lived in *any* given bioregion: the vulnerability of all bioregions to certain homogenizing forces that threaten to transform or destroy them and the degree

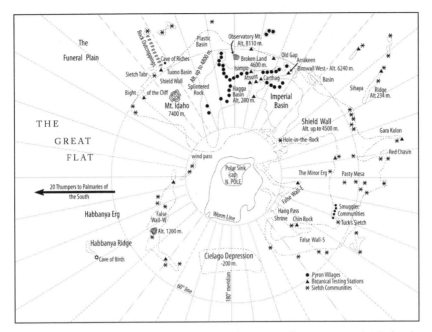

The Planet Arrakis, adapted from Dorothy de Fontaine's map in Frank Herbert's
Dune, © 1965 by Frank Herbert. Used by permission of G. P. Putnam's Sons,
a division of Penguin Group (USA) Inc. For online information about other
Penguin Group (USA) books and authors, see the Internet website at http://www
.penguin.com

to which *any* given person or polity may (or may not) be enfranchised
to make consequential decisions about their lives-in-place. This *something*
held in common by all bioregional experiences *at present* is best characterized as a political and economic context for and of labor called neoliberalism, late capital, globalization, or "unicity."[2]

Snyder observes that those who live in the global North may seem enfranchised to address problems in "the public domain" (29), but as he
further argues, this enfranchisement is largely make-believe. For instance,
"agencies that were once charged with conservation are increasingly perceived as accomplices of the extractive industries" (34). This points to the
most basic class division under neoliberalism. On one side are those who
are able to implement an agenda, through private ownership of the means
to do so; here, Snyder's phrase "extractive industries" works as a synecdoche
for capital's total apparatus of capture.[3] On the other side is the overwhelming majority, scattered to the edges: an "outsourced" proletariat speaking

hundreds of indigenous and mutually unintelligible languages.[4] These people are, as Snyder observes, "literally bulldozed out of their homes by international . . . interests in league with national governments" (34–35). A small few are enfranchised, but most are not. For this reason, personal beliefs, despite Michael McGinniss's concern about personal "values that threaten place-based and bioregional behavior" are in fact *not* the most likely source of risk for bioregions (4). Instead, I find a more plausible suspect in this power differential that allows some to profit from transforming specific bioregions *elsewhere* into strings of commodities and private capital, leaving multitudes to hew wood and draw water knee deep in mine tailings without any legitimized means of effecting meaningful change. Thus, practical engagement with this regime of unequal, undemocratic extraction and distribution of resources must come before questions of personal aesthetics, values, and their expression. To rework Snyder's terms, bioregionalism must make enfranchisement possible through an engagement with power before concerning itself with personal attunement to this or that bioregion's spirit: the latter surely a desirable goal, but a privilege made possible only when one becomes unalienated from one's labors and from nature; this privilege is not yet enjoyed by the disenfranchised majority, even as all beings without exception and without fail *should* enjoy it (Marx, "Economic and Philosophical Manuscripts" 68–79). No libertarian or NIMBY ecotopia at the expense of another or the totality of others is possible in the last analysis.[5] Different as we may be, we are in this together.

In "Toward a Cosmopolitan Bioregionalism," Mitchell Thomashow wrote that "Global economy requires that bioregionalists explore both the landscape (place) and those larger systems that exist beyond the horizon (space)" (126).[6] The problem of private global capital as a largely unspoken but often pointed-toward homogenizing force that threatens bioregional life is exactly one of those larger systems, and in this essay I argue not only that bioregionalist radical democracies would do well to replace it but that, in an unexpected way, Frank Herbert's allegoric novel *Dune* proposes a method for doing so. Thus, following Erin James's consideration in her essay in this volume of the global intersection of bioregional and postcolonial critiques, I propose through *Dune* a more explicit bioregional politics of the postcolonial, of globalization.

Dune (1965) *appears to be* a by-the-numbers heroic journey of a gifted young man, Paul Atrides (who later renames himself Muad'Dib), rising to seize power from an evil regime by dint of his own goodness, the rightness of his Messianic cause, and his capacity for clever violence—it *appears to be* spiritualized pulp fiction. It *is*, however, a novel about globalized capital and its conditions of possibility. This includes descriptions of "necessary" violence toward increasingly vulnerable people and bioregions, beings whose lives and living conditions are made not to count politically and socially except as "bare life," subject to capture and trade.[7] *Dune*'s thoroughgoing critique of this uneven political order opens a utopian space in which one can see capital's ghastly shadow and imagine bioregionally responsible alternatives. These alternatives are presented precisely in terms of local control and full enfranchisement—in other words, radical democracy[8]—thus offering exactly the kind of critical utopianism David Landis Barnhill rigorously advances elsewhere in this volume. In its concern for the ecological conditions and consequences of capitalist extraction and production, *Dune* has long been of interest to those committed to "green" cultural politics; as I show, the bioregionalist method of this novel is uncompromising and much more logically coherent than many green readings of it have yet to grasp.[9]

This confusion about *Dune*'s bioregional implications arises because of the novel's status as a famously popular work of science fiction. Writers in this genre typically find themselves on the horns of a dilemma: their work must appeal to the lowest common denominator of a mass readership to be profitable, but part of that appeal is to seem highbrow, significant, embodying "real values." In practice, these are antithetical demands. Science fiction, as heir to the epic and encyclopedic pretensions of Spenser and Milton, presents alternative conceptual worlds through accessible language and predictable plot points and emotes about "important values" in an uncritical, predictable, commodified way.[10] This utopian appeal is in direct conflict with the traditional sales strategies of science fiction publishers, who seek to appeal to a consuming public made pliable and uncritical, because such public pliability is itself a serious impediment to the sort of democratic participation implicit in the utopian vision.[11] Herbert's solution to this dilemma is to do both at once, by carefully satirizing this generic fictional world and its heroic, imperialistic, and masculine-Messianic narrative, "the crucial Western paradigm of economic interventionism" (Morton 6). *Dune* comes not to praise capital, but to bury it with its own discursive bayonets.

Dune is committed to a rigorous critical or "cognitive" project, as Darko Suvin and Fredric Jameson describe the best of science fiction, or better, *scientific* fiction[12]—not as a mass-cultural and hypermasculine "killer story," but as a satirical representation of such a story that holds the "killing" up for analysis by a critical reader, while inviting masses of uncritical consumers along for the ride.[13] Reading such a novel can be a subtle and subversive education for critical consciousness (Freire). Like any commodity, *Dune's* pillowy and generically spiritualized surface narrative of a heroic crusade against an evil empire by a self-sacrificing lover of freedom resolves on analysis into a precise representation of much larger and more involved social and material processes and their causes.[14] For starters, coercive discourses such as the archetypal-Messianic narrative of Paul Atrides "give way to a contextualized discourse of place" (Cheney 126). Arrakis is an allegory for the way a certain kind of bioregion relates to global, even *intergalactic*, capital, both spatially and culturally.

This bioregion contains a scarce resource extractible only at great risk and by violence to all forms of life present, but necessary for the transportation on which the political economy of Herbert's fictional world totally depends: mélange, or spice. From this fact, one can deduce the significance of the specific geographical features Herbert has assigned to the place, including flora appropriate to hydrocarbon-wealthy Mexico and the Middle East: "*saguaro, burro bush, date palm, sand verbena*" (66), and other forms of life typical not of the global North but of the edges of the map, where materials and labor are extracted from *other* people and places. Culturally, Arrakis is home to stereotyped, homogenous aboriginals. Islamic cultural overtones prevail among the Fremen, the native inhabitants of the planet, but even as they are clearly to be understood as having their cultural origins in Arabia and Persia, they are also firmly linked to Native Americans thematically (Ellis 117). In the imagination of Paul's friend and teacher, Gurney Halleck, the Fremen are presented similarly to "Indians" in James Fenimore Cooper, in that "they were devils on the warpath if you stepped foot where they forbade you to go. And they were so devilishly cunning" (398). In this conflation, Herbert satirizes the generic native-as-other in imperial-capitalistic imaginings and desires (Benjamin 339–422). The Fremen are in this sense stock characters in the stage-act of empire, down to both their lawlessness and the sacredness ascribed to them.

Similarly, Arrakis as a bioregion is presented as a particular kind of political site. Herbert has made it resemble a generic, desertified Petrostate, again recalling Mexico and the Gulf states, by means of the same physical and cultural cues. This resemblance draws immediate correspondences between mélange and petroleum as conditions of possibility for capital, and between Herbert's fictionalized form of capital and that of Herbert's real, twentieth-century moment. Most conspicuously, the Fremen have no local control or even make-believe "enfranchisement." They are instead orientalized, denied recognition both legally or otherwise, and badly oppressed by imperialistic powers. As "will-o'-the-sand people" they are "marked down on no census of the Imperial Regate" (5); they do not *count* as people, and their home is not recognizable as a *place* to any occupying force. Thus, each Fremen is the picture of *homo sacer* or the "sacred man" in Giorgio Agamben's formulation: he can be killed, but he cannot be sacrificed; there are no consequences for killing him.[15] His death is inconsequential, irrelevant, meaningless to power; his existence is something *other* than a life before the law, and for this reason, the Fremen's life is not legitimately political and not capable of becoming-political to power: it is *bare life*, on the margin of the map (Agamben 1–5).

For the dynastic class empowered to do so, the purpose of places like Arrakis is *plunder*. As Hawat explains to Paul, "Harvesting the spice is a process of getting in and getting out with as much as possible" (88), echoing the account of the banana company's regime of virtual reality in *One Hundred Years of Solitude*: it transforms the village and countryside in a whirlwind, and then disappears after taking the profits and disposing of the bodies (Garcia Márquez 215–313). Within capitalism, one purpose for controlling a resource is the ability to exploit it through private excess that is publicly celebrated, as in the ritualized waste of water by the ruling house of Arrakis—enough water "to keep a poor Arrakeen family for a year" (125–26). Mind-altering chemicals and spice as such are historically exchanged and celebrated as luxury commodities, as *Dune* acknowledges (Morton 7). Meanwhile, those integrated with the life of the bioregion, the Fremen, are left in greater squalor than before the precious resource was extracted through their enslavement and sacrifices (see Karl). Nevertheless, the Fremen unobtrusively persist in a kind of labor corresponding precisely to the creative and ecological "practice grounded in bioregional particulars" (their dwellings, their farming, their religious practices) that Norah Bowman-Broz identifies in her essay in this collection.

The role of the ecologist here is ambivalent. Intended as advance men for capital (87), ecologists are formally administrators reporting back to empire (see Anker) on the favorability of material conditions for conquest and exploitation in any given bioregion (107). However, the scientists serving in this role in *Dune*, the elder and younger Kynes, dissent, dissemble, and promote an altogether different agenda—a more democratic one. The elder Kynes claims, "You cannot go on forever stealing what you need without regard for those who come after. The physical qualities of a planet are written into its economic and political record" (268). As this statement attests, ecology and political economy are at this site indistinguishable as forces affecting matter and conditions of continued life and development. Corresponding to Snyder's observations on late capital, the political order in *Dune* bombs and bulldozes beings from their places—anyplace and anywhere, globally—on its own initiative. Herbert's representation of this total political order demonstrates one way in which capital has and continues to reproduce itself by means of its ability to extract material and human resources from bioregions not its own.

This totality of relations is, apparently at least, comprised of many agencies and institutions. The old Reverend Mother of the ultimately political Bene Gesserit order of contemplatives, Helen Gaius Mohiam explains to Paul while he is still a child, "We've a three-point civilization: the Imperial Household balanced against the Federated Great Houses of the Landsraad, and between them, the Guild with its damnable monopoly on interstellar transport" (22). The reader glimpses a map delineating a mess of seemingly multiple and independent powers abutting one another through Paul's eyes. For instance, the Landsraad is intended as a counterbalance of smaller family dynasties against the sovereign power of the Imperium (220). This implies that such a counterbalance was perceived as possible and necessary— these patrician dynasties are competing for something that must be finite among conditions that must be changing and not always predictable, thus making cooperation needful. Keeping all of them in business is the ability to take things by force and to make commodities of them through hired or slave labor, move those commodities around, and sell them at a profit; in other words, the basic formula for capital accumulation holds true on Arrakis (Marx, *Capital* 255). The Guild controls this process because it controls transport of raw materials, persons, and commodities. For this reason, the CHOAM Guild becomes a synecdoche for global capital. CHOAM stands for "Combine Honnete Ober Advancer Mercantiles," per Duke Leto (42)—a parody for the word-salad acronyms dominating American corporate and military life, evoking other mercantile transport monopolies, such as the British East India Company or the informally named "Seven Sisters" of the petroleum racket.

Curiously, although the Guild is willing to transport means of war, and is therefore able to control, regulate, and incite conflict, like global capital, it does not itself formally *make* war. In Paul's thoughts, the Guild is "a force that had specialized for so long that it had become a parasite, unable to exist independently of the life upon which it fed"—bare life, bioregional resources, human labor—"They had never dared grasp the sword . . . and now they could not grasp it" (458). Instead, states as the traditional interface between capital and nature are enlisted to do this work of securing resources (O'Connor 159–77). The collusion of the Imperium with certain dynasties of the Landsraad corresponds precisely to the 1953 Anglo-American intervention in Iran to reclaim the newly nationalized holdings of the Anglo-Iranian Oil Company, deposing the democratically elected government of Mohammed Mosaddeq, and anticipates the CIA-engineered coup that deposed the democratically elected Popular Unity government in Chile on 11 September 1973 in response to Salvador Allende's complete nationalization and democratization of copper mining rights of Anaconda Copper Company and Kennecott Copper Corporation in July 1971. More explicitly, among countless other illegal sovereign state actions that express capital's interests, it parallels the open war Bush and Blair brought to the nationalized oilfields of Iraq in 2003 on false pretenses (see Williams). Again, who is enfranchised? *Dune* presents accurately the relationship between capital and state power, and the sad negligibility of "local control" under these conditions for vulnerable persons and ecosystems that can be killed without legal or political consequence and whose sacrifices have no legitimized political, legal, or public meaning.

As all this suggests, the multiplicity of political institutions that the Reverend Mother narrates to young Paul is reducible to one economic system in which all compete (sometimes cooperatively) for control, and on the terms of which all conform their behavior—and this system is backed in the end by the threat of force. As the omniscient narrator explains, "wealth was the thing. CHOAM was the key to wealth, each noble House dipping from the company's coffers whatever it could under the power of the directorships. Those CHOAM directorships—they were the real evidence of political power in the Imperium" (19). Private capital, then, is the only meaningful form of enfranchisement in this regime; state powers are reducible to organized, unaccountable *interests*, to reformulate Snyder's observation (35). This primacy of capital is demonstrated clearly in *Dune* when, at the pitch of the conflict for control of Arrakis's bioregional integrity and material wealth, it is not a *state* that is able to assert itself, but *capital* as such: the CHOAM banner rises in place of the Harkonnen or Atrides standards (435–39). (Herbert allegorizes the state as absolutist familial dynasties, which is remarkably precise, since such dynasties are the historical origin of the modern state form; see Anderson). In *Dune*, as on Earth, the identity of the state that administers resources is irrelevant to capital, so long as *something* secures the flow of extracted resources so accumulation of wealth can continue.

Ecological conditions complicate CHOAM's control of commodity exchanges and the terms of those exchanges because the addictive spice—a commodity on which CHOAM itself is absolutely dependent—can only be extracted fully formed from a bioregional process (an interaction of certain species under certain conditions specific to Arrakis), not manufactured from other materials synthetically. This extraction is socially and ecologically catastrophic (Ellis 119). So, as with petroleum on present-day planet Earth, a complex regime of exchange and transformation is finally reducible to the production and control of one commodity essential for the current regime of transport. Who controls mélange? Whoever *can* control it, by force of law or state power, or raw force, regardless of indigenous right or ecological responsibility. As I have suggested, more bioregionally appropriate attempts to bring forth local or bioregional control of such a resource, democratizing it away from capital's control (there are obvious historical antecedents, Chile foremost among them), draws serious consequences as a violation of rights to private property.

In short, *Dune* shows capital to be ruthlessly imperial and bent on claiming for itself what belongs to others, to future life, or to nature for the purpose of the accumulation of yet more capital, and discharging the poisonous and violent consequences of its actions in the "backyards" of others.[16] The Baron Harkonnen finds common ground with all enfranchised parties when he professes, "A certain amount of killing has always been an arm of business" (317). They kill, cheat, steal, and destroy to accumulate capital or to be better positioned to do so—not because of deficient values on their part, although their values are surely deficient, but because the totality of relationships in their world is structured so.

Herbert drives home the significance of this point by drawing parallels between this fictionalized account of capital's relation to material nature and the situation of capital at the pitch of the Cold War. Nation-states function as privatized armies of capital proper (the "West") or bureaucratic capital (the USSR and its satellites).[17] All compete globally for resources and advantage; power is reducible to money for the "communistic" Harkonnens, too (229). The surprising lack of contrast between two dynastic families corresponding to the cold war superpowers, the Atrides and the Harkonnens, demonstrates this synchrony. The Harkonnens, with conspicuous Finno-Slavic naming patterns, are recreational murderers with appetites for sexual violence (183) and a Stalinistic willingness to effect a political reorganization through purges and killings (233). Their city, Carthag, is one vowel short of contrasting perfectly against the civilized good of imperial Rome, the cultural capital of the West and ideological antecedent to certain of its empires (see Spenser, Book Two, Canto Ten). The Baron Harkonnen's elephantine body and tempestuous personality recall Krushchev's public figure, and Mao's. The Harkonnens are designed to evoke the midcentury Soviets in stereotype.

By contrast, and reflecting a bit of "them bad; us good" cold war Manichaeism (in order to explode it), the scion of the Atrides family—Mediterranean in features, noble in bearing—poses as a Bible-toting Captain America (with a silent drug habit) against the Soviet menace: "Didn't you learn that Atrides loyalty is bought with love while the Harkonnen coin is hate?" Paul screams to Halleck (420), as if vehement exhortation could make it true. The Atrides do seem kinder and gentler in some respects than the Harkonnens; Halleck, an Atrides hanger-on, is generous with a song and a verse of scripture. But in a mix of love and hate, members from either side *desire violence* against the other in the same way. Piter de Vries, working for the Harkonnens, demands Paul's mother, Jessica, for his own use as a sex slave (16, 161); Halleck demands to kill a Harkonnen for his own pleasure (any one will do) (437, 464–66). This reveals a sadistic symmetry between both houses, equating them by their desires and intentions, which is confirmed when Paul learns he is himself a blood relative of the Harkonnen family (as a grandson of the baron). Complicating matters, the storm troopers of the Imperium, the Sardaukar—themselves under the state of legal exception on the prison planet Salusa Segundus, *homo sacer* like the Fremen—are given creepy Nazi features, "the blond, chisel-featured caste, the look that seemed synonymous with rank among the Sardaukar" (454), a turn of phrase recalling the eugenic hierarchies of Nazi biopower. It is as if Herbert wants to emphasize that this story is not some archetypal good-against-evil myth, but that it instead deals directly with global politics understood analytically, such that the presumably good (the Atrides) may not be so, and the presumably bad (the Harkonnens) may be bad in the same way that the presumably good are.[18] In short, there is no mistaking the intended correspondences between the Imperium's mode of production and the twentieth century's, nor of the novel's hermeneutic of suspicion toward all involved.

Both a basis and an imperative for a critical bioregional program emerge from *Dune*'s representation of the metabolic interaction among neoliberalism, the creative life of particular places, and of human labor. *The basis*: because of irresponsible sovereign power, bioregions are vulnerable to destruction-by-consumption; therefore the conditions of possibility for a future of any kind are precarious (Butler 67–68, 128–51). *The imperative*: this vulnerability demands a responsible, democratic program of action insofar as bioregions are valuable as sites of possibility for capable and creative life and cultural integrity, not only as minimal conditions for bare life.

The cultural experience of the Fremen of Arrakis represents both these claims in that the Fremen as members of a fractured proletariat are wholly marginalized by and vulnerable to the capricious whims of a sovereign power. In other words, they occupy a position where power meets bare life; they are the "many-headed hydra" against which the Hercules of capital has been pitted from the start (see Linebaugh and Rediker). But this multitude also has the potential to become a disciplined force, sweeping off the sea of the desert into the polis from the edges (Ranciere 104). A democratization of land and labor is an alternative to the jihad Muad'Dib most fears (Ranciere 5–37). The Fremen have become uniquely creative and capable by virtue of their bioregional experience, but not fulfilled or self-directed due to their position and manipulation by powers beyond their control: the Imperium, Paul and his mother, the Guild, the Bene Gesserit. This lack of direction can be ameliorated by a coherent and properly implemented program for bioregional control.

Paul, now renamed Muad'Dib, unintentionally points to democratic local control as a feature of such a program: "The Guild is like a village beside a river. They need the water, but can only dip out what they require. They cannot dam the river and control it, because that focuses attention on what they take" (462). The importance of the visibility of what is taken distinguishes resource interventions such as the covert 1973 coup in Chile from the open 2003 war in Iraq, which raised much greater public objections as it was made too obvious, a spectacle. But to return to Muad'Dib's metaphor: what happens if the creatures and cultures in and of the river build their own dam to protect the water and themselves, if they democratize the bioregion and let the simulated life and spectacle of capital go hungry? While Chile's experiment in radical democracy gives much insight here, this must remain an open question.[19]

For now, I propose the following imperative for critical bioregionalists hoping to develop such a program: *To work for the continued reproducibility of capable life as such, of all species, including the specifically capable human species.* "Capable" life can be distinguished from the unenfranchised and hopeless condition of bare life, and both phrases can function as catch-all concepts for the kinds of human potential and utopian tendencies in *Dune* and latent in dialectical thinking broadly inclusive of both historical materialism and the Buddhist concept of *Madhyamika.*[20] This proposal is concerned not only with conditions of life as such, but also with the ability of living beings to do things appropriately to their species nature—for fish to swim and spawn, for people to live not only for subsistence, as the majority of the world's human population struggles to do, but to live and labor creatively and with some measure of joy, cooperatively among others, as the Fremen persist in doing.

For this reason, I call for critical bioregionalism as a philosophy of praxis, not a hermeneutic. Critical bioregionalism views reading not as an end in itself, but as a productive practice "that extracts from the text its revolutionary force," where one does not "apply a theory" to an aesthetic object but rather reads to inform one's broader pedagogic-political project (Deleuze and Guattari, *Anti-Oedipus* 106). Jameson observes that "theory" was absorbed into English departments in the U.S. by the logic of the commodity—with "brand names attached," so that methodologies taken in haste as being suitable to express certain identities are "dramatized as a kind of supermarket of choices . . . and consumed in that way" (Jameson, *Jameson on Jameson* 237). Instead, I propose that the critical bioregionalist resist this and any other "killer story," and instead represent material, processual reality in good faith, with an eye toward a just, sustainable order of development in relation to the ecological totality. This practice is committed first and last to building a bioregionally sustainable radical democracy for all forms of life, without exception.

NOTES

1. Borges, "The Argentine Writer and Tradition"; Debord, *Society of the Spectacle*, 40–41 (section 62).

2. Harvey, *Spaces of Hope*, 21–40; Robertson, *Globalization*, 26.

3. Deleuze and Guattari, *A Thousand Plateaus*, 424–73.

4. Harvey, *Spaces of Hope*, 41–52; Linebaugh and Rediker, *The Many-Headed Hydra*.

5. Cohen, *Self-Ownership*; Shantideva, *The Way of the Bodhisattva*.

6. Aberley, "Interpreting Bioregionalism," 25; Thomashow, "Toward a Cosmopolitan Bioregionalism," 126.

7. Agamben, *Homo Sacer*; Linebaugh and Rediker, *The Many-Headed Hydra*.

8. Laclau and Mouffe, *Hegemony and Socialist Strategy*; Brown, *Towards a Radical Democracy*; Morris, *We Must Make Haste—Slowly*; Aberley, "Interpreting Bioregionalism," 25.

9. Gough, "Playing with Wor(l)ds"; Ellis, "Frank Herbert's *Dune*"; Murphy, "The Non-Alibi"; Stratton, "The Messiah and the Greens."

10. Lem, *Microworlds*, 59; Macdonald, "Masscult and Midcult," 36–50.

11. Lem, *Microworlds*, 85; Debord, *Society of the Spectacle*; Horkheimer and Adorno, *Dialectic of Enlightenment*, 94–136.

12. Suvin, *Positions and Presuppositions*; Jameson, "Reification and Utopia," "Cognitive Mapping."

13. Le Guin, "The Carrier Bag Theory," 152; Macdonald, "Masscult and Midcult," 36–50.

14. Marx, *Capital*, 1: 220–43; Buck-Morss, *The Dialectics of Seeing*, 205–15.

15. Agamben, *Homo Sacer*, 9, 71–74, 124–25.

16. Lenin, "Imperialism"; Luxemburg, *The Accumulation of Capital*.

17. Debord, *The Society of the Spectacle*, 72–73 (section 104); Marx, "Economic and Philosophical Manuscripts," 70–71.

18. Prieto-Pablos, "The Ambivalent Hero," 71–73; DiTomasso, "History and Historical Effect," 321; Minowitz, "Prince versus Prophet," 124–25.

19. Uribe, *The Black Book*; U.S. Senate, *Covert Action in Chile*; Haslam, *The Nixon Administration*.

20. Kalupahana, Nagarjuna; Jones, *The Social Face of Buddhism*.

WORKS CITED

Aberley, Doug. "Interpreting Bioregionalism: A Story from Many Voices." McGinnis 13–41. Print.

Agamben, Giorgio. *Homo Sacer: Sovereign Power and Bare Life*. Trans. Daniel Heller-Roazen. Stanford: Stanford University Press, 1998. Print.

Allende, Salvador. *Salvador Allende Reader: Chile's Voice of Democracy*. Ed. James D. Cockcroft. New York: Ocean Press, 2000. Print.

Anderson, Perry. *Lineages of the Absolutist State*. New York: Verso, 1979. Print.

Anker, Peder. *Imperial Ecology: Environmental Order in the British Empire, 1895–1945*. Cambridge, Mass.: Harvard University Press, 2001. Print.

Benjamin, Walter. *The Arcades Project*. Trans. Howard Eiland and Kevin McLaughlin. Cambridge, Mass.: Belknap Press, 1999. Print.

Borges, Jorge Luis. "The Argentine Writer and Tradition." *Labyrinths: Selected Stories and Other Writings*, Ed. James E. Irby and Donald A. Yates. New York: New Directions, 1964. 177–85. Print.

Brown, Douglas M. *Towards a Radical Democracy: The Political Economy of the Budapest School*. London: Allen & Unwin, 1988. Print.

Buck-Morss, Susan. *The Dialectics of Seeing: Walter Benjamin and the Arcades Project*. Cambridge, Mass.: MIT Press, 1991. Print.

Butler, Judith. *Precarious Life: The Powers of Mourning and Violence*. New York: Verso, 2004. Print.

Cheney, Jim. "Postmodern Environmental Ethics: Ethics as Bioregional Narrative." *Environmental Ethics* 11 (1989): 117–34. Print.

Cohen, G. A. *Self-Ownership, Freedom, and Equality*. Cambridge: Cambridge University Press, 1995. Print.

Debord, Guy. *The Society of the Spectacle*. Trans. Donald Nicholson-Smith. New York: Zone, 1995. Print.

Deleuze, Gilles, and Félix Guattari. *Anti-Oedipus: Capitalism and Schizophrenia*. Trans. Robert Hurley, Mark Seem, and Helen R. Lane. Minneapolis: University of Minnesota Press, 1983. Print.

———. *A Thousand Plateaus: Capitalism and Schizophrenia*. Trans. Brian Massumi. Minneapolis: University of Minnesota Press, 1987. Print.

DiTommaso, Lorenzo. "History and Historical Effect in Frank Herbert's *Dune*." *Science Fiction Studies* 19.3 (1992): 311–25. Print.

Ellis, R. J. "Frank Herbert's *Dune* and the Discourse of Apocalyptic Ecologism in the United States." *Science Fiction Roots and Branches: Contemporary Critical Approaches*. Ed. R. J. Ellis and Rhys Garnett. New York: St. Martin's, 1990. 104–24. Print.

Freire, Paulo. *Education for Critical Consciousness*. Trans. Myra Bergman Ramos. New York: Continuum, 2008. Print.

Garcia Márquez, Gabriel. *One Hundred Years of Solitude*. Trans. Gregory Rabassa. New York: Everyman's Library, 1995. Print.

Gough, Noel. "Playing with Wor(l)ds: Science Fiction as Environmental Literature." *Literature of Nature: An International Sourcebook*. Ed. Patrick D. Murphy. Chicago: Fitzroy Dearborn, 1988. 409–14. Print.

Gramsci, Antonio. *The Gramsci Reader: Selected Writings*, Ed. David Forgacs. New York: New York University Press, 2000. 1916–35. Print.

Harvey, David. *Spaces of Hope.* Berkeley: University of California Press, 2000. Print.

Haslam, Jonathan. *The Nixon Administration and the Death of Allende's Chile: A Case of Assisted Suicide.* London: Verso, 2005. Print.

Herbert, Frank. *Dune.* New York: G.P. Putnam's Sons, 1984. Print.

Horkheimer, Max. "Traditional and Critical Theory." *Critical Theory: Selected Essays.* Ed. Matthew J O'Connell. Trans. Matthew J. O'Connell. New York: Continuum, 1982. 188–243. Print.

Horkheimer, Max, and Theodor W. Adorno. *Dialectic of Enlightenment: Philosophical Fragments.* Trans. John Cumming. Palo Alto, Calif.: Stanford University Press, 2002. Print.

Jameson, Fredric. "Cognitive Mapping." *Marxism and the Interpretation of Culture.* Ed. Cary Nelson and Lawrence Grossberg. Urbana, Ill.: University of Illinois Press, 1988. 347–57. Print.

———. *Jameson on Jameson: Conversations on Cultural Marxism.* Ed. Ian Buchanan. Durham, N.C.: Duke University Press, 2007. Print.

———. "Reification and Utopia in Mass Culture." *Social Text* 1 (1979): 130–48. Print.

Jones, Ken. *The Social Face of Buddhism: An Approach to Political and Social Activism.* London: Wisdom, 1989. Print.

Kalupahana, David J. *Nagarjuna: The Philosophy of the Middle Way.* Albany, N.Y.: State University of New York Press, 1986. Print.

Karl, Terry Lynn. *The Paradox of Plenty: Oil Booms and Petro-States.* Berkeley: University of California Press, 1997. Print.

Laclau, Ernesto, and Chantal Mouffe. *Hegemony and Socialist Strategy: Towards a Radical Democratic Politics.* 2nd ed. London: Verso, 2001. Print.

Le Guin, Ursula K. "The Carrier Bag Theory of Fiction." *The Ecocriticism Reader: Landmarks in Literary Ecology.* Ed. Cheryll Glotfelty and Harold Fromm. Athens: University of Georgia Press, 1996. 149–54. Print.

Lem, Stanislaw. *Microworlds: Writings on Science Fiction and Fantasy.* Ed. Franz Rottensteiner. New York: Harcourt, 1986. Print.

Lenin, V. I. "Imperialism, the Highest Stage of Capitalism." *V.I. Lenin, Selected Works.* New York: International, 1967. 677–777. Print.

Linebaugh, Peter, and Marcus Rediker. *The Many-Headed Hydra: Sailors, Slaves, Commoners, and the Hidden History of the Revolutionary Atlantic.* Boston: Beacon, 2000. Print.

Luxemburg, Rosa. *The Accumulation of Capital.* Trans. Agnes Schwarzschild. London: Routledge, 2003. Print.

Macdonald, Dwight. *Against the American Grain: Essays on the Effects of Mass Culture.* New York: Vintage, 1965. Print.

Marx, Karl. "Capital, Volume One." *Karl Marx: Selected Writings.* Ed. Lawrence H. Simon. Indianapolis, Ind.: Hackett, 1994. 216–300. Print.

———. "Economic and Philosophical Manuscripts." *Karl Marx: Selected Writings.* Ed. Lawrence H. Simon. Indianapolis, Ind.: Hackett, 1994. 56–97. Print.

McGinnis, Michael Vincent, ed. *Bioregionalism.* New York: Routledge, 1999. Print.

———. "A Rehearsal to Bioregionalism." McGinnis 1–9.

Minowitz, Peter. "Prince versus Prophet: Machiavellianism in Frank Herbert's *Dune* Epic." *Political Science Fiction.* Columbia: University of South Carolina Press, 1997. 124–47. Print.

Morris, David J. *We Must Make Haste—Slowly: The Process of Revolution in Chile.* New York: Vintage, 1973. Print.

Morton, Timothy. "Imperial Measures: *Dune*, Ecology, and Romantic Consumerism." *Romanticism on the Net* 21 (February 2001): n. pag. *Romanticism on the Net.* Web. <http://www.erudit.org/>.

Murphy, Patrick D. "The Non-Alibi of Alien Scapes: SF and Ecocriticism." *Beyond Nature Writing: Expanding the Boundaries of Ecocriticism.* Ed. Karla Armbruster and Kathleen R. Wallace. Charlottesville: University of Virginia Press, 2001. 263–77. Print.

O'Connor, James. *Natural Causes: Essays in Ecological Marxism.* New York: Guilford, 1998. Print.

Prieto-Pablos, Juan A. "The Ambivalent Hero of Contemporary Fantasy and Science Fiction." *Extrapolation* 32.1 (1991): 64–80. Print.

Ranciere, Jacques. *On the Shores of Politics.* Trans. Liz Heron. New York: Verso, 1995. Print.

Robertson, Roland. *Globalization: Social Theory and Global Culture.* London: Sage, 1992. Print.

Shantideva. *The Way of the Bodhisattva: A Translation of the Bodhicharyavatara.* Trans. Padmakara Translation Group. Boston: Shambhala, 2003. Print.

Snyder, Gary. *The Practice of the Wild.* San Francisco: North Point, 1990. Print.

Spenser, Edmund. *The Faerie Queene.* Ed. A.C. Hamilton. New York: Longman, 1977. Print.

Stratton, Susan. "The Messiah and the Greens: The Shape of Environmental Action in *Dune* and *Pacific Edge*." *Extrapolation* 42.4 (2001): 303–16. Print.

Suvin, Darko. *Positions and Presuppositions in Science Fiction.* Kent, Ohio: Kent State University Press, 1988. Print.

Thomashow, Mitchell. "Toward a Cosmopolitan Bioregionalism." McGinnis 121–32.

United States Senate. *Covert Action in Chile, 1963–1973: Staff Report of the Select Committee to Study Governmental Operations with Respect to Intelligence Activi-*

ties, United States Senate. Washington, D.C.: U.S. Government Printing Office, 1975. Print.

Uribe, Armando. *The Black Book of American Intervention in Chile.* Trans. Jonathan Casart. Boston: Beacon, 1975. Print.

Williams, Kevin. "Imperialism & Globalization: Lessons from Frank Herbert's *Dune.*" *Reconstruction* 3.3 (2003): *Reconstruction.* Web. <http://reconstruction. eserver.org/033/williams.htm>.

PART THREE

Reimagining

JILL GATLIN

"Los campos extraños de esta ciudad" /
"The strange fields of this city"

Urban Bioregionalist Identity and Environmental Justice
in Lorna Dee Cervantes's "Freeway 280"

B IOREGIONAL PRACTICE BEGINS with understanding place and,
correspondingly, self. Most bioregionalists emphasize that cultivating
sustainable dwelling requires not simply acquiring technical knowledge
about the natural possibilities and limitations of one's geologic, biotic, or
climatic region but also reconnecting to place through personal experience
and rediscovering, in the words of Gary Snyder, "the 'where' of our 'who
are we?'" (*A Place* 184). The movement's most prolific poet and essayist,
Snyder posits that although place and personhood are mutually constitutive, many people ignore their interrelations: "There are tens of millions of
people in North America who were physically born here but who are not
actually living here intellectually, imaginatively, or morally" (*The Practice*
40). Bioregional inhabitation, Snyder proposes, requires paying attention
to place in the pursuit of knowledge, the act of artistic creation, and the
formulation of ethics; it is at once a human- and an earth-oriented practice. Re-seeing "place as an experience" (Snyder, *The Practice* 25) reveals
continual interaction between self and locale and may reverse the trend
of occupying space and using land with little sense of attachment to or
responsibility for it. Similarly, in his bioregionalist manifesto *Dwellers in
the Land*, Kirkpatrick Sale envisions bioregional practice as an experiential
endeavor: "the project of understanding place is neither nostalgic nor utopian but rather the realistic sort of occupation anyone can participate in

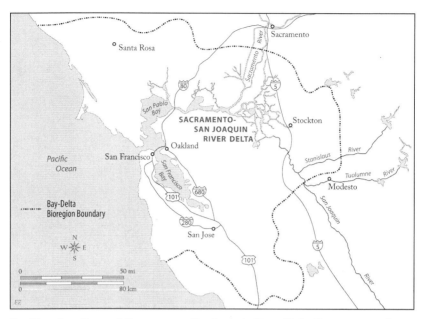

San Francisco Bay and Sacramento–San Joaquin River Delta Bioregion, with San José, California

every day" (48). If we all dwell in places, bioregionalists suggest, we are all equipped to delve in and begin understanding place.

With this participatory ideal underlying a commitment to sustainable human inhabitation of the earth, bioregionalism shares fundamental principles with the environmental justice movement. Advocating sustainability and social equity, environmental justice activists denounce race-, class-, and gender-based hierarchies that have molded mainstream environmentalism while assessing the healthfulness of places of daily human life, labor, and leisure (DiChiro 301, 305–6). Through grassroots action rather than top-down management, both movements direct much of their energy toward the problem of human dwelling, widening their purview beyond that of traditional preservationists. They see that environmental problems and solutions have varied cultural consequences. However, bioregionalists still need to reorient the self-place relationship they champion to account for problems of space, class, and race that undermine sustainable dwelling.

In this essay, I assess the potential and limitations of bioregionalist theory and literature from an environmental justice viewpoint. I propose that Lorna Dee Cervantes's poem "Freeway 280" and other poems by contemporary Chicano/a writers exemplify the urban and minority literatures that must be recognized alongside traditional bioregionalist nature writing for the movement to be truly inclusive and effective. "Freeway 280" productively fuses key theoretical tenets of bioregionalism and environmental justice by illustrating how race and class inform self-place relationships. In contrast to most works discussed by bioregionalist literary critics, the poem imagines the city, rather than the wilderness or countryside, as a site of sustenance, cultural and ecological memory, human and nonhuman resistance to destructive development, and place-based identity: core bioregionalist values and practices.

PEOPLE COLOR PLACES: MOVING BIOREGIONALISM BEYOND UNIVERSALISM

Illuminating the often-interconnected ways in which nonhuman nature and minorities are oppressed, an environmental justice perspective contributes a crucial ethical component to bioregionalism. For bioregionalism to proceed as a culturally and ecologically sustainable grassroots movement, it must attend to the social inequalities that shape people's relationships with their surroundings rather than setting its sights on a colorblind utopia. Presuming that engaging with place is a "realistic sort of occupation anyone can participate in every day" (48), Sale advances a localized, geographically nuanced—but universally human—endeavor that overlooks the culturally mediated complexities of gathering knowledge about place and feeling rooted. African Americans living in neighborhoods adjacent to toxic waste dumps or polluting factories, residents of high-crime neighborhoods, single parents working two minimum-wage jobs, communities displaced by development, and the homeless, for example, may find more barriers to connecting with place than avenues to doing so.[1] Although Sale envisions cooperative bioregional communities that value diversity and expresses concern that "diversity . . . is a complex and possibly problematic phenomenon" that cannot simply be embraced as an "easy lip-service concept," he does not move beyond this lip service (101–4, 107).[2] Even more idealistically focused on a socially just end goal, Snyder conjectures that "a non-nationalistic idea of community, in which commitment to pure place is paramount, cannot be ethnic or racist. . . . anyone of any race, language, religion, or origin is welcome, as long as they live well on the land" (*A Place* 233–34). Anyone "is welcome"—but what will the transformation to an economy where even

the marginalized can "live well on the land" look like, and whose voices
will shape it? Snyder's statement implies that edicts have been established,
and those who agree to follow them will be admitted. The geographer
Dianne Meredith warns of this potential for exclusion, explaining that
imposed ideas of place-based identity tend toward the nostalgic or utopian,
and they often reproduce hierarchical structures of mainstream environmentalism, ignoring those subject to environmental injustices (Meredith
90–91). In the absence of minority voices, Sale's claim that "the project of
understanding place is neither nostalgic nor utopian" (48) loses force.

As environmental studies scholars have pointed out, nature is socially
constructed, though it retains nonhuman and human-influenced material
dimensions (Soper 22–24); similarly, ethnic studies and feminist scholars
have cautioned that while race- and gender-based identity categories are
socially constructed, they have significant material consequences (Moya
7–8). Dissolving nationalism and re-essentializing identity—by inserting
place as "the sole cause or determinant constituting the social meanings of
an individual's experience" (Moya 3)—will not resolve social inequities.[3]
Rather, bioregionalists must examine how multiple and shifting identity
affiliations inform relationships with place. Self-place connections are important; a sense of well-being and an investment in place are affected by
whether people feel grounded, as bioregionalists point out, and whether
they feel mobile, as social justice critics contend.

URBAN PLACE: THE
BIOREGIONALIST COMMITMENT

Whereas mainstream environmentalist organizations commonly disregard
or criticize city dwellers, especially the urban poor, "the predicament of the
'sustainable' city becomes one of the primary concerns" for environmental
justice activists, since most minorities live in cities (DiChiro 314), and for
bioregionalists, who assess cities as one piece of the regional puzzle of sustainability. Snyder declares, "To neglect the city (in our hearts and minds for
starters) is deadly" (*The Practice* 114); likewise, Sale proclaims, "Human life,
to be fully human, needs the city" as well as the countryside (Schumacher
qtd. in Sale 114)—promising departures from environmentalist discourse
painting cities and their residents "as the repositories of waste, garbage,
vermin, disease, and depravity" (DiChiro 314). Although some bioregionalists idealize small-scale development or rural living, many, including San

Francisco–dweller and movement-founder Peter Berg, have advocated for cities as sites of resource efficiency and vibrant human life since the 1970s. The "Green City Project" grew out of Berg's Planet Drum Foundation in 1986 ("Planet Drum," par. 9), and the North American Bioregional Congress established a Green Cities committee at their second convention the same year (Aberley 28). Detailing ways to "ecologize" urban areas, Green City plans are ambitious and varied in their strategies, which range from developing urban food and energy sources to reducing noise pollution to reestablishing land belts with native plants (see Cholette et al. 103; Sale 45, 117–18; Berg, "More" 15, "A Green" 107–8; Snyder, *The Practice* 43).

Moreover, bioregionalists outline cognitive and creative shifts necessary for achieving urban sustainability. Arguing that "the crucial and perhaps only and all-encompassing task is to understand *place*, the immediate specific place where we live," Sale details technical knowledge and solutions relevant to urban dwellers: the intellectual awareness needed to live sustainably (42). He elaborates that the city "could be" a center for trade, services, and the arts, emphasizing technical aspects of urban dwelling but acknowledging imaginative cultural elements as well (45). Similarly, Snyder details cities' ecological components and envisions "Great Brown Bear . . . walking with us, Salmon swimming upstream with us, as we stroll a city street" (*The Practice* 110, 94). His images of urban nonhuman nature emphasize that stereotypical components of city, country, and wilderness continually weave in and out of different spaces, both physically and psychologically.

However, Sale and Snyder, two of the most widely read bioregionalists, have not consistently fused transformative green-cities strategies with the place-based identities and ethical dwelling practices essential to their vision. When it comes to the moral component of inhabitation, for example, both writers revert to valuing the countryside or wilderness over the city. After outlining the city's potential as a cultural center, Sale reproduces the "gulf" between city and country that he himself criticizes: he identifies the countryside as the site of an "earthier voice," "the place of memory, where those closest to the land remember the ways and carry on the traditions of the bioregion, so that the Gaean values are never lost and the urbanites may ever be reminded of ecological reality" (114–15). Sale directs urban dwellers to understand place and live with the land but simultaneously suggests they are too distant from the land to be adequate caretakers of ecological "values" or even to be aware of "reality." For Sale, the source of bioregional identity is the countryside. This view is problematic not only for the socio-spatial hierarchy it reinforces (wherein country dwellers are morally sound and city dwellers deficient), but also for its naturalization of the countryside, which is as much a humanized, materially and conceptually produced place as is the city. Likewise, Snyder rends apart cities and nonhuman nature—and privileges the latter—in his poem "Really the Real," designating a rural wildlife refuge as the repository of authentic meaning, "*really* the real, world" (line 47), in contrast to the nearby city of Davis, California.

In short, Sale and Snyder at times balance precariously over a chasm between sustainable reconstitution of the city and reclamation of self, voice, and reality outside of it. If the purpose of Green Cities projects is to reground the metropolis in its "ecological reality," then urbanites will create and discover these realities all around them, just as they might encounter them in the countryside, in the subalpine forest, or in the dump—and just as Berg contends ("Growing" 141–42) and Snyder hopes elsewhere in his writing (*The Practice* 25).

URBAN BIOREGIONAL LITERATURE: LORNA DEE CERVANTES'S "FREEWAY 280"

With its endless possibilities for imagining place and self, literature provides fertile ground for urban bioregional creative productions and theoretical analysis, yet bioregionalist literary critics have been slow to recognize this potential. Instead, the literature associated with the movement has been limited to rural and wilderness settings. In one of the first published essays on literary bioregionalism, Paul Lindholdt restricts the field to nature writing: "bioregionalism becomes a useful critical orientation insofar as it informs the mass of writing tied so intimately to nature. . . . Admittedly, such an approach would have scarce bearing on the likes of Henry James, Edith Wharton, and many of the postmodernists, alienated by the natural world or, at the very least, separated from its embrace" (122–23). However, if we overlook urban or postmodernist writers, we miss a great deal of the human experience of place, and we have little hope of understanding the conditions that do alienate people from "the natural world." Michael Kowalewski, in his essay "Bioregional Perspectives in American Literature," published two years earlier, acknowledges the need for writers to account for "urban or suburbanized landscapes (where the majority of Americans now reside)," but he primarily discusses the nature writing of Thoreau and

Emerson, and he claims that "the roots of a bioregional vision of human identity" can be found in the works of "[w]riters like Gary Snyder, Barry Lopez, Wallace Stegner, and Wendell Berry, along with many American Indian and Latino authors" (42, 31). Although Kowalewski gestures beyond the Anglo-American canon, he marginalizes these writers in lumped categories while naming individual white authors. In most criticism labeled bioregionalist, the participatory ethic Sale exalts—which surely has the potential for inclusivity—remains hierarchical, with privilege granted to, and guidelines determined by, rural dwellers, wilderness backpackers, the leisured class, and the racially privileged.[4]

Lorna Dee Cervantes's poem "Freeway 280," first published in 1977 and reprinted in her 1981 collection *Emplumada*, illuminates politics of everyday, urban Chicano/a life that most bioregional analyses overlook, and amplifies marginalized voices they silence. Raised in a San Jose, California, barrio, Cervantes declares that poetry saved her life, paving a path away from street gang violence (Moyers 38), nurturing her, and "politiciz[ing]" her (González 177, 165). A highly regarded poet, Cervantes was also the first to publish many now well-known Chicano/a poets in her journal *Mango* in the 1970s. Her American Book Award–winning *Emplumada* presents varied portraits of place, within and beyond the home and the barrio. Cervantes depicts poverty, violence, racism, ignorance, and the dual oppression of the people and the land, as well as hopes, dreams, sustaining relationships, connections to the natural world, and the development of her poetic and political voice.

"Freeway 280" describes a site where homes were razed for the freeway's construction near San Jose: part of the Sacramento–San Joaquin River watershed, which might be broadly termed the "northern California bioregion . . . ringed by mountains on the north, east, and south and . . . the Pacific Ocean on the west" (Berg and Dasmann 400), or more specifically, the "Bay Area/Delta Bioregion" ("Geo Area"). Although the land has been marred and the residents displaced, plants regrow and people return for nourishment of both body and psyche. Cervantes documents the cognitive, creative, and ethical inhabitation Snyder calls for; moreover, she shows that realizing each of these elements requires joint action of humans and nonhuman nature. Painting a nuanced picture of the contingencies shaping human relationships to place, she moves bioregionalist conversations beyond their universalist assumptions about identity. Cervantes presents the difficulties but also the possibilities of impoverished minority communities' producing urban bioregional knowledge crucial to sustainable regional life and food justice.

The poem's first image—of urban homes adjacent to factories, yet surrounded by flowers—establishes a strong sense of interwoven human and nonhuman care for place. Cervantes opens with a description of

> Las casitas near the gray cannery,
> nestled amid wild abrazos of climbing roses
> and man-high red geraniums[.] (lines 1–3)

The "casitas," the little homes, are "nestled" in the roses' "wild abrazos," embraces. The roses, planted and tended by the casita dwellers, nurture the residents in turn. In contrast to their intimate and comforting "nestled" place amongst the flowers, the homes are "near the gray cannery." The neutrality of the word "near" indicates a spatial relationship not of care but of circumstance or functionality. Bursting out against the shadowy image of the "gray cannery," the "red geraniums" are measured in bodily human terms, "man-high," further establishing intimacy between the plants and the people. These few short lines evoke the interrelational, ethical dwelling-in-place that bioregionalists advocate; in this case, it is also intergenerational, as the "red geraniums" and "casitas" recall Cervantes's reference to her grandmother's geraniums and self-built house in "Beneath the Shadow of the Freeway," which appears earlier in *Emplumada* (11–14). Uncharacteristic to bioregionalism, however, this dwelling place is a marginalized barrio community. The poem's grounding image of "las casitas" and the first stanza's most emotional word, "abrazos," both delivered in Spanish, hold not only visual and thematic but also linguistic significance, linking home and care to Chicano/a cultural identity.

Cervantes deftly locates this scene in both the represented physical space of landscape and the psychic space of memory, inscribing the self-place connection, imaginative dwelling, and history of place vital to bioregionalism. After drawing readers into a rooted image, Cervantes delivers a sudden, blunt, forceful disruption of place with a gaping break in meaning and syntax between lines three and four. "Las casitas," we learn,

> are gone now. The freeway conceals it
> all beneath a raised scar. (4–5)

The subjectless beginning of line four, "are gone now," erases the grounded casitas. A new sentence begins midline, turning from the emptiness of the phrase "are gone now" to an image of the freeway, an active agent that "conceals," in contrast to the passive homes that simply "are gone." However, the erasure of the casitas is incomplete. That the phrase "are gone now" occupies a new line, and the houses and plants still stand in the separate space of the first three lines, grants an immediate and enduring presence to the vibrant image of sustainably intertwined nature and culture. Imaginatively immune to its temporal physical absence, this poetic presence manifests the history "of how both the human and natural possibilities of the region have been explored," which Sale implores his readers to excavate (45). In this case, the history is no more visible for its being recent; even to an onlooker who might see past the freeway, the landscape below appears to be an empty space of "abandoned lots" (7). Thus, Cervantes's poetic account of the houses demonstrates how an imaginative space can bring material consequences of development into focus; she demands that her readers see a place of displacement, where landscape and memory together define place and presence.

Furthermore, although this place is now home to an intrusive freeway, sustaining human-nature relationships rematerialize. Underneath the "scar" of the freeway, plant tissues begin to heal the wounded landscape:

> . . . new grasses sprout,
> wild mustard remembers, old gardens
> come back stronger than they were,
> trees have been left standing in their yards. (7–10)

The wild and the cultivated—the mustard and the gardens—regrow together in this urban landscape. Moreover, the trees have reclaimed the abandoned space; although the possessive pronoun "their" may refer to the unnamed community or to the "old gardens," the last subject referred to as "they," it is more directly linked to the trees. Thus, Cervantes grants agency to the plants and ownership of the yards to the trees.

In fact, nonhuman nature is central to this city scene: no visible human subjects enter the poem until the end of the second stanza, where the people resist their displacement in concert with the plants. Requiring interaction with the natural world, their resistant practices exemplify "place as an experience" (Snyder, *The Practice* 25), rather than as a static image or background to human life. Lindholdt writes that "if the basic problem is displacement, one answer is reinhabitation of our bioregions" (126). Cervantes offers a poetic account of reinhabitation wherein displacement is a result not of urbanites' having strayed from the land but rather of their having been rent away from their homes and gardens. These dispossessed residents reestablish their connections to the land:

> Viejitas come here with paper bags to gather greens.
> Espinaca, verdolagas, yerbabuena . . .[.]" (12–13)

Collected by female elders of the community, these fresh plants (spinach, purslane, and mint) sustain the barrio residents. They strikingly contrast the oppressive "smell of tomatoes burning" (18): the industrialized, commodified, contained (literally, canned) plants of the "gray cannery" (1), where many of the barrio dwellers likely work under the intolerable conditions Cervantes describes in "Cannery Town in August" (*Emplumada* 6). Each of Cervantes's lists of plants—first fruit trees (11), then edible greens (13)—ends with an ellipsis, indicating that these are only a few of the plants now flourishing in the lots. The women's harvesting of these plants resists the forgetting and wasting away of the landscape as well as the commodification of food and correspondent production of consumer identities; food justice and the bioregional practice of living off the local land come together beneath the freeway. Furthermore, while documenting the resistant material reclamation of the plants, Cervantes reclaims them linguistically. Presenting both botanical lists in Spanish, she confronts the history of colonizers' dual oppression of the natural world and of Chicano/a language, culture, and identity.[5] In sum, these lists emphasize the intellectual and moral components of dwelling that Snyder advocates: the important local, land-based knowledge of this marginalized Chicano/a community, and the sustaining human-nature relationships that persist even in a seemingly unnatural landscape.[6]

Significantly, Cervantes depicts resistance fueled by both human and nonhuman memory, a radical imaginative gesture that demands re-seeing human and nonhuman roles in reinhabitation. While the women retain and reuse their knowledge of place, the "wild mustard remembers" and regrows. For the plants and the women, this degraded urban land is "the place of memory, where those closest to the land remember the ways and carry on the traditions of the bioregion" (Sale 115). Thus, "Freeway 280" reveals the shortsightedness and exclusivity of Sale's insistence that the countryside serve as the site of memory, where bioregional daily practice can be reinvented. Moreover, by presenting memory as not only a human but also a nonhuman capacity, Cervantes constructs a less anthropocentric Gaean value system than Sale does. Her poem exemplifies and augments Daniel

Berthold-Bond's argument that place is a "relational" construct and that "places and *experiencing subjects* (any being with the capacity for memory, intentionality, and a sense of attachment to and identification with a locale) are inseparable" (17, 15). While plants may not be "experiencing subjects" with the same kind of "intentionality" humans have, they are physically "attach[ed]" to the land. Imagining in the poem's creative space that plants remember their presence in the land, Cervantes grants the nonhuman a role equally important to the human role in reinhabitation, and she suggests that memory has physical as well as intellectual components. She thereby reminds us of the histories of humans' physical placement and their interconnections with other forms of life: the persistent links between the past and present of nature and culture that shape all spaces, wild and urban.

Finally, although the casita-freeway-harvest site does not afford the simple, utopian self-place relationship Sale and Snyder envision, it is a crucial source of identity for the speaker of the poem. The second half of "Freeway 280" shifts from implied memory and observation to first-person experience, revealing the scarred self that fled the scarred landscape:

> I scramble over the wire fence
> that would have kept me out. Once, I wanted out. . . [.] (14–16)

That the poem describes place and community interaction before addressing the individual's sense of self and place suggests that identity can be understood only by considering the multitude of human and nonhuman relationships in which the subject participates. This structure implicitly counters the humanist and Americanist valuation of the individual self over all else as well as essentialist assumptions that identity can be defined outside of cultural and environmental contexts.

For the speaker, who has returned to the urban barrio she once yearned to escape via the freeway, comforting memories of place are counterbalanced by oppressive ones. Crossing the fence, defying the mapped borders of place just as the plants and the viejitas do, the speaker reflects:

> Maybe it's here
> en los campos extraños de esta ciudad
> [the strange fields of this city]
> where I'll find it, that part of me
> mown under
> like a corpse
> or a loose seed. (20–25)

Like the plants, the speaker has been violently overrun by the highway's construction. In her home place, a part of herself has been "mown under," a circumstance that complicates Snyder's idealistic musing, "To know the spirit of a place is to realize that you are a part of a part and that the whole is made of parts, each of which is whole. You start with the part you are whole in" (*The Practice* 38). Many people lay claim to no such place of wholeness and must instead search for understanding of how various fragments of self interact. In selfhood, as in place, the past is never entirely erased.

Rerouting and rerooting herself, Cervantes's speaker returns to "the strange fields of this city" to find the element of self that she is missing. Exactly what she seeks—"it" (22)—remains undefined, an absence that is nonetheless an imagined presence, just as the casitas are. Her return prompts her to consider what finding "that part of [her]" will mean: a death ("corpse") or a potential rebirth ("loose seed"). Cervantes weighs these two options with an inconclusive "or," settling on neither absolute destruction nor simplistic resolution. However, her concluding with the hopeful image of the seed indicates that the speaker may flourish in the city's "strange fields" like the trees, grasses, and greens, and perhaps nurture the community as they do. Envisioning self as seed, Cervantes develops further imaginative connections between nonhuman nature and the human self in the recovery of place and identity. As a "*loose* seed" (25; emphasis mine), this missing part of the self has the potential for both rootedness and mobility. The limited mobility granted by the freeway, with its "rigid lanes" (16), was not the free way to wholeness of self, nor did it liberate the speaker from the place of her past. If the title of the poem erases the casitas like the freeway itself, the poem ultimately reveals that the freeway cannot obliterate self-place connections. Mobility combined with return enables the speaker to imagine possibility for humans and plant life in a place where previously both nature and culture—the ever-present "sun," the "tomatoes burning," the destructive freeway, and the "swing shift in the greasy summer air" (17–19)—had been oppressive. Cervantes illustrates a complicated and still-incomplete process of a community's reclaiming (and an individual's rediscovering) "the 'where' of our 'who are we?'" (Snyder, *A Place* 184).

In her depiction of "the strange fields of this city," Cervantes reveals that if place is linked to self, this relationship is mediated by positionality. "Freeway 280" provides just one example of the many obstacles to affirming self-place relationships. Although the practices Cervantes documents exemplify bioregionalist ethics and paint a hopeful picture of reinhabitation, they should not be romanticized; they are responses to poverty, ways of living in place under even the most difficult circumstances. The poem prompts readers to consider how such daily practices in threatened places might stop being survival responses to oppression and start becoming sustainable ways of life, made viable for more urban dwellers without being recuperated into a consumerist economy that seeks to recommodify all modes of resistance—to turn these vacant lots, for instance, into privatized gardens-for-rent, accessible only to wealthy urban dwellers. What would our cities look like if communities transformed vacant lots into garden commons?

Many more Chicano/a poems offer variations on these urban bioregional themes, finding the "earthier voice" Sale associates with the countryside (114) within the city. Like Cervantes's poem, Pat Mora's "Divisadero Street, San Francisco," for instance, illustrates flourishing, active, boundary-defying urban nature:

> the loud
> orange of nasturtiums running
> unchecked among the prim-
> rose and the purple bursts of lilies of the Nile
> in the cement heart of the city[.] (lines 2–6)

The woman tending this garden has intimate knowledge of nature's cycles— she "sniffs / the pollen-heavy air for last year's bees"—and she declares the land essential to humans' spatial and psychological grounding: "*Lost without dirt*, she says, / so she greens this hidden square" (13–14, 15–16). Mora presents nonhuman nature as integral to the urban self-place connection.

For Alma Luz Villanueva and Luis J. Rodriguez, nonhuman nature and poetic voice rooted in place simultaneously challenge the deadening concrete of San Francisco and Los Angeles, respectively. In "The Harvest," Villanueva, like Cervantes, describes the difficult yet necessary process of revisiting the city:

> . . . when I
> returned . . .
>
> . . . . . .
>
> the city was always
> as it was: cold
> cement and the blossoms
> bursting forth[.] (lines 2–3, 6–9)

These blossoms, "bursting" like Mora's, grow beyond the contained space of "the prescribed / park" (10–11); they "sing / through" (25–26) "the cracks" (24) in "the grey cement" (22), just as the poetic speaker will "sing" (36) "in that crack" (35) after listening to and observing her surroundings (29–36). If the city is at first "cold," it becomes a site of "new connection" (4), new voice, and renewed sustenance grounded in knowledge of place. Though Rodriguez writes of a protest rather than a song in "This Tree, this Poem," he similarly portrays the persistence of nonhuman nature and poetic voice:

> This tree, this poem,
> is smothering in the city's crush.
> It rises through cement cracks
> like the earth invading,
> reminding,
> protesting,
> and demands the sky. (lines 33–39)

Paved cities need not serve as the vision of the future, all four poets indicate: "cracks" in the cement symbolize space for urban changes catalyzed by attentiveness to details of place and acknowledgement of humans' connections to nonhuman nature.

Rodriguez highlights the intertwined well-being of humans and nonhuman nature in his warning that "We make of trees / what we make of ourselves" (48–49). He illustrates this phenomenon in his depiction of the parallel devastation of urban nature and street-dwelling factory workers in the title poem of *The Concrete River*. For these urban workers, the "dried banks / Of a concrete river" (lines 10–11)—the channelized, polluted Los Angeles River—offer an inadequate but necessary site for makeshift shelter: "Home for now. Along an urban-spawned / Stream of muck" (28–29). As in "Freeway 280," Rodriguez's poetic speaker seeks to escape this deficient home—in this case, through inhalant-induced hallucinations and even death. Notably, however, neither Cervantes nor Rodriguez accept escape from the city as a viable solution, no matter how damaged and damaging the city may be.

Indicating that humans must remake the cities that have suffocated them, Villanueva directly exemplifies Rodriguez's proclamation that "we make of trees / what we make of ourselves" ("This Tree, this Poem" 48–49) in "View from Richmond Bridge," another San Francisco poem. After describing a "hill glow[ing] red / with life" (lines 6–7) at sunset, she asserts that the buildings reflecting the light are "burning and beautiful / but dead" (20–21) and then observes:

> the image of man . . . struggling
> out of a dead tree
> trunk in the city's
> empty lot. (22–25)

Villanueva interrupts the scene with a collage of traditional images of humans and animals carved in wood and molded in clay, all sacred and liberating, fashioned "that we / may soar" (34–45); however, in this city scene, "the body" remains

> . . . locked
> into wood
> staring out
> at the traffic. (49–52)

The juxtaposed uplifting and entrapping human-nature unions of Villanueva's poem encapsulate the urban tension between enlivening and deadening productions of place; these images present humans and the natural world as inseparable, their destinies intertwined.

Whether these poems offer damning accounts of urban destruction, hopeful portraits of burgeoning urban life, or a combination of the two, they point to the need for a much more complex account of the cognitive, creative, and ethical dimensions of bioregionalism, and they counter Sale's claim that "a total understanding of ecological principles . . . is at present so astonishingly lacking" in "urban process[es]" (118). Including urban and minority literatures in the bioregionalist corpus will help ensure that, rather than producing totalizing and potentially violent regional stories, bioregionalism will reach its transformative potential through coalitional activism of diverse communities. Environmental justice must not be simply a goal of bioregionalism, but rather an integral element of its process.

NOTES

1. Several studies document the disproportionate number of toxic facilities in minority neighborhoods (Bullard xv; Bullard et al. x–xi).

2. Notably, Van Andruss, editor of *Home! A Bioregional Reader*, declares, "The problem of racism remains poorly understood in the bioregional movement"

(174). *Home!* contains only two single-page selections addressing racial inequality (78, 162).

3. In fact, nationalism has played crucial roles in civil rights movements (Moya 2) and environmental justice politics, especially within the Chicano/a community, where the metaphorical, and sometimes material, reclamation of Aztlán, mythical ancestral homeland of Chicanos/as, has fueled resistance and built solidarity in the face of the violent history of colonization. Erasing nationalism may mean erasing significant foundations of group identity among marginalized communities.

4. Two recent articles stand out as exceptions to this trend. In "Bringing Nature Writing Home," Karla Armbruster states that "there are limits to how far" traditionally defined "nature writing" "can push readers toward sustainable, intimate relationships with their own places," which may exhibit "geographic and cultural" differences (4). In "Toward a Symbiosis of Ecology and Justice" Tom Lynch advocates "bioregionally informed" environmental justice in his discussion of several writers' accounts of Anglo-Chicano water-rights conflicts in southern Colorado (262–63).

5. For a discussion of this history, see Gloria Anzaldúa, *Borderlands/La Frontera*, and Devon G. Peña, *Mexican Americans and the Environment*.

6. Although Raúl Homero Villa deemphasizes the importance of the agency of the plants in his analysis of "Freeway 280" ("the crucial element here is not simply the resilience of the plant life and its symbolic associations"), he also identifies the importance of "the knowledge the women exercise in identifying and making use of these urban gardens" (218) "for the subsistence and survival of themselves, their families, and their community" (219–20).

WORKS CITED

Aberley, Doug. "Interpreting Bioregionalism: A Story from Many Voices." *Bioregionalism*. Ed. Michael Vincent McGinnis. London: Routledge, 1999. 13–42. Print.

Andruss, Van, Christopher Plant, Judith Plant, and Eleanor Wright, eds. *Home! A Bioregional Reader*. Philadelphia: New Society, 1990. Print.

Anzaldúa, Gloria. *Borderlands / La Frontera: The New Mestiza*. 3rd ed. San Francisco: Aunt Lute, 1999. Print.

Armbruster, Karla. "Bringing Nature Writing Home: Josephine Johnson's *The Inland Island* as Bioregional Narrative." *Reading Under the Sign of Nature: New Essays in Ecocriticism*. Ed. John Tallmadge and Henry Harrington. Salt Lake City: University of Utah Press, 2000. 3–23. Print.

Berg, Peter. "A Green City Program for San Francisco Bay Area Cities and Towns." Andruss et al. 104–9.

————. "Growing a Life-Place Politics." Andruss et al. 137–44.

————. "More Than Just Saving What's Left." Andruss et al. 13–16.

Berg, Peter, and Raymond Dasmann. "Reinhabiting California." *The Ecologist* 7 (1977): 399–410. Print.

Berthold-Bond, Daniel. "The Ethics of 'Place': Reflections on Bioregionalism." *Environmental Ethics* 22.1 (2000): 5–24. Print.

Bullard, Robert D. *Dumping in Dixie: Race, Class, and Environmental Quality.* Boulder, Colo.: Westview, 1990. Print.

Bullard, Robert D., Paul Mohai, Robin Saha, and Beverly Wright. *Toxic Wastes and Race at Twenty: 1987–2007.* Cleveland: United Church of Christ, 2007. Print.

Cervantes, Lorna Dee. *Emplumada.* Pittsburgh: University of Pittsburgh Press, 1981. Print.

————. "Freeway 280." *Latin-American Literary Review* 5 (1977): 175–79. Print.

Cholette, Kathryn, Ross Dobson, Kent Gerecke, Marcia Nozick, Roberta Simpson, and Linda Williams. "Green City: An Introduction." Andruss et al. 103.

DiChiro, Giovanna. "Nature as Community: The Convergence of Environment and Social Justice." *Uncommon Ground: Toward Reinventing Nature* Ed. William Cronon. New York: Norton, 1995. 298–320 Print.

Dodge, Jim. "Living By Life: Some Bioregional Theory and Practice." Andruss et al. 5–12.

"Geo Area—Information by Bioregion." *State of California.* 1994–2005. Web. 19 Mar. 2010. <http://ceres.ca.gov/geo_area/bioregions/index.html>.

González, Sonia V. "Poetry Saved My Life: An Interview with Lorna Dee Cervantes." *MELUS* 32.1 (2007): 163–80. Print.

Kowalewski, Michael. "Bioregional Perspectives in American Literature." *Regionalism Reconsidered: New Approaches to the Field,* Ed. David Jordan. New York: Garland, 1994. 29–46. Print.

Lindholdt, Paul. "Literary Activism and the Bioregional Agenda." *ISLE: Interdisciplinary Studies in Literature and Environment* 3.2 (1996): 121–37. Print.

Lynch, Tom. "Toward a Symbiosis of Ecology and Justice: Water and Land Conflicts in Frank Waters, John Nichols, and Jimmy Santiago Baca." *The Environmental Justice Reader: Politics, Poetics, and Pedagogy.* Ed. Joni Adamson, Mei Mei Evans, and Rachel Stein. Tucson: University of Arizona Press, 2002. 247–64. Print.

Meredith, Dianne. "The Bioregion as a Communitarian Micro-region (and its Limitations)." *Ethics, Place and Environment* 8.1 (2005): 83–94. Print.

Mora, Pat. "Divisadero Street, San Francisco." *Communion.* Houston, Tex.: Arte Público, 1991. 17. Print.

Moya, Paula M. L. "Introduction: Reclaiming Identity." *Reclaiming Identity: Realist Theory and the Predicament of Postmodernism.* Ed. Paula M. L. Moya and

Michael R. Hames-García. Berkeley: University of California Press, 2000. 1–26. Print.

Moyers, Bill, ed. "Lorna Dee Cervantes." *Fooling with Words: A Celebration of Poets and their Craft*. New York: Morrow, 1999. 31–45. Print.

Peña, Devon G. *Mexican Americans and the Environment: Tierra y Vida*. Tucson: University of Arizona Press, 2005. Print.

"Planet Drum Foundation." *The Volunteer Center*. 2010. Web. 19 Mar. 2010. <http://www.thevolunteercenter2.net/org/10287028672.html>.

Rodriguez, Luis J. "The Concrete River." *The Concrete River*. Willimantic, Conn.: Curbstone, 1991. 38–41. Print.

———. "This Tree, This Poem." *The Concrete River*. Willimantic, Conn.: Curbstone, 1991. 118–19. Print.

Sale, Kirkpatrick. *Dwellers in the Land: The Bioregional Vision*. San Francisco: Sierra Club, 1985. Print.

Schumacher, E. F. *Good Work*. New York: Harper, 1979. Print.

Snyder, Gary. *A Place in Space: Ethics, Aesthetics, and Watersheds*. Washington, D.C.: Counterpoint, 1995. Print.

———. *The Practice of the Wild: Essays*. San Francisco: North Point, 1990. Print.

———. "Really the Real." *Danger on Peaks*. Washington, D.C.: Shoemaker & Hoard, 2004. 50–51. Print.

———. "Regenerate Culture!" *Turtle Talk: Voices for a Sustainable Future*. Ed. Christopher Plant and Judith Plant. Philadelphia: New Society, 1990. 12–19. Print.

Soper, Kate. "Nature/'nature.'" *FutureNatural: Nature, Science, Culture*. Ed. George Robertson, Melinda Mash, Lisa Tickner, Jon Bird, and Barry Curtis. London: Routledge, 1996. 22–24. Print.

Villa, Raúl Homero. *Barrio-Logos: Space and Place in Urban Chicano Literature and Culture*. Austin: University of Texas Press, 2000. Print.

Villanueva, Alma Luz. "The Harvest." *Planet, with Mother, May I?* Tempe, Ariz.: Bilingual Press, 1993. 8–10. Print.

———. "View from Richmond Bridge." *Bloodroot*. Austin, Tex.: Place of Herons Press, 1982. 9–10. Print.

ERIN JAMES

Bioregionalism, Postcolonial Literatures, and Ben Okri's The Famished Road

T HE PRIMARY GOAL of this book is to consider what it means to read a text bioregionally. As we ask ourselves this question, it is important to also ask what kind of bioregional literary criticism particular texts can offer. How does the bioregional imagination of one writer differ from the next? How does the place-based aesthetic of one bioregion differ from the next? In this paper I'm particularly interested in considering what contribution postcolonial literatures can make to our growing understanding of bioregional literary criticism. The marriage of the two discourses promises to be fruitful: at first glance bioregionalism and postcolonialism appear to have much in common. Both are interested in critiques of dominant power, be it power that stems from the nation, from imperialism, or from globalization. Both are concerned with the recovery of indigenous knowledge and language. Practitioners of both often have a strong, inherent political stance and have long dealt with accusations of provincialism. Despite these compatibilities, however, bioregional critics have generally overlooked postcolonial texts, limiting their purview to American literature.

Inspired by these common grounds, I approach Ben Okri's award-winning novel *The Famished Road* from a bioregional perspective to question what type of aesthetic is put forward by a postcolonial bioregional imagination. In addition to questioning how Okri's place-based aesthetic may differ from the Western texts studied elsewhere in this collection, I also explore what challenges a postcolonial text might pose to our growing understand-

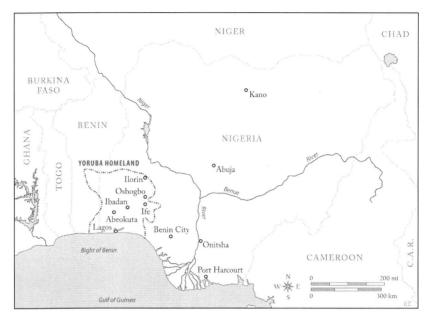

Yoruba Homeland and Niger Delta

ing of bioregional literary criticism, as well as how a bioregional approach may push popular postcolonial readings of Okri's work. The exercise of marrying an emerging sense of bioregional literary criticism with post-colonial literature is important; the global environmental crisis is not limited to one type of place and, as such, we must become skilled at reading place-based aesthetics beyond our own places and cultures. Contemporary environmental pressures emphasize the need to ask how postcolonial literatures prompt us to develop a nuanced and international bioregional criticism that is able to consider how we *and* our neighbors imagine our ecological homes.

POSTCOLONIAL READINGS OF *THE FAMISHED ROAD*

Ben Okri was born in Minna, Nigeria, in 1959, and his career has been heavily influenced by his childhood experiences in civil war–era Nigeria. Although he spent the first ten years of his life in London, he returned to Nigeria in 1969 in time to witness the violence and political corruption that fueled the Biafran War. Funded by a grant from the Nigerian government,

Okri left Nigeria a second time in 1978 to study comparative literature at the University of Essex, England. Since graduation, Okri has produced critically acclaimed poetry, short stories, and novels that explore the tensions of contemporary Nigeria, including the novel *Incidents at the Shrine*, winner of the 1987 Commonwealth Writers Prize (Africa Region); he has also written the short-story collection *Stars of the New Curfew*, short-listed for the Guardian Fiction Prize in 1988, and *The Famished Road*, winner of the 1991 Booker Prize. Okri was awarded an Order of the British Empire in 2001 and continues to live and write in London.

The Famished Road, Okri's best-known work, may seem at first an unusual candidate for a bioregional reading because of its interest in the postmodern and the supernatural: interests that differ from the nature, realism, and empiricism that bioregionalists tend to gravitate towards.[1] The novel describes the experiences of Azaro, a spirit-child who migrates between the world of the living and the world of the dead on the eve of Nigerian independence. Azaro is what is known as an *abiku*, a spirit trickster figure from Yoruba mythology that masquerades as a human baby to repeatedly die and be reborn to the same mother. The Yoruba are a populous Nigerian ethnic group who live in the southwest of the country along the borders of the Niger Delta and neighboring Benin and who conceive of the cosmos as composed of two different yet inseparable realms: *aye*, the world of the living, and *orun*, the spiritual realm of the ancestors, gods, and spirits. Metaphoric crossroads known as the *orita meta* pass between these two worlds, symbolizing the movement of the living to the otherworld and the unborn or ancestors into the world of the living (Drewal 14). Mythical beings such as *abiku* children and celebrants in *egungun* masquerades—a custom in which ancestors return to the living by possessing elaborately costumed dancers—regularly transverse these crossroads.[2]

The *abiku* is a familiar trope of Nigerian writing, appearing most notably in Wole Soyinka's poem "Abiku" and the Half-Child character in his early play *A Dance in the Forests*. Derek Wright notes that in Soyinka's work the *abiku* motif is "interlarded with suggestions of a doomed embryo, a stillborn, newborn innocence and demonic evil" (10). Okri's *abiku* differs from these earlier examples; instead of an evil or doomed spirit who brings sadness to his parents and highlights the cruelty of Nigerian infant mortality rates, Azaro is a child who struggles to stay among the living because he "want[s] to make happy the bruised face of the woman who would become my mother" (*The Famished Road* 5). The spirit world does not share

Azaro's enthusiasm for life, and spirits who attempt to coax him back to the otherworld persistently visit him. Okri's long novel tracks Azaro as he slips between the world of the living and the otherworld in the midst of the political and ecological turmoil leading up to Nigerian independence; it gives voice to the character's prophetic visions of the future, dominated by corrupt politics and environmental devastation.

Postcolonial scholars have found Okri's *abiku* a useful symbol of the struggle for Nigerian independence, as well as a vehicle for the novel's postmodern form that stresses the interaction of Yoruba perceptions of the world with that of Western realism in contemporary Nigeria. Wright is illustrative of critics who read Azaro's *abiku* status as a metaphor for the as-yet independent nation of Nigeria: "Read through the *abiku*'s round of premature, inopportune deaths, postcolonial Africa is at the same time a case of arrested political development and a resilient survivalist, a latter-day Lazarus who keeps coming back from the dead when the modern world has given him up" (10). For Wright, the *abiku* tradition provides Okri with a sophisticated symbol for the struggles of Nigeria to establish a viable and peaceful independent government. In his reading of Okri's *abiku*, Olatubosun Ogunsanwo argues that the figure is a distinctly postmodern vehicle that allows Okri's protagonist to observe the goings-on around him in a social realist manner but also continually slip into an otherworld that disturbs this realism. For Ogunsanwo, the *abiku* is essential to the novel's form, made fragmented and dreamlike by its "astonishingly swift shift[s] from the conventional verisimilar description of the world of discrete things in the Western manner of narration to the mythopoetic description of the 'other reality'" (43). The *abiku* is thus not only symbolic of Nigerian politics, but also of the multicultural interactions of contemporary Nigeria, illustrated by the pastiche of Western and African literary modes Ogunsanwo reads in Okri's text.

Ogunsanwo is not alone in associating *The Famished Road* with postmodernism. Other critics, such as Wright and John C. Hawley, argue that the novel's juxtaposition of Western realism with the Yoruba mythology of the *abiku* is best interpreted as a postmodern critique of the dominance of Western ideas of truth, history, and identity.[3] Hawley bases his interpretation on comments from Okri himself, in which the writer states a "true invasion takes place not when a society has been taken over by another society in terms of infrastructure, but in terms of its mind and its dreams and its myths, and its perceptions of reality" (qtd. in Hawley 32). Resistance to this invasion of perception leads Okri to favor a Yoruba aesthetic that is "not something that is bound only to place" but "bound to a way of looking at the world . . . in more than three dimensions" (qtd. in Hawley 31). Such an approach, Hawley argues, "moves African literature closer to the postmodern movement" (31). Wright agrees, arguing that the novel contains "many of the features, techniques and devices of what, internationally, goes under the name of 'postmodernist' fiction," including unstable fictional ontologies and the problematic treatment of the relations between fiction and history (7). Stressing the way it resists Western versions of truth and history, readings interested in *The Famished Road*'s postmodern elements position Okri's text as an eloquent statement of cultural politics in postcolonial Nigeria.

THE FAMISHED ROAD AS A BIOREGIONAL TEXT

Missing from these readings of *The Famished Road* as postmodern national allegory is a consideration of the novel's treatment of a local sense of place. Indeed, some postcolonial readers criticize Okri's novel for its lack of local specificity. Eleni Coundouriotis, for example, states that the novel "presents us with distinct spaces, but no real places. . . . [Okri] describes outdoor spaces with no distinct contours, no recognizable geography" (41). Coundouriotis' reading is concerned with the "absence of a sense of place" in Okri's text: a result, she argues, of the problematic lack of historical memory addressed through the text's postmodern critique of Western hegemony and realism (41).

Coundouriotis' reading, however, fails to appreciate the specifications of place present in Okri's novel, both encoded in the postmodern form of the novel and clear in the biological realism presented in that form.[4] Indeed, we can even read Okri's postmodernism as *integral* to his place-based aesthetic. Azrao's travels between the world of the living and the otherworld form an important basis of Okri's questioning of Western hegemonies, as they disturb the perception of reality offered by Western versions of history and literary realism. Yet I suggest these seemingly strange and unfamiliar elements of Okri's texts, including spirits ranging from monstrous beasts to the ghost of a policeman's son, do not detract from a local sense of place but offer a local version of realism rooted in a site-specific understanding of culture and environment. It is in this local realism that Okri finds an alternative perception of reality to that of the West, a point stressed by

Anjali Roy when she states that the Yoruba reality portrayed by Okri—
spirits included—is only unreal to some: Okri's novel "looks at the world
from a particular African point of view, the Yoruba, which is presented
as a holistic, self-contained 'culture of totality' independent of Europe's
theories" (25). Hawley concurs with the idea that Okri's novel offers Yoruba
realism when he writes, "We are dealing with a type of realism here . . . but
the world that shapes [Okri's] character's consciousness is shaped by a non-
Western mythology, an animistic appreciation of a surging and constantly
transmogrifying reality" (36).

Essential to a bioregional reading, the aesthetic Okri derives from a Yoruba perspective of reality is firmly rooted in the topography and biology
of southwest Nigeria. Maggi Phillips, in the closest thing to a bioregional
reading of *The Famished Road*, argues that Okri's attempt to undermine
notions of an empirically founded realism is rooted in an important element of the Nigerian landscape: the river (169). Phillips notes that rivers
are essential in West Africa as sources of food and communal well-being
and likens the postmodern form of *The Famished Road*, with its indirect
and flowing narrative and emphasis on plurality and convergence, to the
river itself. "Technically then," she argues, "Okri shapes his narratives with
structural elements that highlight phenomenal multiplicity, simultaneity
and flux, all of which can be seen to accentuate the river-like, non-linear
quality of the writing" (173). Phillips' reading of the novel's form as mim-
icking the movement of a river suggests an emphasis should be read in
Okri's statement that his aesthetic is "not something that is *only* bound to
place" (qtd. in Hawley 31; my emphasis). Okri's aesthetic may be tightly
bound to seeing the world in new ways via new perceptions, but the perception he does offer is also one clearly rooted in the Yoruba homeland of
Southwest Nigeria.

In addition to its mimetic representation of the river, the strange sense of
indirectness and nonlinearity created by Okri's postmodern form is aided
by his depiction of the region's climate.[5] During the annual dry season of
harmattan the sun is so relentless that it obstructs the view; as Azaro notes,
"[s]ometimes it seemed that the brightness of the sun burned people out
of reality" (*The Famished Road* 270). In addition to hiding things from
view, the harshness of the sun distorts what can be seen: "The sun was
remorseless. Shadows were deep. Where the sun was brightest, objects were
blackest. Antagonists and protagonists twisted in an extraordinary dance
and all I could make out were the confusing shapes of glistening bodies

moving in and out of visibility. The lights made everything unreal" (242). The sun throws light that creates fantastic images, adding to the reader's sense of dislocation. The relentless precipitation of the region's rainy season functions in a similar way, at times making things appear alien, and at other times completely obstructing Azaro's vision: "It poured down so hard that sometimes I couldn't see. . . . The forest was distorted. The houses quivered" (286). The weather conditions Okri describes are certainly not fantastic: southern Nigeria is known for its harsh sun and heavy rains. The weather is locally accurate, helping to lend a sense of meteorological realism to Okri's novel and explain the seeming nonreality of its postmodern form as rooted in a realistic depiction of a specific place and climate.

Finally, the link between Okri's postmodern interests and his place-based aesthetic is strengthened by *The Famished Road*'s biological realism. Although the novel's setting is never specified, critics like Ato Quayson and Brenda Cooper have long read Okri's text as set in Nigeria because of its focus on the political corruption surrounding the forthcoming independence elections, as well as the writer's own Nigerian roots.[6] A more precise identification of the novel's setting, however, is indicated by the species Okri mentions. The novel features over one hundred and thirty species of flora and fauna, ranging from those familiar to a Western reader— chickens, dogs, and tomatoes—to those more easily associated with a Nigerian setting—flame-lily, baobab, and yam. The flora Azaro finds as he explores the forest that borders his ghetto, such as mistletoe and palm, obeche, iroko, rubber, and mahogany, help to localize *The Famished Road* to tropical Africa.[7] The fauna Okri mentions, including the antelope and the duiker, help to localize the text even further to the Yoruba home of the southwest part of Nigeria's rainforest, which is particularly known for these two species, both endangered by hunting pressure.[8] These species are mentioned at integral parts of the novel—iroko and obeche trees feature heavily in an extended "otherworld" scene in which Azaro confronts a beast reminiscent of that in W. B. Yeats' "The Second Coming" (242–48), and a duiker is released from its sacrificial captivity as Azaro's father confronts political thugs (466–67)—reinforcing the need to read *The Famished Road*'s biological realism in the local context of its Yoruba worldview.

The Famished Road stresses the importance of form in bioregional readings. This focus on form, raised here and in additional essays in this collection,[9] stands to become an important aspect of bioregional literary criticism of all texts, not just postcolonial ones. In Okri's case, a bioregional reading sensitive to the nuances of *The Famished Road*'s form shows Okri's postmodernism not as distancing his writing from the realistic depictions of nature usually associated with bioregionalism, but rather as integral to his place-based aesthetic. The novel's form, illustrative of postmodern concepts of nonlinearity and plurality, is mimetic of aspects of its topography and meteorology, and the species featured in Okri's work add a biological realism essential to a bioregional reading. Azaro's movement between the world of the living and the otherworld and the juxtaposition of Western realism and Yoruba mythology created by his *abiku* status not only make important claims about the interaction of cultures in postcolonial Nigeria, but also help Okri accurately depict a bioregional imagination of a southwest Nigeria Yoruba homeland.

THREATS TO A PLACE-BASED AESTHETIC

In addition to its interest in postmodernism, *The Famished Road* may also appear an unusual candidate for a bioregional reading because of Okri's interest in movement. While writers associated with bioregionalism such as Gary Snyder emphasize the importance of staying rooted in the bioregions they live and work in,[10] Okri is not "rooted" in the bioregion he depicts. Okri was raised and educated in both the U.K. and Nigeria and currently lives and writes in London; thus, his biography straddles lines of geography and culture and often informs the metaphorical and literal border crossings that frequent his work. This interest in movement is clear in *The Famished Road*, in which Okri's characters—both botanical and human, and threatened by both political and environmental pressures—have a difficult time staying still.

In his essay "Toward a Cosmopolitan Bioregionalism," Mitchell Thomashow is interested in the movement caused by a problem increasingly common to postcolonial communities: environmental refugeeism. Arguing that the problem of global refugeeism is increasingly acute, Thomashow urges bioregionalists to consider the relationships between species and humans who are forced to move due to environmental pressures such as deforestation. In an age of changing climates, we can extend Thomashow's concerns to also embrace those regions affected by the drought, rising sea levels, and natural disasters associated with global warming and increasingly familiar to postcolonial bioregions. Indeed, Thomashow's concerns are particularly relevant to residents of southwest Nigeria: in a 1993 study, "Environmental

Refugees in a Globally Warmed World," Norman Myers notes that roughly half of the world's ten million environmental refugees at the end of the twentieth century were from sub-Saharan Africa and goes on to predict that worldwide environmental refugee numbers could rise as high as 150 million by the year 2050 (758). The threat of environmental refugeeism is particularly high in coastal and delta areas such as the Niger Delta due to sea-level rises and storm surges, as well as regions susceptible to drought such as north and west Africa. Concerns of environmental refugeeism have only increased since Myers' study, with a recent report based on a UN study estimating that up to a billion people may be forced to relocate in the next fifty years as the effects of climate change worsen (Guterres).

Stating that "having a homeland will represent a profound privilege" in the twenty-first century, Thomashow poses important challenges to bioregionalists, asking, "[H]ow are those rooted in place-based communities to be allowed to become aware of their collective responsibility to lend support to those who are caught in diasporas? . . . how are the scale of dislocation and the correspondence between threats to biodiversity, to cultural integrity and to human survival to be shown?" (123). One approach to Thomashow's challenges is to turn to literature for answers. Ben Okri's work not only shows us what environmental change and consequent refugeeism looks like from a bioregional perspective, but also stresses that postcolonial unrootedness is not simply a local problem. Through his metaphorical writing on forced migration and refugeeism in *The Famished Road* and its sequel *Infinite Riches*, Okri both points to our collective responsibility in the creation of diasporas and shows how a local imagination of such problems is illustrated.

The environmental refugeeism of *The Famished Road* is largely metaphorical, as it is confined to the trees that border Azaro's ghetto. Okri's protagonist is disturbed by the destruction of the forests he often wanders and envisions the clearings in a way that emphasizes the bloodiness of the act: "The clearing was the beginning of an expressway. Building companies had levelled the trees. In places the earth was red. We passed a tree that had been felled. Red liquid dripped from its stump as if the tree had been a murdered giant whose blood wouldn't stop flowing" (16). Sap becomes blood in Okri's depiction of deforestation, with the trees themselves personified as dying giants. Azaro envisions the trees fleeing this violence. He sees the plants "retreat screaming into the blue earth" and notes "[i]t took longer to get far into the forest. It seemed the trees, feeling that they were losing the argument with human beings, had simply walked deeper into the forest" (457, 104). The loss of the forest is traumatic for plant and human alike and in humanizing the trees Okri makes clear both the brutality of environmental degradation and its link to forced migration.

The metaphorical threat of environmental refugeeism in *The Famished Road* becomes literal in its sequel, *Infinite Riches*. In this later text, Azaro watches as "[a]nimals gasped for breath in the undergrowth" and worries about the "rising seas and shrinking forests . . . [and] the unstable earth and misery to come" (94, 109). Misery comes in the form of a devastating heat wave that kills twenty people and threatens to displace many others, symbolized by a wandering spirit:

> And the Wandering Spirit, released from its dream of centuries, went from city to city, from country to country. And then, because it was permanently homeless, it began to roam the entire world, spreading its erratic heatwaves and spontaneous combustions and curious weather conditions wherever circumstances were favourable. It created droughts, extended desert spaces in lands of rich vegetation, and created roads on which nothing would grow and along which the god of chaos would travel. And it mingled with the other negative forces released in the new times, and found affinities with the pollutions and radiations of the century. (142)

The wandering spirit—formed by the industrial dreams of the past two hundred years and now affecting weather conditions the world over—is a clear metaphor for climate change, and the droughts that turn formerly fertile land into deserts is the exact threat faced by many in contemporary Nigeria. Affected by the global environmental crisis, the characters of *Infinite Riches* find it impossible to stay rooted.

Of course, the fact that Okri illustrates climate change as a wandering, permanently homeless spirit should not go unnoticed in a bioregional reading. I've tried to point to the bioregional importance of spirits in Okri's texts, as they are both a formal tool of the writer's postmodern critique of Western hegemony and a central aspect of his bioregional imagination. Here the tables are turned. Instead of symbolizing indigenous Yoruba culture, a spirit, originating in the industrialized West, poses a direct threat to the indigenous spirits rooted in Okri's forests. In this metaphor of climate change, the bioregional formula of "wandering = bad; rootedness = good" resurfaces with a twist. Unable to stay rooted, the species and humans of Okri's text are forced to migrate because of centuries of industrial abuse.

They should not be judged for leaving, but read as an illustration of the difficulty of staying rooted in this postcolonial place. Beyond this, Okri's text shows us that postcolonial unrootedness is a collective problem. The wandering spirit is in large part the doing of the industrialized West—a revelation that stresses the importance of cooperation of all regions in the type of climate change policy that will prevent unrooted environmental chaos, as well as put a stop to the deforestation and pollution that aids its spread.

THE NECESSITY OF
POSTCOLONIAL BIOREGIONALISM

This essay imagines what a bioregional reading that considers postcolonial literatures and perspectives might look like. The exercise is important, for what is at stake is an understanding of how place is lived in and imagined around the world: an understanding that international environmental policy depends on. Through my reading of Okri's work, I've tried to show that postmodern literature and bioregional literary criticism can complement each other to make important statements about what it means to live-in-place outside of North America. I want to stress that bioregional literary criticism needs to develop sensitivities to reading aesthetics of place that do not correspond with those easily recognized by a Western sense of realism and rootedness. Okri's work shows us that attention to form can be an important aspect of such reading, for it is at this level of the text that much of his bioregional imagination is encoded; Okri's postmodern form does not distance his work from nature, but provides a sophisticated image of what it is like to live in a community in which the indigenous environment and culture is affected by the legacy of colonization. In addition, *The Famished Road*'s metaphorical depiction of climate change and Okri's personal experience as a Nigerian writer living and writing in London suggests that bioregional literary criticism should be alert to threats to the rootedness associated with a place-based aesthetic, whether the result of worldwide actions manifesting themselves in environments vulnerable to the effects of climate change or of movement within postcolonial diasporas.

The exercise of considering what type of bioregional imagination is offered up by a postcolonial text is not only important to the development of bioregional literary criticism, but also for literary criticism at large. Bioregionalists stand to gain crucial insights from bioregional imaginations in postcolonial literatures, and postcolonial scholars equally stand to gain from engaging with bioregional ideas. The celebration of migration and cosmopolitanism has long been a staple of much postcolonial scholarship, but a bioregional perspective can illuminate the importance of paying attention to place. In Okri's novel, such attention to place helps to specify the location of Azaro's wanderings, as well as suggest an alternative reading of local realities—largely defined by fears of environmental destruction—to accompany the popular metaphorical reading of *The Famished Road* as Nigerian national allegory. The fresh interpretation of Okri's novel made available by a bioregional perspective promises to extend our understanding of many additional postcolonial texts, be they those similarly concerned with postmodern ideas and form, such as Amos Tutuola's *Palm-Wine Drinkard*, Wilson Harris's *The Palace of the Peacock*, or Salman Rushdie's *Midnight's Children*; or others from the postcolonial canon, such as Chinua Achebe's *Things Fall Apart* (which, like *The Famished Road*, includes discussions of indigenous mythology in its representation of local realism) or Jamaica Kincaid's *A Small Place*, which shares Okri's interest in documenting the environmental destruction of formerly colonized regions by Western industry.

Indeed, the new insights provided by a bioregional perspective would go far to answer recent calls within the academy for such work, such as Rob Nixon's argument that "the isolation of postcolonial literary studies from environmental concerns has limited the field's intellectual reach" (247). With its critique of dominant powers, strong political stance and interest in the recovery of indigenous knowledge and practice, bioregionalism offers postcolonial scholars a useful tool in linking narratives of human history with considerations of ecology and contemporary environmental pressures. Such work is not only interesting but necessary, as a global environmental crisis demanding cooperative solutions requires us to better understand how place is imagined and lived in around the world.

NOTES

1. Although little bioregional work on postmodern literature exists, Jim Cheney's argument that bioregionalism *is* postmodern is a notable example. Cheney sees bioregionalism as postmodern in the sense that it encourages us to pay attention to local myths based in place: myths that can help resist the totalizing and es-

sentialist identities promoted by modernist ideas of "'Truth.'" See "Postmodern Environmental Ethics."

2. *Egungun* masquerades are mentioned several times in *The Famished Road*. Examples include Azaro's landlord, who looks like "a travesty of an Egungun" after losing his clothing in a crowd (125), the spirit that breaks into Azaro's house following a bar fight—"the great monstrous Egungun, belching white smoke from seven ears, bursting into our room and devouring us all with his bloodied mouth" (228)—and pictures from a fishing festival depicting *Egunguns* that are "bizarre, fantastic, and big: some were very ugly; others were beautiful like those maidens of the sea who wear an eternal smile of riddles" (263).

3. There is also a significant tradition of reading *The Famished Road* as a magic realist text. Because magic realism is a mode often concerned with hybridity and crossing boundaries, these readings tend to focus on Okri's work as existing on the margins, inhabiting the borders between perceptions, cultures and identities. See Brenda Cooper's *Magical Realism in West African Fiction* and Gerald Gaylard's *After Colonialism.*

4. For example, even though Coundouriotis discusses scenes that heavily features duikers and antelopes, she fails to appreciate the significance of these species to southwest Nigeria (see discussion in the following paragraphs of this essay).

5. This is a point also discussed by Phillips. In her analysis of the novel's climate, Phillips is more interested in humidity than sunlight. She argues the humidity "provides Okri with an alternate means through which to test the parameters of vision while remaining true to the sensations of invasive humidity experienced by tropical climes" (175). Of the novel's rain, she writes: "Clearly, the solidity of objects and, by extension, of reality tends to be destablized when seen through the rain and this tendency fits well into Okri's project" (175).

6. See *Strategic Transformations in Nigerian Writing* and "Landscapes, Forests and Borders Within the West African Global Village," respectively.

7. Robert Smith, in *Kingdoms of the Yoruba*, identifies the oil-palm bush as an important crop in the forests traditionally inhabited by the Yoruba (7); K. M. Buchanan and J. C. Pugh stress the prevalence of mahogany of the high forests of the same area in *Land and People in Nigeria* (35).

8. Jan Lodewijk R. Were, in a study for the World Wildlife Fund, labels this region the "Nigerian Lowland Forests" ecoregion. Although it lacks many endemic species, it is known for antelopes and duikers in particular. Both species appear in Okri's novel: a duiker is featured heavily in the fight scene that concludes *The Famished Road*, while antelopes are mentioned throughout.

9. For additional discussions of the importance of form to bioregional readings in this collection, see Christine Cusick's interpretation of Tim Robinson's Connemara writing, in which she highlights the way Robinson's ambulatory and cor-

poreal prose style reflects the bioregion it depicts; Harry Vandervlist's exploration of Jon Whyte's unfinished poem *Minisniwapta*, which he suggests mimics the topography of the Bow River in its meandering form; and Ruth Blair's reading of Beverly Farmer's *The Seal Woman*, in which she detects the novel's emphasis on an interconnected and weblike ecological worldview through narrative techniques such as the stitching together of disparate fragments of time and citing verbatim pieces of other kinds of texts (newspapers, magazines, etc.).

10. See, for example, Snyder's "The Place, the Region and the Commons" or Scott Russell Sanders's *Staying Put*.

WORKS CITED

Buchanan, K. M., and J. C. Pugh. *Land and People in Nigeria: The Human Geography of Nigeria and Its Environmental Background.* London: University of London Press, 1961. Print.

Cheney, Jim. "Postmodern Environmental Ethics: Ethics as Bioregional Narrative." *Environmental Ethics* 11 (1989): 117–34. Print.

Cooper, Brenda. "Landscapes, Forests and Borders within the West African Global Village." *Mapping the Sacred: Religion, Geography and Postcolonial Literatures.* Ed. Jamie S. Scott and Paul Simpson Housley. Amsterdam: Rodopi, 2001: 275–93. Print.

———. *Magical Realism in West African Fiction: Seeing With a Third Eye.* London: Routledge, 2004. Print.

Coundouriotis, Eleni. "Landscapes of Forgetfulness: Reinventing the Historical in Ben Okri's The Famished Road." *The Post-Colonial Condition of African Literature* Vol. 6. Ed. Daniel Gover, John Conteh-Morgan, and Jane Bryce. Trenton, N.J.: Africa World Press, 2000: 41–48. Print.

Drewal, Henry John, and John Pemberton III. *Yoruba: Nine Centuries of African Art and Thought.* New York: Museum for African Art, 1989. Print.

Gaylard, Gerald. *After Colonialism: African Postmodernism and Magical Realism.* Johannesburg: Wits University Press, 2005. Print.

Guterres, Antonio. "People on the Move." *The Guardian.* 11 December 2007. Web.

Hawley, John C. "Ben Okri's Spirit-Child: Abiku Migration and Postmodernity." *Research in African Literatures* 26.1 (1995): 338. Print.

Myers, Norman. "Environmental Refugees in a Globally Warmed World." *BioScience* 43 (1993): 752–61. Print.

Nixon, Rob. "Environmentalism and Postcolonialism." *Postcolonial Studies and Beyond.* Ed. Ania Loomba, Suvir Kaul, Matti Bunzl, Antoinette Burton and Jed Esty. Durham, N.C.: Duke University Press, 2005: 233–51. Print.

Ogunsanwo, Olatubosun. "Intertextuality and Post-colonial Literature in Ben Okri's *The Famished Road.*" *Research in African Literatures* 26.1 (1995): 40–52. Print.

Okri, Ben. *The Famished Road.* 1991. London: Phoenix, 1998. Print.

———. *Infinite Riches.* 1992. London: Anchor, 1993. Print.

Phillips, Maggi. "Ben Okri's River Narratives: *The Famished Road* and *Songs of Enchantment.*" *Contemporary African Fiction.* Ed. Derek Wright. Bayreuth: Breitinger, 1997: 167–79. Print.

Quayson, Ato. *Strategic Transformations in Nigerian Writing: Orality and History in the work of Rev. Samuel Johnson, Amos Tutuola, Wole Soyinka and Ben Okri.* Oxford: James Currey, 1997. Print.

Roy, Anjali. "Postmodern or Post-Colonial?: Magic Realism in Okri's *The Famished Road.*" *The Post-colonial Condition of African Literature.* Ed. Daniel Gover, John Conteh-Morgan and Jane Bryce. Trenton, N.J.: Africa World Press, 2000: 23–39. Print.

Sanders, Scott Russell. *Staying Put: Making a Home in a Restless World.* Boston: Beacon, 1993. Print.

Smith, Robert. *Kingdoms of the Yoruba.* 3rd ed. Madison: University of Wisconsin Press, 1988. Print.

Snyder, Gary. "The Place, the Region and the Commons." *The Practice of the Wild.* San Francisco: North Point, 1990: 25–47. Print.

Thomashow, Mitchell. "Toward a Cosmopolitan Bioregionalism." *Bioregionalism.* Ed. Michael Vincent McGinnis. New York: Routledge, 1999: 121–32. Print.

Were, Jan Lodewijk R. "Nigerian Lowland Forest (AT0123)." *World Wildlife Fund.* World Wildlife Fund, 2001. Web. 20 Sept. 2009.

Wright, Derek. "Pre- and Post-modernity in Recent West African Fiction." *Commonwealth* 21.2 (1999): 5–17. Print.

LIBBY ROBIN

Seasons and Nomads

Reflections on Bioregionalism in Australia

As the world moves beyond nationalism into larger global corporate communities, one response has been to retreat to proximity and, in Kirkpatrick Sale's terms, to "dwell in place." The "imagined community" (Anderson) of the bioregion is human sized: it is a homeland not a nation. The notion of the "bioregional imagination" as explored throughout this book is created by place-conscious literature, art, natural-history writing, and thoughtful daily living. It is an effort to cultivate the sort of community Sale and others imagine, one that, many believe, might enable us to dwell more sustainably in place. What I investigate here, however, is how in the Australian context a bioregionally inspired attunement to place may lead away from rooted forms of dwelling and toward the very sort of nomadic or migratory lifestyles that so much bioregional discourse critiques.

A TIME FOR ALL THINGS: SEASONAL THINKING

Bioregional living is not just about place; it is often also about time. For example, Barbara Kingsolver's *Animal, Vegetable, Miracle* celebrates her family's year of minimizing their ecological footprint by eating seasonally and locally. Dwelling in place demands attention to seasonal time.

Not all places are equally seasonal, however. Kingsolver's opening chapter sees her leaving her home in Tucson, Arizona, to move to a more temperate climate in Virginia for her experiment in place-based living. Some things never had a season in Arizona: living there demanded outside in-

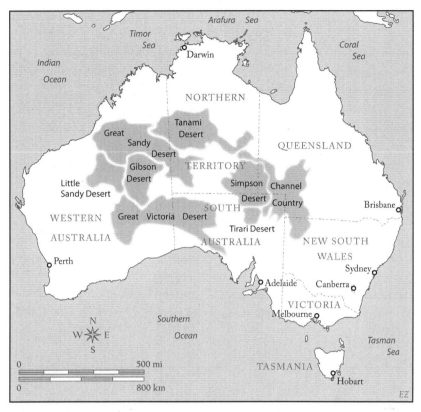

Australian arid zone and deserts

puts, including energy for the air-conditioning, water from imported and fossil sources, and food from temperate climates.

Kingsolver's experience suggests that implicit in the "ethic of proximity" in the twenty-first century is a "normal seasonal life" in a place that is small enough to be imagined as a community and large enough to sustain a Western lifestyle. If (and only if) such an assumption is supportable can individuals be empowered by "dwelling in place." In places that cannot support people in this way—like Kingsolver's Tucson, a place she loved and where she raised two children—a different sort of living is the only possibility. Kingsolver felt "giddy and tragic" (*Animal* 2), she writes, about leaving her "far-flung little community of erstwhile Tucson homesteaders, raising chickens in our yards and patches of vegetables for our use, frequenting farmers' markets to buy from Arizona farmers, trying to reduce the miles-per-gallon quotient of our diets in a gasoholic world.

But these gardens of ours had a drinking problem. So did Arizona farms. That's a devil of a choice: Rob Mexico's water or guzzle Saudi Arabia's gas?" (6). Kingsolver's move east was driven by a long drought and a sense that she was staring global warming in the face. But her family's retreat to the southern Appalachians "like rats leaping off a burning ship" (2) was also a return home for Steven Hopp, her husband and one co-author of the book, as well as a return to the bioregion of Kingsolver's own childhood. Her daughter Camille, the other co-author, was a Tucson native, but she had also developed a seasonal relation with the farmhouse they were approaching, having spent three months in a log cabin in the woods behind the farm over many summers. Over the years, they had "migrated like birds" between Steven's home place and theirs. The migratory cycle itself had kept pace with the movement of the sun, allowing the Kingsolvers to avoid the harsh and relentlessly hot Tucson summer, benefiting from the convenience of the long break in the school year.

Seasons are very important in Kingsolver's story. Eating seasonally creates and sharpens the sense of place. The sun's annual cycle sets the rhythm for the writing. Kingsolver's descriptions of the first green asparagus spikes forcing their way through the soil after the winter frosts are both mouth-watering cooking prose and great nature writing. The spirit of the fresh asparagus spike offers something uplifting to the soul as well as tempting to a palate sharpened by long winter deprivation. The cyclical, seasonal world of food is a great way into a community, even in Tucson, where the local was supplemented from elsewhere. The idea that there is a "seasonal balance" that will return cyclically each year is hardwired into European consciousness (and is also prominent in much Asian cultural discourse, for example, in the festival of cherry blossoms in Japan). It made a "natural" structure for Kingsolver's book, with the seasonal eating beginning with those first asparagus spikes of spring.

PLACES BEYOND SEASONS

Seasonality is the privilege of the temperate world where most major world civilizations evolved. It is not a universal fact of place and is certainly not descriptive of the climate in either tropical or desert Australia, biomes that together constitute four-fifths of the continent.

Tropical places do not have four seasons or variable day-lengths. Nor, in most cases, do they support first world economies and expectations. The only tropical climates paired with first-world economies are at the southern tip of Florida and in the tropical regions that span across northern Australia. The tropics, governed by monsoon (mostly summer) rainfall, extend across roughly ten percent of Australia (about the area of Texas and Oklahoma combined). Darwin is only 12 degrees south of the equator, with a stormy "wet" season and a long dry season. Whitefellas (Settler Australians) talk about two seasons; Aboriginal people in the region, for example, the Jawoyn at Nitmaluk (Katherine), recognize up to six, including a "knock-em-down" season around early March, when tropical storms flatten the long grass at the end of the wet season.[1]

In tropical northern Australia, the seasons vary in length and character from year to year. By contrast, day lengths vary little year round. Most years, more than six months are without rain. Growing seasonal things is a challenge. When rains come, they are so heavy that roads become impassable. There is little arable soil: it is a terrain of rugged outcrops, fissured rocks and, for much of the year, no water. Rainfall feeds the rivers near the coasts (where it runs quickly out to sea) not in the upper reaches, where dams might be possible (Ross 22). If you eat a Western diet, there is little choice about importing food. It has been hard for settler Australians to develop a different lifestyle and a different economy suited for dwelling in such a place.

Next there is desert Australia, some 70 percent of the land mass—over two million square miles (five million square kilometers). Here there are no reliable seasons at all: there may be no rain for several years. Rain may come from the north ("summer" rain), or from the south ("winter" rain), or not at all. Average rainfall figures are meaningless. You take it when you can get it.

Even in the rest of Australia, particularly the southeast and southwest coastal areas, where climate is more temperate and where winter rain is more reliable, weather is becoming unstable. Climate change is making rainfall more unpredictable even in these traditionally seasonal places. An Australian writer does not really have the option to create a sense of place through seasonal sensibilities, although "bad" seasons are a recurrent motif in Australian writing.

REGIONS, BIOREGIONS, AND COUNTRY

Following his expedition to Central Australia in 1894, Baldwin Spencer divided Australia into three regions, naming them for prominent explorers and using them to classify plant and animal habitats. The largest region, the Eyrean, corresponded to the desert; the Torresian region was the tropics; and the Bassian was the temperate coastal fringe in the South (Robin, *Flight of the Emu* 18–20). The vast majority of people in Australia live in the Bassian region, most of them in cities of a million people or more. All the major cities are Bassian. The governance of the other regions is filtered through the economic and political imagination of the temperate South, where European settlement began because seasonal rains enabled Old World foods and agricultural practices.

Another great anthropologist and archaeologist, Norman Tindale, divided the country differently. He drew up a map of Australia in 1974 that divided the land into hundreds of regions, based on the tribes of Aboriginal Australia before European contact. Tindale's map has been much discussed since; it is a cultural map of places richly localized by hundreds of languages, a surprising counterpoint to Australia today, where Aboriginal languages are fewer, and those that remain are endangered by the dominance of English in the mainstream culture.

Most Australians would not be familiar with either Spencer's ecological or Tindale's linguistic regionalization of the country. By contrast, state boundaries, with their sharply ruled surveyors' edges, have a political significance and high recognition. The Federation project of "imagining" a singular nation has been largely successful.

"Bioregional" has a different dominant meaning in Australia. It is unrelated to the movement in the United States that responds "to the challenge of reconnecting socially just human cultures in a sustainable manner to the region-scale ecosystems in which they are . . . embedded," to use Doug Aberley's definition (12). It is seldom about human cultures at all, socially just or otherwise. It is a government word. A bioregion is "a large, geographically distinct area of land with common characteristics such as geology, landform patterns, climate, ecological features and plant and animal communities" ("Australia's Bioregions"). This centralized and singular definition is at odds with the "defiant decentralism" that Aberley describes in the United States context. The Australian bioregion hyperseparates human from animal and plant communities, and emphasizes "types" rather than connections. A bioregion is just physical, beyond the human world. Decentralized, subjective self-definition is not part of the policy makers' dry vision. The IBRA (the Interim Biogeographic Regionalization of Australia) is the basis for a cartographic carve-up of places. It underpins the

National Reserve System's planning framework and is "a fundamental tool for identifying reservation targets and setting priorities to meet them." It does not facilitate creativity. Place-conscious thinkers are left to find words other than "bioregion" to talk about the humanity of place.

Literary academic and poet Philip Mead discusses writing about place in Australia. Using "critical regionalism" and "place-consciousness," Mead traces a historical trajectory in Australian literature, noting emerging trends away from the national after nearly a century using the "civilizing" arts to establish and legitimize a "unisonant nation": "Terms like region and state, with their etymologically embedded dyads—metropole and nation—seem increasingly outmoded," he writes (555). Mead prefers the indigenizing term "country," a choice also made by Tim Bonyhady and Tom Griffiths in their book *Words for Country*. Bonyhady and Griffiths shied away from "landscape," a word "which suggests a view that is remote and painterly" (1), and chose instead the more emotionally engaged "country." "Country" is a cross-cultural and complicated word in Australia. It is the word that Aboriginal people use to mean land and also soul and knowledge. Nonindigenous people also talk about the health of the country encompassing the state of the soil, the water, the vegetation and the people. Country has fewer edges than "region." It is not a synonym for "territory." Country can extend to the horizon and beyond and is subjective and emotionally laden.

Mead explored a range of locales to demonstrate the rise of a writerly place-consciousness, beginning with Western Australia. Like the founders of bioregionalism in the United States, Gary Snyder and Kirkpatrick Sale and others, Western Australians write to mark their difference from the dominant eastern states. Published in the 1970s, some of the earliest regional anthologies of Australian writing hail from the West (Brady, *Soundings*; Bennett, *New Country*; Bennett and Grono, *Wide Domain*).[2] The Indian Ocean is one important focus for prominent Western Australian writers, including Tim Winton and Robert Drewe. The wheat belt, inland from the capital Perth and extending many miles north and south, is the source of the writing of the poet John Kinsella and the literary criticism of Tony Hughes-d'Aeth. The Kimberley region in the Far North is also a literary and artistic frontier, with the former pearling town of Broome famous for cross-cultural community music. Much new art and writing is emerging from this northwest corner. "The Kimberley" is the setting of Baz Luhrmann's movie, *Australia* (2008). Yet until recent years, East and West Kimberley were isolated from each other, with culturally differ-

ent traditions on either side of the rugged Bungle Bungle mountains. The
Great Northern Highway that joins the two Kimberleys was not sealed
until 1986.

Kimberley is North as well as West, part of what Nicolas Rothwell has
argued to be the heart-place for a new and emerging literature, something
altogether free of the old classical world. The North is, in his words, "un-
written country." But it is a complicated place, difficult to be close to, to
"dwell in." People come "to northern Australia . . . because they're lost,
or searching, or on the edge of life, and silence, and they're chasing after
some kind of pattern, some redemption they think might be lurking, on
the line of the horizon, out in the faint, receding perspectives of the bush,"
Rothwell writes in his latest book (*Red Highway*, 126). Rothwell is critical
of outsiders who write Australia's monsoon North (and Red Centre) from
brief sojourns. He suggests that it is impossible for a writer on the Australian bush to sense the significant presence or absence of Aboriginal people
in country "unless he feels it as a matter of identity; unless it acts like a pressure, tangible inside the geometry of his own life" ("The Outsiders" 20).
This is an argument for the authority of dwelling in place, even if the place
is in the mind, because the North is a place where a "traveling-through"
relationship with country is the way of dwelling. The *highway* is, in a sense,
the *home*, and this is the fount of bioregional imagining here.

In the literature of Australia's temperate southern places, small islands,
especially Tasmania, have been a focus, as Philip Mead noted. This theme
echoes the notion of the *Littoral Zone* chosen by CA. Cranston and Robert Zeller as the title for their edited volume billed on the back cover as
"the first collection of ecocritical essays devoted to Australian contexts and
their writers." The littoral zone plays with the national-regional tensions in
an island-continent (Lewis and Wigen 21–46). The world's largest island/
smallest continent has long been a trope for Australia. Cranston takes this
further in her chapter, "Islands," in which she considers insularity in its
physical and emotional forms, reminding her readers that the "island" of
Tasmania is "in fact an archipelago state, composed of 334 islands," and
that Western Australia "has 3,747 islands" (221, 222).

The *Littoral Zone* alludes to the prehistoric Inland Sea as well. In a
stimulating chapter, Tom Lynch considers the literature and art of Australia's arid zone, where evidence of marine incursions long-past shape the
landscape, and shells can be found thousands of miles from the sea. Sometimes the ancient salts rise from within the landscape and kill the fields,

as Tony Hughes-d'Aeth describes in the Western Australian wheat belt. Both Lynch and Hughes-d'Aeth write of the interactions between art and science in their respective places. Australian regional literature is highly scientifically engaged. In remote places it is often scientists who shape place-consciousness through the way they envision the ecological structures of the country.

INDUSTRIAL HERITAGE

In Australia, local places can be grim and are far from utopian. Ecological carnage was created in the historical crucible of simultaneous agricultural and industrial revolutions. Industrial agriculture is not a pretty sight. John Kinsella's actively antipastorale poetry is aggressive and thoughtful at the same time. He argues that in the Australian language, "pastoral" is "a construct to re-create European, specifically English, rural power-structures, the reconfiguration of 'home' in an alien landscape. Such language usage comes out of a politics of oppression and degradation of indigeneity. A new pastoral must come out of this that re-examines what constitutes rural space and how that is mediated" (*Disclosed Poetics* 3). George Main's *Heartland: The Regeneration of Rural Place*, about his home in another wheat belt, is also antagonistic to the idealized pastorale. He paints the farm country on the southwest slopes of central New South Wales as "industrial," stripped of nature: "New, powerful machines made clearing an easy task. . . . [But there were] unforeseen consequences. Noisy flocks of green budgerigars disappeared. Curlews no longer wailed at night," he writes (231). There is human loss as well as ecological:

> Something more than dead trees and uneven terrain disappeared from
> the land my father and our neighbour cleared. Maybe a sense of vanished
> potential for dialogue and connectivity keeps evoking the haunting dream.
> Tractors and ploughs erased intricate patterns—cultural and natural . . .
> Possibilities for new, mutually nourishing relationships between land and
> people evaporated. When my family sold the farm almost thirty years ago,
> we lost any chance of finding alternative ways to engage with the paddocks
> of Ardrossan. (*Heartland* 241–42)

Heartland is a relentless critique of the myth that agriculture is good for rural places. It shows ecological and social fragmentation, but also draws hope from a little regeneration. Biological diversity, natural integrity, and human hope are mutually supportive in this long meditation on place. Main struggles to develop a language for healing ecological damage and the separation of human communities from place by engaging with his own haunted dreams.

Nicolas Rothwell acknowledges the tensions of colonization too, referring to "a mood of nostalgia, a yearning, a desire so strong" that "highlights a primary distance between writers and subject." The Aboriginal presence "in the outback, the inland and the remote north defines the landscape . . . and their absence in other parts of the continent communicates a tone as well" ("Outsiders" 20). Seasons are part of "elsewhere places," but the question remains in their absence: How do you acculturate "this place," this rural, regional or even urban Australia, with a Western-educated imagination and a locally informed ecological understanding? What sorts of literature of place are possible without annual seasonality?

DESERT KNOWLEDGE

In the Australian desert, there are many forces creating an "imagined community." There is a vibrant international desert art movement, infused with storytelling (Johnson). The desert is a powerfully Aboriginal place, and this Aboriginality is the fount of its literature. T. G. H. Strehlow, who was fluent in English, German, and several Aboriginal languages, published *Songs of Central Australia* in 1971. He recorded the literary, lyrical form of Arrernte songs as the fundamental poetry of this place, as poet Barry Hill has argued in his important biography of Strehlow, *Broken Song*. Strehlow's work is often classified as "anthropology" and overlooked by literary writers, but he wrote Aboriginal lyrics as high art, as "literature" in a language of oral tradition.

In the last few years, an ecological picture of Central Australia began to emerge in parallel with the appreciation of traditional society. This holistic framework for understanding arid Australia was conceptualized by ecologists, including Steve Morton and Mark Stafford Smith, who have worked closely with Aboriginal people over many years. Morton calls the Australian desert "the land of uncertainty" and writes lyrically in scientific journals about the need for "stewardship" of a fragile system. Ecologists describe the patchiness of desert life, the mosaic of pockets of biodiversity separated widely and unpredictably (Morton and Stafford Smith, "A Fresh Framework for Arid Australia"). They see hearths and homes for people and animals scattered across the red landscape. Variable rainfall and poor soils create big spaces between possible living places in this spatial view. Aboriginal stories connect these places. Country is not about the patches but rather about the journeys between them. The journey is the country. When Aboriginal people talk about conservation, it is the songlines they want to conserve (Keogh). As historians Heather Goodall and Allison Cadzow write, "Mobility was and is as much a defining characteristic of Aboriginal cultures as affiliations with meaningful bounded places" (21).

Ecologists have been living and working in Alice Springs for over fifty years; they are now local people, too. Initially they went out from the big cities to support and develop pastoral industries. Increasingly they saw the destruction that sheep and cattle (and their companion travelers, rabbits) wrought on the old soils and fragile, patchy vegetation. "It was like triage," Steve Morton commented at an ecological forum recently. How to choose which species to save? Australia leads the world in mammalian extinctions, a doubtful honor. In the end, all the extinctions suggested a different sort of economy, a new "imagined community" for desert Australia. Ecologists now promote a hybrid cross-cultural field, Desert Knowledge, which combines conservation, livelihoods, health, and cross-cultural engagement. Desert Knowledge embraces moral as well as scientific and economic imperatives to dwell in this place.

The desert is known as the Red Centre, yet it is the forgotten corner of every mainland state in Australia, politically speaking. "You have little say in your own future. Your voice is a distant one, muffled by closer political thunder" (Stafford Smith and Cribb, *Dry Times* 123). Alice Springs is just a small town of 23,000 people, but its local hospital serves a hinterland the size of France. Scientists define the "arid zone" precisely and mathematically, but they also want to engage with it politically to re-center the political agenda for the desert and to embrace the ecologically similar parts of five states and a territory. The population of Australia's arid zone is comparable to the Nunavut territory of northern Canada, which is also sparsely populated but is its own Inuit state. Alaska, another sparsely populated, ecologically complex region, also has a strong regional identity. Ecologist Mark Stafford Smith is promoting an Outback Capital Trust modeled on the Alaska Permanent Fund to enable the Red Centre to set and receive natural resource rents and ensure that mining and pastoralism do not take all the region's economic and knowledge capital elsewhere (Stafford Smith and Cribb, *Dry Times* 135–36). He wants to support diffuse evolutionary

processes in the landscape and "develop persistent community local knowledge" (Stafford Smith, "Rangelands" 15). Science has moved a long way
from techno-fixes for soil deficiency. Scientists, as they dwell in this place,
are curious about its literature, its history, and its art. The humanities are
part of their endeavors to sustain life. Art is already an important part of
the desert economy as people on the ecological edge create distinctive lives
and lifestyles.

NOMADIC LIFESTYLES

In the Red Centre, dwelling in place paradoxically demands mobility.
When there are no rains for many years, some waterholes dry up and landscapes lose animals and plants altogether. Traditional Aboriginal lifestyles
adapt to what ecologists call the "pulse and reserve system." People travel
lightly, with sufficient mobility to move into an area at the time of a "pulse"
of life (after rain or fire) and to move to a safer place and wait out the
long "reserve" periods. The secret of success is to move in quickly when
food supplies are rich and to move out before they dry up. Nomadism is
thoughtful loving of a patchy landscape with very little water. The past
century has shown that there are places where the European agricultural
revolution and settlement should never have occurred.

In *Boom and Bust: Bird Stories for a Dry Country*, I and other Australian
authors tell stories of ten different birds. Our voices are diverse—some
scientific, some anthropological, some historical. We offer our bird stories
as parables for people who live in the southern thirstlands. Even in Bassian
Australia, where most Australians live, water is scarce. The parables are also
relevant to a wider world of increasing variability. What the stories of these
birds reveal is that mobility, more than rooted dwelling, may be a survival
skill for an increasingly arid and unpredictable world.

Nomadism is no longer just associated with Aboriginal lifestyles. Increasingly it is the European-Australians who pass through the desert seasonally. Indigenous people walk their songlines, singing up country, but
the new "fly-in-fly-out" nomads do not create place as they travel. Their
nomadism and even the place itself may be incidental to their purpose.
One Aboriginal man asked wryly, "Who are the nomads here?" when a
host of foreigners came from Melbourne, Canberra, Sydney, Europe, and
the United States for a meeting to discuss "nomadic lifestyles" in Timber
Creek in the Northern Territory. The Aboriginal nomads walked there or

drove. They knew the country as home. It was the Western "investigators of nomads" who flew in from elsewhere. Nomadism is not morally good or bad, nor is it necessarily ecological or economic. Neither is it "primitive" or "noble." It is just another way to live in country. Transience is a byproduct of the booming mining economies of northern, western, and central Australia. It also defines the growing tourist economies of these places. However, mobile lifestyles are absolutely at odds with the settlement ethic of pastoralism, the original raison d'être for rangeland ecology, which started as a science of "making deserts bloom." The angst and ambivalence about nomadism in settler Australia has the same roots as in North America: mobility in the direction of pastoral dreams is socially good, but culturally ambivalent (Heise 49). Unless the mythic settler pastoral is achieved—unless the travelers find their Beulah home, in North American terms—the traveling is all in vain. Traveling is subservient to the settlement ideal, not an attentive mobility that cares for country in the indigenous tradition.

Where dwelling in place is not an option, bioregional thinking needs to embrace multiple ways to create communities. It needs to collect rent from the transients, as the Outback Capital Trust may achieve. It also demands a bigger home place, a place big enough to provide scope for retreat in tough times. "Dwelling" beyond places of comfortable, reliable seasons and rich soils is an art form. It demands *high* culture, in fact. There is an urgent need on a planet affected by anthropogenic climate change to consider how humanity can live with variability, extreme events, and uncertainty. Instead of focusing on communities in richly resourced and reliable places, it is worth observing life in places like the Australian desert. Here, in what is arguably the most variable and unseasonal climate on earth, Aboriginal peoples have lived successfully—even sustainably—for thirty-five thousand years or more, through many extreme (natural) climate change events (Robin and Smith).

Perhaps the next great project for the humanities is to restore dignity to nomadism rather than to reinforce the romantic yeoman farmer ideal of many western nations, both in old Europe and in the settler lands of the neo-Europes. In the United States, rather than being anxious about "nomads without roots forever on the road" (Heise 48) and "restless" mobile lifestyles, we need to shed the ambivalence and see nomadism as another response to place. Australian Aboriginal nomads have roots in their traveling and it creates their country. Their bioregion is enormous, and their nomadism leaves a light footprint, kind to that country. The idea that one can see to the horizon (or fence line) of one's place is based in the rich soils of old European thinking. This needs to be rethought for other places, particularly for displaced Europeans bringing old mind-sets to places with different rules (Robin, *How a Continent*).

"Local places" are sized by human demands and ecological resources, not horizons. Where it is possible to buy local food and make a "handshake deal in a community gathering place," where farmers have first names and come every week to a market, it is important to do as Barbara Kingsolver urges and make "small stepwise changes in personal habits" that can change the story of who we are on this planet ("Stalking the Vegetannual" 53). But places are not all the same, and the size and possibilities of a place depend on its ecological richness. There is great variation in what might constitute a "nourishing terrain," as Deborah Bird Rose calls the country of Aboriginal groups in Australia. Different climes support different numbers: one area of "territory," according to geographer Ian Simmons, might support three people in the Arctic, eleven in semidesert, 54 in grassland, and 136 in subtropical savanna (7).

The challenge, when writing about places, is to weigh up their richness and the ecological cost of living there. For those of us in privileged Western lifestyles with enormous ecological footprints, living in "place" may also demand a global imagination, as we surely use the equivalent of more than a planet's worth of resources on a per capita basis. But settling down in the few pockets on earth that support a pastoral idyll is not the only thing our best critical thinkers can do in the age of the Anthropocene, where people have already changed every biophysical system on earth (Robin and Steffen; Crutzen). Bioregional writings must recognize ecological limits as they also enable hope. Science is important here, alongside humanism. In 1972, René Dubos was part of the UNESCO scientific team that wrote the report *Only One Earth: The Care and Maintenance of Our Small Planet*. At the same time he was also writing *The God Within*, a book about the "distinctive genius of each place and each person" (ix). Dubos reflects, "These two attitudes are not incompatible. . . . We can develop a rational loyalty to planet earth while maintaining an emotional attachment to our prized diversity" (13). Technology has given people immense power over the cosmos, but it also deprives us of the "sustenance" derived "from direct contact with nature" (4). Dubos urges his readers to discover the "*entheos*" ("the god within," the root of the word *enthusiasm*), in the "subconscious chiaroscuro region of the mind" and the spirit of place (5). The Australian desert is most often seen through a scientific lens. If we want to celebrate its "place," and not just its biophysical dimensions, we need more humanistic readings and writings to enchant it, to complement the strong oral indigenous traditions of "singing up" country. Bioregionalism is a tool for imagining diverse places and a diversity of manners of dwelling. Australian deserts offer a microcosm for imagining possible ways to dwell on an increasingly ecologically limited and unpredictable planet.[3]

NOTES

1. Nitmaluk Visitor Centre, pers. obs.

2. See also a monograph: Bruce Bennett's *The Literature of Western Australia*.

3. A variety of conversations shaped this piece. I am grateful to the editors for a brief that enabled comparison and reflection on differences and shared sensibilities and to comments and insights from Philip Mead, Jenna Mead, Tom Griffiths, Steve Morton, Mark Stafford Smith, Mike Smith, George Main, Cameron Muir, and Elizabeth Robin.

WORKS CITED

Aberley, Doug. "Interpreting Bioregionalism: A Story from Many Voices." McGinnis 13–42. Print.

Anderson, Benedict. *Imagined Communities: Reflections on the Origins and Spread of Nationalism*. London: Verso, 1983. Print.

Australia. Department of Environment, "Australia's Bioregions." Web. 9 Oct. 2009.

Bennett, Bruce. *The Literature of Western Australia*. Perth: University of Western Australia Press, 1979. Print.

———. *New Country: A Selection of Western Australian Short Stories*. Fremantle: Fremantle Arts Centre Press, 1976. Print.

Bennett, Bruce and William Grono, eds. *Wide Domain: Western Australian Themes and Images*. Sydney: Angus and Robertson, 1979. Print.

Bonyhady, Tim and Tom Griffiths, eds. *Words for Country: Landscape and Language in Australia*. Sydney: University of New South Wales Press, 2002. Print.

———. "Landscape and Language." In Bonyhady and Griffiths 1–13. Print.

Brady, Veronica, ed. *Soundings: A Selection of Western Australian Poetry*. Fremantle: Fremantle Arts Centre Press, 1976. Print.

Cranston, CA. "Islands." Cranston and Zeller 219–60. Print.

Cranston, CA., and Robert Zeller, eds. *The Littoral Zone: Australian Contexts and their Writers*. Amsterdam: Rodopi, 2007. Print.

Crutzen, P. J. "Geology of Mankind." *Nature* 415 (2002): 23. Print.

Dickman, Chris, Daniel Lunney, and Shelley Burgin, eds. *Animals of Arid Australia: Out on Their Own?*. Mosman: Royal Zoological Society of New South Wales, 2006. Print.

Dubos, René. *A God Within*. New York: Scribners, 1972. Print.

Goodall, Heather, and Allison Cadzow. *Rivers and Resilience: Aboriginal People on Sydney's Georges River*. Sydney: University of New South Wales Press, 2009. Print.

Heise, Ursula K. *Sense of Place and Sense of Planet: The Environmental Imagination of the Global*. New York: Oxford University Press, 2008. Print.

Hill, Barry. *Broken Song: T. G. H. Strehlow and Aboriginal Possession*. Milsons Point, New South Wales: Knopf, 2002. Print.

Johnson, Vivien. *Papunya Painting: Out of the Desert*. Canberra: National Museum of Australia Press, 2007. Print.

Keogh, Luke. "The Forum Is a Campfire, the River Is a Story." Robin, Dickman, and Martin 264–83. Print.

Kingsolver, Barbara. "Stalking the Vegetannual: A Road Map to Eating with the Seasons." *Orion* (March–April 2007): 50–53.

Kingsolver, Barbara, with Steven L. Hopp and Camille Kingsolver. *Animal, Vegetable, Miracle: A Year of Food Life*. London: Harper Perennial, 2007. Print.

Kinsella, John. *Disclosed Poetics: Beyond Landscape and Lyricism*, Manchester: Manchester University Press, 2007. Print.

Lewis, Darrell. Pers. comm., 30 September 2006.

Lewis, Martin W., and Kären E. Wigen. *The Myth of Continents: A Critique of Metageography*. Berkeley: University of California Press, 1997. Print.

Lindenmayer, David, Stephen Dovers, Molly Harriss Olson, and Steve Morton. *Ten Commitments: Reshaping the Lucky Country's Environment*. Melbourne: CSIRO, 2008. Print.

Main, George. *Heartland: The Regeneration of Rural Place*. Sydney: University of New South Wales Press, 2005. Print.

McGinnis, Michael Vincent, ed. *Bioregionalism*. London: Routledge, 1999. Print.

Mead, Philip. "Nation, Literature, Location." Pierce 549–67. Print.

Morton, S. R. "A Land of Uncertainty." Recher, Lunney and Dunn 122–44. Print.

Morton, S. R., et al. "A Fresh Framework for the Ecology of Arid Australia." *Journal of Arid Environments* 30 (2010): 1–17. Web. 6 Jan. 2010. <doi:10.1016/j.jaridenv.2010.11.001>.

Morton, S. R., et al. "The Stewardship of Arid Australia: Ecology and Landscape Management." *Journal of Environmental Management* 43 (1995): 195–217. Print.

Pierce, Peter, ed. *The Cambridge History of Australian Literature.* Cambridge: Cambridge University Press, 2009. Print.

Recher, H., D. Lunney, and I. Dunn, eds. *A Natural Legacy.* 2nd ed. Sydney: Pergamon Press, 1986. Print.

Robin, Libby. *The Flight of the Emu: A Hundred Years of Australian Ornithology 1901–2001.* Melbourne: Melbourne University Press, 2001. Print.

———. *How a Continent Created a Nation.* Sydney: University of New South Wales Press, 2007. Print.

Robin, Libby, and Mike Smith. "Science in Place and Time: Archaeology, Ecology and Environmental History." *Animals of Arid Australia: Out on Their Own?* Ed. Chris Dickman, Daniel Lunney, and Shelley Burgin. Mosman: Royal Zoological Society of New South Wales, 2006. 188–96. Print.

Robin, Libby, and Will Steffen. "History for the Anthropocene." *History Compass* 5.5 (2007): 1694–1719. Print.

Robin, Libby, Chris Dickman, and Mandy Martin, eds. *Desert Channels: The Impulse to Conserve.* Melbourne: CSIRO, 2010. Print.

Robin, Libby, Rob Heinsohn, and Leo Joseph, eds. *Boom and Bust: Bird Stories for a Dry Country.* Melbourne: CSIRO, 2009. Print.

Rose, Deborah Bird. *Nourishing Terrains: Aboriginal Views of Landscape and Wilderness.* Canberra: Australian Heritage Commission, 1996. Print.

Ross, Joe (Chair, Northern Australia Land and Water Taskforce). *Sustainable Development of Northern Australia.* Canberra: Department of Infrastructure, Transport, Regional Development and Local Government, December 2009. Web, 17 February 2010. <http://www.nalwt.gov.au/files/337281_NLAW.pdf>.

Rothwell, Nicolas. *Red Highway,* Melbourne: Black Inc., 2009. Print.

———. "The Outsiders." *Australian Literary Review* 2.10 (November 2007): 14–15, 20. Print.

Sale, Kirkpatrick. *Dwellers in the Land: The Bioregional Vision.* San Francisco: Sierra Club, 1985. Print.

Simmons, I. G. *Global Environmental History 10,000 BC to AD 2000.* Edinburgh: Edinburgh University Press, 2008. Print.

Stafford Smith, D. M., and S. R. Morton. "A Framework for the Ecology of Arid Australia." *Journal of Arid Environments* 18 (1990): 255–78. Print.

Stafford Smith, Mark. "Conserving Desert Australian Livelihoods." Robin, Dickman, and Martin 249–63. Print.

Stafford Smith, Mark, and Julian Cribb. *Dry Times: Blueprint for a Red Land.* Collingwood, VIC: CSIRO Publishing, 2009. Print.

―――. "Rangelands." Lindenmayer *et al.* 11–18. Print.

Strehlow, T. G. H. *Songs of Central Australia*. Sydney: Angus and Robertson, 1971. Print.

Tindale, Norman. "Tribal Boundaries in Aboriginal Australia." [cartographic material, drawn by Winifred Mumford on a base map produced by the Division of National Mapping, Department of National Development, Canberra, Australia]. *Aboriginal Tribes of Australia*. Berkeley: University of California Press, 1974. Print.

PAVEL CENKL

Reading Climate Change and Work in the Circumpolar North

> *The long, long road over the moors and up into the forest—*
> *who trod it into being first of all? Man, a human being,*
> *the first that came here. There was no path before he came.*
> *Afterward, some beast or other, following the faint tracks over*
> *marsh and moorland, wearing them deeper; after these again*
> *some Lapp gained scent of the path, and took that way from*
> *field to field, looking to his reindeer. Thus was made the road*
> *through the great Almenning—the common tracts without an*
> *owner; no-man's-land.*
>
> Knut Hamsun, *Growth of the Soil*

M Y STUDENTS AND I typically begin the first day of our "Literature and Film of the North" class by considering the question, "What is North?" We start by looking at a wide range of documents that includes the 550 CE *Voyage of Saint Brendan*, which recounts the episodic narrative of Brendan's crossing of the North Atlantic in an ox hide boat; passages from Homer and Dante; and for a visual cornerstone, Gerhard Mercator's 1595 map, *Septentrionalium Terrarum Descriptio*.

Our foray into the literature and cartography from medieval and early modern Europe challenges from the outset student preconceptions of the circumpolar North and immediately implicates the region within a global framework of exploration, commodification, and cultural history. Mercator's map, for instance, in its development of a fanciful narrative about resource availability, circumpolar navigability and cultures—not to mention topography—attempts to frame the Arctic in terms that might have

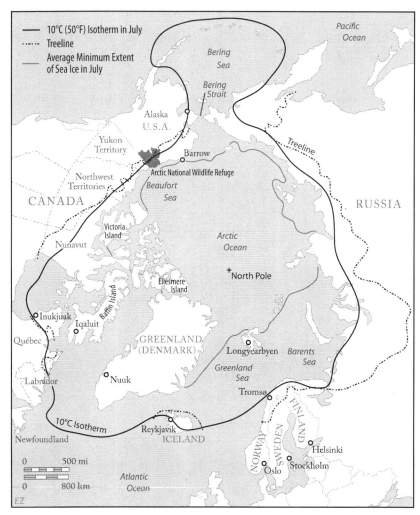

The Circumpolar North

Mercator's 1595 map of the Arctic. Library and Archives Canada (Web).

been both familiar and attractive to European explorers and their financial sponsors. Well before Europeans set foot in what is now the Canadian High Arctic, the region's Inuit inhabitants were already situated in the commercial context of early modern European conceptions—often, tragic misconceptions—of the hyperborean regions that potentially lay beyond the hostile northern seas. These centuries-old narratives help the class to frame more recent examples of polarizing politicized language about the North—a North in which, for instance, the Arctic National Wildlife Refuge is represented as either the "last hope for retaining a piece of the world in its natural state" (Readicker-Henderson 383) or, in the words of U.S. Senator Lisa Murkowski, as "North America's best and last hope of a giant oil discovery" ("The Debate").

The Arctic can be defined in a variety of both complementary and conflicting ways: as a region within which the mean annual temperature never

rises above 10° Celsius; as the area of the earth north of 66°30' north lati-
tude; as the terrestrial and marine ecosystem north of tree line; as home to
specific groups of indigenous and colonizing cultures; or even, described
tongue-in-cheek by a colleague, as that region where caribou have been in
residence anytime in the past ten thousand years. Most of these definitions
are subject to variations in climate, species migration, precipitation, and
wind and ocean currents, variations which continually shift our understanding of the region's actual boundary. And it is this very absence of a
discrete, identifiable boundary that challenges definitions of the North as
a single, unified region. More clearly defined, I believe, are the environmental and cultural histories from across the circumpolar North that trace
linked paths through the daily lives and place rootedness of both native and
transplanted cultures, which wend their way through a landscape that is at
once immense and intimate. To make sense of such an illimitable territory,
and one that continues to see abrupt and destabilizing shifts in climate that
challenge conventional notions of bioregional stability, I propose that it is
within the context of the quotidian experience of daily work—of intimate
human interaction with the terrain underfoot—that the identity of culture
and place begin to cohere to define the North as one of our planet's largest bioregions.

Work, whether directed toward the survival of cultures in Rachel Qitsualik's story "Skraeling," or involved with reindeer herding in the verse of
Sámi poet Nils-Aslak Valkeapää, or engaged in by rural farmers and shep-
herds as described in works by nonindigenous writers, such as Halldór Laxness's *Independent People* and Knut Hamsun's *Growth of the Soil*, consists of
repetitive, seasonal gyres across subarctic or Arctic landscapes. A working
individual's relationship to the land in these texts is resolutely affective and
can serve to break down singular depictions of place and narratives that describe the North as any sort of unified territory. Seen in this way, individual
or communal labor is the very antithesis of a totalizing narrative. Among
cultures such as the Inuit, Inupiat, Yupik, and Sámi, peripatetic vocations
like herding and hunting in the North impel a revision of place as unique
and rooted; in working the land, the individual comes to embody the land
itself. In the very movement sketched in poems and narratives and determined by both climate and culture, inhabitants of the circumpolar North
confront daily the dynamic northern landscape through the very work of
their travel across the landscape; it is thus the travel itself—travel more and
more frequently regulated, curtailed, or simply made impracticable—that

can help to define place and region in the North. Central to developing an understanding of the interbraiding of culture and environment in the circumpolar bioregion is an exploration of work as an individual, experiential engagement with the land, with the physical terrain and the very ground underfoot.

The Inuit author and journalist Rachel Qitsualik centers her 2004 short story "Skraeling" on the imagined meeting of three cultures near the southern tip of Greenland's west coast at the end of the first millennium: the Thule people, the predecessors of the modern Inuit; the Dorset or Tunit people, whom the Thule culture had completely replaced by the end of the fifteenth century; and the Vikings, whose settlement in Greenland coincided with the medieval warm period between approximately 950 and 1400. Qitsualik's story follows an Inuit protagonist, Kannaujaq, as he begins to recognize his position and identity in the midst of environmental and cultural transition.

Following an attack on a Viking raiding party near the conclusion of the story, Kannaujaq watches as the Viking leader is left adrift in his boat, subject to the whims of the "odd" ocean currents and staring back at Kannaujaq on shore with, as Qitsualik writes, "no hatred in those ice-blue eyes, but only despair, and resignation" (65). Kannaujaq, and by extension, Qitsualik, pauses to reflect on this moment and to consider whether all cultures are destined to succumb to this same fate as the process that this region has become implicates culture, region, and climate in a complex relationship. The author intimates, in the story's final paragraphs, that all of us are subject to odd currents of sea and climate: "The world would grow much colder," Qitsualik writes, "and [Kannaujaq's] kind would be the only survivors here. And they would speak of Tunit only in their own legends" (66). The slow drifting of the Viking character in "Skraeling" into the sea underscores the dynamic nature of the North as much as it foreshadows the climatic shift that enabled both the transition of local indigenous cultures and a rapid cooling that effectively evicted the Vikings from their territories in southwestern Greenland in the fifteenth century. Qitsualik's choice to emphasize the intertwining of region and climate that was evident one thousand years ago clearly resonates with contemporary issues surrounding ties between cultural identity, climate, and region.

It is not possible in an essay, of course, to "get off into the country and sleep on the ground" in order to, as Barry Lopez writes in *Arctic Dreams*, "begin to sense the timeless, unsummarized dimensions of a deeper landscape" (256). However, informed by the entwined contexts of ecocriticism, climatology, and ethnography, it is possible to trace a path "between the stones and the ocean, [on] a surface so narrow it is no more than a possible line for a possible balance" (115) and to outline an approach to reading within the context of the circumpolar North as both a unique place and as one implicated in the global impacts of economic, cultural, and environmental transformations pushing steadily northward. If work is the thread that insinuates and coheres cultural identity in the northern landscape—"as a literature of lived life"—it "must be experienced in place to be fully felt and known" (Spirn 81). I am suggesting here that "the North" as bioregion can be defined through the intentional engagement with place that is the embodiment of everyday labor—here the work of survival—of hunting, subsistence farming, and the daily trials of a group's survival in the North. It is as well the narrative of that work—as it is the experience of writing that narrative—that both defines and is defined by the unique fabric of climate, region, and cultural identity.

Rachel Qitsualik's "Skraeling" imagines a moment of contact more than a thousand years ago; however, the type of climatic and cultural transition that she sketches in her story is both real and far from unique. Narratives of abrupt climate change or rapid landscape change brought about by dramatic, localized or regional temperature fluctuations pervade the historical record of northern cultures and communities. Abrupt regional changes in mean annual temperature are apparent both in the paleoclimatic record and in surveys of more recent fluctuations in the early and mid-twentieth century that have influenced traditional hunting practices among the Inuit of southwestern Greenland. For example, in the 1920s, seal hunting was abruptly replaced by cod fishing as the principal marine-based economy, and only a half-century later, in 1970, this cod-fishing industry was just as abruptly replaced by a move to shrimp fishing. These changes were precipitated both by changes in ocean temperatures in the region as well as by poor resource management. The challenges faced by Greenland's indigenous population were not too far removed from those challenges that saw the extirpation of Norse settlement in the same region in the fifteenth century; a combination of cooling climate and poor farming practices on marginally arable land contributed to the rapid demise of more than four centuries of settlement on Greenland's southwest coast.[1]

Regional climate fluctuations have on many occasions affected relationships between a region's inhabitants and their traditional work roles and subsistence practices. In a 2008 study of hunting practices among the indigenous population of Newfoundland, Trevor Bell and Priscilla Renouf speculate that, given the anthropological evidence from the period around approximately 700 CE (1200 years before the present), "pack ice might have been much lighter and present for a shorter duration thereby reducing the period of harp seal availability; the timing and distribution of the pack ice and associated harp seal herds might have been less predictable thus undermining an important aspect of the hunt" (83). They conclude that a shift in the native population's reliance on fish and birds to an almost total reliance on harp seals indicates that "continuously rising temperatures might have undermined the conditions of site use to the point where its large population was no longer supportable" (84). Hunting techniques practiced over centuries in that area were, therefore, no longer viable to support the indigenous community. In its conclusion, the study speculates that a correlation between resource exploitation and climate variability in this area of Newfoundland contributed to significant cultural changes in the native population's attitudes and approaches to hunting.

Much of the literature at the forefront of a collective cultural concern with our global environmental crisis, including Jared Diamond's bestselling 2005 book, *Collapse*, makes clear that change in climate is in only a few instances wholly responsible for dramatic changes in cultural traditions or a population's engagement with particular work practices. In a presentation at the 2005 GLOBEC Symposium on Climate Variability, for example, Lawrence Hamilton cautioned "against a simple view that climatic change determines societal outcomes" to argue, through a survey of resource shifts in Newfoundland, Iceland, and the Faroe Islands, "important resource shifts can result from complex interactions between physical, biological and social systems." The cultural identities of northern cultures are ever shot through with the region's dynamic nature, yet the North's fragile ecology is often indelibly marked by millennia of human use. In a 2006 interview with Clare Kendall for *The Ecologist*, Inukjuak resident Eva Inukpuk laments, "It is very sad. My daughter Qulliq will not grow up eating caribou every day like I did. She will eat junk food and Pepsi. But we can't move. We can't live in the city. We hunt. That's what we do. That's who we are" (Kendall 28). Whether in the guise of opportunities or challenges, the combined pressures of the tangible, noticeable effects of global climate change and of an expanding global economic system render impossible the reconstruction of traditional relationships to specific places or regions. The inability to move freely—to become familiar with the intimate rhythms of weather, ecosystem, and topography—whether as a result of regional or global climate change or of specific social or economic concerns, can impel northern communities to redefine themselves according to an emerging series of external forces.

Whereas mobility and movement across a landscape are often perceived as the antithesis of place rootedness and attentiveness to one's bioregion, migration and nomadism can, contrarily, build closer connections to place— the very travel across terrain gives meaning to place and building communities around shared experience of place.[2] Australian Aboriginal songlines are a clear example, as are emergence and migration stories of native North American peoples and story maps and platial descriptors used by native peoples across the Arctic. The work of herding and hunting necessitates a movement that is directly tied to topography, season, local climate, distribution of flora, and migration of fauna. The labor made explicit by individual movement across a landscape can be seen to define a bioregion—or, conversely, to be defined by it. The reindeer herding culture of the Sámi in northern Scandinavia is one such group—directly tied to the terrain and challenged by southern economic, political, and social pressures as well as by a climate change that is likewise largely precipitated by more industrial southern neighbors.

As a way to celebrate cultural and ecological identity and, at least in part, to help ground unfamiliar readers in a unique landscape, Sámi poet Nils-Aslak Valkeapää's 1997 book, *The Sun, My Father*, invites readers to traverse a sequence of 570 linked, numbered poems that emphasize the place, people, and regional identity of the Sámi. The book, itself a translation of Valkeapää's 1988 *Beaivi, Áhčážan*, interbraids language with the particulars of the landscape and culture of the Sámi region of northern Finland, Sweden, Norway, and Russia. With catalogs of flora and fauna particular to the region, and a deep consciousness of place, the poems are a literal invitation to explore the region's particular landscape. The sequence of poems 69–71, for instance, identifies key ecological and topographic touchstones in an effort to entice readers to engage with the Sámi region:

> 69. step by step
> smell of green, the first grass
> blue heather
>   Angelica

wood sorrel

upland waters

towards the sky

from peak to peak

these lands

the valleys

the high mountain slopes

over the forests

towards the coast

meadows
reindeer calf moors
land where calves are born

70. come
and I will show you
secretly
these paths,
      that begin, disappear
come
and I will point
with wonder
          to the antlers, the water flowers
the blowing of whales,
            flocks of eider

proud bold peaks
stony, crumbled beaches . . .

71. the land
is different
when you have lived there
wandered

sweated
frozen

see the sun
set rise
disappear return

. . .

While Valkeapää demonstrates his connection to even the minutiae of the Sámi region, from the broad topographic features of peaks and beaches to a landscape resonating with narrative in the "land where calves are born," the potentially marginalizing specificity of his home place is balanced by a continuing invitation to his readers—originally only readers of Sámi—to participate, celebrate, and engage in the unique attributes of this northern landscape. At the very center of Valkeapää's poetic sequence, the reader encounters, in poem 272, a seven-page textual representation of a reindeer herd traversing the book from right to left, from the end of the book to the beginning, meeting the reader headlong when both reader and reindeer arrive at the middle of the book. Harald Gaski traces in the poem a complex layering of "sounds pertaining to migration, words for working the herd, for the baying of dogs, and the sounds of a thousand hoofs on frozen ground, for undulating moors over which reindeer horns move, for the sound of bells that, like a blanket of clouds, lift the sky up and give the basis for life in these northern regions" (qtd. in Dana, *Áillohaš* 90). Grounded in specificity and detail, the poem minimizes the distance between language, self, and the world, thereby beginning to build a path toward a clearly intentional relationship between people and place.

Gaski identifies and offers translation of most of the terms in Valkeapää's poem 272; however, at the same time he asserts that the poem is untranslatable—as is apparent in the numerous words specific to the identity of particular reindeer and to the practice of herding reindeer. The language of the poem and the work of writing the poem are parallel to the work of reindeer herding itself: the work of writing and the work of being in place. Poems 272 and 273 are the only untranslated poems in *The Sun, My Father*, which asserts explicitly that the language regarding reindeer is untranslatable and inseparable from the culture and environment of the Sámi region in a manner that Douglas Reichert Powell might describe as using "rhetoric to describe these intricate interactions" between individual, culture, and place (21). The very periods that follow the poem exist as traces of herding's environmental and cultural legacy. Furthermore, without the context provided by the extensive photos throughout *Beaivi, Áhčážan*, which frame the poem in photos of reindeer herds, herders, and the tools of their trade, poem 272 both marginalizes and incites dialogue with the context of the poem's content.

Dana makes clear that reindeer are identified by the Sámi with a precision that allows clear identification of distinct individuals by verbal description alone: "Throughout this aural, linguistic trance, the reader is brought into the essence of a Sámi way of life. . . . On the recorded version, their characters and behavior are audible in their names and the voices of the layered voices, chanting this herd into reality" (Dana, *Áilloháš* 90–91). This precision underlies the language in poem 272 of *The Sun, My Father* and asserts the proficiency of the herding culture within the particular landscape of the Sámi region. Valkeapää's poetry, offers Dana, represents "no idle walk in the highlands, seeking beauty, but an expression of traditional ecological knowledge of an experienced reindeer herder, who recognizes the value of this spring pasturage appropriate for calving" (Dana, "Robert Frost" 70). The poem's movement across the pages of his book, then, is a deliberate engagement of Sámi cultural traditions as well as an invitation to readers to celebrate the specific and irreplaceable nature of particular language and place.

More recently, Sámi reindeer-herder and current Saami Council President, Olav Mathis Eira, has offered his personal observation of climate change in a 2011 interview, in which he asserts that the results of changing snow conditions, migration of tree line, and parasites has had a significant impact on reindeer-herding practices and, by extension, cultural traditions: "The worst thing for reindeer is that the condition of snow has changed," he says, which makes it "too hard for reindeer to get down to the food. The result is starvation." The reality of today's changing climate in northern latitudes is apparent across Sámi as it is throughout northern Canada, Alaska, Greenland, and Russia. Mathis Eira cites his own observation of a tree line that is perceptibly trending north, thereby causing birch leaf–cover to kill the grass on which the reindeer and their herders depend; the ice and snow conditions are less stable, and as a result, he laments, "if reindeer herding disappears, it will have a big effect on the entire Saami culture" (Mathis Eira). The narrative of work here draws attention to the daily experience with place, cultural identity, and the dynamics of climate in the North. It is the cultural, economic, and environmental threats to continued traditional work in the North that presents the tableau on which Sámi, like Valkeapää and Mathis Eira, describe both a land under shadow of inevitable change and the work that continues to hold the land and culture together.

The poetry of Valkeapää makes explicit these ties between environment and culture through language. As Gaski explains, Valkeapää shows us that "Whether we journey *with* the herd or only pass by it as we wander, it is impossible for us to survive into the future without the tracks, without nature" (Dana, *Áilloháš* 90; Harald Gaski, "A Language to Catch Birds With"). The periods that trail the poem's six pages of layered reindeer lan-

lándesteadáji   *uuuuuuu*   *uuuuuu*   *roahpebiellu*   *guŋká njunuš*   *duoddarat*   *eallun*   *bárusteame*   *báraideame*   *máraideame máraideam*
                                                                                      njunušmanni   ovdamanni   oaivugas   njunušgeahkka
                                                                                      eallima   johtola

Poem 272, a textual representation of reindeer herd migration, from Nils-Aslak
Valkeapää's *The Sun, My Father* (in Sámi language, not translated into English).
Used with permission.

guage effectively denote a trace of cultural and environmental legacy that
is at once hopeful, as a historical record, and concerning, as evidence of
decline in this traditional craft. The labor of herding runs parallel to the
work of writing and adds what Kent Ryden has called a "geography . . .
thickly layered with significance" (*Mapping* 95) to create a written record of
movement across a landscape, which inevitably develops into an ambiguous palimpsest of meanings, each trod into the fragile, undulating terrain.

The definition of place through an interbraiding of culture and ecological perspectives points again to the fluid nature of region—that region is
"not a thing in itself, a stable and bounded object of study" (Powell 21). The
fluctuation of mean annual temperature, sea-ice extent, or precipitation
calls into question the ways that cultures define themselves and indeed the
indelible marks with which they tend to circumscribe their home places.
With their perception of the northward movement of aspen and birch trees
in northern Scandinavia, the decrease in sea ice that leads to storm surges

coarvemearran

guolbanat   čoarvin   sugadeame   sojadeame   ruvgaleame
biellobalvan   leavvedolgin girjjohallá   dihhát   eallun
áldobiellu   bielloáldu heargebiellu   bielloheargi
               severjesmuzetčuoivvat
                              spiirtamuzet

silbasiidu   sietnjanjunni
gierddočalbmi   gearddočoarvi
beavvránit čazat sarvvačoarvin dolvvásteame njolggásteame
duottar   eallá   davviguovllu eallenvuoddu
duottarboazu máttaboazu vuovdeboazu njárgaboazu
             doalvi dolvvedit doalvvástit
             njolgi njolggedit njolggástit
             cirgut gurgalit šávihit
                    skavgalit
                              gomogazzii

along Alaska's northwestern coast, and changes in migration patterns of
land mammals in Nunavut, a growing number of indigenous witnesses
attest to contemporary changes in climate, changes which alter traditional
work customs. Such changes, coupled with economic or social factors, dramatically influence both cultural identity and the identity of region in the
circumpolar North.

The North, perhaps more than any defined bioregion, is far from static.
The icecap at the pole itself, though a mythic place for many North American children, is in constant motion—occasionally at speeds of up to 400
meters per hour. Both climate-related changes (whether localized, regional,
or global in extent; whether rapid or longer term) and the ties between
culture and climate are perhaps more starkly apparent in the North than
elsewhere. That said, the implication of fictional and poetic works from
a broad range of northern cultures that engage work as a central trope of
cultural identity help to define a region as more unified than the movement
of the Arctic ice sheet or the magnetic pole might suggest.

It is through work, which I have defined in this essay as an intimate, yet

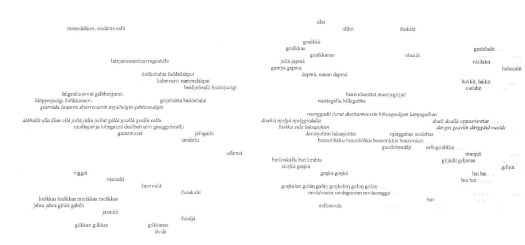

dynamic relationship between humans and the land, as well as in sketches of work in writing from the North, that a more complete picture of the fluidity of northern identity begins to emerge. Kent Ryden has offered that "A place—any place—is much more than a chunk of geography" (*Mapping* 95). Indeed, the richly layered terrain of the North (itself a diverse and multifaceted region) demands a close reading that is attuned to the changing relationship of people and place in the face of dramatic change. In *For Space*, Doreen Massey has similarly written that a thoughtful study of region asks us to recognize "space as the product of interrelations; as constituted through interactions, from the immensity of the global to the intimately tiny" (7). By looking at the native and Western perspectives on working and community in the North, it becomes clear that the North's specific biotic resonance as perhaps the world's largest bioregion has particular impact on the literary representation of work and of the cultures that perform it. Many northern authors limn an identity directly tied to a working landscape that is defined in the narrative by an individual's relationship to place. Furthermore, the work in these texts emphasizes the

discrete nature of local places and circumscribes the northern bioregion—
the laboring individual not *against* the climate and terrain of the Arctic,
but *with* it.

The North has never existed outside of the context of the global environment or, since early modern (or even medieval) European explorers
first set foot in the Arctic, outside of a global economic system. Southern
fascination with, dependence on—and, in the face of melting glacier ice,
great fear of—this region along the upper margin of the world continues
to attract an increasing rhetorical attention. "Insofar as the center is utterly
dependent upon the periphery," Wendell Berry writes, "its ignorance of
the periphery is not natural or necessary, but is merely dangerous" (116).
Perhaps it is through the methodical engagement of the land that labor can
craft a regionalism that sees itself as within the broader paradigm of global
economics and cultural relationships but does not allow itself to be written
into them in such a way that the rural/pastoral becomes subsumed by the
global marketplace and becomes just another commodity (Hess 95). The
currency of narrative about labor in the North and our *reading* of work

in the North—whether in social science treatises, fiction, poetry, or other forms—extend the possibilities of place when "literally unknown places become literarily known" (Ross 5).

NOTES

  1. For discussion of regional climate fluctuations in Greenland, see Nyegaard Hvid's *Climate Change* and Hamilton et al.'s "West Greenland's Cod-to-Shrimp Transition."
  2. See Heise, 50–62, and Deleuze and Guattari, 380–85.

WORKS CITED

Bell, Trevor, and M. A. P. Renouf. "The Domino Effect: Culture Change and Environmental Change in Newfoundland, 1500–1100 cal BP." *Northern Review* 28 (Winter 2008): 72–94. Print.

Berry, Wendell. *The Way of Ignorance*. Washington, D.C.: Shoemaker & Hoard, 2005. Print.

Dana, Kati. *Áillohaš the Shaman-Poet and his Govadas-Image Drum: A Literary Ecology of Nils-Aslak Valkeapää*. Oulu, Finland: University of Oulu Press, 2003. Print.

———. "Robert Frost in the Fields and Nils-Aslak Valkeapää at the Treeline: Ecological Knowledge and Academic Learning at the Northern Forest Edge." *Nature and Culture in the Northern Forest: Region, Heritage, and Environment in the Rural Northeast*. Ed. Pavel Cenkl. Iowa City: University of Iowa Press, 2010. 61–76. Print.

"The Debate over Oil Drilling in the Alaskan Wild." *Current Events*. 9 Mar. 2001. Web. 28 Oct. 2009. <http://findarticles.com/p/articles/mi_m0EPF/is_20_100/ai_71875058/pg_2/?tag=content;col1>.

Deleuze, Gilles, and Félix Guattari. *A Thousand Plateaus: Capitalism and Schizophrenia*. Minneapolis: University of Minnesota Press, 1987. Print.

Gaski, Harald. "A Reindeer Herd on the Move." *Sámi Culture*, nd. Web. 31 Oct. 2009. <http://www.utexas.edu/courses/Sámi/diehtu/siida/reindeer/comp-intro.htm>.

Hamilton, Lawrence. "Human-Environment Interactions: Social drivers and impacts of change in the North Atlantic Arc." GLOBEC Symposium on Climate Variability and Sub-Arctic Marine Ecosystems. Victoria, B.C., 16–20 May 2005.

———. Benjamin C. Brown, and Rasmus Ole Rasmussen. "West Greenland's Cod-to-Shrimp Transition: Local Dimensions of Climatic Change." *ARCTIC* 56.3 (2003): 271–82. Print.

Heise, Ursula K. *Sense of Place and Sense of Planet: The Environmental Imagination of the Gobal.* New York: Oxford University Press, 2008. Print.

Hess, Scott. "Postmodern Pastoral, Advertising, and the Masque of Technology." *ISLE: Interdisciplinary Studies in Literature and Environment* 11.1 (2004): 71–100. Print.

Kendall, Clare. "Life on the Edge of a Warming World." *Ecologist* 36.5 (2006): 26–29. Print.

Laxness, Halldór. *Independent People.* Trans. J. A. Thompson. New York: Vintage, 1997. Print.

Mann, Daniel, et al. "Environmental Change and Arctic Paleoindians." *Arctic Anthropology* 38.2: 2001. 119–38. Print.

Massey, Doreen. *For Space.* London: Sage Publications, 2005. Print.

Mathis Eira, Olav. "Climate Change Costing Herders Deer." Euronews. 4 Apr. 2011. Web. 29 July 2011. <http://www.euronews.net/2011/04/04/climate-change-costing-herders-deer/>.

Nyegaard Hvid, H. *Climate Change and the Greenland Society.* Denmark: WWF, 2007. Print.

Powell, Douglas Reichert. *Critical Regionalism: Connecting Politics and Culture in the American Landscape.* Chapel Hill: University of North Carolina Press, 2007. Print.

Qitsualik, Rachel A. "Skraeling." *Our Story: Aboriginal Voices on Canada's Past.* Ed. Tantoo Cardinal, et al. Toronto: Doubleday Canada, 2004. 33–68. Print.

Readicker-Henderson, Ed, and Lynn Readicker-Henderson. *Adventure Guide to the Alaska Highway.* Edison, New Jersey: Hunter Publishing, 2006. Print.

Ross, Patricia. *The Spell Cast by Remains: The Myth of Wilderness in Modern American Literature.* New York: Routledge, 2006. Print.

Ryden, Kent. *Landscape with Figures: Nature and Culture in New England.* Iowa City: University of Iowa Press, 2001. Print.

———. *Mapping the Invisible Landscape: Folklore, Writing, and the Sense of Place.* Iowa City: University of Iowa Press, 1993. Print.

Spirn, Anne Whiston. *The Language of Landscape.* New Haven: Yale University Press, 1998. Print.

DAN WYLIE

Douglas Livingstone's Poetry and the (Im)possibility of the Bioregion

I N HIS WONDERFUL BOOK *The Star Thrower*, Loren Eiseley relates how, walking along a beach one evening, he encountered a man diligently picking up stranded starfish and hurling them back into deeper sea. The "star thrower" admitted that this was quixotic but simply could not leave the fish to die. I can't remember if he—or Eiseley—considered the lives *lost* as a result of his philanthropy: the microbiota invisibly embedded in the sands, tiny carnivorous worms, scavenging crabs, and spiral-shelled plough mollusks that were being deprived of vital fleshy detritus.

South African poet Douglas Livingstone (1932–96) also writes of a beached starfish, a "minute, arid artefact" whose unusual six-pointed structure reminds him of the Star of David, of the Holocaust, and of all the world's

> countless starfish, children
> with no historian (Livingstone 41–42)

For this poet, *A Littoral Zone*—the title of his key volume (hereafter *LZ*)—is the interface of extremes, of life and death and the multiple interchanges between them. It is also the place he knows best: his bioregion.

Littoral zones both sandy and rocky support unique ecosystems, at their richest crammed with species of bacteria, algae, kelps, crabs, shellfish, octopi, urchins, and birds that can subsist under no other conditions. At this patently singular seam between the geological and the marine, there seems little reason not to apply the term *bioregion*. After all, many scientists have

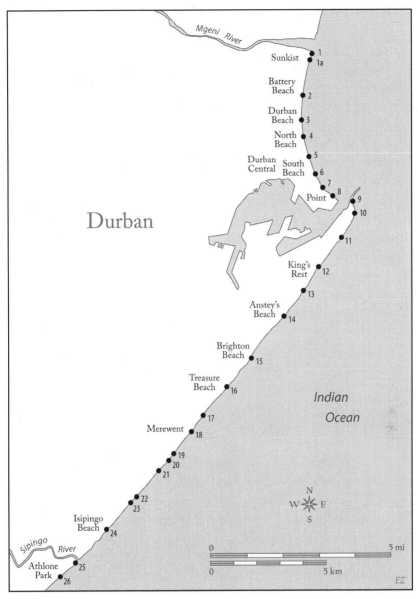

Durban, South Africa, and Douglas Livingstone's water-pollution measuring
stations

made their living studying estuarine mudflat or tidal pool ecosystems and
would unhesitatingly assert that their biological uniqueness and levels of
species-endemism are no less localized, worthy, or diverse than those of,
say, a tropical forest or the unique Cape Floral Kingdom fynbos biome.

As almost every observer of the littoral has noted, however, it is also a
zone of particularly dramatic dynamism: the relentless crashing of waves on
coral, rock, or sand, the diastole-systole rhythms of tides, the erosion and
infinitesimal rebuilding of beaches and dunes. It has become a widespread
symbol of the common fragility of natural and human affairs. Laurie Ricou
considers the intertidal zone "an ideal metaphor for a place in constant
transition . . . a place of deposition, of layering, of a mix of communities, of crevices and hidden pools" (qtd. in Mason 79). Though shoreline
conditions are extreme, they raise the difficulty of defining or retaining the
concept of a bioregion more generally. Even in relatively isolatable "systems," what we all now take as a truism—that ecology *is* dynamism—any
distinctiveness, stasis, or "balance" ever attained or discerned is necessarily
temporary, contingent, and relative. The turbulence of the littoral only
makes unavoidably obvious what holds for all the natural world.

It nevertheless often seems to make good sense to see the bioregion as
a "useful territorial container" (Aberley 31) with more or less discernible
boundaries. Some areas wear the epithet more easily than others: an oasis,
a patch of isolated forest, even a river catchment system. This perception
allows one to find oneself "at home" in the given area, to exercise what
Kirkpatrick Sale has termed "querencia" (Sale 3) and Peter Berg, in his
founding statement of bioregionalism, "reinhabitation" (Berg). One's very
sense of selfhood may be predicated on the comfortable familiarity with
certain species of tree, animal, or grass, their colors and sounds and textures, together ineffably constitutive of the place. Berg originally pointed
out—and this has remained a staple of the bioregional literature—that
the bioregion is definable by both natural and cultural elements, is both
"a geographic terrain and a terrain of consciousness." In "natural" terms,
Berg further defined the bioregion as exhibiting "a continuous geographic
terrain and includ[ing] a particular climate, local aspects of seasons, landforms, watersheds, soils, and native plants and animals." In cultural terms,
Berg reverts to the "ecologically adaptive cultures of early inhabitants,"
evidently in contrast to the "catastrophic effects on Earth's biosphere due to
human activities since the inception of the industrial era" (Berg). Another

stock definition calls a bioregion "an area that shares similar topography, plant and animal life, and human culture" (bioregionalism.org).

This notion of the bioregion-as-container, or "traditional" bioregionalism, has been widely critiqued recently. Critic Lawrence Buell notes, "Traditional writing about place tends to interest itself especially in bounded areas of small size" and that such ecolocalism is likely to be most "concerned about countering threats to the bounded holistic community from the outside." This is changing, so that "what especially differentiates modern bioregionalism, be it rural or urban, from traditional regionalism is the sense of vulnerability and flux . . . the increasing sense that regions remain permeable to shock waves potentially extending worldwide" (Buell 77, 81). Mitchell Thomashow concurs: "Bioregional theorists and activists are confounded if not disempowered by the conceptual challenges of interpreting dynamic global events and processes. How does a bioregional vision accommodate the bifurcation of economic globalization and political decentralization, the instability and dislocation of ecological and cultural diasporas, the elusiveness of pluralistic identities and multiple personas?" (121). Don Alexander similarly points out, in a brief but provocative essay, that one's delineation of a bioregion is dependent on "which geographical criteria one is using" and expresses grave doubts about the possibility of simplistically correlating natural areas with cultural units, even those of autochthonous people, let alone today's globalizing cultures (3). Sitting on my own home ground, an escarpment slope in South Africa's Eastern Cape, I might choose (as bioregionalists insist) to delineate it by natural rather than political criteria (the provincial boundary, or that of the more local Makana Municipality). I might choose to align my bioregion with the range of endemic species such as the broad-leaved Oldenburgia trees which shade me, the thorny complex of so-called Eastern Cape Thicket visible on a facing slope, and the earthy underworld of golden moles invisible beneath me. Well and good. However, if I were to look for distinctive geological or climatic criteria, I would have to admit that the Table Mountain sandstone rock on which I sit is of a type continuous throughout the Cape fold mountains stretching a thousand kilometers west of me (well beyond my "home ground") and that with a dry "Berg wind" blowing across my back from the northern deserts even as the rim of a cold front of southwesterly storm, born just yesterday in the South Atlantic, approaches across the distant coast, I am perched not within a distinctive container but at the intersection of many systems. Not to mention the European swallows and Russian yellow-billed kites hunting above me, the protea flowers that have been here since before Gondwanaland broke up and can be found identically in Argentina, and the vigorous mess of invasive English bracken, Scottish thistles, and Australian wattles (one of which I now enthusiastically uproot, in defense of the putative "integrity" of "my bioregion"). Such global intersections are equally multiple in human cultural terms: there is simply no one cultural presence—Bushman, Xhosa, white settler, or any other—coterminous with natural features, and indeed, my region is punted in the tourist literature as "Frontier country."

Alexander proposes four different ways of approaching the definition of a bioregion, not all necessarily mutually exclusive, and despite his cautions, not necessarily destructive of the bioregional ideal. They are the "determinist position" (nature determines culture); a correspondence between nature and culture (mutual affectiveness); a possibilist position (resources set certain limits); and one in which "the terrain of consciousness is everything" (what we think we are is what we are). None of these, in my view, goes very far in helping actually delineate a bioregion. It may be more helpful to think of "hard" (possessing clear boundaries) and "soft" (recognizing a higher degree of porosity) methods of delineation. The hardness of a boundary may be set by "natural," materialist features (which assumes we can objectively "know" what's out there, though even what we select as natural resources is partly governed by cultural imperatives or aesthetics) or by political or legislative fiat (as in setting the borders of a national park, which may well not precisely correlate with ecosystems like catchment areas). As it is, a political dimension has been an integral feature of bioregionalism from Berg onwards, given bioregional movements' deliberate defiance of the validity of larger political units. In effect, most definitions and practices seem to allow a variable degree of "softness" in their assertion of defensible "boundaries" to the bioregion: a certain arbitrariness is recognized, as is an inevitably fluid composition of intersecting "imagined communities," to use Benedict Anderson's famous phrase. Nor is such indeterminacy a ploy of poets or writers: a standard ecology textbook states, "The safest statement we can make about community boundaries is that probably they do not exist. . . . The ecologist is usually better employed looking at the ways in which communities grade into each other" (Begon 478).

Consequently, bioregionalists find it increasingly difficult coherently to harbor utopian "harmony-" or "balance-" driven programs. Aberley's belief that "bioregionalism offers the best hope we have for creating an inter-dependent web of self-reliant, sustainable cultures" (McGinnis 4) seems remote at best, even internally self-contradictory. Aberley quotes, but does not critique, Sale's list of features of this kind of "bioregional paradigm," which attempts idealistically to incorporate both stability *and* evolution, both cooperation *and* decentralization. Harking back to an alleged "condition of symbiotic balance" (House and Gorsline qtd. in Aberley 21) amongst so-called primitive peoples as a baseline for a "future primitive" state of similar balance, also, as Alexander has argued, appears illusory.

Some "soft" version of bioregionalism, founded on intimate local knowledges, may yet prove essential to saving our environments. I suggest, however, that the concept of the *ecotone* may be a more useful and accurate one than the container-like *bioregion*. The ecotone may be defined as the "zone of transition . . . having a set of characteristics uniquely defined by space and time scales, and by the strength of the interactions between adjacent ecological systems" (di Castri qtd. in Mason 4). John Elder suggests that an ecotone partakes "of some of the physical attributes of each constituent environment and harbours some of the creatures from each as well. Within such a meeting-ground, 'edge-effect' prevails, in a diversity of species that exceeds those of the separate ecosystems" (qtd. in Mason 4). I suggest further that, rather than being a mosaic of putatively independent and exclusionary units, any biotic environment is effectively *all* edge-effect: ecotones or fuzzy boundaries "all the way down." This conception of environment, especially when natural and human cultural influences mesh, conflict, and cross-fertilize, has rather different ethical and methodological implications for anyone claiming to "belong" in a chosen locale and wishing to defend or improve it. It is not so much that "belonging" vanishes or becomes incoherent, but rather that its expressions and motivations are processual rather than regional, integrative rather than defensive, progressive rather than backward looking, global as well as local.

Douglas Livingstone's poetry both exemplifies and explores precisely these difficulties and charts a way through them, albeit a rather unsettling one. Livingstone was born in 1932 in Malaya but settled in southern Africa, finally becoming a marine biologist with a particular brief to help protect South Africa's east coast (north and south of the port city of Durban). For some two decades he "sallied in / rapt attendance on the sea's health" (*LZ* 48)—measuring water-pollution levels at a series of selected stations. He increasingly integrated his scientific work into a substantial body of poetry

of a tough, knotty, often raunchy, sometimes delightfully satirical kind. He
depicts himself setting out in his little Cortina car

> loaded with boxes
> of wide-mouthed glass sampling bottles,
> aluminium racks of plastic ones
> and a sampling stick that clacks its jaws.
> To horse! (*LZ* 9)

Later,

> A sea sample gets hooked, grappled
> with ancient tricks through practiced scoops,
> flicks of the wrist, the excess spilled. (*LZ* 35)

Although during the turbulent 1970s and 1980s, when the struggle against
apartheid was uppermost in the national consciousness, Livingstone was
accused by many of being inadequately politicized, his ecological vision is
now regaining relevance. By the time he died in 1996, he was—and still
is—widely considered South Africa's premier poet, yet his poetry remains
critically neglected, especially in its environmental aspects. This is com-
pounded by a complete absence of bioregional literary studies in South Africa: though material suitable for such study is abundant in our literatures,
as far as I know the word hasn't even entered the locally embryonic fields
of ecocriticism and environmental history.

As the discussion above indicates, it's doubtful whether in *A Littoral Zone*
Livingstone can be said to be writing of a bioregion at all. To characterize
the collection as being the exploration of an ecotone makes much more
sense of it. Nevertheless, his commitment to saving this strip of territory
from some of its anthropogenic damage is not in doubt. His numbered
measuring stations remained fixed—the volume includes a map which sets
them out, as nodes around which most of the poems are written—and his
work, literally at the microscopic level, exemplifies the attentive miniatur-
ization which, in Jonathan Bate's formulation, best makes loving a place
possible. Bate reworks Gaston Bachelard thus: "the more attuned I am as I
miniaturize the world, the better I dwell upon the earth" (Bate 161). That
sea and love are constant metaphors for one another in Livingstone's oeuvre
is just one indication of his feelings for the "place," unbounded though it
intrinsically is. Like many bioregionalists, he also eschewed provincial, na-

tional, and other political borders, and indeed used biological scales and
continuities as a critical lever against them. He would have approved, along
with Buell, that the "new environmentalist writing and criticism is also
always in some sense a post-nationalist persuasion" (Buell 81).

Livingstone had no illusions about the difficulties he faced, though he
was not unsuccessful in helping improve water quality along that increasingly built-up coastline (his strip is today lined virtually end-to-end with
hotels, casinos, and rich holiday suburbs). Like Eiseley's star thrower, he
overtly characterized his little crusade as quixotic, even

> futile,
> scientifically delivered blows at sullage,
> against the republics of ignorance and apathy,
> with bust lance, flawed shield,
> lamed steed of action. (*LZ* 10)

In an inadvertent but telling congruence with Eiseley, Livingstone included
this epigraph from *Don Quixote* in *A Littoral Zone*: "I have always heard,
Sancho, that doing good to base fellows is like throwing water into the sea"
(*LZ* 6). To the degree that he permitted himself hope for fruitful change,
he was a romantic, but in a quite severely unspiritual vein; hence Mariss
Stevens, in the only major study of this work to date, characterizes him as
a "Romantic materialist" (Stevens). She also calls him an ecopessimist: Livingstone abhorred much of human behavior as grimly destructive, likely to
leave no more than "A legacy of dust, and no more green" ("Premonition"
qtd. in Hacksley 498).

But he never allowed this prognosis to curb his energetic campaign to
do what he could. He considered the South African coastline a microcosm of the country, and the country that of the planet; the planetary
perspective also rescues his poetry from accusations of narrow or exclusionary provincialism. Indeed, the poems, despite being so knowledgeable
about and redolent of their places of origin, defy the traditional models
of bioregionalism in at least three main ways. First, they are constantly
intersected by the incursion of extra-littoral, even global influences, both
natural and human cultural, both temporal and spatial. Second, Livingstone evinces little interest in utopian schemes of balance and harmony; his
imagery is characteristically of unstable motility, evolutionary in its scope
and assumptions. Even the body, which he repeatedly describes in terms

suited to the bioregion, almost *as* a bioregion in itself, is porous and unintegrated. Third, he is as interested in human presences (including literary and imaginative ones) as in the natural. Indeed, as most bioregionalists now recognize, humans have to be counted as integral to "the community" of biota as well, with all their destructive foibles. Human denizens of this ecotone, from hoteliers to impoverished beachcombing children, feature prominently in Livingstone's wry purview. In the remainder of this chapter, I explore each of these aspects in more detail.

First, then, Livingstone's poems consistently show how the littoral zone, virtually by definition, is not sealed off from its adjoining regions—ocean and land. He would doubtless agree with biologist Joseph P. Dudley that "bioregional parochialism . . . places great limitations on our ability to comprehend and communicate the pervasive effects of anthropogenic and ecological phenomena of continental and global significance" (Dudley 1332). The poet himself is a node of coalescence:

> Drinking, I drink
> old mythologies—
> men, gods, strange beasts;
> the stones, slaked bottles, seas. (Hacksley 122)

On the one hand, from the ever-suggestively fluid resources of the sea, food arrives for the beach residents, bodies wash up alongside flotsam from passing ships, legends are imported on the back of global maritime trade. More profoundly, Livingstone regards the sea as our ultimate evolutionary origin:

> vestiges in me
> recall a time I once breathed in [evolution's] sea. (*LZ* 18)

The interstitial zone of "Haunted Estuary" is a birthplace of coiling mists

> where river & sea
> the fresh & the saline
> rehearse in the air
> the grapplings of cubs. (*LZ* 11)

In "Address to a Patrician at Station 8," Livingstone apostrophizes the coelocanth, a species which has survived virtually unchanged in deep-sea trenches for millions of years. The final stanza contrasts the astonishing persistence of this species with the "makeshift" nature of almost everything else, but also celebrates a profound ancestral interconnection:

> What awes me—fish from long ago—
> is not the muddying of your chaps
> when waves clawed 200 metres up
> or below today's makeshift shores
> nor your changeless chinless lineage,
> but your fathers squirting on eggs
> to sire everyone I know. (*LZ* 24)

He has a reverent sense of the mysterious, overwhelming depths of time and space of the ocean, which is the

> great menstruum
> solvent and transmuter
> of men and ships. (*LZ* 42)

Against its immensity the poet is

> a mere excrescence
> on a giant's spine dreamed up
> by seas still veiled to fettered man. (*LZ* 48)

Nevertheless, if in the ocean we began, then language itself must have begun there, too; in an earlier poem, "Aspects," Livingstone envisages "a tropic sea-floor / beyond divers, submarines / the nosings of bathyscaphes" where "On a patch of clean sand / both god the father and his son / have shyly signed their names," an originary tablet as it were, "where Earth's / old volcanic basalt floods / quietly made some words" (Hacksley 373–74). Our own art is analogous or derivative, serious but not to be taken too seriously; so he wryly toasts his own poetic métier in "Libation to the Geoid, Station 23" (*LZ* 56):

> Here's to the sea in its restive quest
> intent on drowning land;
> even the saddest poem's a jest
> writ on the ebb-tide's sand.

Repeatedly, Livingstone figures the advent of both life and death, of consciousness itself, as a fraught transition across the foreshore from ocean to land,

> the mind
> groping its way, hand over hand,
> north to murderous oceans of sand. (*LZ* 39)

Section II of the poem, "Thirteen Ways of Looking at a Black Snake" (*LZ* 16), depicts another creature crawling across the beach, apparently fruitlessly:

> Baked dry by the sun, the stiff black snake
> forms a parched question-mark between
> highwater-mark and the dunes.
> Eden was ever too far for the crawling back.

The littoral zone represents nothing so strongly as the infirmity of Edenic or utopian ideals. Although in one poem, "Eland about Station 17" (*LZ* 44), Livingstone seems to valorize the lives of "symbiotic" San or Bushman peoples, whose rock art he discovers in a hidden cave, he decides to tell no one about it. That autochthonous world is no longer retrievable. Mostly, the littoral embodies the improbability of ever attaining either a settled environment or a reformed human nature:

> The approximation to justice,
> the perfectibility of man,
> the conservation of beauty,
> the final attainment of truth
> are salients that ever evade us. (*LZ* 12)

Puzzling at the meaning of life and thought's ephemerality—and of death itself—is a persistent theme in Livingstone's oeuvre. In "Bad Run at King's Rest" (*LZ* 37) a beached turtle, "shell split by an errant propellor-blade," lies dying, tormented by gulls, urchins, and trophy hunters. The speaker, "asking pardon, cut[s] the leathery throat," and appeals "dumbly" for meaning "to the incoming tides." No meaning is forthcoming. Similarly, when encountering a beached dolphin, the poet tries in vain to return it to the sea: the bystanders to whom he appeals for help want only to kill it with "a long and rusted bayonet" (*LZ* 55). It is his own impulse to compassion which puzzles the poet; clumsily he tries to persuade himself that dolphins and humans alike are carnivores, caught up in the evolutionary cycles, and perhaps "dolphins are no more / than raw fish-dogs of the sea; or bait," the well-known smile an anthropomorphic illusion. On the verge of this "paradox" the poet feels similarly helpless, stranded, dying, alien.

The paradox is that the erratic progressions of evolution, its "rash chromosomal loops" and "random nightmares" (*LZ* 18), have somehow bred in us sympathies, sentiments, and fears arising in part from our consciousness of death. These feelings are ever a source of tension between acceptance of our being "natural" organisms, and our ephemeral glorying in those cultural productions with which we attempt to assuage or explain our lot. In "Coronach at Cave Rock" (*LZ* 29), the poet discovers a "small, silent piece" of driftwood, "the holster-stock of a machine-pistol issued / to U-boat crews." The piece bears the name A VON WEBERN—not the musician of that name, the poet assumes, but the coincidence sends him off on a tightly interwoven meditation on the meanings of music and the horrors of the Nazi Holocaust, and above all how they could possibly coexist. The poet fondly imagines that *this* A von Webern was a mere conscript and, like him, "an indignant pacifist," but he is also then obliged to envisage his own end, his own "crumbling essence drowned in blood or water."

While on the one hand the sea delivers up life, death, and the material for paradoxical meditations on human origins, on the other, the urban landscapes of the immediate hinterland also impinge on the littoral zone. A number of poems relate trips to or from the shoreline, some labeled "traffic interludes": land is governed by a highly mechanized, mobile, globally networked culture. As Leonard Lutwack has pointed out, the "quality of a place in literature is subtly determined by the manner in which a character arrives at it, moves within it, and departs from it" (qtd. in Love 111). "Starting Out," for example, is a detailed narrative of driving out from the city of Durban to the measuring stations, the early morning streets all but empty. As dawn rises and the suburbs thin, he notes

> stacked heaps of concrete lumber,
> the high-rise cabinets where more folk are filed.

The press of those bureaucratically anonymous "millions" is suffocating, rendering his work all but "futile." There is, however, a recognition that the urban and natural are intricately interlinked; the urban environs are described in marine metaphors: "Gnarled leaves" are "like keloidal crustaceans / crabbed in sight and sound"; a prostitute is "dolphin-dusky."

Even on the beaches the "sullage" of those "millions" is inescapable. In "The Christmas Chefs of Station 1A" (*LZ* 12), postparty "mess on the sand [is] incredible," prompting the gloomy prognostications on the elusiveness of human perfectibility quoted earlier. In "Reflections at Sunkist" (*LZ* 13), "the paper cups, the empty tins . . . a silver slice of mirror," "Monday's debris from Sunday's crowd" makes it hard to "face the shattered sea uncowed." Indeed, this shame of human carelessness prompts an excursion into the nature of madness, couched as memories of an insane asylum.

These ruminations end with the poet turning to the sea for renewal: "the brain [is] as untameable as any ocean," he says, and though a "cauterized synapse" might shrivel and die,

> it could be some cerebral referee
> clicks on new relays to spark in that sea.

This tentatively optimistic figuring of the brain as oceanic and self-healing brings us to the second focus: the body as bioregion. It is striking how often Livingstone returns to the yearning, hurting body as an emanation, almost, of the spaces within which it moves. At best the body feels like a temporary habitation,

> little but a glove
> stretched from metatarsals to neocortex
> on a stiffening frame. (*LZ* 7)

But it is intrinsically heterogeneous: the boundedness of skin and the autonomy of "self" are really superficial and temporary "mirages" (*LZ* 38). In fact, Livingstone wrote, "Each of us is a walking universe of complexly disparate worlds, continents and seas, with immense and differing populations, all organized together into some sort of functioning coherence with the single inherent determination (if we are sane) to preserve life and what is left of our planet" (qtd. in Stevens 57).

The poem "A Tide in the Affairs of Station 18" (*LZ* 46) sharply explores the paradoxical "inherent determination[s]" of love and survival. The "affairs" of the poet's body are envisaged as a tidal system caught between restraint, attainment, and allure. A man is both "Cool Jekyll" and "manic Hyde," as two-faced as the littoral zone itself. Man's "obsessions collide / with self-possessed coasts forever anointed / with his ditherings, his slimes, his ebbs and flows"; on the one hand he is a "hunter-killer," on the other "fouled up by sublimities"; and sometimes it seems that only his rampant, evolutionary sexual drive is "durable and permanent as any tide." This is to see love as analogous to, or an extension of, what Livingstone elsewhere—most unscientifically—discerned as a "Creative Principle" in the universe (Stevens 81). Yet there is a hint that this too will pass, or at least our consciousness of it will.

The ephemeral nature of the human body is most vividly depicted in "Cells at Station 11" (*LZ* 35), in which death, interconnection at the molecular level, and incursion on the littoral zone from outside, simultaneously intersect. The poem describes the poet finding "a blackened corpse" tumbling sluggishly in the surf,

> the sea unsure
> about relinquishment.

He dutifully takes his water sample as usual, aware that his microscope might well reveal cells that have drifted in from the rotting body. This prompts a meditation (drawing on the research of Lynn Margulis) on the cellular and molecular foundations of our life:

> Billion-year-old invaders
> the silent mitochondria—
> propel our mobile towers, shared cells
> sparking, colonized by vandals:
> a fifth column of DNA
> in interstellar sequences,
> bland in their promiscuity.

Like the littoral itself, our very consciousness seems under siege by outside forces, almost at war with itself. To consider the way in which, at this molecular level of blindly "interned energies," "life pump[s] through us anyhow," is to seriously question our notions of "autonomy." We only "think we choose." Yet this view has a curious ethical outcome: "Woe will betide, betimes, the man / who kills his brother," or burns him, for he "burns shared cells." To injure another is to injure oneself. Furthermore, to the extent that we are all "interstellar," made from and subtly interchanging common physical materials, we are "bound lovers under the sun," all alike "lolling there in an unchecked sea." In short, the body itself is more an ecotone than a bioregion, a nexus of "connection of desires, conjunction of flows, continuum of intensities" (Deleuze and Guattari 161); its sense of coherence and autonomy is illusory, its pretensions, in the final analysis, touchingly absurd.

Everywhere along this littoral, in fact, humans and their endeavors, though ineluctably present in (mostly) deleterious effects, are described as transitory. Even so massive an enterprise as a whaling station is now abandoned, "ship-wrecked" (*LZ* 36). At a number of points in the collection, hotels are figured as icons of transience; though their inhabitants seem often decayed to the point of indifference, Livingstone acutely observes both their touristic dependence on, and subjection to, the natural forces of the littoral. In the crumbling "Beachfront Hotel at Station 5" (*LZ* 19), the rails are "salt-stained," the stairs "sand-crunching," the banisters "crab-clawed," as if the environment is about to recolonize it. At the same time, Livingstone lifts the tawdry details of the place into ironically mythic perspectives: the door is like that of a "dead-man's-chest"; furnitures "confront each other in sword and trident stances"; the "outcopulated springs" of the bed amount to a "Golgotha for males." Yellowed pages from old issues of the famous magazine *Drum*, a prime vehicle in its day for up-and-coming black middle-class urban readers, recall a heyday of South African writers:

> . . . sheets of Nat Nakasa and Bloke Modisane;
> of Casey Motsisi and Arthur Maimane;
> pages of Lewis Nkosi; while a piece signed
> Ezekiel Mphahlele sticks.

But the pages have been ignorantly relegated to "shallow warped flimsy ill-fitting drawers"—those adjectives a concise comment on the entire, weirdly conglomerate culture of the modern South Africa. Countering this sardonic comment on the demeaning of creative writing, however, is the sense that these writers have nevertheless survived, a global company amongst whom Livingstone is happy to place himself. This littoral/literal meeting and melding of previously, ostensibly divided cultures is as much an integral part of the ecotone as natural crossings-over. Most importantly, then, the poem's final stanza insists on the tenacity of love, significantly couched once again in both marine and cosmic metaphors:

> Yet love vaults unbidden from memory's dungeon,
> its lyricism whirled from the seabed of this world
> to bounce off heedless constellations . . .

Characteristically, such valorization of love as Livingstone finds is haunted, if not wholly compromised, by an apocalyptic sense of humanity's impending, deserved demise. In a key poem, the fantasial "The Wall beyond Station X" (*LZ* 27), the poet walks out along a narrow wall angling away "across the shallows." But as the poem puts it, "The history of walls is not too good." This one narrows, becomes ever more precarious, the weather stormy, return impossible. It ends:

> Equilibrium
> at risk, you try a quick glance back:
> the wall behind you is dissolving as you pass.

This is precisely the quality of the ecotone. Nowhere is the tension between love and misanthropy more evident to Livingstone than at the symbolically shifting borderline of all intersections, the littoral zone where global natural and cultural influences, both destructive and creative, necessarily converge, conflict, and coalesce.

In sum, the littoral zone is a region of "impossible compromises" and "insupportible interfusions," as he puts it in the collection's last poem, "Road Back" (*LZ* 60). In one guise, the sea is his "old ally against psychic apathy, who saves [his] soul from atrophy"; but it (or, in Livingstone's gendered characterization, "she") also teases him with

> her obverse face: a negligence verging
> without cruelty on maternal indifference.

The insanity of the highway along which he finally drives home is a reflection of humans' crazy inner world of unquenchable desires,

> the whole substructure steered and toed
> by the doomed and hurtling microcosm within.

Humanity, Livingstone believes, is destined for self-destruction, like everything else that lives tending

> to excrete
> its entropy.

Once we overwhelm our resources, planetary systems will reassert themselves. Despite the fact that the planet ultimately "must win," and so perhaps does not need him as one of its "quixotic knights," he has no choice but "to accept the gage and buckle to," take his water samples, write his "words, words, words," throw the starfish back. Livingstone evidently draws on James Lovelock's Gaian conceptualizations here, to produce a sad closing paean to miraculous life on what is, effectively, the only bioregion, the whole Earth:

> The planet counter-attacks.
> Its choice is plain: kill or be killed.
> Ours too: symbiosis or death

at the hands of a bright blue cell
—the only living thing in known space.

WORKS CITED

Aberley, Doug. "Interpreting Bioregionalism." McGinnis 14–42.
Alexander, Don. "Bioregionalism: The Need for a Firmer Theoretical Foundation." *Trumpeter* 13.3 (1996): 1–7. Print.
Bate, Jonathan. *The Song of the Earth*. London: Picador, 2000. Print.
Begon, Michael, Colin R. Townsend, and John L. Harper. *Ecology: From Individuals to Ecosystems*. London: Blackwell, 2006. Print.
Berg, Peter. "Bioregionalism (a definition)." Diggers.org, 2002. Web. 3 April 2010.
Buell, Lawrence. *The Future of Environmental Criticism*. London: Blackwell, 2005. Print.
Deleuze, Gilles, and Félix Guattari. *A Thousand Plateaus: Capitalism and Schizophrenia*. Minneapolis: University of Minnesota Press, 1987. Print.
Dudley, Joseph P. "Bioregional Parochialism and Global Activism." *Conservation Biology* 9.5 (1995): 1332–34. Print.
Hacksley, Malcolm, and Don Maclennan, eds. *A Ruthless Fidelity: The Collected Poems of Douglas Livingstone*. Cape Town: David Philip, 2007. Print.
Livingstone, Douglas. *A Littoral Zone*. Cape Town: Carrefour, 1991. Print.
Love, Glen. *Practical Ecocriticism: Literature, Biology and the Environment*. Charlottesville: University of Virginia Press, 2003. Print.
Mason, Travis V. "Ornithology of Desire: Birding in the Ecotone and the Poetry of Don MacKay." PhD thesis. University of British Columbia: Vancouver, 2007. Print.
McGinnis, Michael, ed. *Bioregionalism*. London: Routledge, 1999. Print.
Sale, Kirkpatrick. *Dwellers in the Land*. 1991. Athens: University of Georgia Press, 2005. Print.
Stevens, Mariss. "'Symbiosis or Death': An Ecocritical Examination of Douglas Livingstone's Poetry." MA thesis. Rhodes University, Grahamstown, 2004. Print.
Thomashow, Mitchell. "Towards a Cosmopolitan Bioregionalism." McGinnis 121–32. Print.

ANNE MILNE

"Fully motile and AWAITING FURTHER INSTRUCTIONS"

Thinking the Feral into Bioregionalism

WHAT DOES THE FERAL HAVE TO DO WITH BIOREGIONALISM?

I F BIOREGIONALISM IS VIEWED narrowly, with a bioregion seen as a distinct natural region or a local place touted for its specialities, the feral may function as an unwelcome or invasive intrusion. In this narrow view, the energy of the local is focused on expelling, demonizing, marginalizing, and even destroying the feral. Generally, the feral can be understood as a state that lies somewhere between domesticated and wild. Ferality is implicitly accepted as a natural process: what happens when a domestic escapes, is released, or is transported into another bioregion; or conversely, what happens when the wild thing shifts or is shifted out of its wild. Yet once ferality is achieved, fait accompli, a perceptual reconfiguration takes place and the feral suddenly becomes unnatural; in this view, as Nicholas Garside explains, the feral is "disruptive" and "*out of place*," losing "any sense of intrinsic value" (62). Furthermore, ferality risks being seen as working against the ideals of bioregionalism and place-based perspectives. Feral animals may be equated with invasive species, with the focus on eradicating the invaders before they eradicate us. As we prepare ourselves to kill the feral (or euphemistically, "cull" them), we describe them as pests, vermin, and garbage.

I suggest that this antagonistic view of the feral enacts a negative energy and emerges from a misperception of the dynamic and positive nature of

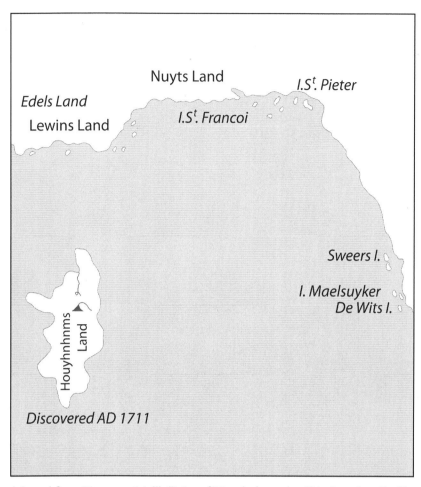

Adapted from Hermann Moll's "Map of Houyhnhnms land" in Jonathan Swift's *Gulliver's Travels*

bioregionalism itself. The bioregion needs the feral and the idea of the feral because the feral makes the bioregion think harder about place. Indeed, if as Lynch, Glotfelty, and Armbruster suggest in the introduction to this book, early bioregionalists began by "forming a sort of parallel culture" as a way of "address[ing] matters of pressing environmental concern through a politics derived from a local sense of place" (2), bioregionalism itself could be described as feral or once feral. Perhaps it is now time for bioregionalism to remember its outsider origins and resist its own domestication. If bioregionalism takes the opportunity to integrate its own feral status and history into all of the varied contemporary manifestations of the local, the bioregional imagination can easily thrive, for the feral supports and embodies processes that engender multiplicities and lateral flows in perspectives and perceptions. As Garside suggests, the feral "repoliticizes spaces" and engenders a healthy "democratic tension" (76–79). Indeed, at some level, the feral—the thing that cannot be definitely one thing or another—*is* the energy that nurtures bioregionalism and throws place open to its ineffable vicissitudes. And ineffability is what ultimately characterizes place: ineffability, that ephemeral, darting spirit that makes one place like no other on earth even as, just in the nick of time, it pulls the rug out before the taxonomizers glue it down and try to name that place and tell us definitively what it is and what belongs there. What I offer to the bioregional imagination here is some feral ecocritical thinking to discomfort our fine and earnest notions of place. Like the wild, the feral disrupts our categories, but unlike the wild, the feral is recognizably and comfortably familiar. The feral lives among us *almost as if it belongs.*

As we look more closely at the feral, I suggest that rather than attempting to change or eliminate it, instead we should engage in what Frances Westley, Brenda Zimmerman, and Michael Quinn Patton call "standing still." They appropriate this term from David Wagoner's poem "Lost" and apply it to complex human organizations with a view to engendering and sustaining meaningful social activism and change (see Westley, Zimmerman, and Patton 82–91). In "Lost," from Wagoner's 1978 collection *Who Shall Be the Sun?*, the speaker exhorts the listener/reader to "Stand still," both at the beginning of the poem and near its end (lines 1, 11). In this way, he emphasizes not only the commonplace of taking the time to carefully observe your surroundings and learn from them but also the more profound notion of opening yourself up to "be[ing] known" (4) and "lett[ing] it find you" (12). Such a consideration of how the feral seems from where we stand, a new openness to how we seem from where it stands, as well as a fresh recognition of the natural world, of place or "Here" (2) as "a powerful stranger" (3) that encompasses a myriad of coevolving agencies is aided by the methodologies recommended by Westley, Zimmerman, and Quinn Patton. These include reflective practice, pattern recognition, and developmental evaluation to facilitate the processes of innovation within a context of uncertainty where, as Jamie A. A. Gamble asserts, "innovation drives change" (15). With respect to the feral, bioregionalism, and a feral bioregionalism, developmental evaluation can be helpful in conceptualiz- ing and living well in place by acknowledging that change, coevolution and new knowledges can be simultaneously and exquisitely marginal, folded into place, and revelatory.

Indeed, simply thinking the feral into bioregionalism results in a dy- namic, lateral, and reflexive way of approaching the feral not as a problem but as a participant. A deliberately feral bioregionalism can encompass what Nicholas Garside calls "feral citizenship" as a democratic tool or strat- egy for social change in which performative "feral citizens" intervene to generate or expose synergies within communities that work to accelerate or illuminate change appropriate for and reflective of the needs of that com- munity. Such an interventionist feral bioregionalism can also be connected to Kate Rich's redefinition of the feral to "describe a process that is wilfully wild . . . as opposed to nature wild" (Rich).[1] Less clear is how the bioregion and the bioregional imagination can include and sustain their own feral details (organisms, animals, people) as they become more deeply domesti- cated and institutionalized. In this chapter, I both inscribe and inhabit the feral spirit and, using Mitchell Thomashow's concept of bioregional cos- mopolitanism, describe several possible strategies for satisfactorily coming to terms with the feral in the bioregion and in the concept of bioregional- ism. Thomashow's assertion is that "the most daunting task facing the con- ceptual integrity of bioregionalism" lies in lending meaning to the complex interplay of local and global environmental relationships" ("Toward" 121). I suggest that the feral and its richness are also part of that complex interplay, and that understanding its role is part of the challenge facing bioregional- ism. A "feral bioregionalism" encourages rooted, place-based communities to "lend support to those who are caught in diasporas," calls attention to "the magnitude of extinction," and demonstrates "the scale of dislocation and the correspondence between threats to biodiversity, to cultural integ- rity and to human survival" (Thomashow, "Toward" 123).

I do not, though, appropriate Thomashow's "cosmopolitan bioregionalism" wholesale. Although Thomashow is accurate in his assessment of patterns of migration and immigration and in his description of the inevitable physical, cultural, and psychological dislocation, his impulse toward "centering" strikes me as less satisfying than Stuart Kauffman's coevolutionary idea of "fitness landscapes," in which places and states of mind are constantly redefined even as "foundation[s] [are] laid to take on new challenges" (Westley, Zimmerman, and Quinn Patton 202–5). Although "centering" offers a comforting image of place, it implies stillness and perhaps even a conclusiveness or momentary conclusiveness. There is something beautiful and inclusive in Kauffman's explanation of how symmetries "breaking give rise to . . . an expanding Adjacent Possible that is both real ontologically and without yet 'defeat[ing]' the second law of thermodynamics . . . lead[s] to a non deductive account of how the universe, partially lawlessly, and creatively, becomes complex" (Kauffman). Though both bioregional cosmopolitanism and fitness landscapes emphasize a kind of mindfulness in the way that they employ meditative discernment to generate new knowledges, the radically uncentered feral honestly embodies Kauffman's idea and accounts for the challenges of globalization and the desire for place; it has the potential to teach us how to live well within chaos and fragmentation. Thomashow too implicitly recognizes the value of the feral in his observation that "bioregional sensibility must also cultivate a language for expressing the connections between regions" ("Toward" 129), for the feral crosses regions and lives in the spaces along their boundaries. To promote this process, I suggest that rather than attempting to displace the feral we "avoid the illusion of contrived stability" ("Toward" 131) and appropriate both Thomashow's perceptual guidelines and social justice methodologies so that the feral can be freshly "seen" in place. From there it makes sense to engage in a deep consideration of how the feral from "where it stands" works to produce bioregional knowledges.

I start with the Canada goose, an increasingly displaced and becoming-feral animal: in its wild state, it provides a potent symbol of Canadian nationalism through its sweeping migrations and its purposeful sense of spaces and communities. Even flattened on currency, corporate logos, and "tactical outerwear," it reverberates in the ephemeral yet palpable collective Canadian imagination. But earthbound and un-wilded in its suburban invasions, its eagerness for flat, green, open spaces, mowed lawns, and golf courses, the Canada goose hearkens a bioregional knowledge that is a truth about another kind of Canadian nationalism: the one of globalized consumer monoculture, a feral, human truth we prefer not to hear.[2] Perhaps our fear of hearing the truth of our places embodied *in* the feral is what separates us from it.

Nicholas Garside recognizes the ways in which our marginalization of the feral undermines democracy and democratic practices. He encourages an intentional, interventionist ferality within bioregions as a form of social activism and reengagement. This impulse to act fits well with Thomashow's opening question in "Toward a Cosmopolitan Bioregionalism": "[H]ow are personal and community actions relevant to the formidable complexities of global environmental change?" (121). Both Garside and Thomashow's calls-to-engagement are illustrated powerfully in the Australian-American mechanical engineer/artist Natalie Jeremijenko's 2002–3 work, "Feral Robotic Dogs." In this project, Jeremijenko reengineers commercial robotic dog toys to help locate environmental contaminants. "Released in a pack, the Feral Robotic Dogs use sophisticated programming to sniff out contaminants" (Thompson 68). In what Mitchell Thomashow would call a "profound cultural vision," Jeremijenko directly addresses Thomashow's question about the relevance of personal and community actions through her direct intervention into global market capitalism and consumerism. Using the very technologies that drain us of our bioregional identification and inculcate us into a monocultural consumer capitalist mode, Jeremijenko, as feral engineer/artist, playfully reappropriates and reconfigures domesticated consumer products intended to be ephemeral and disposable into feral change agents.[3] Powerfully, the feral robotic dogs as toys "play" on the user at least as much as the user "plays" with them. Urban youth, in particular, are engaged in several important ways. In her role as teacher both at UCSD and NYU, Jeremijenko trains emerging engineers into flexible, untraditional ways of thinking about technology, the environment, and place. Further, Jerimijenko offers an instruction kit on her website so that the public can retool their own robotic dogs. Less-enfranchised youth are engaged by and reoriented to their place through their use of the feral robotic dogs (organized feral dog releases have taken place in Orlando, Florida, and at the Bronx River in New York). These youth become feral citizens through their engagement with the feral robotic dogs. They increase their understanding of place and local issues related to land use and toxicity. Here the local and global are simultaneously addressed by Jeremijenko's manifestation of the feral. Furthermore, Jerimijenko's process of subverting and reappropriating her own education and training as a mechanical engineer to retool herself as an "aesthetic activist" who challenges the domestication and institutionalization of knowledge production is feral as well. In the context of this positive manifestation of a feral citizenship and a potential for becoming-human in new, engaged ways, it is important to recall the depths to which feral humans have also embodied our discomfort with the feral.

Despite evidence of Jeremijenko's feral citizenry and her effect on both robotic and human "offspring" (repurposed toy dogs and student engineers), feral humans are more often described as "immanent, detached, and soulless" (Newton 198). Indeed, Jeremijenko has been subjected to some of this kind of compartmentalization through the "highest-rated" comments section posted on *You Tube* in response to her October 2010 TED talk, "Let's teach fish to text! and other outlandish ideas." One viewer, for example, rhetorically hedges praise of Jeremijenko's work within this comment: "She was hot, and very clever, but I think she might be insane." The tendency to sexualize feral humans and make the assumption that they are insane is common in the histories of feral humans, where the focus is on their inhumanity and whether they have the potential to be rehabilitated and redomesticated. The feral human is frightening and unfathomable—what is not supposed to be there in the rubric of what defines the human.[4] Carl Linneaus refused to classify feral humans, preferring to "suspend them as an anomalous and ahistorical category that belonged nowhere" (Nath 253–54).

And perhaps no one understood this human perceptual hesitancy and its dire implications as well as Jonathan Swift, who in 1726 imagined the exploited body of the feral boy, Peter of Hanover (found wandering in the German forest in 1725, eating raw meat and later imported to Britain as a curiosity and adopted "pet" of King George I, the Elector of Hanover) into Lemuel Gulliver, the apparent author of the *Travels into Several Remote Nations of the World in Four Parts. By Lemuel Gulliver, First a Surgeon, and then a Captain of several Ships.*[5] By masking this fictional work as travel narrative, making a great show of its veracity in the final chapter (part 4, chapter 12), as well as by concluding each of the voyages with Gulliver's return to England where his reports are met with disbelief,[6] Swift allows his Gulliver and potentially his reader to become painfully, ontologically unstuck four times, as he assumed Peter perpetually was, in order to ask his essential question, "Who are we as humans?" In answer, Swift radically changes how we think about who we are and what ground that "who we are" is founded on. If, as Dipika Nath theorizes, feral children generally work to raise this question about "what is *natural* or *human* in *human nature* and about the place of culture and education in crafting 'the human'" (Nath 252), Swift's Gulliver functions in much the same way except that Gulliver is able to give voice to his estrangement through his gift for language.[7] Yet Swift's question, shimmering in its ferality, is not ultimately answered; it is left both resolved and unresolved at the end of Part 4, with Gulliver struggling to reconcile himself to his own teeming animality and "to the *Yahoo* kind in general," unable to bring himself to touch his family and finding their smell "very offensive" (*Gulliver* 271). Even five years after his return to England, he prefers the stable and his horses who "understand me tolerably well; I converse with them at least four Hours every Day" (266). Gulliver remains confused, enamoured with his memory of the rationality and gentility of the horselike Houyhnhmns, whom he has no proof of ever having met.[8] This is despite the fact that he assumes Houyhnhmns lie at the core of the ordinary stable horses he owns and controls in England.[9]

But humans resist Gulliver just as he resists his reintegration into place and specifically into Englishness, and Swift leaves Gulliver between the stable and the hearth at the end of the *Travels*, sacrificing his fictional character to ontological indeterminacy in order to make a more important point about the structures of belonging and not-belonging in eighteenth-century England. In this way, *Gulliver's Travels* embodies what Garside sees as the feral's disruptive potential to "create discursive moments that can orient the community toward seeing its activities in relation to broader democratic goals of freedom and equality" (Garside 64–65).[10]

This discursive work is the enactment of a positive ferality. When we continuously read and enact the feral as invasive and destructive, our discomfort with its in-betweenness only entrenches the wild and the domestic as inherently antagonistic binaries that cannot coexist. We do harm by conceptualizing the feral as a wasteland between the two binaries, blinding ourselves to ferality's beauty and promise. Surely, ecology has taught us by now to revel in the apparently ugly, and to love, as Thoreau so wisely recognizes, "the impervious and quaking swamps" (274). Surely, Gulliver should be able to talk to both his horses and his wife! Surely satire of place as a feral and highly effective tool of reorientation, social activism and change is recognizable in Swift's text.

Speaking to this promise of the feral's multiplicity, Ralph Acampora writes that "the construction of a cultural home . . . does not have to be *oppressively* domestic—rather than repressing wild animality, home might be flexible enough to let the animal in us emerge and return occasionally to the wilderness" (8; emphasis in original). Feral thinking in this way has potential, and we often resist it (or embrace it) precisely because it evades control. Perhaps, too, we idealize the feral state as one from which anything can be said and done: an escape from and resistance to domestication, an articulate wildness. This beautiful resistance in the feral is positively named and discussed in philosophy, performativity, psychoanalysis, and ecosophy, and it is touted as a powerful potential for self and community actualization. Deleuze and Guattari's stretchy thresholds and borderlines become visceral from this perspective, as do Donna Haraway's companion species. This spandexed feral is also dynamic and active; it positively embodies what Michael Newton calls ferality's condition of "absolute materiality" by upending the view (which emerged as a predominant eighteenth-century view and held) that the feral human (and Peter of Hanover, specifically) was "unsettling[ly] perplexing," "a body without a soul," "a surface appearance . . . deprived of any rational intentionality" (197–98). According to Newton, eighteenth-century observers of Peter (Newton uses Daniel Defoe's 1726–27 pamphlet, *Mere Nature Delineated* as his example) "project themselves and constitute a sense of their own identity [and genuine humanity] through . . . Peter's difference"—in particular, by contrasting it with the silence of ferality, Peter's "unmeaning and hollow" laughter, as well as his "perceptual detachment" and absence of a "reciprocating interest in others" (203–5). In contrast to this view, I propose that a feral bioregionalism relishes such "absolute materiality" as a reminder of the dynamism of ecosystems and of nature that challenges the smug stagnation of knowing what (and who) should be there.

WHAT, THEN, IS THE BIOREGIONAL FERAL; OR, WHAT IS THE FERAL IN BIOREGIONALISM AND THE BIOREGIONAL IMAGINATION?

Simply put, it is a challenge to the smug stagnation of knowing what should be there. And, perhaps, it is what Michael Vincent McGinnis means when he talks about "learning to dwell" and returning to "the place 'there is'" (3), which includes the feral. Indeed, the feral may be evidence of Dan Flores' assertion that "place is endlessly created" and not "formed exclusively by local populations" (qtd. in McGinnis 52, 49). If bioregionalism is, as Flores suggests, a dialogue between nature and human culture, listening to the feral is integral to bioregional practice. In the context of increasing vernacular lip-service paid to phrases such as "the local," Thomashow's call for the preparation of "perceptual groundwork" ("Toward" 131) has the benefit of reconnecting bioregionalism to its feral core, since that groundwork will reveal the unsettled nature of the bioregion.

Clearly the feral is not about the comfort zone. We have been domesticated into a particular way of thinking about home place and bioregionalism that may be too circumscribed, too nostalgic, too controlling. It would be helpful to put aside our environmental romanticism about place and expand beyond selective topophilia to acknowledge that the part of place in which the sun does not shine is unabashedly also part of place. Paraphrasing Brian Luke's analysis of going feral in an animal liberation context, to "go feral" in a bioregional context means to reject rationalist, hierarchical, and adversarial approaches and methodologies and *break through* to adopt a semi-wild state and expose the controls on our agency (Luke 314). Gary Snyder, for example, in unpacking the terms *wild* and *nature* reveals Asian associations with illegitimacy, prostitution, fiction, and the uncouth (Snyder 6). Though Snyder uses these associations to construct a discourse of the wild, they are, fundamentally, feral institutions. They are highly integrated transgressors. And, just as Snyder illuminates the ways in which a culture of wilderness permeates our human experience in "The Etiquette of Freedom," he tacitly acknowledges the feral. Indeed, when Snyder describes language as an "infinitely interfertile family of species spreading or mysteriously declining over time, shamelessly and endlessly hybridizing, changing its own rules as it goes" (8), is this not the process of ferality, of becoming, something Snyder not only celebrates but also connects to the potential for holistic, spiritual, and material survival? This way of thinking enriches the burgeoning bioregional imagination in ways that Doug Aberley, Mitchell Thomashow, and Gary Snyder recommend, and it is fully embodied in Garside's feral citizen who, in her purposeful ambivalence, ferrets into gaps and creates disruptive moments that "are able to become . . . part of a broad counter-hegemonic methodology or politics of disruption" (143, 146).

THE FERAL AND/IN CONTEXT(S)

Metaethically, to extend Brian Luke's argument, the feral bioregion or the feral in the bioregion expands the capacity for democratic decision making by providing fuller information. One can come to a self-understanding of the intrinsic value of caring within moral agency through deeper, broader exposures to greater diversity (see Luke 313). This ethic of care is also in keeping with Thomashow and others' bioregional cosmopolitanism in promoting "the acquisition of substantive knowledges about global interconnections" as a way to cultivate "open-mindedness . . . which [as a value] corresponds with bioregionalists' efforts to regenerate biodiversity" (Li 394). In the context of globalization, the feral supports bioregionalism's "response to the formidable power relations of global political economy and the ensuing fragmentation of place" (Thomashow, "Toward" 121) by becoming diasporic, by making unexpected appearances in new places and knitting knowledges past and present and far and wide into new contextual manifestations of the local.

Knowing the feral in the bioregion is similar to the strategy ecofeminists have used to reconceptualize the hegemony of the rational into a politicized ethic of care that transforms "caring about" into "caring for." As Deane Curtin describes it, "caring about" is generalized and "occurs in a context where direct relationships to specific others is missing." For ecofeminists, "caring about" is contrasted with "caring for," which is "marked by an understanding of and appreciation for a particular context in which one participates" (Curtin 94). "Contextualization" is distinguished from "localization" because localization "resists the expansion of 'caring for' to the oppressed who are geographically remote from us, or to nonhuman nature" (95). The goose on the golf course is a local pest, but a contextual player "caring for" and worthy of care. Similarly, Peter of Hanover is an inarticulate human but "says" much about the ethics of care for children in eighteenth-century Germany (how did a boy disappear in the first place?) and a land use that would both enable a child to be raised by the wild and make it possible for him to be found years later by villagers who, presumably, had no idea who he was.[11]

Swift's and the many other Peter of Hanover stories from the eighteenth century illuminate the challenge of contextualization in practice and point to the responsibilities that writers and recorders of place bear. Eighteenth-century commentators in general decontextualize Peter, who then functions as an embodied figure through which satire (obviously directed at the "civilized") can be performed. The result is that the tame, domesticated (albeit deeply flawed) psyche is exclusively privileged and Peter's psyche is split.[12] Although records indicate that Peter's eventual integration into a rural English community was never completely successful, his lived experience may have been quite different and, perhaps, full of feral potential. These records, though, stand as templates and rubrics for treating the feral and for thinking about the feral in specific, categorical ways that may do harm. Where fiction served Swift by enabling him to imagine Peter into a speculative Englishman's lived experience of the feral that ultimately had only abstract implications, the feral-in-place challenges us in its real presence.

And its presence is not so easy to resist or destroy, after all, often proving resistant, insistent, and persistent. Indeed, we often cannot quite bring ourselves to destroy it. Consider again the ferality of the Canada goose. The goose's insistence that it belongs to specific, shorn, suburban bioregions (regardless of the evolution of these bioregions) speaks to epistemological and ontological potentials that have until now only been read from the human perspective.[13] That the goose is complicated by its affiliate meanings, its positive and historically symbolic value, is only to suggest an even deeper feral potential. For example, in place-based terms, the goose hardly stands still in place, and its elemental flexibility changes the ways it means to humans. On lawns, the feral goose disturbs, while in the water and especially in the air, it delights us. Can the knowledges of the twenty-first-century goose-pest help bring flexibility to our thinking about the bioregion where its disturbing groundedness becomes grounds for new ideas about coevolution and coexistence?

If the embodied feral disturbs and delights simultaneously, the feral horse has a similar potential. Swift may have recognized this potential in his conceptualization of Gulliver as a becoming-Houyhnhnm-becoming-human. What we can recognize in Gulliver and in Swift's offer of Gulliver to us as someone "good to think on" is what Walter D. Mignolo calls "sustainable knowledge," where Gulliver's story and his difference, his tensile resistance to both the wild and domesticated challenge us to include him in our future-thinking. If one role of the feral is, as Philip Armstrong suggests, to reject commodification (39), the implication is that the individual subject must matter collectively in how it is constituted in the whole other and, indeed, in the wholeness of self. Since the process and result of commodification in Marxian terms is alienation, by resisting commodification, the feral casts off alienation. In fact, I would suggest that the self-in-nature of the feral is inherently unalienated. This has great value for us bioregionally as we "learn to dwell." By standing still and experiencing the unalienated feral actor in the place "there is," we are interpellated into a feral knowing that realigns our ways of being in place. If the domesticated, wild, and feral are no longer "kept from a potentially confusing proximity" (Armstrong 41), the problem of the Canada goose, of Gulliver, of the Yahoos, for example, can no longer be framed or spoken of as invasive or marginal, for each possesses no exclusivity but is fully constituted in place. The feral as the "unintentional or uncanny element that inevitably accompanies the 'ordering and improving' project of enlightened modernization" (Clark qtd. in Armstrong 35) is rising, "fully motile and AWAITING FURTHER INSTRUCTIONS" (Jeremijenko "Feral").

How we engage with the feral to write us, and how we write the feral and write the feral in us, is at the core of the bioregional imagination. Border thinking, sustainable knowledge, the feral goose, the feral horse, the feral Englishman within bioregionalism remind us of the inherent, constituent, biophilic longing for survival-in-place and the ecological conditions that invite all manner of players into a community of potentials: a feral bioregional imagination inherent to the bioregional imaginary.

NOTES

1. Rich's project, *Feral Trade*, offers alternative live courier services "outside commercial networks." Services are negotiated via social networks for the exchange of goods with a "high potential for sociability" to harness "the surplus freight potential of recreational, commuter and cultural travel for the practical circulation of goods" (Rich).

2. Two recent examples of this conflation of Canadian identity with corporate culture are Molson's "Joe Canadian" beer campaign and the Tim Hortons' coffee chain's ongoing construction of itself, as Prime Minister Stephen Harper put it in a 2009 speech, as "the essential Canadian story" ("Prime Minister").

3. One of Jeremijenko's projects is a robotic goose that humans can send out to interact with live geese (see Thompson 68).

4. Clearly Jeremijenko's international status and reputation as an artist and her faculty and research positions at a number of prestigious universities belie such comments.

5. Swift's original text disguised Swift's authorship and promoted the fiction of truth; that is, that Lemuel Gulliver was a real man who had published a factual account of his travels.

6. This is much less obvious with Part 3 because Gulliver finds it necessary to disguise himself as a Dutchman and travel under a false name in order to get permission to return to Europe. His need to hide his real identity means that he

interacts very little with his shipmates on the return voyage, where the narration of his adventures and their reception in Part 1 and Part 2 had occurred.

7. Everywhere Gulliver ventures, the kings and masters are amazed by his facility for language. The Houyhnhnms, for example, looked on Gulliver's ability to learn their language "as a Prodigy, that a brute Animal should discover such Marks of a rational Creature. . . . that in five Months from [Gulliver's] Arrival, [he] understood whatever was spoke, and could express [himself] tolerably well" (*Gulliver* 218–19). Gulliver's four voyages are "A Voyage to Lilliput," "A Voyage to Brobdingnag," "A Voyage to Laputa, Balinibarbi, Luggnagg, Glubbdubdribb, and Japan," and "A Voyage to the Country of the Houyhnhnms." In the final chapter of Part 4, Gulliver informs his "Gentle Reader" that he has "given thee a faithful History of my Travels for Sixteen Years, and above Seven Months" (Swift 1726, vol. 2:184–85).

8. Interestingly, Gulliver has artifacts which prove the truth of his tales from Lilliput, Brobdingnag, and Struldbruggs but except for "the scar on the inside of [his] left knee," he apparently brings nothing back from Houyhnhmns Land (*Gulliver* 261).

9. The Houyhnhnm Master is appalled by Gulliver's elaboration of the treatment and uses of horses in England (*Gulliver* 222–24).

10. Indeed, Gulliver asserts in the final chapter of his travels that his "sole intention [in writing] was the PUBLIC GOOD" and he refuses to accept the idea that "what ever Lands are discovered by a subject belong to the Crown" because "I could never give my Advice for invading them" (*Gulliver* 268–69). But I must also add Philip Armstrong's observation that the Yahoos are feral, too: "the feral outbreak of an introduced species"; in Swift's satire, they are former, now feral, colonizers whose "ancestors may have been English" (Armstrong 37). Swift's subtitles for the final chapter of part 4 (chapter 12): "The Author's Veracity," "His Design in publishing this Work," "His Censure of those Travellers who swerve from the Truth," etc. reveal both Swift's satire and his social/moral project.

11. Peter's feral status, especially the assumption that he was raised in the wild, has been challenged numerous times since the eighteenth century. Indeed, the community may well have known that Peter was the mentally challenged son of a local man and that disability and domestic abuse may have been why he was living in the wild (see Benzaquén 92–93, for example).

12. Peter was eventually sent to live with a farmer in Hertfordshire, where he was managed and cared for by the community until his death in 1785. At his death he was about seventy-two years old.

13. Mignolo promotes *gnoseology* as a type of knowledge "beyond the culture of scholarship" (9), a revelatory experience in which "the illusion of truth through illumination replaces rational argument" (12).

WORKS CITED

Acampora, Ralph R. "Nietzsche's Feral Philosophy: Thinking through an Animal Imaginary." *A Nietzschean Bestiary: Becoming Animal beyond Docile and Brutal.* Ed. Christa Davis Acampora and Ralph R. Acampora. Lanham, Maryland: Rowman & Littlefield, 2004: 1–13. Print.

Armstrong, Philip. *What Animals Mean in the Fiction of Modernity.* London: Routledge, 2008. Print.

Benzaquén, Adriana S. *Encounters with Wild Children: Temptation and Disappointment in the Study of Human Nature.* Montreal: McGill-Queen's University Press, 2006. Print.

Curtin, Deane. "Towards an Ecological Ethic of Care." *The Feminist Care Tradition in Animal Ethics: A Reader.* Ed. Josephine Donovan and Carol J. Adams. New York: Columbia University Press, 2007. 87–100. Print.

Deleuze, Gilles, and Félix Guattari. *A Thousand Plateaus: Capitalism and Schizophrenia.* Minneapolis: University of Minnesota Press, 1987. Print.

Flores, Dan. "Place: Thinking about Bioregional History." McGinnis 43–60.

Gamble, Jamie A. A. *A Developmental Evaluation Primer.* Montreal: The J. W. McConnell Family Foundation, 2008. Web.

Garside, Nicholas. "Feral Citizens, Democratic Ideals, and the Politicization of Nature." Diss. York University, 2006. Print.

Haraway, Donna L. "Cyborgs to Companion Species: Reconfiguring Kinship in Technoscience." *The Animals Reader.* Ed. Linda Kalof and Amy Fitzgerald. Oxford: Berg, 2007. 362–74. Print.

Jerimijenko, Natalie. "Feral Robotic Dogs". *XDesign.* February 7, 2011. http://www.nyu.edu/projects/xdesign/feralrobots. Web.

———. "Natalie Jeremijenko: Let's teach fish to text! and other outlandish ideas." TED talk. Oct 14, 2010. Web.

Kauffman, Stuart. "Why Is the Universe Complex? Cascading Broken Symmetries." *Cosmos and Culture* 13.7. National Public Radio. Web.

Li, Huey-li. "Bioregionalism and Global Education: Exploring the Connections." *Philosophy of Education.* 2000: 394–403. Print.

Luke, Brian. "Taming Ourselves or Going Feral: Toward a Nonpatriarchal Metaethic of Animal Liberation?" *Animals and Women.* Ed. Carol J. Adams and Josephine Donovan. Durham, N.C.: Duke University Press, 1995. 290–319. Print.

McGinnis, Michael, ed. *Bioregionalism.* London: Routledge, 1999. Print.

Mignolo, Walter D. *Local Histories/Global Designs: Coloniality, Subaltern Knowledges and Border Thinking.* Princeton: Princeton University Press, 2000. Print.

Nath, Dipika. "'To Abandon the Colonial Animal': 'Race,' Animals, and the Feral Child in Kipling's Mowgli Stories." *Animals and Agency: An Interdisciplinary*

Exploration. Ed. Sarah E. McFarland and Ryan Hediger. Leiden: Brill, 2009. Print.

Newton, Michael. "Bodies without Souls: Peter the Wild Boy." *At the Borders of the Human.* Ed. Erica Fudge, Ruth Gilbert, and Susan Wiseman. London: Macmillan, 1999. 196–214. Print.

"Prime Minister Harper Welcomes Tim Hortons back to Canada." *Stand Up for Canada.* Conservative Party of Canada, September 23, 2009. http://www .conservative.ca/EN/1004/110783. Web.

Rich, Kate. "Feral Trade Grappa, FER-1578." *Feral Trade (Import-Export).* February 7, 2011. http://www.feraltrade.org. Web.

Snyder, Gary. *The Practice of the Wild.* Berkeley: Shoemaker & Hoard, 1990. Print.

Swift, Jonathan. *Gulliver's Travels.* 1726. London: Penguin, 2003. Print.

———. *Travels into several remote nations of the world. In four parts. By Lemuel Gulliver, first a surgeon, and then a captain of several ships. . . .* 2 Vols. London, M,DCC,XXVI. [1726]. *Eighteenth Century Collections Online.* Gale. LMU Muenchen. 8 Feb. 2011. Web.

———. *The Most Wonderful Wonder that Ever Appeared to the Wonder of the British Nation.* London, 1726. Print.

Swift, Jonathan, and John Arbuthnot. *It cannot Rain but it Pours, or, London strow'd with Rarities, subtitled Of the wonderful Wild Man that was nursed in the Woods of Germany by a Wild Beast, hunted and taken in Toyls; how he behaveth himself like a dumb Creature, and is a Christian like one of us, being call'd Peter; and how he was brought to Court all in Green, to the great Astonishment of the Quality and Gentry.* London, 1726. Print.

Thomashow, Mitchell. *Bringing the Biosphere Home.* Cambridge: MIT Press, 2002. Print.

———. "Toward a Cosmopolitan Bioregionalism." McGinnis 121–32. Print.

———. *Ecological Identity: Becoming a Reflective Environmentalist.* Cambridge: MIT Press, 1995. Print.

Thompson, Nato. *Becoming Animal: Contemporary Art in the Animal Kingdom.* North Adams, Mass.: Mass MoCA Publications, 2005. Print.

Thoreau, Henry D. "Walking." *Civil Disobedience and Other Writings.* Ed. William Rossi. New York: Norton, 2008. 260–87. Print.

Wagoner, David. "Lost." *Who Shall Be the Sun?* Bloomington: Indiana University Press, 1978. Print.

Westley, Frances, Brenda Zimmerman, and Michael Quinn Patton. *Getting to Maybe: How the World is Changed.* Toronto: Vintage Canada, 2002. Print.

PART FOUR

Renewal

LAURIE RICOU

Out of the Field Guide

Teaching Habitat Studies

> *To walk out of the field guide*
> *and listen.*
>
> . . . .
>
> *To open the grammar of being seen*
> *and let the creatures name* you.
> Sue Wheeler, "Understory"
>
> *It's like waking up*
> *to discover the language you used to speak*
> *is gibberish, and you have never really*
> *loved.*
> Stephanie Bolster, "Many Have Written Poems
> about Blackberries"

I LIKE EPIGRAPHS: they focus what follows and simultaneously upset it.[1] When you return to them minutes or months later, they seem to question the very propositions you thought were so stable. I begin with Sue Wheeler—you will recognize the poem from the course description on the department website—because it comes from a collection titled simply *Habitat*. And because while honoring the field guide(s) you will depend on in this course, it hints that other sources of information might be more important. Those sources, the ones not found in print, require us to be *good listeners*. To be a good listener is to attend closely (beyond just *hearing*), with respect, and expecting to be differently informed. To

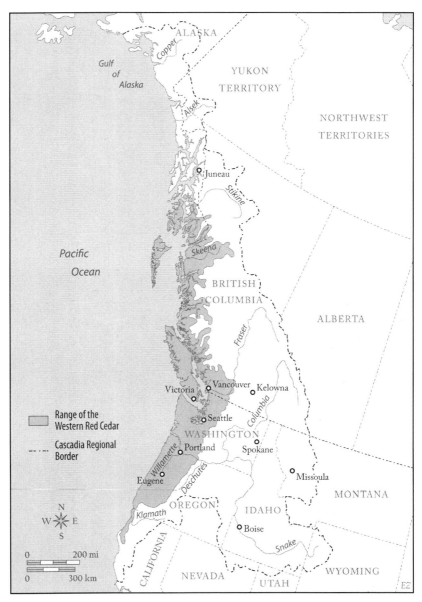

The Cascadia Bioregion and coastal territory of *Thuja plicata*, the western red cedar

listen is to *wait*—patiently—for a sound to be absorbed, maybe to become a message. Perhaps to *heed*. Perhaps to listen *in* on. Wheeler's opening lines catch the curiosity and secrecy that accompany overhearing and eavesdropping.

Stephanie Bolster's poem—also probably familiar to many of you—wonders at the (sometimes ominous) fecundity of the Himalayan blackberry. As the poem closes, Bolster extravagantly describes tasting a blackberry: "like kissing the whole world / at once." "It"—presumably the blackberry's literal and imagined habitat, its complicated range of habit and association—alerts us to the limits of the language we routinely, unthinkingly use and receive. Maybe we need to listen for another tongue, open to the possibility of the creatures naming *us*. That's what this course asks you to do—however impossibly. How does the woodland skipper communicate? What language does bull kelp speak? Let's ask, adapting Don McKay's challenge, not "What is the northern alligator lizard to me?" but "What am I to the northern alligator lizard?" (17).

I want to welcome you, and thank you for registering in this course. I'm a little surprised, I'll admit, that so many of you have chosen this course. So I want to salute a certain daring: for the website description predicts a course completely unlike any other you've taken in this department. Moreover, my admonitory e-mail of a month ago seems to have discouraged very few.[2] Oh, I suspect at least some of you didn't quite believe that the course has no prescribed texts? Maybe some of you checked at the bookstore just in case.

Later, we'll go on a short "field trip." It won't be far, just a few hundred meters, where we'll stand under a western red cedar, touch its bark, smell its leaves, and listen for what bird might be perching within it. This short walk out of the field guide on Day One will remind us that much of the research in this course must take place outside classrooms, libraries, beyond the reach of computers. At the end of our encounter with our region's totemic tree, each of you will draw from this hat a species ticket; on it will be the common name of a species of flora or fauna whose characteristics and habitat will become your singular focus for the semester.

Let me explain by distributing now the rather speculative guidelines for your term project.

The names on those tickets are printed at the bottom. (The course outline, which after all is alarmingly vague, can wait.)

This is not the sort of water in which one could meander
in a storied boat. She thinks
if this place has any stories they would not be spoken
in her tongue.
Stephanie Bolster, "In which alice visits pacific rim national park," *White Stone*

Habitat Project: Some Suggestions

Each participant prepares a comprehensive research notebook focusing on a particular species, most of which inhabit, in one way or another, the Pacific slope region of North America. These "field notes" lack precise definition; part of the project is to discover a form for reporting. Try to respond to or incorporate at least several of the following projects/possibilities:

- the "literary ecology" of the plant or animal: where and how it appears in poems, plays, novels, short stories; where it appears in other written texts (nature essays, journalism, cartoons, advertisements, government regulations, etc.).
- where and how your focus item appears in the visual, spoken, and musical arts, in film, on CDs, on TV, on the Web, etc.
- what contexts, and meanings, and implications, and associations can you find/develop?
- habitat: the ecological interdependencies . . . crucial.
- uses in food, medicine, in/as artifacts—in various cultures.
- include illustrations if you can. (Sources must be carefully, completely acknowledged and identified.)
- To look closely and not to take for granted. (Leslie Marmon Silko)
- how many names, in how many languages, can you find for your item? Test the limits and resonances of translating these.
- think of yourself composing a *biography* of gull, a *story* of red huckleberry, an *archaeology* of the purple star, a *poetics* of snow goose.
- a record, at least partial, of dead ends: detective work proceeds by pursuing leads. If you don't find what you're looking for, consider what *not* finding something means.
- adventure—outside of the usual texts and Web sources that might be used in a literature course. Incorporate archives.
- attend to the dance of the particular (roy kiyooka).
- remember the end-of-term lunch.

The research project has two aspects: obsessive pursuit of your focus species and collaborative study of species selected by the rest of the research team. Acknowledge in some detail in your completed project where others have helped.

The results of your research can be submitted in a notebook/report, in a form you find appropriate to your subject and to our evolving sense of how its habitat might be imagined. Think of comparative, cross-genre, and interdisciplinary forms. Think of forms that embody the first law of ecology. The report need not be assembled into a coherent, linear argument. Evaluation will include consideration of variety and amplitude. (So, for example, ten references to ten Audubon guidebooks might lack the variety signaled by the possibilities indicated; a guidebook reference "unpacked" is preferred to one simply recorded.) Follow the project far enough to surprise yourself. Then go back to it. Be patient and relentless. Dream. Surprise yourself again. Wear heavy socks. Always travel lighter than the heart.

Each week, in the seminar meetings, you will be presenting aspects of your research. Your completed report is due 9 April 2009.

Himalayan blackberry
purple loosestrife
skylark
western pond turtle
red Irish lord
snow goose
Douglas-fir tussock moth
bull kelp
deer mouse
sea lettuce(s)
European rabbit
red tree vole
woodland skipper
shore pine
northern alligator lizard
yellow sand verbena
Roosevelt elk

I chose to include the complete guidelines in my project document because. . . . I wanted a record of all the class participants and
their extraordinary species to remind me of the ecosystem that we
created.

(Erin Samuda)

So, let's proceed with a few elaborations.

The head note emphasizes "experiment" and "discover." I picked the species mostly randomly, not because I've done the work to know they would
lead to great projects supported by ample resources. At this moment, I am
as uninformed about the Douglas-fir tussock moth as you are.

Literary Ecology. Here you begin to make up for the absence of assigned
texts by creating together a "classroom anthology." How is your species
written? How is it read? How does language—which after all might be
understood as an *ecology*, an intricate system of interdependencies—signal
connections within and among species?

Film . . . the Web. This suggestion invites you to range widely. In particular, it should prompt a critical reading of media and analysis of implicit
ideologies. How does Ducks Unlimited configure purple loosestrife?

Contexts. Think representation and construction. When you're bewildered
or just awed—rely on yourself to create contexts that generate meaning.

KNOWING GREEN

I come from a dry land. I know the thin green of cottonwood on a gravel
bank, the cool high green of lodge pole pine, and the flat pungent green
of sagebrush. These colors tint my semi-arid home. . . . But on the coast, I
did not know green from green from green.

AGAINST DESCRIPTION

I went to the blackberries
on the vine.
They were blackberries
on the vine.

They were
blackberries

Black
berries.
George Bowering, *West Window:*
Selected Poems

In the long, dry days of my first September on the "Salish Sea" the sheer
mass of the emerald banks of blackberry told me that I was not home—
but this knowing was sweet . . . .

(Shasta Grenier)

Habitat. I set out almost no strict requirements for your project. But I do
require that you *get the science right.* Now, I know many of you last took
a biology course in Grade 10, and when you got to university you heard
the soft science option was astronomy (so you seized it). And I realize that
many arts students believe that capital-S science is a linear tool, an extension of the empiricist, racist, capitalist patriarchy. I'm not asking you to
jettison your convictions, but please park them long enough to immerse
yourself in *The Canadian Journal of Botany* and *The Annals of the Entomo-
logical Society of America.* Read and reread, look up terms, unpack them,
make an earnest effort to translate and incorporate. Essential.

Uses. In this zone, you examine human uses: this enquiry should lead you
to raise cross-cultural, cross-occupational, and status considerations.

Illustrations. And try drawing yourself.

How Many Names. Remember that the course, and your project, have a
continuing anchor in language studies. You want to query all the common
names for your species and unpack carefully the Latin binomial. (Sometimes you will find more than one.) Ask what your species is called in
Spanish, German, Cantonese—and especially in the original languages of
this bioregion: Tillamook, Lushootseed, Haida, Nisga'a. If you can't find a
name, what does this tell you about the epistemologies implicit in different
language systems? Here your local goes globalling.

In *Thompson Ethnobotany*, Nancy Turner makes no note of var. *contorta* although she records that native people used var. *latifolia* (lodgepole) for its pitch, as a polish, as a fragrance, as a poultice and as a
topical unguent during cleaning rituals. In the Thompson Indian culture,

coniferous trees (spruce, fir, pine) are referred to as "/kem'-y'=éke? . . .
needle-bearing trees" (1990 63). It seems that . . . lodgepole pine, white
pine and ponderosa pine were virtually interchangeable. Still within the
shore pine's habitat range, the Nitinaht Indians live on the west coast of
Vancouver Island in the Carmanah Valley north of Port Renfrew.

In *Ethnobotany of the Nitinaht Indians*, Nancy Turner records that both
var. *monticola* (white pine) and var. *contorta* (shore pine) grow in this
area. Even though "they were recognized as being different they were
called by the same name": *ʔišipt*. While many Nitinaht words describe a
specific species, *ʔišipt* is a generic term for pines (1983 49). (Note that
Turner includes lodgepole pine in her list of common names for var.
contorta).

                                                              (Karen Taylor)

Composing. Test the genre and form through which you might most con-
genially explore the habitat of your species.

Dead Ends. You should document all stages of your search. Some of you
will have great difficulty finding information, or at least the information
on aspects of your species that you think would be important for your
project. But it will reassure you if you keep track and incorporate into
your project the knowing that inheres in being lost. Read Rebecca Solnit's
A Field Guide to Getting Lost or Don McKay's "Five Ways to Lose Your
Way" (85–93).

I was able to locate few literary references to English ivy in North
America, particularly along the Pacific Northwest. I scanned/combed/
perused/studied/glossed/skimmed/read eyefuls of local literature. After
a few days of fruitless searching, I decided to approach English ivy with
less industry. I began staring at the spines of poetry books, trying to
'intuit' which books contained English ivy.

In the poem "Brother Ivy," Denise Levertov articulates English ivy's
pervasiveness in the urban Pacific Northwest environment. The poem's
opening lines even include six visual representations of ivy. Look at a
comma (,). It looks like a seed with a plunging root. If English ivy were
represented as punctuation, it would be a comma—unobtrusively,
quietly pervasive, a twisted connector and separator. After all, commas go largely unnoticed by the eye. Look at the opening lines reading
the commas as tiny ivies: "Between road and sidewalk, the broad-

leafed ivy, / unloved, dusty, littered, sanctuary of rats, / gets on with its life" (45).

(Shane Plante)

Brunch. Our last meeting will celebrate your projects at a potluck meal. Not all of you will be able to bring an edible form of your species, but try where a chance exists (for example, sea lettuce) and, again, keep track of your search.

'THEY' SAY IT TASTES LIKE PORK

Rat Recipes

When Paris was under siege during the Franco-Prussian War, Parisians openly ate brown rats and black rats. In Ghana rat is a staple food. And, Canada has a versatile recipe for the Muskrat, which may be used with any other large rodent (Schwabe 204–5). Bon appétit!

ENTRECÔTE À LA BORDELAISE (GRILLED RAT BORDEAUX STYLE)

Alcoholic rats inhabiting wine cellars are skinned and eviscerated, brushed with a thick sauce of olive oil and crushed shallots, and grilled over a fire of broken wine barrels.

(Lisa Szabo)

Acknowledge. Some of you will readily find material—hundreds of skylark poems are singing somewhere—while others will find frustration. But I hope it's some reassurance that I will take into account the differing levels of difficulty inherent in your assignments. Also, a crucial aspect of the document you are preparing is an ample, generous, detailed, specific acknowledgements section. Each of you is responsible to help with all sixteen projects; when you are skimming through forty volumes of poetry, looking for that elusive poem on the tussock moth, delight in finding something on deer mouse or the Roosevelt elk. I will look to your acknowledgements, as well as to our Google Docs file, for evidence of your generous help in sharing habitat.

Frederic was right when he said that at the rate we were all exchanging information we would soon need a Dewey Decimal system just for our biotopes . . . although being called Noah's librarian . . . hmmmm.

(Lisa Szabo)

At this point in the seminar's first meeting, we leave the classroom building to smell, touch, listen, sometimes to taste. I identify three or four species and talk briefly about their naming and some aspects of their ecology. Then, each participant draws a scrap of paper from the hat. I designate one recorder to make a list.

FIELD TRIP #1 12 SEPTEMBER 2007

We are outside standing amongst the shrubbery just outside Buchanan B awaiting our fate. Flora and/or fauna are to be distributed by
hat or . . . something. I feel a little like Alice, out of place, out of the
classroom. We are to eat, sleep and breathe our choice. He's enjoying
this I think and reminds us more times than is comfortable that if we had
not done due diligence and checked the synopsis for this seminar and
wished to drop it, that we should do it soon. If we decide to stay, we are
to discuss our chosen topic, with others, at every opportunity. We jockey
for position along the narrow path and around Laurie. We discuss Sword
fern and Salal and are challenged to eat some kind of purple berry. If
the fates are kind, it will kill me on the spot. I am . . . the European Pine
Shoot Moth. Never heard of it. . . . First class I sit beside a girl name Kita.
We don't talk too much at first, we don't discuss right away, but we immediately agree. Her lichen and my moth co-exist as it turns out. I have
an idea about this, signs—sometimes they knock me off my feet. I have
the bruises to prove it.

(Claire Nicol)

Then we dismiss with a final enthusiastic urging: I know you have been glancing furtively at the list of species now for the last 90 minutes. And you've been thinking "Please God, let me not pick the red tree vole." Or, conversely, you've been praying to be allowed to chase the cuddly European rabbit. But, whatever you have chosen, I now want you to spend every waking hour, and some sleepless nights, finding out about your species. First thing in the morning, while you are brushing your teeth, ask yourself, "I wonder what the red Irish lord is doing now (And does it have teeth? How many? And how does it keep them clean?)?" Ask the person next to you on the bus, the one whose soggy umbrella is dripping down your neck, what he knows about the western pond turtle. And when you go clubbing this weekend, and you're staring longingly across the dance floor, remem-ber what a great pickup line you now have: "Would you like me to tell you about the yellow sand verbena?"

⅔

In the ecologist's mapping, my region contains multiple bioregions or ecological zones.[3] Presumably, a strictly bioregional approach in the humanities
classroom would demand focusing on just one ecosystem classification—
Coastal Western Hemlock Zone, for example—a tactic not particularly
congenial to literature's more fluid mapping of regions.

Habitat studies, so I persuade myself, provides a congenial way to recognize
both senses of bioregion. A student selecting a species of flora and fauna
before a set of texts, already has her own rather singular bioregion: all the
places in which the sand verbena or the snow goose finds it congenial or
possible to live and reproduce. Intersecting that food-and-shelter delineation of space is the region worded in the various textual realizations of the
snow goose. And, for an individual reader, this region will also extend to
the locations in which he is reading. Reading about the sand verbena on a
beach on Anguilla, where the sea grape is everywhere the verbena would be
on Vancouver Island, shifts your understanding of verbena and island-edge
biogeography.

⅔

Surprise lingers in our collective search for literary habitat. Both researcher
and participants delight that they have found a literary reference where they
had expected none. Angela Waldie, for example, found the rufous-sided
towhee in David James Duncan (237), Thoreau (191–92), and Emily Carr,
one of whose lesser-known works teaches through an attentive parable of
Father Towhee (67–69).

Angela opened her "[Towhee] Field Notes" with a working-from-dream
sequence found in Audrey Thomas's story "The Man with Clam Eyes":

> Now I open the door—
> (West-coast birds, the towhee with its strange cry, and the waves). (561)

Towhee surprises because it is a bit hidden—syntactically. As Angela
mused,

> "You inhabit parentheses—the edges of thoughts."

And then, picking up on an Audubon guide's description of towhee habitat—forest edges, thickets—she continues,

> "You live, I like to think, on the edges of things."

Angela greets Thomas's half-hidden towhee with a meditation I have since frequently turned to as a foundational expression of my aspiration for habitat studies.

> And so I am introduced to you by your call. You cry "drink-your-tea" or "towhee," announcing your presence, engaging in an act of self-naming. I wonder, sometimes, what my name would be were it determined by my own voice.

Here Angela connects name to body—sounding in that originary sense so sensitively explored in David Abram's *The Spell of the Sensuous.* Thinking towhee from the edge, she listens to her own shifting identity.

The course outline for habitat studies is deliberately spare and cryptic. Its absence of detail proposes the centrality of the project and invites the participants to take us where their species leads them.

In Week 2, I ask each student (briefly, about 5 minutes each) to introduce her species to the full group and to describe a research problem that, at this early stage, she anticipates will be a prominent focus of her study. Then in Week 3, a field trip on some ecological topic is important. Sometimes, I ask the university's sustainability office to provide a tour of campus sustainability initiatives.[4] Or, I recruit a graduate student from geography or environmental studies to teach us about a campus site. In 2008 and again in 2009, Toktam Sajedi, a PhD student in forestry, showed us succession patterns in Pacific Spirit Park, a second growth forest that surrounds the campus. Toktam studies soil nutrients, comes with a spade, and shows us how to read the layers of the forest floor.

> Toktam lays the shovel down, and with her bare hands she peels away the top layer of the soil to expose to us the hidden workings of the forest biome. She brushes away twigs and dry leaves like friends, covering her hands in dirt. Someone points out her obvious comfort with the soil, and she giggles, saying she has probably made "around a

thousand" of these soil plots. I am suddenly fascinated by how I imagine she sees the world. I see "the woods," but she sees a series of interconnected soil cross-sections and biochemical make-ups. I envy her deep knowledge of the ground we stand on.

(Erin Samuda)

By Week 4, participants will have located a sample of writing about their species: it might be a poem, a paragraph from a novel, a field guide description, or a portion of a scientific article. The assignment is to do a "close reading" and share it with the group. The Week 4 assignment is to be handed in, and I return it with comments, queries, suggestions, cautions, and a mark (which I assure the students I will only use in calculating the final mark if it improves their result). Usually we take two classroom sessions to read these pieces. By this point, the group is beginning to call one another by their species names rather than their given names.

By Week 6, I try to arrange another field trip. We might go to the Museum of Anthropology to discuss ecological principles inherent in the aboriginal art of our bioregion, or to the UBC Farm, an on-campus research farm testing methods of organic stewardship, or to a gallery, where I usually make the visit self-guided. I ask the students to range about the gallery, choose a work of particular interest, keeping in mind their species and concepts of habitat, and stare at it intently enough and for long enough that they can show us features of content and technique the museumgoer's typical ten-second glance would not notice. Reassembling, each student teaches us about his piece. This relaxed format, mostly involving students with no formal studies of the fine arts, typically draws a half-dozen casual gallery patrons who follow around with us.

An encouraging thing happens between my first and second skylark hunts. Our class visits the Vancouver Art Gallery to conduct ourselves through an "erratic guided tour," an exercise in which each of us finds a work and presents it to the other class members.

For me the choice is easy, because the first thing I hear is birdsong. Trying to find it, I explore Hadley Howes and Maxwell Stephen's video installation *1 + 1 = 1* (part of the "How Soon is Now" exhibit of contemporary art, Spring 2009), in which the artists have cannily hidden their birdsong-producing apparatus amid various artifacts and screens displaying chopped-up bits of Jean-Luc Godard's experimental Rolling Stones documentary *Sympathy for the Devil* (originally titled *1 + 1*). Entering the installation (backward, as I discover, in an unintentional tribute to Godard's Situationist past), I learn to filter with my ears, to scrutinize the barrage of sensory information piece by piece for use. It is a process I have been trying to become more comfortable with since my first walk; "birdwatching is really birdlistening," several wellwishers have told me, and here my visual inputs are designed to mislead.

Closing my eyes, I imagine myself a creature of pure aurality, superbly adapted to his surroundings. I track down the birdsong, emanating from a knocked-over Klieg light. I try to hold onto the feeling of crossing over, the almost visceral metamorphosis. I am gratified to note that several of my classmates do not pick out the birdsong at all until it is pointed out to them. I am learning to approach nature differently, at least on a sensory level.

                                                                    (Martin McCarvill)

In Week 7, we meet in small groups of three or four to workshop the projects. I ask for a prepared document that includes one to two pages of writing so polished the writer is convinced it will feature significantly in the final project document, plus an annotated table of contents testing the likely form of the whole. These are circulated for written comments from each workshopper; then we discuss ideas, organization, and problems. I ask for these emergent forms to be handed in for my further responses.

The workshop leads into a session—deliberately postponed until the projects are taking form—in which I show students examples of projects in habitat studies. I show them single-species studies, such as Michael Cohen's *Garden of Bristlecones*, and collections of shorter creative nonfiction pieces, such as Patricia Lichen's *River-Walking Songbirds and Singing Coyotes*. I also bring a generous sample of past students' projects, chosen to show range and variety. I describe these not as models but as inspiration.

In Week 9, our session often combines theory and representation. One of my graduate students, Sonnet L'Abbé, likes to lead this session. She asks us to read Deleuze and Guattari on rhizomatics and Foucault on classifying. She distributes a few days in advance Karen J. Warren's "Ecological Feminist Philosophies: An Overview" and Jacques Derrida's "And Say the Animal Responded?" from *Zoontologies: The Question of the Animal*. Then, she leads a field session that combines our trying to draw a patch of duff, or a leaf. Then, she gives us a select few letters from the alphabet and asks us to use them to name the objects we have drawn.

> Sonnet helped us to engage with language in another way as well. First she guided us through a creative interaction with some of the plants from her house. We were asked to, not describe (this word may have limited us to scientific language), but to "give" the plant to someone else through words. After we wrote five or six lines, we drew the plant over and over and connected more deeply through observation and artistic reproduction of what was in front of our eyes. After drawing we returned our focus to our original plant and again wrote our observation about the plant.
>
> (Ali Costigan)

In Week 10 a session might attempt some "conventional" literary ecocriticism. I often use Aldo Leopold's "Marshland Elegy," a poem by John Clare or Seamus Heaney, and always one or two pieces reading the immediate bioregion.

In either the penultimate week or at the lunch, each student introduces a piece of music or a video concerning her species. A good many at this point write their own songs.

> Travellin' freshwater like a largemouth bass
> Or underground like a gopher, emerging for grass
>
> . . . .
>
> There is not a species my life does not need
> Including Japanese knotweed to root my feet
> ("Butterfly [Woodland Skipper]" written, recorded and performed by Paul Watkins)

Although bioregionalism has a sixty-year history (Aberley), the term did not become prominent in habitat studies until about 2004. Ecocriticism, however, had been very much on my mind since Glen Love's Western Literature Association address in 1990 and the subsequent meeting in Reno that resulted in the founding of ASLE. But the course's genesis lay in a grassroots localism that obviously responded—if not explicitly or deliberately—to an emerging culture of bioregionalism.

Soon after, with Glen Love and Cheryll Glotfelty as models and guides, I began to add to my Northwest courses a small assignment (10 marks out of 100) to write a one-pager on a single native species. I was uneasy that we were studying regional writing but few of us knew much about the flora and fauna that shared our place. My students quickly acknowledged my uneasiness with enthusiastic curiosity. One-pagers grew into eight-pagers, and, by the second testing of this mini-assignment, several students, faced with such term paper projects as "Concepts of History in Northwest Writing," were asking me, "Is it okay if I do my *whole* term project on Oregon grape (or the American dipper)?" So it was English literature students fascinated by the lives of others, and frustrated at their ignorance of their immediate surroundings, that led to a course where a single species became the starting point. For a while, I assigned some texts—a few nature essays, a packet of poems, a single novel—to provide some literary focus. But gradually I realized that activist scholars dedicated to home place would create a more richly layered literary texture to our study than any I could prescribe.

Habitat studies could also be titled "bioregionalism studies." I have stuck with the habitat label partly because it seems less intimidating, less programmatic. It implies dwelling and liveability—and invites the reimagining implied by rein*habitat*ion. Habitat requires us to think about the climate, and soil, and air, and topography, and other species that any single animal or plant needs to thrive and reproduce. It's inherently placed, yet mobile.

But the course surely is bioregional in its objectives. Even if these are not explicit or advocated in so many words. Bioregion upsets the implicit homogeneity and insularity of regionalism. It also counters the root sense of *region* ("to rule"), the dimension of the term that signals political power and space controlled from afar. The control element in bioregion is the power of life—of blood pulsing, oxygen transforming, nectar feeding—and hence the space of a bioregion is continuously transforming, at once growing and decaying. Sixteen habitat projects overlap and reach for interconnections. The course is tribal in that students quickly recognize that assigned such difficult tasks, they must work together. Play-community is fostered on field trips more relaxed than seminar rooms: storytelling occurs spontaneously. Participants try to adopt other identities, and doing so they become celebrants of the uncelebrated, the ignored, the invisible, and the underfoot.

NOTES

1. This article is a teaching guide to a course that's been evolving over the past fifteen years. Accordingly, much of what follows is in the form of an imagined transcript of the instructor's opening-day monologue (in a course that subsequently has *no* lecturing). I call the course "Habitat Studies"—rather than, for example, "Literature and the Environment" or "Ecocriticism"—because the term *habitat* insists on a close examination of the essentials of water, food, shelter, and protection from predation that define any species' home. Yet the term also has an amplitude that allows for all forms of living-in, including the cultural (that is, human) and imagined. The term *habitat* comes from *habere*, "to have, to hold." As my student Derek Woods, reflected, it's valuable to think of any organism "holding to a place" within a "gathering of creatures that have learned to hold together."

The website referred to in the opening paragraph is www.english.ubc.ca. The archives of "English Courses Offered" record some of the "calendar" descriptions of the course.

I would like to thank W. H. New for his editorial acumen. Students in this course sign an acknowledgement giving permission to quote their term projects, verbatim or edited, in future publications. Special thanks to the many students who have taught me what habitat studies could be within a department focusing on literature and language.

2. Email to the students in English 490: Majors Seminar: "Sorry to intrude on your busy term with this blather, but I wanted to be sure you realize that the course you've registered for in next term begins by asking you to study a species of flora or fauna, rather than say an intricate poem, or an upholstered novel, such as you might legitimately expect to be studying in a course whose designation begins ENGL. And worse, you don't even get to choose which species. Past experience suggests that it might get weirder still, with field trips and stuff. Oh, we will get round to a fair bit of fabulous literature, and we will find some poem that surprises us with the way it teaches habitat. But you might find the sidewayness of this course a bit too upside down. I just wanted to send this caution, because I have a stretching waiting list of people I would like to accommodate. If you have questions at this point, I am not sure I can answer them, but I'll sure try."

3. Some sense of ecological zones can be found, for example, in the prefatory material in Boersma's *Invasive Species in the Pacific Northwest*. These would

include, to recognize some of the differentiated ecoregions, the Cascade Mountains Leeward Forests, the Fraser Plateau and Basin complex, and the Palouse Grasslands (xviii).

4. See <www.sustain.ubc.ca>. The University of British Columbia has, for example, built Sustainability Street and some buildings have compostable toilets.

WORKS CITED

Abram, David. *The Spell of the Sensuous*. New York: Pantheon, 1996. Print.

Boersma, P. D., S. H. Reichard, and A. N. Van Buren, *Invasive Species in the Pacific Northwest*. Seattle: University of Washington Press, 2006. Print.

Bolster, Stephanie. *Two Bowls of Milk*. Toronto: McClelland & Stewart, 1999. Print.

Bowering, George. "Against Description." *West Window: Selected Poems*. Toronto: General Publishing, 1982. 135. Print.

Carr, Emily. *The Heart of a Peacock*. 1953. Toronto: Irwin, 1986. Print.

Duncan, David James. *The River Why*. Toronto: Sierra Club, 1983. Print.

Levertov, Denise. *Evening Train*. New York: New Directions, 1992. Print.

McKay, Don. *Deactivated West 100*. Kentville, Nova Scotia: Gaspereau Press, 2005. Print.

Schwabe, Calvin W. *Unmentionable Cuisine*. Charlottesville: University Press of Virginia, 1979. Print.

Solnit, Rebecca. *A Field Guide to Getting Lost*. New York: Viking, 2005. Print.

Thomas, Audrey. "The Man with Clam Eyes." *Anthology of Canadian Literature in English: Revised and Abridged Edition*. Ed. Russell Brown, Donna Bennett, and Nathalie Cooke. Toronto: Oxford University Press, 1990. Print.

Thoreau, Henry David. *Thoreau on Birds*. Ed. Helen Cruickshank. Toronto: Oxford University Press, 1990. Print.

Turner, Nancy J. *Ethnobotany of the Nitinaht Indians*. Victoria: B.C. Provincial Museum, 1983. Print.

Turner, Nancy J., Laurence C. Thompson, M. Terry Thompson, and Annie Z. York. *Thompson Ethnobotany: Knowledge and Use of Plants by the Thompson Indians of British Columbia*. Victoria: Royal B.C. Museum, 1990. Print.

Wheeler, Sue. *Habitat*. London, Ontario: Brick Books, 2005. Print.

WES BERRY

Switching on Light Bulbs and Blowing Up Mountains

Ecoliteracy and Energy Consumption in General Education English Courses

I'M A NATIVE KENTUCKIAN teaching Kentuckians, a strange bird in higher education where so many teachers find employment far from their roots. Having a background similar to many of my students—religious, provincial, basketball obsessed—I'm uniquely situated to develop courses in which students can better understand their native state.

I'm also aware of the complexities bound up with this word *native*. Shawnee people roamed my home county, called "Barren," long before I did. I've found their arrowheads near the creek bordering my grandfather's farm. And does merely living in a place make one "native"? Wes Jackson's essay collection *Becoming Native to This Place* suggests that nativity requires more than establishing residency: it requires knowledge of place gained from long-term dwelling and interaction. Jackson urges universities to educate students in "homecoming": "Our task is to build cultural fortresses to protect our emerging nativeness. They must be strong enough to hold at bay the powers of consumerism, the powers of greed and envy and pride. One of the most effective ways for this to come about would be for our universities to assume the awesome responsibility to both validate and educate those who want to be homecomers—not necessarily to go home but to go someplace and dig in and begin the long search and experiment to become native" (97).

Bioregional thinker Wendell Berry, never one to use fancy language or claim allegiance to "isms," summarizes succinctly the requirements for such

nativity in his essay "Conservation and Local Economy," a vision he revisits
frequently in his work:

> In our relation to the land, we are ruled by a number of terms and limits
> set not by anyone's preference but by nature and by human nature:
>
>   I. Land that is used will be ruined unless it is properly cared for.
> II. Land cannot be properly cared for by people who do not know it
>   intimately, who do not know how to care for it, who are not strongly
>   motivated to care for it, and who cannot afford to care for it.
> III. People cannot be adequately motivated to care for land by general
>   principles or by incentives that are merely economic. . .
> IV. People are motivated to care for land to the extent that their interest
>   in it is direct, dependable, and permanent.
>   V. They will be motivated to care for the land if they can reasonably
>   expect to live on it as long as they live. They will be more strongly
>   motivated if they can reasonably expect that their children and
>   grandchildren will live on it as long as they live. In other words, there
>   must be a mutuality of belonging: they must feel that the land belongs
>   to them, that they belong to it, and that this belonging is a settled and
>   unthreatened fact.
> VI. But such a belonging must be appropriately limited. . . . there is a
>   limit to how much land can be owned before an owner is unable to
>   take proper care of it. (3–4)

Put in scholarly terms, Berry advocates here what Berg and Dasmann call,
in their bioregional tract "Reinhabiting California," "living-in-place," defined as "following the necessities and pleasures of life as they are uniquely
presented by a particular site, and evolving ways to ensure long-term occupancy of that site" (399).

The cynic in me wants to say that my students' native place is the computer screen and text windows of their cell phones, since that's where they
often place their attentions. Even in a largely rural state like Kentucky,
where some of my students have lived on farms and experienced outdoor
play during childhood, electronic media now occupies much of their days.
I'm pretty sure my students spend more time on Facebook than they do
observing details of the world outside of the numerous screens that hold
them captive. In short, teaching bioregional ideals to today's wired students
poses special problems. I'm no longer amazed that my students, growing
up in a major coal-producing state, don't realize that over 90 percent of
the electricity they use to power their computers comes from coal. Fewer

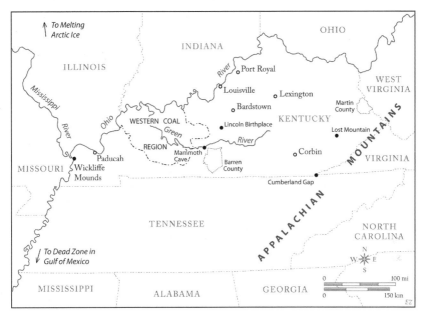

Kentucky and notable energy regions

understand how that coal is mined. Hardly any of them know that Kentucky's per capita electricity use is much higher than the national average because of so-called cheap energy linked to our abundant coal supply. Students should know that when they flip on that light switch, a mountain is exploding somewhere in Appalachia—and they should understand the connection. Mountaintop removal mining (MTR) is burying our streams, and Appalachian coal burned at power plants in Kentucky and many other states is linked to fast-melting ice in Alaska. You would think college students would know these things, but few of my students do, and few of them are learning this urgent information in other courses.

Knowing one's energy sources is an essential part of knowing where one's at, and even though I'm a teacher of writing and literature—subjects not easily aligned with learning about energy sources (the specialization of geologists and engineers)—I have knitted together successful English classes centered on the motif of energy economics (supply and demand). My home state is blessed with a strong environmental writing base, including prominent writers with conservationist/agrarian/social justice visions: Wendell Berry, Silas House, Barbara Kingsolver, and Erik Reece. In teaching upper-level literature courses, I also choose fictions that feature regional settings and thematic land-use issues by writers representing various parts of Kentucky, such as Harriet Arnow, Jesse Stuart, James Still, and Bobbie Ann Mason. Every two years I teach a course called "Kentucky Literature," which is a perfect venue for exposing students to agrarian issues. But I don't want to wait every two years to disseminate ecological literacy, so I've developed ways of working such learning into my regular writing classes that all students at the university have to take—classes like "Freshman Composition" and "Introduction to Literature." The most effective method I've used to capture students' attention and get them to see connections between their own places and the broader world is to focus on our fossil-fueled economy and their own roles in it.

Energy consumption in an English class? This ain't "Environmental Science"! What the durn hell?

Getting students to think honestly about their places takes some work. It's far easier for them to see their home state as a collection of symbols than as a network of particular regions with unique plants and animals, soil formations, language patterns, and economies. The symbols that create the "Kentucky myth" include Daniel Boone, Colonel Sanders, and horses. Those savvy to the tourist packaging of our state may also name mint juleps, hot browns, and the Hatfield-McCoy family feud. An incredible number of people of my home state consider themselves to be "property of" the University of Kentucky basketball program—a rabid loyalty that may for many fans surpass actual devotion to one's place. A postcard I picked up in "Bourbon Capital" Bardstown, Kentucky, encapsulates humorously some of my state's identity baggage: "You Know You're from Kentucky," says the headline, "If you can spit tobacco juice and talk at the same time"; "If the trim on your car is duct tape"; "If the bathroom is located 75 feet behind the house"; "If you consider a saw and washboard to be musical instruments"; "If your sister is also your cousin and your aunt"; "If your idea of 4th of July fireworks is a shotgun and box of shells." *The Onion* ran a story in 2003 with the headline "Iraq, Kentucky Vie for World Shooting-into-the-Air Supremacy." No surprise that when I ask students to tell me about their home state, they make a sort of redneck shopping list that includes many of the aforementioned stereotypes. Since cultivating a bioregional imagination involves knowing how human identity is bound up with places, beginning courses with a discussion of Kentucky mythology makes sense. Kentucky-the-myth carries a fair amount of beauty (horse farms) and heroics (Abe Lincoln), combined with a sense that, as a people, we somehow missed modernity, especially those backward folks of the eastern mountains who, limited by vertical geography, just can't quite make it over the next ridge to discover what is happening in the broader world of commerce—good things like shoe manufacturing and bonded whisky. In my literature and writing courses, we begin by evoking the myths—which lures many students into the discussion immediately, because most of them love talking about their home state—after which we make the shift to texts that deal honestly with regional land-use issues.

I don't fool myself into thinking my students are getting a bioregional education in my courses. A bioregional education requires a long time of getting-to-know, and in my courses we have less than four months. Besides, my students come from many parts of Kentucky, other states, and foreign countries. There is not one bioregion we hold in common. Moreover, the best bioregional education is hands-on and multidisciplinary. While I've attempted to get students into the field by taking them on trips to local organic farms and on hiking trips in Mammoth Cave, the experiential component is more difficult to achieve in English courses than, say, biology courses. Of necessity, my approach is more general, addressing issues that are connected to students, issues that students usually don't realize they are connected to—like the link between their energy use and MTR mining and its effects.

Moreover, the focus on Kentucky isn't exclusive—at different times we've studied texts such as the documentary film *Oil on Ice*, dealing with oil production in the Arctic, and read testimonies by Appalachian dwellers outside of our state about the effects on coal mining in their places. Furthermore, this focus on energy economy can be tweaked to appeal to students all over the country, whether your energy source is coal, nuclear, or hydroelectric, because it involves investigative work that requires students to learn how their region is connected to other regions. For example, a power plant in Monroe, Michigan, burns coal from Black Mountain, Kentucky. Monroe is near Toledo, Adrian, and Ann Arbor, sites of colleges and universities; perhaps students at those midwestern schools power computers using coal from Appalachia. Understanding one's energy sources and the connections between regions—and discovering beneficial texts to support this understanding—is paramount to this pedagogy.

In "Interpreting Bioregionalism: A Story from Many Voices," Doug Aberley notes that the "bioregional story can only be learned through long participation in local and continental bioregional gatherings, and by assimilating ideas penned in ephemeral journals and self-published books that rarely appear in libraries or mass distribution outlets" (13). I assume Aberley is alluding to books akin to the *Foxfire* series that documents the folkways of southern Appalachia, or local fishing reports and agricultural extension newsletters, or maybe the cookbook put out by local homemakers. As a teacher of literature, I'm responsible for boosting my students' knowledge of books that have literary merit. I realize that *literature* is a slippery term; accordingly, I begin my "Introduction to Literature" courses by asking students to define it. Almost always, a student says that literature is words on a page, broadly conceived, so that there's literature of economics, literature of the medical field, etc. Other students think literature is limited to imaginative prose and poetry. In his 1949 Nobel Prize speech, William Faulkner said good writing deals with "the problems of the human heart in conflict with itself." This definition could apply to much writing about consumer society, from *Walden* to *The Great Gatsby* to *Into the Wild* to *Lost Mountain*. After all, don't many of us live paradoxical lives, desiring clean air but enjoying our mobility fueled by airplanes and cars? Don't we value our computers that operate on the juice from strip-mined coal and relish delicious coffee shipped from South America, even while deploring climate change? Salman Rushdie says, "Literature is where I go to explore the highest and lowest places in human society and in the human spirit, where I hope to find not absolute truth but the truth of the tale, of the imagination and of the heart" (62). Again, much writing about our economic and ecological predicament, like Lester Brown's *Plan B* series and most essays by Wendell Berry, while not conventionally literary, live up to the spirit of Rushdie's description, especially the part about exploring the highest and lowest places in human society, which investigative work into our energy economy reveals.

In choosing books for my literature and writing courses, I interpret literature broadly, not confining text selections to fiction and poetry, and this opens up possibilities for bioregional pedagogy. At my university, the boilerplate goals of "Introduction to Literature" include "examining representative works in the major genres of literature with attention to different time periods, cultures and diversity," and also "thinking and writing critically about literature." This course description allows for flexible content. I interpret "literature" as "story" and "narrative," which makes room for memoirs, journalistic prose, and documentary film, in addition to the standard fiction, poetry, and drama. What benefits students and society most? Having them read another canonical short story from an anthology or having them learn urgent issues of interspecies health care (you know, how to live in peace and health on this small planet)? The two don't have to be mutually exclusive—there are canonical stories in literature anthologies that are instructive, that can make students better for having read them— but we have limited class time, and if we believe Bill McKibben and other climate change heralds, then we also have limited time to make drastic changes in how we produce and consume. Creating courses that allow students to analyze their own consumption is vital pedagogy.

Even considering my generous assessment of what deserves placement on a literature syllabus, I nevertheless would not include many of the aforementioned fishing reports or cookbooks or even the *Foxfire* books in most English classes. However, feeling the urgency of our world ecological predicament and the need to educate consumers in this nation where our energy usage is grossly out of balance with our population, I have used more regularly books and film that may seem a bit strange to traditionalists of English studies: books like Erik Reece's *Lost Mountain: A Year in the Vanishing Wilderness*, a piece of environmental journalism; the essays of Wendell Berry; and documentary films like *Sludge*, produced by a Kentucky community-based filmmaking organization called Appalshop (see Appalshop.org) and *Kilowatt Ours: A Plan to Re-energize America* by Nashville filmmaker Jeff Barrie. Students thus get exposed to narratives that have the added benefit of teaching them something useful about being a human in this world that is being consumed far too quickly.

Motivated by self-preservation, my students' concern for nearby regions elevates when they learn the concept of "living downstream." Accordingly, early in my courses focusing on sustainability we read Wendell Berry's article "Contempt for Small Places," as it succinctly sums up in seven paragraphs the concept of porous borders. Berry begins by noting how newspaper editorials deplore the "dead zone" in the Gulf of Mexico and such practices as MTR mining in eastern Kentucky, adding that "[s]ome day we may finally understand the connections." Berry then states clearly the concept of "living downstream" without naming it as such: "The health of the oceans depends on the health of rivers; the health of rivers depends on the health of small streams; the health of small streams depends on the health of their watersheds. The health of the water is exactly the same as the health of the land; the health of small places is exactly the same as the health of large places. As we know, disease is hard to confine. Because natural law is in force everywhere, infections move" (7).

Berry's work reinforces the point that the headwater mountain streams buried under the "overburden" of the MTR process are connected with the health of downstream creeks and rivers. Many people are ignorant about their drinking water source—and I'm talking about major rivers, not obscure streams 100 miles from the household—so if my students finish a course knowing more about their water source, then a small step towards bioregional awareness has been taken. If they learn how that water source is affected by what happens in other regions, even better.

Erik Reece's *Lost Mountain* helps students see how a light switched on in central Kentucky is linked to a mountaintop being exploded and leveled in eastern Kentucky. Reece's investigative purpose, he announces early on, is to "see up close what an eastern mountain looks like before, during, and after its transformation into a western desert" (13). Reece documents one year of Lost Mountain's demise and in doing so radiates outward, helping readers understand how this mountain is attached to places far away, to a broader American cultural wrongheadedness, to habitat loss worldwide, and to readers' own dorm rooms and apartments.

Lost Mountain is an eloquent bioregional text with distinctive literary qualities, such as a unique speaking voice, an expertly drawn setting, and an urgent vision. Although it's a collection of essays, the book even has something like a plot, as Reece returns to the mining site each month to observe the destruction, putting himself at considerable risk by doing so (he tells several stories in *Lost Mountain* of thug tactics used by coal company watchmen and coal truck drivers). Reece is well schooled in American conservationist writing, and one hears echoes of Rachel Carson, Aldo Leopold, and Wendell Berry in his arguments. He regularly quotes from E. O. Wilson's work and alludes to Walt Whitman, John Muir, and Robert Frost. *Lost Mountain* can thus serve as a conservationist primer for readers uninitiated in ecological writing. Of additional benefit for my students are Reece's conversations with local residents of Eastern Kentucky affected by MTR.

It seems ridiculous that we share a statewide identity as Kentuckians—a loyal and proud identity in our symbols and heroes (Bluegrass pastures and music, the University of Kentucky wildcat logo, tobacco farming)—but that we citizens outside of the coal mining areas know so little about the stories of the people whose lives are affected by the industry that supplies our low-cost-per-kilowatt-hour electricity. Reece remedies this by giving voice to the mountain folk whose stories are not often covered in mainstream media, noting that when Martin County, Kentucky, suffered a coal slurry spill in 2000, thirty times the size of the Exxon Valdez oil spill, the *New York Times* "didn't print one word about it" (129). Reece writes about mountain families whose homes are flooded because of increased erosion caused by dynamite blasting of the mountaintops by absentee mining companies. He tells of many people injured and killed by overloaded coal trucks speeding on mountain roads, and of people like Teri Blanton, who grew up in Harlan County, Kentucky, whose children broke out in a "measles-like rash" after bathing because their groundwater was poisoned with vinyl chloride, trichloroethylene, and other "volatile organic contaminants" irresponsibly dumped by the McGraw-Edison Company who was rebuilding mining equipment nearby. Elsewhere, Reece notes that the number of Kentucky children treated for asthma has risen nearly 50 percent since 2000, and how because of "acid rain and acid mine runoff, there is so much mercury in Kentucky streams that any pregnant woman who eats fish from them risks causing serious, lifelong harm to the child she carries" (25). Reece's expose of environmental injustices helps students realize that as consumers of electricity that comes primarily from Kentucky's mountains they are complicit. Guilt can be a prime motivator in changing behavior—maybe not the ideal motivator like empathy and spiritual goodwill, but nevertheless effective. Images and statistics from *Lost Mountain*, students have told me, make a powerful impact, enough to change the way they consume electricity.

To reinforce for students how their actions in cave country are linked to lives in other regions, and also to provide some hope after the emotional drain of *Lost Mountain*, we watch a well-edited documentary by Nashville filmmaker Jeff Barrie, whose fifty-five-minute narrative *Kilowatt Ours* traces our electricity usage from raw material to the home. This documentary has proven to be a successful capstone to the energy unit, as it illustrates with striking visuals and personal stories the connections Berry and Reece make in their writings—such things as MTR, global warming, the nuclear power cycle, and mercury pollution. The initial twenty minutes of the film explore serious consequences of our heavy use of coal and nuclear power. Noting that the average American home uses 900 kilowatt hours monthly at the ratio of 1 lb. coal/kWh, Barrie presents a cartoon image of boxcars filled with coal, extending from coast to coast and back and then circling the earth three times—a striking visualization of the 1.1 billion tons of coal burned each year in the United States. The film presents aerial shots of MTR in Appalachia, an accessible primer on global warming with expert testimony, and a personalized look into the nuclear power industry with an interview of Navajo "elder" Melton Martinez, who explains the incredibly high cancer rate in his community because of exposure to toxic radioactive yellowcake leavings from uranium mining operations. Martinez says, "Everywhere you turn you hear people dying of cancer or having respiratory leukemia, newborns having leukemia. Most of our people don't even have electricity in our Navajo reservation. Most of our elders are gone from here. . . . We're the elders now, and we're only in our 40s." From such examples, students can see connections between the Appalachian people whose lives are disrupted by MTR and the Navajo people who suffer from uranium mining by absentee corporations producing electricity for people far away from the mining sites. Barrie's film also helps students realize their own complicity in these cases of domestic colonialism—that our wasteful energy consumption has much more negative consequences than high electricity bills, including waterways polluted by mercury from coal burning power plants and childhood asthma rates on the rise. The remaining 35 minutes of *Kilowatt Ours* shows how each of us can make positive changes in our consumption, highlighting simple tasks like buying Energy Star electronics, using compact fluorescent bulbs, and sealing air leaks in homes. Barrie looks at homes, schools, and businesses that have become much more efficient by using geothermal technology, daylighting, LED bulbs, and by doing such sensible things as shutting down computers when people aren't using them. In another segment on green power, Barrie interviews a family in Iowa with a private wind turbine and a dairy farmer who generates energy using a methane digester. After watching, we discuss the extent to which the film uses narrative techniques such as plot, setting, characterization, use of symbols, dialogue, and imagery.

In addition to *Kilowatt Ours*, I've shown students video clips from the "America's Most Endangered Mountains" video series on the website iLoveMountains.org, which features interviews with mountain people about how MTR affects their lives, and I've also shown the film *Sludge*, about the massive coal slurry spill in Martin County, Kentucky, in the year 2000. Each text helps students understand more clearly how we are connected bioregionally and how in this global absentee economy we are all "living downstream." At the end of the unit, students write an essay that analyzes the use of rhetoric in these written and visual works of storytelling.

Assessing my oddball "Introduction to Literature" unit, the following student comment summarizes what others have said regarding their increased knowledge and desire to make positive change:

> In particular I really felt drawn to the film *Kilowatt Ours*. This film stressed the using up of natural resources like coal; and the importance of reducing your use to save the planet. Usually I don't care much about these issues or at least don't do my part. But from this film and discussing it in class, I really had a change of heart; and now I recycle much more and reduce my energy use. One thing the film brought to light for me was *all the ways I could benefit personally* from reducing my use and just how easy it is. This video kept an upbeat non-boring side to what usually is a boring topic. It taught me a lot about the issue and I even found myself taking notes when I wasn't required to do so. I went back home and replaced my light bulbs with more energy efficient ones, as a means to begin reducing my use. (my emphasis)

Note the student's comment about benefitting personally from conservation. Self-interest, whether for economic gain or for improved health, remains a prime motivator for my students, and this energy unit taps into that drive.

In the end, bioregional learning with an energy focus will, of necessity, be expansive and nonprovincial, requiring learning that goes beyond the native soil to see how one's actions here affect people who live over there. The majority of my students wish to remain in Kentucky and deepen their roots here. I'm inspired by how many of them feel an intense loyalty to some place that lies within the political borders of our state, and by how many of them feel proud of our shared symbols. The kind of learning acquired in the energy unit models the "homecoming" that Wes Jackson advocates for university education, as it cultivates a deepening "nativeness" that will, at best, "hold at bay the powers of consumerism . . . greed and envy and pride." It goes beyond our collective symbols, beyond mere living in a place, inching a little further towards a more authentic patriotism, or love of place, that is more responsible because of heightened awareness of how actions in one place are linked to land use in other places. It cultivates a bioregional awareness that students can pack with them if they are relocated to a different state or country—a cosmopolitan care of places that, like the students' beloved "interwebs" (humorous slang for the Internet), understands no region is an island unto itself.

WORKS CITED

Aberley, Doug. "Interpreting Bioregionalism: A Story from Many Voices." *Bioregionalism*. Ed. Michael Vincent McGinnis. London: Routledge, 1999. 13–42. Print.

Berg, Peter, and Raymond Dasmann. "Reinhabiting California." *The Ecologist* 7.10 (1977): 399–401. Print.

Berry, Wendell. "Conservation and Local Economy." *Sex, Economy, Freedom & Community*. New York: Pantheon, 1993. 3–18. Print.

———. "Contempt for Small Places." *The Way of Ignorance and Other Essays*. Berkeley: Shoemaker and Hoard, 2005. 7–8. Print.

Jackson, Wes. *Becoming Native to This Place*. Washington, D.C.: Counterpoint, 1996. Print.

Kilowatt Ours: A Plan to Re-energize America. Dir. Jeff Barrie. KilowattOurs.org, 2007. Film.

Reece, Erik. *Lost Mountain: A Year in the Vanishing Wilderness*. New York: Riverhead, 2006. Print.

Rushdie, Salman. *The Rushdie File*. Ed. Lisa Appignanesi and Sara Maitland. Syracuse: Syracuse University Press, 1990.

LAIRD CHRISTENSEN

Teaching Bioregional Perception—at a Distance

AT 1,919 FEET IT'S NOT much of a mountain, even by northern Taconic standards, but still people climb through the hickory, beech, and maple to take in the view from Haystack Mountain: Adirondacks to the west, Green Mountains to the east, and the basin of Lake Champlain opening to the north. There's nothing visible to suggest where a mapmaker's line separates Vermont from New York, or Rutland County from Bennington and Washington Counties—never mind the fainter lines between the towns of Pawlet, Granville, Rupert, or Danby. That's why I bring my graduate students here each September, in the company of writers such as Bill McKibben and Gary Nabhan. It's a good place to talk bioregions.

From up here it doesn't take students long to grasp the idea that political boundaries have little to do with how the world orders itself. As we watch the Mettowee River roll north, none of us can tell just where it passes into New York. Away from the maps and road signs, we are a step closer to experiencing place the way a moose does, browsing her way to the next mouthful of willow buds, oblivious to any change in jurisdiction. We can almost imagine the world she inhabits—and yet we do so, as Yi-Fu Tuan reminds us, from within symbolic "mental worlds" that humans construct "to mediate between themselves and external reality" (13). Is it even possible for us to see past our mental worlds to one more fundamental? Since these students are pursuing degrees in environmental studies, we can at least try to find a less obstructed view of the environment they'll be studying.

The first step, of course, is simply to set aside the boundaries we're used

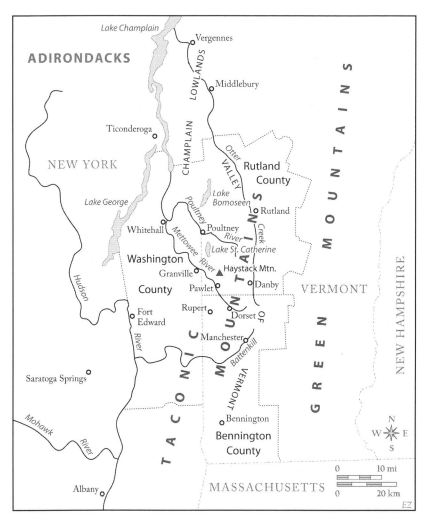

Southern Lake Champlain Basin in Vermont and New York

to working with. But is a world without *our* boundaries really a world without boundaries? I ask the students to consider the ranges of different species: they won't find these chestnut oaks north of here or sugar maples in such numbers further south. Isn't an ecological limitation a kind of boundary? If so, the next step is to decide which natural boundaries most accurately define our bioregions. Where does *here* end and *there* begin?

The students turn in slow circles, taking in miles and miles of rumpled green. Since watersheds are naturally defined regions, I point to the spot where rainwater begins to follow the Battenkill to the Hudson, rather than the Mettowee to Lake Champlain. Does that seem like a distinct boundary, I ask, that imperceptible rise of land north of Dorset? Gary Snyder suggests starting with indigenous homelands, so I gesture toward Mahican territory, then toward Western Abenaki and Mohawk territories, and explain how malleable those boundaries seem to have been ("On Earth Geography" 24). Some prefer physiographic regions: yes, these Taconics are geologically distinct from the Greens and Adirondacks, but should we also separate these hills from their drainages and imagine those Champlain Lowlands as a different bioregion? Where do we draw the lines?

As we start down from the bare summit on this final day of our graduate residency, I hear students sorting out the questions they will ask of their own landscapes when they get home. Since they will be attending my class online, each will be the only one trying to define the bioregion that exists beneath Las Vegas, Nevada, or Birmingham, Alabama. Oshkosh, Wisconsin. Temecula, California. Lima, Peru.

Strange as it may sound, these students will be learning how to perceive their own bioregions through distance education.

When the administration of Green Mountain College proposed offering a Master of Science degree in environmental studies online, our faculty was skeptical. After all, we were drawn to this tiny Vermont college by the chance to work closely with students, teaching environmental liberal arts in applied settings. Distance education seemed the antithesis of this approach. We pictured lonely graduate students at their computers, isolated not only from each other but from the very environments they wished to study.

Over the course of several years and countless meetings, however, as we recalled those environmental professionals we knew living far from any university, we began to appreciate the need for such a program. The turning point came when we realized that we could *ground* the curriculum by requiring students to use case studies from their local bioregions in all of their online courses, from Natural Systems Ecology to Environmental Law and Policy. So that working professionals might earn their degree in two years, we designed a series of six-week courses, each requiring at least fifteen hours weekly. Students log on as their schedules allow, as long as they can access computers several times each week.[1]

In "Bioregional Theory and Practice" (ENV 5040), the program's introductory course, my primary goal is to help students perceive the places they live in ecological rather than political terms. Toward that end, they learn to define their homes according to various bioregional models; they research the natural and cultural history of their places; they create an inventory of local environmental issues and stakeholders; and they compile an annotated bibliography of bioregionally relevant resources. By the end of this course they have established a foundation that the rest of their graduate work will build on, and so their education in environmental studies will be applied, from residency through thesis, to the places they call home.

Our primary textbook is *LifePlace: Bioregional Thought and Practice*, by Robert Thayer Jr., but I prepare students for the course by first assigning Barry Lopez's *The Rediscovery of North America*: a compact but devastating critique of our national disconnection. Students also read Michael McGinnis's anthology, *Bioregionalism*, Wendell Berry's *The Art of the Commonplace*, and dozens of articles available through the online platform. Among the supplemental works, perhaps the most useful introductions to bioregionalism are Jim Dodge's "Living by Life" and a trio of pieces from Gary Snyder: "The Place, the Region, and the Commons," "Reinhabitation," and a 1971 interview entitled "On Earth Geography."[2]

Since the program went online in 2006, the kinds of graduate students we've attracted have had a notable effect on how I teach this course. As we suspected, our program draws employees of state and federal agencies, especially the National Park Service; we hadn't anticipated, however, attracting so many from the military—including a fighter pilot attending classes from her base in Iraq. Most of our students have been out of school for some time, and they bring a wealth of experience to our discussions. But many are less eager than the typical Green Mountain student to embrace radical critiques of our government and economy. As a result, I find myself emphasizing a distinction between bioregional perception and ideological bioregionalism.

By "bioregional perception," I mean the act of transforming how we understand the places we live by learning to pay closer attention to their character and composition. It begins with developing a sense of home rooted in the knowledge of landforms, natural communities, and even "perceptual indicator species," which Thayer describes as being so characteristic of a region that they help define it (37). Bioregional perception also requires an expanded sense of time so that the essential identity of a region is broad enough to include historical changes in species composition. Knowing where we live includes knowing what happened there before.

My emphasis on bioregional perception doesn't mean that students avoid more ideological positions, such as the argument that bioregionally sound governance would benefit from the absence of a centralized government. But they also read authors who describe meaningful bioregional practice within existing political and economic systems. I try to draw students into conversation with the more doctrinaire approaches, as in the following discussion prompt:

> Doug Aberley points out that "the language of bioregionalism has been appropriated to assist in conceptualizing experiments in institutional and organizational reform," but that "these initiatives are generally devoid of a crucial bioregional value—the redistribution of decision-making power to semi-autonomous territories who can adopt ecologically sustainable and socially just policies" (34–35). This is a charge that might well be aimed at Green Mountain College's graduate program, since we do not advocate any specific political agenda. First, does it seem to you that the insights of bioregionalism do inevitably lead to the kind of decentralization that Aberley describes? And second, because we do not formally advocate political decentralization in our curriculum, are we misappropriating the language and ideas of bioregionalism?

These threaded discussions are the highlight of the course, as the medium allows for more thoughtful and thorough conversations than typical classroom discussions.[3] Engaging graduate students in dialogues like this offers them the chance to decide for themselves how far to take the political and economic implications of bioregionalism. (And those students who enjoy sharing what they've learned with agency colleagues and supervisors are free to omit the demands for regulatory decentralization.)

Of course, the basic practice of bioregional perception is in itself a radical act, as might be inferred from the fact that it begins by throwing out official descriptions of place in favor of less arbitrary boundaries. As we unearth an ecological sense of place from beneath the socially constructed lines and labels, and begin to identify where we live in more fundamental ways, so do our own identities begin to evolve. We *mean* something different, individually and collectively, when our new definition of place is interested in humans only as one among many resident species (albeit one with a pronounced environmental impact). Through the lens of bioregionalism, I do not identify myself as a native Oregonian, a recent Vermonter, or even an American, but as a bipedal primate of mostly northern European stock following a set of culturally determined interpretive strategies through this place where the oaks and hickories give way to beech and maple forests.

While epistemological reconstruction is not listed among my course objectives, two assignments in particular seem to encourage the transformative impact of bioregional perception: the first requires students to define where they live bioregionally, identifying new boundaries by drawing on a range of models, while the second asks them to research and recount the deep histories of their local bioregions, from geological formation to the present. Each of these assignments ultimately enacts a shift of perspective that breaks students out of more anthropocentric interpretations of place.

The assignment that opens the course—a formal report proposing bioregional boundaries based on geological, hydrological, and biotic circumstances—may sound simple, but it is an almost immediately frustrating task. Student Michelle Stubbings recalls that even her initial research was challenging: "[W]hat I was looking for crossed political and cultural lines, making it necessary to think outside those parameters and redefine my search terms and limits. Maps and charts stop at township and state lines, but mountain ridges and rivers continue north; you have to learn to cut, paste, and layer bits of information together to gain the full story of the landscape." I refer students to resources such as the Environmental Protection Agency's "Surf Your Watershed" page and Robert Bailey's "Description of Ecoregions of the United States," produced for the U.S. Forest Service, but I also discourage students from replacing one established set of boundaries with another.[4] Simply substituting what Bailey calls the "Atlantic Coastal Flatlands" for Horry County, South Carolina, may be an improvement, but I want students to try out multiple ways of defining their bioregions and eventually to explain why they chose one over the others.

Introducing them to a variety of models can complicate the project in useful ways. Students read an interview in which Gary Snyder suggests we might do well to "correlate the overlap between ranges of certain types of flora, between certain types of biomes, and climatological areas, and cultural areas, and get a sense of that region, and then look at more or less physical maps and study the drainages, and get a clearer sense of what drainage terms are and correlate those also" ("On Earth Geography" 24). Kirkpatrick Sale offers a cleaner approach by dividing the landscape into nested ecoregions, georegions, and morphoregions, though his definitions can be a bit vague (56–59). Jim Dodge does a fine job of consolidating "the criteria most often advanced for making bioregional distinctions"; his list includes "biotic shift, watershed, land form, cultural/phenomenological, spirit presence, and elevation. Taken together, as I think they should be, they give us a strong sense of where we're at and the life that enmeshes our own." Dodge goes on to point out, however, that strict bioregional definitions are "unnecessary, and perhaps dangerous. Better to let definitions emerge from practice than impose them dogmatically from the git-go" (8).

This is the second major frustration for students still at work on their first assignment: not only are there many ways to define a bioregion, but most definitions are inherently imprecise or contingent. It doesn't help that the models for designating bioregional boundaries are inconsistent: students are quick to notice, for example, that Sale's georegions and morphoregions do not parallel Bailey's domains and provinces. Even borders that initially seem pretty firm frequently dissolve when examined more closely. If the eastern boundary of a student's bioregion is marked by the predominance of Ponderosa pine, for example, how precise is that moment of biotic shift? The boundary may be miles wide, swelling and shrinking and wobbling to accommodate different landforms. Eventually most students learn to accept fuzzy, porous boundaries—even those in coastal bioregions, who often end up extending the saltier edge of their maps past the beach and onto the continental shelf.

One way I help students through the confusion is by defining my native bioregion in a lecture. To use Sale's terms, the place where I grew up is on the edge of two morphoregions (the Columbia River gorge and the

Willamette Valley) within a georegion (the Columbia River drainage) that intersects an ecoregion. That ecoregion can in turn be defined in several ways: to some it is the Cascadian Bioregion of the Great Rain Coast, lying between the Ish and Shasta Bioregions. According to Bailey, it belongs to the Marine Division of the Temperate Humid Domain, and can be further reduced to the Pacific Lowland Mixed Forest Province.[5] But this particular province is a long band stretching 400 miles from the southern Willamette Valley to Puget Sound, and it would be longer if Bailey hadn't stopped at the Canadian border. Trying to configure a consistent set of policies at that scale would be difficult. The more likely move, I suggest, would be to divide the Pacific Lowland Mixed Forest Province between rivers that flow to the Columbia or into Puget Sound. Within those two divisions, some policies might then be made at the level of individual watersheds.

Of course it is disconcerting to replace a precise set of political boundaries with a conditional definition chosen from an array of competing possibilities, but one humbling lesson of this assignment is that our tidy categories are too simplistic to fit the world beyond our minds. Students find some comfort in the words of Christopher Klyza, who observes, "I don't think we are particularly well served if we simply use bioregionalism to substitute one more ecologically rational set of boundaries for an existing set of ecologically less relevant boundaries. Rather than wed ourselves to new boundaries, I hope that bioregionalism can help us focus on the fundamentally social nature of boundaries and to think of overlays of borders and boundaries" (81). Such a postmodern balancing act reminds us that we may never fully escape the interpretive models that mediate our experience of the world. After all, even our most ecologically correct maps are still mental constructions—but we can learn to see them as constructions and reevaluate them in the context of other possible models.

Once I've managed to complicate students' spatial orientation, it's time to do something similar to their sense of time. In each new cohort, I find local histories are distorted in a fairly consistent way. The emphasis tends to fall on the last century, in which our places assumed most of their current form: paved roads, telephone lines, and department stores. Before that lies an indeterminate rural period—a blurry continuum stretching from Crevecoeur to the Dustbowl days—and before that came the pioneers to clear the forests. In the very beginning, so this version of history goes, native people lived in harmony with a wilder version of the local environment.

Of the many problems with that history, most fundamental is the fact that the nonhuman elements of the bioregion function merely as a backdrop to the human action. The best way I've found to correct this impression is to put our species in its place by recounting history broadly enough to leave the human role substantially diminished. The central assignment of "Bioregional Theory and Practice" is for students to research the geological, biological, and cultural history of the bioregion, reaching back hundreds of millions of years, and then to put this deep history into a narrative form suited to a general audience.

I was familiar with the notion of deep history from my graduate studies of environmental literature. Works such as Gary Snyder's "What Happened Here Before," David Rains Wallace's *The Klamath Knot*, and John Hanson Mitchell's *Ceremonial Time* are useful models of the shift in perspective that occurs when we take the long view of our home places. If time permitted a book-length model of deep history, I would certainly assign Thomas Fairchild Sherman's classic text, *A Place on the Glacial Till*, which is the most thorough, well-researched, and lyrical model I've encountered. And yet even the best literary account offers only a secondhand experience. To gain the perceptual benefits of deep history, we're better off conducting our own research into the places we live.

I experienced those benefits firsthand in 1999, while helping students in central Michigan research, write, and publish what I then called a "bioregional biography" of the local watershed.[6] This was not a region I was familiar with, but by the end of that semester I found myself living in a landscape made of stories. I saw the tracks of glaciers in nearly imperceptible hills; in the shadows of farms and neighborhoods, I saw the great pine forests that stood before the land was logged and drained; I listened to stories of the Anishinaabeg and visited their old village sites. As a result, my surroundings came to life for me. And once I learned to see a tiny piece of Michigan that way, I found myself trying to make a deeper sense of other landscapes I encountered as well. Why are those mountains more rounded than the ones east of here? Why does this place have so much spruce? What species lived here before these? The bioregional intimacy earned by such curiosity can hardly compare to that of inhabitory cultures, living in the geography of their mythologies, but it's a good place to begin the process of reinhabitation.

From historian Dan Flores, students learn that "good bioregional history ought to aim for the 'big view' not so much through wide geographic generalizations in shallow time, but through analyzing deep time in a single space" (51). The deep history that Flores describes moves from geological formation to the region's climate history, which "can then position us to understand the ebb and flow of floral and faunal species across space and time the way our eyes enable us to track cumulus clouds drifting across an open basin by the shadows they cast on the ground" (51).

While my students must reach back many millions of years in their histories to describe the creation of local landforms, important details can get lost in so vast a chronology. So I encourage them to tell the story in broad strokes until they arrive at the last ice age, and then to zoom in for a closer look. Of course, that much time spent on the Holocene can encourage students to overemphasize the human story. But when a broader view reveals that the real action is a series of evolving habitats, then what we are used to seeing as background information becomes causal—and those people we thought were the main characters appear more properly as effects.

One common mistake of students is to minimize or overlook the distinct postglacial shifts in climate and habitat, so I refer them to E. C. Pielou's *After the Ice Age* (which would certainly be an assigned text if only it applied as well to all of my students' bioregions). Another common mistake is the assumption that Native Americans living at the time of European contact accurately represent earlier American populations. I urge students to pause at each cultural transformation since the ice age, and to connect those technological and social innovations to changes in climate, habitat, and availability of food sources. When we recognize Paleo-Indian, Archaic, and Woodland cultures as distinct forms of human inhabitation, each lasting thousands of years, then we have a broad enough view of North American history to reveal the last few centuries of European-American impact as an aberration. (I do find it necessary, however, to make sure students compare the environmental effects of different populations in terms of technology, values, and economics, rather than race.)

By the time they are finished, my students have each produced a document that is ready to be shared with others in their bioregions. Although their information comes from scholarly sources, I ask them to synthesize and narrate their histories in ways that make them accessible and interesting to a general audience. There's real value in knowing that terms like *thrust-faults* or *hypsithermal* are going to leave some readers confused or bored. In fact, because the translation of specialized concepts into common language requires that students understand them very well, it's quite an effective way to process new material. In all but a few cases the completed assignments tend to be the first attempt at a local deep history, and I encourage students to circulate these essays through libraries, schools, or local organizations.

To know the story of one's place is not only to live in an animated landscape, but also to understand better how one fits into that story. Lauren Imlay, a graduate student living in Vernal, Utah, discovered this while writing her deep history:

> As I move through my bioregion I am constantly thinking about the research I have done and relating it to what I am seeing. For example, when I see a drilling rig I know how and why this area has such rich oil reserves (and right now I am exploring the problems that the extraction of this oil causes), when I see the ruins of the historic cabin down the road from me I know who lived there and why they settled here, and when I see a cave I know how Native Americans might have utilized it. . . . It makes me feel good to know the history of my home and it is amazing how this knowledge really makes me experience a sense of belonging and connection to this area. (Online discussion posting)

When our frame of reference expands like this, not only do we better understand *where* we are, but we have a different sense of *who* we are as individuals defined, in part, by the place we call home.

Over the past four years I have been convinced of the transformative effects of these assignments in bioregional perception. I continue to adjust them, usually hoping to offer a clearer sense of what I'm looking for, though at the same time I realize that asking too precisely for something can discourage more original insights. But there are plenty of opportunities for originality, as well as for reflection on the learning process.

Toward the end of the course, I ask students to consider a point made by Robert Thayer: "Within any particular life-place lies a laboratory so well equipped as to keep countless students of all ages and persuasions busy learning for lifetimes. Yet in the age of the computer and the Internet, it is remarkable how little we rely on this real-world laboratory to teach our students; here-and-now learning has been displaced by 'distance' learning, the educational buzzword for the new, presumably electronic, millennium" (232). I ask the students what they think Thayer would make of a class like ours. Is there something about the technology we're using that is antithetical to learning from our "real-world laboratories"? The students generally disagree with Thayer, arguing that our combination of distance technology and a bioregional curriculum serves our students better than a more conventional residential program might. After all, they point out, how many of Thayer's students in Davis, California, actually come from the Central Valley? How many will remain after graduation?

I must admit that I would love the chance to work with graduate students residentially, spending a semester exploring this bioregion in the company of geologists, biologists, and local citizens—but I would prefer to do that with students who are making a home here. In the meantime, I am delighted that our online courses are helping graduate students become more familiar with the places they call home. It's true, in our program they miss some chances to study with scientists working in their own bioregions, although we do encourage students to find local experts to supervise their practicums and independent studies. We have also built requirements into our curriculum that lead students to make connections with local agencies and organizations, and on occasion these contacts have led to opportunities after graduate school.

In the end, my greatest reassurance comes from gathering with our graduate students at each September's residency. The variety of students who have found their way to our program has been remarkably diverse in education, age, and professional experience. They have created a community that some might dismiss as "virtual," though many of our students insist they are closer to their graduate colleagues than they ever were to their undergraduate classmates. The residencies are essential to creating this sense of community, but so are the discussions: students typically post more than double the required number of entries each week, in addition to more casual postings in our "Virtual Cafe." They learn so much from each other, as you might expect of a class filled with environmental professionals, and I learn so much from them.

As successful as our program has been in helping graduate students discover their local bioregions, I would never wish to see distance education replace residential colleges. Students clearly benefit from an environment where they can work together in laboratories or in the field, where classroom ideas bounce around the hallways and dining rooms, and where exposure to people from other backgrounds hints at a world of possibilities. But I have been convinced, by class after class of my graduate students, that truly transformative education can take place over the Internet. The irony, of course, is that until our brick-and-mortar institutions begin integrating bioregional education into their curricula, distance education just may provide the most natural way to teach environmental studies.

NOTES

1. In the terminology of distance education, such courses are described as "asynchronous."

2. I also assign readings from Kirkpatrick Sale, Peter Berg, Thomas Berry, Murray Bookchin, J. Baird Callicott, E. F. Schumacher, Bill McKibben, Stephanie Mills, Freeman House, and Aldo Leopold, among others.

3. For one thing, unlike a traditional classroom setting, no one sits quietly in the back of the room. Not only is everyone fully involved in each discussion, but students also reference readings specifically and have a chance to draft and revise their comments before posting.

4. The Environmental Protection Agency's "Surf Your Watershed" site is located at <http://cfpub.epa.gov/surf/locate/index.cfm>; Bailey's "Description of the Ecoregions of the United States" is found at <http://www.fs.fed.us/land/ecosysmgmt/index.html>.

5. Bailey's description of the Pacific Lowland Mixed Forest Province can be found at <http://www.fs.fed.us/colormap/ecoreg1_provinces.conf?54,104>.

6. For a full account of this experience, see my essay, "Writing the Watershed."

WORKS CITED

Aberley, Doug. "Interpreting Bioregionalism: A Story from Many Voices." McGinnis 13–42. Print.

Berry, Wendell. *The Art of the Commonplace: The Agrarian Essays of Wendell Berry.* Ed. Norman Wirzba. Washington, D.C.: Counterpoint, 2003. Print.

Christensen, Laird. "Writing the Watershed." *Teaching in the Field: Working with Students in the Outdoor Classroom.* Ed. Hal Crimmel. Salt Lake City: University of Utah Press, 2003. 124–36. Print.

Dodge, Jim. "Living by Life." In *Home!: A Bioregional Reader.* Ed. Van Andruss, Christopher Plant, Judith Plant, and Eleanor Wright. Philadelphia: New Society, 1990. 5–12. Print.

Flores, Dan. "Place: Thinking about Bioregional History." McGinnis 43–60. Print.

Imlay, Lauren. Online discussion posting. 29 March 2009. Web.

Klyza, Christopher. "Bioregional Possibilities in Vermont." McGinnis 81–98. Print.

Lopez, Barry. *The Rediscovery of North America.* New York: Vintage, 1992. Print.

McGinnis. Michael Vincent, ed. *Bioregionalism.* New York: Routledge, 1999. Print.

Mitchell, John Hanson. *Ceremonial Time: Fifteen Thousand Years on One Square Mile.* New York: Anchor, 1984. Print.

Pielou, E. C. *After the Ice Age: The Return of Life to Glaciated North America.* Chicago: University of Chicago Press, 1992. Print.

Sale, Kirkpatrick. *Dwellers in the Land: The Bioregional Vision.* Philadelphia: New Society, 1991. Print.

Sherman, Thomas Fairchild. *A Place on the Glacial Till: Time, Land, and Nature within an American Town.* New York: Oxford University Press, 1996. Print.

Snyder, Gary. "On Earth Geography." *The Real Work: Interviews and Talks, 1964–1979.* Ed. William Scott MacLean. New York: New Directions, 1980. 23–30. Print.

———. "The Place, the Region, and the Commons." *The Practice of the Wild.* San Francisco: North Point, 1990. 25–47. Print.

———. "Reinhabitation." *The Old Ways: Six Essays.* San Francisco: City Lights, 1977. 57–66. Print.

———. "What Happened Here Before." *Turtle Island.* New York: New Directions, 1974. 78–81. Print.

Stubbings, Michelle. Message to the author. 1 Sept. 2009. E-mail.

Thayer, Robert L., Jr. *LifePlace: Bioregional Thought and Practice.* Berkeley: University of California Press, 2003. Print.

Tuan, Yi-Fu. *Topophilia: A Study of Environmental Perception, Attitudes, and Values.* New York: Columbia University Press, 1974. Print.

Wallace, David Rains. *The Klamath Knot: Explorations of Myth and Evolution.* Twentieth Anniversary Edition. Berkeley: University of California Press, 2003. Print.

KATHRYN MILES AND

MITCHELL THOMASHOW

Where You at 20.0

W E ARE COMPELLED to educate a new generation of environmental leaders. This means we must also understand what our
students care about, their views and how they form them. We also recognize
that these views and values may not be our own. Mitch was born in 1950;
Kate was born in 1974. Our students were born after 1990. Thus, we represent three distinct generations of place-based experience. In this essay, we
seek to tease out the distinctions that arise from such generational differences and how these distinctions affect a person's sense of bioregionalism.

We begin with a hypothesis: to be a college student in the 21st century
is to be a person of the world. Characterized by such monikers as the
"Millennials," the "Net Generation," "The Digital Natives," and, increasingly, "The Google Generation," the cohort of contemporary students is
one defined by digital mediums and an access to information never before
witnessed. The current generation of students must navigate the vast terrain between local natural history and global electronic connectivity. We
wondered, then, whether concepts such as place and community remain
relevant to this generation—whether bioregionalism can still be a salient
lens through which to view our place in the world.

In short, we wondered where this new generation was at.

We suspected our students would locate themselves in a bioregional milieu quite different than our own. We even worried that our commitment
to this concept would seem antiquated to these students, or that we would
have a hard time finding common ideological ground. However, we also

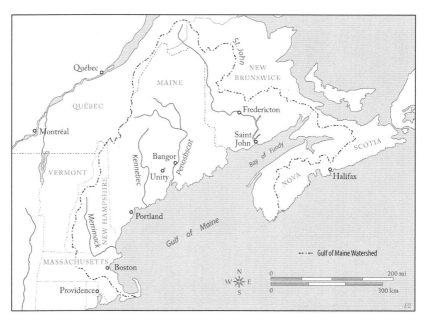

Gulf of Maine Watershed

believed that the college classroom provides a powerful link in contemporary space and time. This got us thinking: Can we use the classroom space to better understand our common aspirations? More specifically, can we find common ground in ideas about place and the formulation of our ecological identities? Can we, by comparing our experiences and what's most important to us, create a stream of authentic narrative about generational responses to bioregionalism?

Such questions are at the heart of much of our own work. As scholars, we both focus on questions of cognition and ways of knowing. We are committed to the Romantic Era idea of stepped development, perhaps best articulated by John Locke, that we begin as blank slates and slowly become the sum of our experiences. What this means, then, is that everything from our schooling and religious beliefs, to our particular cultural and social milieu, to our hobbies and entertainment, becomes the lens through which we view place and bioregionalism. As William Wordsworth so lyrically put it, "Heaven lies about us in our infancy! / Shades of the prison-house begin to close / Upon the growing Boy" (lines 67–69). These shades—books, relationships, the stresses and opportunities of life—all create filters that affect our ability to have an unadulterated relationship with a place. So, too, does the generation into which we were born.

Peter H. Kahn Jr. refers to this phenomenon as "environmental generational amnesia." In brief, Kahn's theory suggests that our relationship with the world stems from what we might call a shifting sense of environmental reality. He writes that "in childhood people construct a standard, a baseline, for what is the 'normal' environment, and they use that baseline to assess environmental degradations later in their life" (204). In other words, if a place was degraded when we first came to know it, our sense of its health, or beauty, or importance, will be based solely on that compromised state. The downside, of course, is that this prevents us from coming to understand a landscape in what we might call a natural state. The upside, Kahn says, is that this limited view can liberate us to consider novel approaches to being in a particular locale.

Certainly today's student arrives at college or university with a different perception of a landscape than our own. Ask just about anyone how a beloved home space has changed in a decade or less, and more often than not you will hear stories about new housing developments, the erection of cell phone towers and wind turbines, the increased congestion and crowding or, in the case of many cities, the urban decay caused by the continuing diaspora to the suburbs. Factor in the twenty or more years that separate most college faculty from their students, and you're bound to see even starker differences in terms of what any given space means to different people.

Thus, we knew that our students and others in their generation would come to campus with their own distinct notions of landscape: one in which planetary boundaries and significant environmental degradation have become global realities. We also suspected that they would arrive entrenched in a virtual landscape as well. These students were born into a world of cell phones, the Internet, instant messaging, and social networking. If we accept Kahn's theory, then this digital background also creates both an amnesia and an opportunity to rethink all our theories about bioregionalism. Through their experiences, we sought to explore this new way of thinking and what it might say for the future of environmentalism.

At the center of our investigation is a course we team-teach entitled "The Future of Life on Earth." The genesis for this interdisciplinary seminar arose out of a shared concern: climate change and threats to biodiversity are extraordinary and urgent challenges that require our very best thinking. We believe that sustainable resource use and life choices present everyone with the foundation for sound ecological alternatives. And so we sought to design a course that introduces basic concepts of place, biodiversity, and climate change. Perhaps more importantly, we sought to give students lifelong learning tools to promote creative solutions and a continued sense of wonder.

When constructing our syllabus, we began by envisioning the goals for this course. While it was important for students to master theoretical content, we also wanted them to leave with a new dispositional awareness that reaffirmed or even strengthened their connection to place and also demonstrated the value of integrating analysis and imagination in interpreting the natural world.

To do so, we needed a methodology and an investigative instrument—something that would allow us to square our students' thinking on bioregionalism against that held by previous generations. And so we settled on what may be one of the most enduring artifacts of the original bioregional movement: the somewhat cheeky (and now seminally serialized) quiz, "Where You At?" (see facing page).

First published in *CoEvolution Quarterly* in 1981, the quiz teases out basic understandings of place, as defined by plant associations, land-use history, water sources, and more. And for years it served as the touchstone for assessing one's understanding of a particular landscape.

This quiz will soon celebrate its thirtieth birthday. And so it seemed fitting to test its relevance for this new and increasingly digital generation. What do tools such as the "Where You At?" quiz mean in the globalized, hyperdigitalized world of the twenty-first century? Does it resonate with the generations born well after the launch of the bioregional movement? Does place have meaning for them? How do they define their own relationship with the natural world?

To tease out such thorny questions—not to mention their responses—we sought first to foster a sense of engagement among the students: a real commitment to the importance of these subjects in their own lives. And so, to begin the course, we decided to foreground the notion of place as it relates to home. One of the best articulations of this idea as it relates to bioregionalism is Gary Snyder's essay "The Place, the Region, and the Commons." Therein, Snyder makes a persuasive case that, by our very nature, we all feel an emotional pull and sense of grounding when we reflect

WHERE YOU AT?

What follows is a self-scoring test on basic environmental perception of place. Scoring is done on the honor system, so if you fudge, cheat, or elude, you also get an idea of where you're at. The quiz is culture bound, favoring those who live in the country over city dwellers, and scores can be adjusted accordingly. Most of the questions, however, are of such a basic nature that undue allowances are not necessary.

1. Trace the water you drink from precipitation to tap.
2. How many days until the moon is full? (Slack of 2 days is allowed.)
3. What soil series are you standing on?
4. What was the total rainfall in your area last year (July–June)? (Slack: 1 inch for every 20 inches.)
5. When was the last time a fire burned in your area?
6. What were the primary subsistence techniques of the culture that lived in your area before you?
7. Name five edible plants in your region and their season(s) of availability.
8. From what direction do winter storms generally come in your region?
9. Where does your garbage go?
10. How long is the growing season where you live?
11. On what day of the year are the shadows shortest where you live?
12. When do the deer rut in your region, and when are the young born?
13. Name five grasses in your area. Are any of them native?
14. Name five resident and five migratory birds in your area.
15. What is the land-use history of where you live?
16. What primary ecological event/process influenced the land where you live? (Bonus special: what's the evidence?)
17. What species have become extinct in your area?
18. What are the major plant associations in your region?
19. From where you're reading this, point north.
20. What spring wildflower is consistently among the first to bloom where you live?

Scoring

0–3	You have your head up your ass.
4–7	It's hard to be in two places at once when you're not anywhere at all.
8–12	You have a firm grasp of the obvious.
13–16	You're paying attention.
17–19	You know where you're at.
20	You not only know where you're at, you know where it's at.

"Where You At?" quiz, by Leonard Charles, Jim Dodge, Lynn Milliman, and Victoria Stockley. Used with permission.

on the most intimate spaces that have formed us. Home is where our earliest perceptions and ideas are formed, and emotionally it's where most of us find the strongest ties. This makes good etymological sense. The word *home* comes from the Old German, *heim*, or "habitation." Both are also derived from the Old English root, *heorth*, or "hearth," which is conveniently similar to *heart*, or *heorte*. From heart and hearth come knowledge and connection.

From an epistemological perspective, those early connections seem to carry a particular weight when it comes to the formation of future ideas— even when a sense of place feels somewhat lacking. Thus, we devoted the early sessions of the course to the anecdotal, personal stories we tell about who we are and where we come from. We also liked the idea of building on these tellings with what Snyder calls the specificity of place: the information and discrete experiences that define a locale. And so, during these first classes we asked students to create place maps and to reflect on their personal histories with regard to landscape.

In addition to fostering engagement, we saw this exercise as the first opportunity for the students to tell us where they're at, both ecologically and cognitively. And we were curious about the degree to which they would use digital mediums and technologies to express that sense of location. We suspected it would be a significant one. After all, these students were born in the last decade of the twentieth century, long after the eruption of the Internet, twenty-four-hour cable news, and digital entertainment. The idea of stepped development—that we begin with the nucleus of the house, and gradually widen that perspective to encompass the multiplicities of a region—risks serious antiquation where they're concerned. These were people born into that multiplicity to begin with, whose associations and ideas have been part of an enormous web from the start.

If contemporary scholars on digital media are correct, they are also a generation of people experiencing a dissociative tendency when it comes to sustained analysis or depth of inquiry. In a recent briefing paper published by the British Library and JISC, an education think tank, scholars described this generation as one defined by "horizontal, rather than vertical" thought processes. Their research suggests that this generation approaches most cognitive activities with the same tendencies they demonstrate on the Internet, a process described in the briefing paper as "scan, flick, and powerbrowse." Would the students' place maps reflect that?

Some did. But what struck us most was the overwhelming variety and range of responses we received. Some students relied on multiple digital mediums, creating Powerpoint slides and Web pages, incorporating You-Tube videos, iTunes, Google Earth images, and more. Others chose to make collages out of old photos or even pen-and-ink sketches of the flora, fauna, and historic landmarks in their towns. The diversity of response was an important reminder for us as college professors: it can be all too easy to make sweeping generalizations or expectations about a cohort of students based on their generational identification. Doing so risks overlooking the wide-ranging spectrum of individual responses and the degree to which a student adheres to any such categorization.

We discussed this range and the cultural expectations of their generation with the students, particularly as both relate to place. They all admitted that they worry, for instance, that the idea of bioregional identification holds even less currency for their generation than it does ours—that even the term itself is not part of their lexicon. One student told us that, while she relishes the ease of access provided by the Web, it also means that she and her peers are losing a sense of what is unique within any given place—that they spend more time exploring the global instead of the local. Others disagreed; they spoke about the advantages of technology like Facebook and Skype, which give them what they see as unfettered access to our planet and many of its occupants. They also said that technologies such as Google Earth were a useful way to get back a home place: locating material for maps of their sense of place or even being reminded of a cherished apple orchard or city park was all the easier when they could call up an image of the place on the Web.

Throughout our discussion, the students remained divided in terms of the value of this shift. However, they all seemed to agree with the idea that they are the Google Generation. Or, perhaps more exactly, that they are the Social Media Generation, one driven by what the JISC report calls "involving, dynamic and personalised content experiences."

This discussion provided the perfect segue to larger questions of bio-regionalism. After all, we can think of no better way of describing a relationship with a landscape than involved, dynamic, personal, and experientially based. And once someone understands the way in which household ecology works (whether or not said ecology is a digital one), it's an easy step to broaden that vision to encompass a distinct biome. It is, as Scott Russell Sanders explains in *Staying Put*, a matter of entering a "series of nested rings," which widen out from home but ultimately remain connected as a series of concentric circles. This idea is shared by Jim Dodge, one of the primary authors of the "Where You At?" quiz. In his essay, "Living by Life: Some Bioregional Theory and Practice," Dodge writes that, etymologically, "bioregionalism means life territory, place of life, or perhaps by reckless extension, government by life." He also suggests that one way of distinguishing between notions of place and bioregionalism is the importance of natural systems.

We read and discussed both Sanders and Dodge with the students, along with Terry Tempest Williams's lovely, lyrical account of place, *Red: Passion and Patience in the Desert*. Although none of our students hail from the Red Rock Desert depicted in Williams's work, this text nevertheless resonated deeply with them, and many indicated that it was their favorite of all the assigned readings.

One of the reasons for this might be the accessibility and applicability of the work's defining tenet. In the opening pages of *Red*, Williams offers a deceptively simple equation: "people + place = politics" (3). This statement, which Williams explores at length throughout the remainder of her book, gets at the heart of Dodge's notion of territory and "the government by life" as it relates to bioregionalism. It's also an equation that has defined much about the United States and how we interact with the landscape. Our culture's connection to place, though sometimes contradictory and confusing, is deeply held and very political.

Our students understood not only this equation, but also its ecological and political consequences, on a deep and meaningful level. Essays composed in response to the readings evoked deeply rooted concepts of home and place as reflected in landscapes, relationship, and identity.

For instance, our student Rachel wrote,

> I whole-heartedly agree with the equation from *Red* that says "people + place = politics." It doesn't matter where in this country you go, as long as there is land and there are people, there will always be some kind of political controversy. . . . I think that in order for you to have a significant connection to a bioregion, you have to have a personal connection to a place within the bioregion first. If you begin by getting to know a place within a bioregion, it gives you a stepping stone to use on your journey to discovering more about the bioregion as a whole. Everyone needs somewhere to start from. Then, once you have gotten to know the general area of that starting place, and you have begun to become connected to it, you begin to wonder what else there is around your place. If you have con-

nected enough with your place to become curious as to what surrounds it, you have reached the point where you are now connecting place to bioregion.

For Rachel, this issue came down to an ethic of care. A bioregional sensibility, she explained, depends on an emotional connection to a place, which in turn demands an awareness of the relationships—both inter- and intraspecies—formed there. "I am connected to my home," she concluded. "I am connected to my town. I am connected to my bioregion. I care about what happens here. People, places, animals, memories that I love live here. I care."

Our student Marc emphasized a similar need for personal connection:

> I think that the place we grow up in has a life changing impact. I've grown up loving the countryside and forest and wish to preserve these areas. So why do some people grow up in a rural area and have a desire to move to the city, or people that grow up in the city have a desire to move to the country? I try to figure out what drives people to a place. Is it because of the memories they have as a child? Do people with good memories wish to stay in the area they grew up and people with bad memories wish to leave? A sense of place, I think, must be influenced by the way we perceived the world as a child. . . . I think the importance of bioregionalism is that it is what ties us to a place. The language, the culture, the people, the land, the natural environment are all things that draw us to a place and give us a sense of home.

These are timeless comments. Both Marc and Rachel explore how they come to care about a place. They devise implicit educational and political strategies for how to cultivate an ethic of care, couched in a bioregional fabric. Marc feels tied both to his personal past and to the larger cultural one. Rachel explains how the core of her affiliation lies in the people, animals, and memories of her ecological landscape.

We are inspired by this transcending sensibility. Rachel and Marc, along with the rest of our students, exude a sense of gratitude and reciprocity. Their home landscapes are deeply ingrained in their appreciation of life. They identify their landscapes as seamless with their personalities, values, and ethics. This is the very essence of ecological identity. Implicit in their responses is a great desire to give back to the places from where they came: what Jim Dodge calls an ecopolitical system based on egalitarian thinking and "interdependent self-reliance" (8).

This idea of "interdependent self-reliance" is, of course, at the heart of any conversation about ecology and bioregionalism. And so it seemed to us a natural transition to introduce the "Where You At?" quiz at this point in the semester. We began by asking the students to complete the quiz based on the place they call home and for the bioregion in which our college is located; the students then entertained a lengthy discussion about the saliency of the quiz—and its underlying concepts—for their generation.

When it came to the original "Where You At?" quiz, the students' response was lukewarm. They liked its commitment to general ecology but worried about its specificity. Identifying five edible plants in a region, they said, is both too detailed and reductive when it comes to knowing a bioregion. Or, as one student incisively put it, "Just because you have ecological facts memorized, does not mean you know a place."

Instead of these so-called facts, the students wanted more attention paid to our lived environment. They wanted an emphasis on sustainability: asking questions about how to source grass-fed meat, find public transportation, or learn about the politicos dictating local policy. Knowing a place, they said, is an important first step. However, they also contended that knowing our relationship to that place is at least—if not more—important. To this end, they created a corollary quiz that they called "How You Live?" (see facing page). In it, they posed questions pertaining to the above issues of sustainability, along with questions about energy consumption, the efficiency of our homes, the routes taken by our waste water, and the location of both the nearest fast food restaurant and local farm stand.

And, yes, they said: these questions were at least in part based on their adherence to the ideologies and experiences of the Google Generation.

We of the older generations would do well to acknowledge that, while these experiences may not be our own, there is a real authenticity to them. It's tempting to assume that the Google Generation's outlook is defined by one more shade on the prison door, or one more step away from an immediate relationship with place. But many of our students say they think otherwise. This temporary dislocation can inspire a new and valuable cognitive process, they say, so long as we marry that experience with the physical geography beyond our computer screen. And, if we accept Kahn's theory, then this knowledge really is creating both an amnesia and an opportunity to rethink all our theories about bioregionalism.

Certainly many of us in older generations would benefit from making this kind of correction. Whereas our generations saw themselves as

1. On what day is your local farmers market?
2. What type of energy is used to heat your home? How many days a year is it employed in this capacity?
3. Where is the closest fast food restaurant to your home?
4. List three invasive species in your region. What is the most damaging to the ecosystem?
5. Where does your water go when it goes down the drain?
6. How many independently owned shops exist in your area?
7. What facilities in your area accept universal hazardous waste?
8. Describe in specific detail your governor's environmental policy.
9. What types of plastic are accepted by your regional recycling center?
10. To what degree does light pollution obfuscate the night sky in your region? (Extra credit if you answer using the Bortle Dark-Sky Scale)
11. What is the closest state park to your home?
12. Trace the electrical energy in your home from source to outlet.
13. What is the mpg of your vehicle? How many miles per year does it travel?
14. What type of tax credits are offered by your state and local governments for installations of energy-efficient devices (such as solar hot water heaters)?
15. What is the proper tire-inflation pressure for your car tires to maximize efficiency?
16. What is your current water footprint?
17. List five game animals that can be hunted in your region and the permissible hunting season of each.
18. What form of public transportation is closest to you? When does it operate and where does it go?
19. Who are your senators and how can you contact them?
20. What is the average temperature and precipitation for your region? How has it changed in the past three decades?

Scoring

0–3	Don't bother making future plans.
4–7	Paging Charles Darwin . . .
8–12	You have a firm grasp of the obvious.
13–16	You're paying attention.
17–19	You know how you live.
20	You not only know how you live, you know how to keep the planet alive.

"How You Live?" quiz.

increasingly uprooted, our students understand the very real ways in which the entire planet has become so. They are not confronting the effects of the 1970s oil crisis, but rather, the reality of myriad peak resource scares that won't go away. Their lives have been marked by continual tipping points, the rapid acceleration of climate change, and the distinct possibility of another mega-extinction. Place, for them, is an ever-shifting plane.

Again and again, their response to these challenges is to emphasize the immediacy of relationships. Phone calls from helicopter parents, the constant flow of text messages, the idea that *friending* is not only a verb, but something to do robustly and continuously, are very much at the heart of their collective identity. Their revisions to the original "Where You At?" quiz bear this out.

What struck us most about the students' assessment was their ability to make a persuasive case for the ways in which humankind functions within this system as well. Several students wrote about what is probably best described as a human ecology: they see the way in which we shape a particular environment and, just as importantly, the way it shapes us. Implicit in their understanding is an admirable attention to ethics and questions of what is right. Their definitions of biodiversity not only allow for but ultimately demand that we acknowledge the ever-growing impact of humankind on any place. Such a focus is largely missing from the original quiz and from early definitions of biodiversity.

We would even go so far as to suggest that this new model of interconnectedness should be at the heart of any environmental conversation. Our students' generation gets that. And while their sense of place may not be ours, they definitely know where they are. To their minds, there is no separation between the natural and the human or the wild and the civilized. All are part of the same worldwide web. And any ethical decision made by members of this generation has implicit within it a recognition of that belief.

We are inspired by the fidelity to place witnessed in these seminar students: their sense of reciprocity and gratitude regarding the natural world, their vigilance about the Internet, and their yearning to incorporate bioregional precepts in their lives. They may not represent any kind of mainstream view. Most of them had rural upbringings, and we are aware that they are a self-selected group of environmental studies aspirants. That's okay. We are constantly reminded of the idiosyncratic quality of personal experience, and we eschew any profound sociological patterns. However, we have a hunch. We believe that if you ask any college freshman to explore the meaning of place and community in his or her life, that person will have a great deal of insight, and you will find levels and layers of affiliation and meaning. It's a short pedagogical step from making that link to broader considerations of place and planet.

We find that idea both heartening and inspiring. More than that, though, we're inclined to believe, when it comes down to defining environmental identity in a new age, this generation really does know where it's at.

WORKS CITED

Charles, Leonard, Jim Dodge, Lynn Milliman, and Victoria Stockley. "Where You At?" *CoEvolution Quarterly* 32 (1981): 3. Print.

Dodge, Jim. "Living by Life: Some Bioregional Theory and Practice." *Home! A Bioregional Reader.* Ed. Van Andruss, Christopher Plant, Judith Plant, and Eleanor Wright. Philadelphia: New Society, 1990. 5–12. Print.

JISC. *Information Behaviour of the Researcher of the Future: A* CIBER *Research Paper.* JISC, 11 Jan. 2008. Web.

Kahn, Peter H., Jr. "The Child's Environmental Amnesia—It's Ours." *Children, Youth and Environments* 17.2 (2007): 199–207. Print.

Sanders, Scott Russell. *Staying Put: Making a Home in a Restless World.* Boston: Beacon Press, 1994. Print.

Snyder, Gary. "The Place, the Region, and the Commons." *The Practice of the Wild.* Washington, D.C.: Counterpoint, 2003. 25–47. Print.

Williams, Terry Tempest. *Red: Passion and Patience in the Desert.* New York: Pantheon, 2001. Print.

KYLE BLADOW

A Bioregional Booklist

Andruss, Van, Christopher Plant, Judith Plant, and Eleanor Wright, eds. *Home! A Bioregional Reader*. Philadelphia: New Society, 1990. Print.

    A collection gathering many early bioregional articles, including reprints from *Raise the Stakes*, the *Catalist*, and the *New Catalyst*. A repository of definitions suggesting multiple perspectives and initiatives as well as trends (e.g., attention to watersheds, appreciation for indigenous traditions, promotion of decentralized self-government). Features multiple selections by Peter Berg, Freeman House, and Judith Plant; sidebar articles, excerpts, a bioregional quiz, and ceremonies; and intersections of bioregional thought with ecofeminism, urban design, and community planning.

Berg, Peter. *Envisioning Sustainability*. San Francisco: Subculture Books, 2009. Print.

    A valuable introduction to one of bioregionalism's founding figures, which gathers essays by artist and activist Peter Berg, representing over forty years of his work with bioregionalism. Arranged chronologically, the articles, interviews, talks, and artwork attest to the wide, holistic range of his vision; the collection, which includes the groundbreaking essay "Reinhabiting California," highlights Berg's engagement with various groups (e.g., The Diggers, Planet Drum) as well as his commitment to including urban communities within bioregional thought and planning. Berg provides an introduction and original publication information for each selection.

Berg, Peter, ed. *Reinhabiting a Separate Country: A Bioregional Anthology of Northern California*. San Francisco: Planet Drum Foundation, 1978. Print.

    Published by the Planet Drum Foundation founded by Berg, this celebratory anthology forms a "bundle" that "respond[s] to the need for a new synthesis between natural history and culture." Substituting "natural country" for bioregion, it suggests "identity with a natural country is a way to address the biosphere without backing into it and knocking it over." Includes personal narratives, oral history, poetry, prose, drawings, and photography of northern California, with Peter Berg and Raymond Dasmann's landmark essay "Reinhabiting California" serving as the afterword.

Berry, Wendell. *The Art of the Commonplace: The Agrarian Essays of Wendell Berry.* Ed. Norman Wirzba. Washington, D.C.: Counterpoint, 2002. Print.

A compilation of reprinted essays representing Berry's agrarian vision, characterized by a strong critique of current dominant economic systems that fail to concede their dependence on natural resources and environments. As "much of Berry's writing refers to and is inspired by his farm home in Henry County, Kentucky" (xx), the first essay describes ecological and cultural aspects of this region. Proposes a less exploitative paradigm for Western culture via holistic, inclusive perspectives on work and community. While much bioregional philosophy has ties to indigenous or Eastern spiritualities, Berry argues a Christian perspective, particularly in the final section, "Agrarian Religion."

Cheney, Jim. "Postmodern Environmental Ethics: Ethics as Bioregional Narrative." *Environmental Ethics* 11 (Summer 1989): 117–34. Print.

Engaging a postmodern focus on situatedness, this essay questions the "epistemological function of place in the construction of our understandings of self, community, and world" (117). Asserting a contextualized, place-based epistemology, Cheney argues, guards against the "totalizing, colonial discourse" prevalent in modern thought. Taking a situated approach to place—engaging in "bioregional narrative" (134)—should also involve extending "notions of context and narrative outward so as to include not just the human community, but also the land" (128). Cheney draws on postmodern feminist philosophy and the work of Paul Shepard, Biddy Martin, and Chandra Taplade Mohanty, among others, to promote a bioregional approach to postmodern ethics.

Evanoff, Richard. *Bioregionalism and Global Ethics: A Transactional Approach to Achieving Ecological Sustainability, Social Justice, and Human Well-Being.* New York: Routledge, 2011. Print.

This philosophical synthesis brings the local and the global into dialogue as Evanoff proposes a new global ethic that values ecological sustainability, social justice, and human well-being. He argues that a cross-cultural, confederated bioregional model is better suited to achieve this three-fold ethic than is the dominant development paradigm. His transactional approach attempts to harmonize relations between individual, society, and nature while granting each a degree of autonomy. Evanoff's extensive bibliography is subdivided into sections on bioregionalism, capitalism and its critics, coevolution, development, economics, politics, globalization, indigenous cultures, environmental ethics, social construction of nature, and others.

Heise, Ursula K. *Sense of Place and Sense of Planet: The Environmental Imagination of the Global.* New York: Oxford University Press, 2008. Print.

   Casts new light on the relationship between the local and global by putting "environmental reflections on the importance of a 'sense of place' in communication with recent theories of globalization and cosmopolitanism, in an attempt to explore what new possibilities for ecological awareness inhere in cultural forms" (13). Grounded in literary analyses of authors including Ursula K. Le Guin, Don DeLillo, Karen Tei Yamashita, and Christa Wolf, the book also engages in a larger cultural critique by examining environmentalist movements, mapping technologies, and visual art. Employs risk theory (manifested in such contexts as chemical and nuclear pollution and climate change) and Heise's concept of "eco-cosmopolitanism" to envision a global environmental outlook.

House, Freeman. *Totem Salmon: Life Lessons from Another Species.* Boston: Beacon, 1999. Print.

   A former commercial salmon fisherman, House offers in his first book an engaging narrative of species coexistence within a bioregion, namely between humans and salmon in the Mattole River watershed (and the Pacific Northwest in general). House complements his own experiences with references to natural history, folklore, and environmental science. He creates a well-crafted story of "codependence" between entities within a bioregion, reinforcing his conviction that if stories of a bioregion and the life within it "are not kept alive in the collective memory" (206), the risk of degradation to the bioregion increases. In particular, House's stories emphasize habitat restoration efforts to benefit salmon populations.

Lopez, Barry. *The Rediscovery of North America.* Lexington: University Press of Kentucky, 1990. Print.

   A slim, honed work describing the European discovery of North America as an incursion that "quickly became a ruthless, angry search for wealth" and "set a tone in the Americas" (9); Lopez links this history to contemporary environmental degradation on the continent. He argues, however, that "this violent corruption needn't define us" (11), and through bioregional approaches—learning to appreciate land for more than just its physical resources by experiencing it firsthand and recovering stories about it—we can find in landscape a *querencia*, "a place on the ground where one feels secure" (39).

Lynch, Tom. *Xerophilia: Ecocritical Explorations in Southwestern Literature.* Lubbock: Texas Tech University Press, 2008. Print.

   Employs a bioregional focus to analyze literature of the American Southwest, including writing by Leslie Marmon Silko, Terry Tempest Williams, Edward

Abbey, Ray Gonzalez, Charles Bowden, Susan Tweit, Gary Paul Nabhan, Pat Mora, Ann Zwinger, and Janice Emily Bowers. Chapters are themed around southwestern characteristics: acequia culture, borderlands, nonhuman inhabitants (particularly invertebrates), and multisensory perceptions of the desert. While engaged in literary criticism, Lynch also draws on environmental justice theory, ethnography, and environmental history; he provides helpful definitions of bioregionalism and ecocriticism as well as insightful personal narratives and photographs of the Southwest. Exemplary interfacing of bioregionalism and literary studies.

McGinnis, Michael Vincent, ed. *Bioregionalism*. London: Routledge, 1999. Print.

A foundational, interdisciplinary anthology, with selections from community activists and scholars in such areas as law, history, regional planning, political science, and environmental studies; together, the contributors "offer contrasting views of the importance of place, the locale and the bioregion in global economy" (8). This vital work includes a historical survey of bioregionalist movements, a section on "regionalization" and the intersections of bioregionalism with national and global frameworks, a section on local knowledge and modern science, and a concluding section about bioregionalism's future as expressed in pedagogy and practice.

Ricou, Laurie, *The Arbutus/Madrone Files: Reading the Pacific Northwest*. Corvallis: Oregon State University Press, 2002. Print.

A bioregional cultural study of the Pacific Northwest (or Cascadia), assembled into twelve "files" that seek to compile rather than rigidly order varied aspects of the region. Ricou examines many authors—including Emily Carr, Ken Kesey, Joy Kogawa, Ursula K. Le Guin, and David Wagoner—asking how they "write their version of the Pacific Northwest region: in particular to ask what words they choose to describe setting, community, work, speech patterns" (3). This fine example of place-based scholarship invites a broad audience of critics, educators, policy makers, and residents of the region.

Sale, Kirkpatrick. *Dwellers in the Land: The Bioregional Vision*. San Francisco: Sierra Club Books, 1985. Print.

Provides for bioregionalism "an attempt . . . to lay some of its groundwork, suggest some of its basic outlines, and gather in one place some of its wisdom" (xxiii), with an emphasis on ecological influences and sociopolitical applications. The book critiques Western epistemologies for drifting away from nature into an "industrio-scientific paradigm," which Sale suggests should be abandoned for a bioregional paradigm. Chapters focus on scale, economy, politics, and social configurations; later chapters argue for the "historical realities" of bioregional movements and the imperative of adopting bioregionalism in order to reverse ecological destruction.

Sanders, Scott Russell. *Staying Put: Making a Home in a Restless World*. Boston: Beacon, 1994. Print.

Eight essays centered on Sanders's childhood and adult homes in Ohio and Indiana, in which he ruminates on home, family, and belonging to place in a sometimes elegiac, but often celebratory tone. Invokes a variety of writers (e.g., Henry David Thoreau, John James Audubon, Salman Rushdie, Thich Nhat Hanh) and interweaves bioregional sentiments throughout. "Settling Down" (chapter 5) focuses especially on the connection between rootedness and sustainability, the idea that "those who root themselves in places are likelier to know and care for those places" (106).

Snyder, Gary. *The Practice of the Wild*. San Francisco: North Point, 1990. Print.

Written in a meditative style, this collection includes personal narrative, myths, and philosophical essays, though every selection maintains an ethical imperative for humans to reevaluate our conduct toward nature and our home environments. At the heart of this volume is Snyder's elegant conceptualization of wildness, a complex, self-organizing order that largely escapes human control or understanding but that he sees as the origin of human culture. Building on Thoreau's famous dictum, Snyder writes, "Wildness is not just 'the preservation of the world,' it *is* the world" (6). For Snyder, wildness is a quality that is most fully expressed in the places we call wilderness, but can be found anywhere, including the weedy vacant lots of cities and even the human body and subconscious. Snyder's bioregionalism builds on the recognition that place-based cultures are most likely to achieve wholeness by resolving "the dichotomy of the civilized and the wild" (23).

Thayer, Robert L., Jr. *LifePlace: Bioregional Thought and Practice*. Berkeley: University of California Press, 2003. Print.

An excellent model showing how a text might feature a particular bioregion. Thayer's study of the Putah-Cache watershed in California's Sacramento Valley competently extends beyond his own expertise in landscape architecture to address important and varied concerns for understanding a bioregion, ranging from geography, climate, and biology to human culture and economy. Thayer's clear, anecdotal style makes this work accessible to a wide audience; he uses *lifeplace* interchangeably with *bioregion*, arguing that "a life-place framework will be judged not on how 'warm and cuddly' it makes people feel but on whether it contributes in a physical sense to the fulfillment of needs of life on earth" (5).

Thomashow, Mitchell. *Bringing the Biosphere Home: Learning to Perceive Global Environmental Change*. Cambridge: MIT Press, 2002. Print.

Continuing to develop ideas from his essay "Cosmopolitan Bioregionalism," Thomashow argues that a bioregional focus need not reject global realities, but can help foster deeper understandings of the relationships between places. This important book argues for the need to develop a "place-based perceptual ecology," the "ability to observe, witness, and interpret the ecological patterns of the place where you live" (5); it suggests ways to develop perceptual ecology and explores "various approaches to learning about global environmental change" (14). Thomashow's background in environmental studies provides a solid foundation onto which he adds cultural, social, and spiritual insights and implications for a bioregional worldview.

Vitek, William, and Wes Jackson, eds. *Rooted in the Land: Essays on Community and Place.* New Haven: Yale University Press, 1996. Print.

Features "new and previously published essays that take as their central theme the importance of 'placed' human communities" (xi), with contributions from scholars in theology, philosophy, community development, and environmental studies, as well as from social activists and nonacademics. Many of the essays move capably between personal anecdotes and theory or analysis. Civics and agriculture are predominant topics, with particular emphasis on rural communities and landscapes. Section titles include "Rootlessness," "Valuing Community," and "The Ecological Connection."

Daniel Gustav Anderson, who notes that he is "homesick for the Palouse," has recent and forthcoming publications on Deleuze and Guattari, post-Marxism, and integral theory in the *Quarterly Journal of Ideology* and the *Integral Review*. He is pursuing a PhD in cultural studies at George Mason University, emphasizing critical theory, ecological Marxism, and historical materialism. He recently became a Buddhist priest (his title is "doshu") after training at the Tendai Buddhist Institute.

Karla Armbruster is professor of English at Webster University in St. Louis, where she teaches American literature, interdisciplinary humanities, and professional writing. With Kathleen R. Wallace, she is the editor of *Beyond Nature Writing: Expanding the Boundaries of Ecocriticism* (University Press of Virginia, 2001) and the author of numerous articles and essays, including "Bringing Nature Writing Home: Josephine Johnson's *The Inland Island* as Bioregional Narrative" (*Reading under the Sign of Nature: New Essays in Ecocriticism*, ed. John Tallmadge and Henry Harrington, University of Utah Press, 2000). She is also a past president of the Association for the Study of Literature and Environment. Armbruster's appreciation for sense of place was dramatically heightened by moving from Ohio to Michigan to Colorado to Missouri in the course of four years in the late 1990s. She is now happily nestled near a big river (the Mississippi) in a place not too different than the one where she grew up (along the Little Miami River, a tributary of the Ohio River in the southwestern corner of Ohio).

David Landis Barnhill received his PhD in religious studies with a minor in Japanese literature from Stanford University. His erosional life has taken him from the Sierras to the Cascades to the Blue Ridge and now to the Central Sand Hills of Wisconsin. Barnhill's publications include *At Home on the Earth* (an anthology of American nature writing), *Deep Ecology and World Religions* (coedited with Roger Gottlieb), and a two-volume translation of the Japanese nature poet Basho. Recent articles include "The Spiritual Dimension of North American Nature Writing," "The Social Ecology of Gary Snyder," and "East Asian Influence on Recent North American Nature Writing." He is currently working on a book on radical politics in American nature writing. He is director of environmental studies and professor of English at the University of Wisconsin Oshkosh. His courses have included American nature writing, Japanese nature writing, bioregionalism, ecosocial activism, environmental ethics, and East Asian religions.

Wes Berry grew up among green hills, hardwoods, beef cattle, and tobacco fields in cave country, Barren River drainage, Kentucky, where he's returned (after a long dozen years away) to teach at Western Kentucky University. He lives on a ridgeline near the confluence of the Green and Barren Rivers, where he's fixing up an old property and managing a small flock of laying hens. He specializes in twentieth-century American literature and environmental humanities and has published essays on Walter Anderson, Wendell Berry, Cormac McCarthy, Anne LaBastille, Toni Morrison, Annie Proulx, Leslie Silko, and Barbara Kingsolver. His novel *Boating with the Dead* was a finalist for the Bellwether Prize for Fiction of Social Change in 2008. He also taught for a spell in Sichuan province, China, where the cuisine is as savory as western Kentucky barbecue, the topic of his current "research."

Kyle Bladow originally hails from Michigan's Upper Peninsula, where he received his BA in English and his MA in literature and creative writing from Northern Michigan University. He is currently pursuing his PhD at the University of Nevada, Reno, and learning to appreciate the Truckee River watershed of the Great Basin. His research interests include bioregionalism and postcolonial studies. His master's thesis examined perceptions of landscape occurring in four novels set along the southern shore of Lake Superior, and he sports a bioregional tattoo of the lake on his forearm.

Ruth Blair grew up in Brisbane, Australia, where she now lives, following stretches of time in Paris; Ithaca, New York, where she completed a PhD in comparative literature; and Hobart, Tasmania, Australia's island state and the cradle of contemporary Australian environmentalism. Her interest in environmental literature began when she was teaching at the University of Tasmania. There, and subsequently at the University of Queensland, she taught American literature alongside courses on literature and the environment. Now retired and a research associate at the University of Queensland, she is glad to have more time to devote to environmental concerns and to writing about the environment. She has recently published on bioregional writing in CA. Cranston and Robert Zeller, eds., *The Littoral Zone: Australian Writers and Their Contexts* (Amsterdam and New York: Rodopi, 2007); and on postcolonial perspectives on the environment in the Pacific in Helen Tiffin, ed., *Five Emus to the King of Siam: Environment and Empire* (Amsterdam and New York: Rodopi, 2007).

Norah Bowman-Broz grew up in the Cariboo-Chilcotin in Northern British Columbia. Having lived on islands and plateaus and cities, she now resides in the dry and coniferous Okanagan Valley in British Columbia. She has published poetry in Canadian literary journals *CV2* and *Prairie Fire* and a critical essay in the *Canadian Journal of Native Studies*. Norah is a freelance writer and a PhD student in the English department at the University of Alberta. Currently, Norah is working on a book-length project about living on the front lines of climate change in Northern B.C.

Pavel Cenkl was born and raised in New England. Having spent his youth in the Boston area for a decade, Cenkl moved slowly northward through New Hampshire until settling in the Northeast Kingdom of Vermont, some 30 miles from the Canadian border. He is dean of academics and professor of humanities and regional studies at Sterling College in Vermont. His recent scholarship and teaching focus comprises intersections of literature, culture, and environment in the Northern Forest of the United States and the Canadian and European Arctic. He is the author of *This Vast Book of Nature: Writing the Landscape of New Hampshire's White Mountains, 1784–1911* (Iowa, 2006) and *Nature and Culture in the Northern Forest* (Iowa, 2010), an interdisciplinary anthology of essays that engage culture, economy, and environment in the U.S. Northeast.

Laird Christensen is professor of English and environmental studies at Green Mountain College, an environmental liberal arts college in Poultney, Vermont, where he was founding director of the graduate program in environmental studies. His poems and essays have appeared in a number of books and journals, including *The Utne Reader, Northwest Review*, and *Wild Earth*. He served as coeditor of two books released in 2008: *Teaching about Place: Learning from the Land* (University of Nevada Press) and *Teaching North American Environmental Literature* (Modern Language Association). He writes, "I'm a native Oregonian, but I spent more than a decade drifting around the country, living out of a backpack while searching always for someplace more interesting. Now, having spent ten years in western Vermont, I'd just as soon stay put."

Christine Cusick currently makes her home in the foothills of the Laurel Highland Mountains of southwestern Pennsylvania and feels most at rest when rambling in the west of Ireland. She is associate professor of English and composition at Seton Hill University and has published ecocritical readings of contemporary Irish poetry, landscape photography, and American nature writing as well as nationally recognized creative nonfiction. Her interview with Tim Robinson is included in her edited collection *Out of the Earth: Ecocritical Readings of Irish Texts* published by Cork University Press.

Jill Gatlin, currently cultivating New England roots after a Rocky Mountain up-bringing and Pacific Northwest education, serves on the liberal arts faculty at New England Conservatory. She received her PhD in English from the University of Washington and is completing a manuscript on environmental justice in U.S. literature. Her article "An Epistemology of the Everyday: Occupational Health and Environmental Justice in Hubert Skidmore's *Hawk's Nest*" appears in *Literature and Medicine*, and her essay "Experience Is All We Have: Postpositivist Realist Ethics in Terry Tempest Williams' *Refuge: An Unnatural History of Family and Place*" appears in the collection *A Wilderness of Signs: Ethics, Beauty, and Environment after Postmodernism*. She has also contributed to the Washington Center's curriculum for the bioregion initiative.

Cheryll Glotfelty is professor of literature and environment and director of graduate studies at the University of Nevada, Reno, where she cofounded the literature and environment graduate program. She coedited with Harold Fromm *The Ecocriticism Reader: Landmarks in Literary Ecology* (University of Georgia Press, 1996). She recently edited *Literary Nevada: Writings from the Silver State* (University of Nevada Press, 2008) and has published essays in *ISLE*, *Western American Literature*, *ATQ*, *Women's Studies*, and many edited collections and reference works. She is past president of the Association for the Study of Literature and Environment. Itinerant during her formative years—Montana, Colorado, Maryland, California, Hawaii, Germany, and New York—Glotfelty has devoted the last two decades to sinking a taproot into Nevada's high desert.

Serenella Iovino is a native of the Vesuvian area, a volcanic and coastal bioregion embracing the Bay of Naples, but is now life-placed some six hundred miles north, in the southwestern slope of the Po Valley. Author of four books, she is professor of ethics at the University of Turin, Piedmont, at the foothills of the Cozie Alps. From 2008 to 2010 she served as president of the European Association for the Study of Literature, Culture and the Environment (EASLCE) and is currently a member of the editorial board of *ISLE* and of the scientific committee of *Ecozon@: European*

Journal of Literature, Culture and Environment (www.ecozona.eu). Her Web page is http://unito.academia.edu/serenellaiovino.

Erin James is a native of Nova Scotia who spent five years in the U.K. and is currently living in the Great Basin. She is an assistant professor of English at the University of Nevada, Reno. She is coeditor of *What Is the Earthly Paradise?: Ecocritical Responses to the Caribbean*, and her latest article, "Doomed Kyoto: Language, Environment and National Interests," appears in the *Journal of Commonwealth and Postcolonial Studies* (both are published under her maiden name, Erin Somerville). She has published articles or is currently conducting research on writers including V. S. Naipaul, Ben Okri, Ken Saro-Wiwa, Ngugi wa Thiong'o, Kamau Brathwaite, and Sam Selvon. Her forthcoming book project examines the role of literary narratives in encouraging the ecological awareness and understanding demanded by the global environmental crisis.

Heather Kerr is senior lecturer in English and associate dean of higher degrees (research) in the faculty of humanities and social sciences at the University of Adelaide, South Australia. She publishes in the areas of early modern literary studies, women's writing, cultural studies, and fictocriticism. She is an associate of the Australian Research Council Centre of Excellence for the History of Emotions.

John Lane, a healthy portion of whose genetic material can be traced to the Carolina piedmont, has had his work published in *Orion, American Whitewater, Southern Review, Terra Nova*, and *Fourth Genre*. His prose books include *The Best of the Kudzu Telegraph, Circling Home, Chattooga, Waist Deep in Black Water*, and *Weed Time*, a gathering of his early essays. His *Abandoned Quarry: New & Selected Poems* (Mercer University Press) and his book-length narrative *My Paddle to the Sea* (University of Georgia Press) were recently published in 2011. In 2008, the Texas Tech University library purchased his literary papers for inclusion in the James Sowell Family Collection in Literature, Community, and the Natural World. Lane is cofounder of the Hub City Writers Project. He was recently named director of Wofford College's Goodall Environmental Studies Center, where he teaches environmental writing and humanities. His website is http://www.kudzutelegraph.com.

Tom Lynch dwells in the tallgrass prairie of the central United States, arguably the most degraded and endangered biome on the planet. He is associate professor of English at the University of Nebraska, Lincoln, where he specializes in ecocriticism and place-conscious approaches to literature. In 2005 he published *El Lobo: Readings on the Mexican Gray Wolf*. His book *Xerophilia: Ecocritical Explorations in Southwestern Literature*, which won the 2009 Thomas J. Lyon award from the

Western Literature Association, is a bioregional approach to the literature of the American Southwest. He is currently at work on a comparative study of literature of the American West and the Australian Outback from bioregional and post-colonial perspectives. His website can be found at http://www.unl.edu/tlynch2 /Homepage/Home.html.

Kathryn Miles, who currently resides on the coast of Maine, is an award-winning writer whose recent essays have appeared in publications including *Best American Essays, Ecotone, Flyway, PMLA, Reconstruction,* and *Terrain.* She is the author of *Adventures with Ari* (Skyhorse / W. W. Norton, 2009) and *All Standing,* forthcoming in 2012 from Simon & Schuster. Miles currently serves as director of the environmental writing program at Unity College, as scholar-in-residence for the Maine Humanities Council, and as editor in chief for *Hawk and Handsaw: The Journal of Creative Sustainability.*

Anne Milne, who has mostly always lived in Southern Ontario, teaches in the bachelor of arts and sciences program at the University of Guelph in Guelph, Ontario. Her research and published work focuses on representations of animals, laboring-class poets, and agrarian studies in Restoration and eighteenth-century British texts. She published *"Lactilla Tends her Fav'rite Cow": Ecocritical Readings of Animals and Women in Eighteenth-Century British Labouring-Class Women's Poetry* with Bucknell University Press in 2008. She is a 2010–11 Carson Fellow at the Rachel Carson Center (Ludwig Maximilians University / Deutsches Museum) in Munich, Germany.

Laurie Ricou is a Canadian who questions how borders are written in the Pacific Northwest. Until retiring in 2009, he taught English at the University of British Columbia, where over the past 15 years he developed seminar courses in habitat studies. He is author of two recent books on the Pacific Northwest literary bioregion: *The Arbutus/Madrone Files: Reading the Pacific Northwest* (Oregon State University Press, 2002) and *Salal: Listening for the Northwest Understory* (NeWest Press, 2007). He is currently finishing a book on invader species.

Libby Robin had a peripatetic childhood within and beyond Australia. She currently lives in urban Australia and works on the desert outback. She is an interdisciplinary scholar working at the intersections between science, humanities, and environment. She is senior fellow at the Fenner School of Environment and Society, Australian National University; senior research fellow at the Centre for Historical Research at the National Museum of Australia, Canberra; and guest professor of environmental history at the Royal Institute of Technology in Stockholm, Sweden.

Trained as a historian of science, she has published widely in environmental history, environmental literature, ornithology, ecology, museum studies, global history, and the ecological humanities. Her book *The Flight of the Emu* won the Victorian Premier's Literary Award for Science Writing in 2003; her *How a Continent Created a Nation* won the New South Wales Premier's History Award for Australian History in 2007. Her recent books include two major edited collections about Australian desert country: *Boom and Bust: Bird Stories for a Dry Country* (2009) and *Desert Channels: The Impulse to Conserve* (2010), both from CSIRO Publishing.

Kent C. Ryden teaches in the American and New England studies program at the University of Southern Maine. He holds a PhD in American civilization from Brown University. He is the author of *Mapping the Invisible Landscape: Folklore, Writing, and the Sense of Place*, *Landscape with Figures: Nature and Culture in New England*, and *Sum of the Parts: The Mathematics and Politics of Region, Place, and Writing*, as well as many articles and reviews on ecocritical, regional, and environmental topics. Ryden has lived in New England since 1982 (and in Maine specifically since 1994).

Mitchell Thomashow grew up in the Long Island suburbs—Woodmere, New York. He lived on what was essentially a landfill, although he didn't know it at the time. His family lived only ten minutes from the Atlantic Ocean, and during his formative years he spent hours a day on the beach. Since 1975, he has become a full-fledged inhabitant of northern New England, spending 30 years in the Monadnock Region of New Hampshire (where he still has a home and will eventually return) and now in midcoast Maine. Still, he considers himself a cosmopolitan bioregionalist. Thomashow was the president of Unity College from 2006 to 2011. His books include *Ecological Identity: Becoming a Reflective Environmentalist* (MIT Press, 1996) and *Bringing the Biosphere Home: Learning to Perceive Global Environmental Change* (MIT Press, 2001). He is the founder of *Hawk and Handsaw: The Journal of Creative Sustainability* and the cofounder of *Whole Terrain*.

Harry Vandervlist grew up next to the Niagara Escarpment but now lives in the foothills of the Canadian Rockies, where he teaches at the Department of English in the University of Calgary. He is the editor of *Jon Whyte: Mind Over Mountains: Selected and Collected Poems* (Calgary: Red Deer Press, 2001), and he contributed the entry "Jon Whyte" in the *Dictionary of Literary Biography: Canadian Writers of the Twenty First Century* (Detroit: Gale Research, 2006). In 2000 he created the inquiry-based course "Writing the Mountains," which involves undergraduate students in the annual Banff Mountain Book Festival while they complete research projects on mountain writing.

Bart Welling, a child of the U.S. Air Force, has lived in six states and three countries. He feels most at home in the mountains of Utah, but for the past seven years he has been living just a few miles from Janisse Ray's home bioregion in the Altamaha River watershed of south Georgia. He is an associate professor of English and an Environmental Center fellow at the University of North Florida in Jacksonville, near where the historic St. Johns River flows into the Atlantic. His writing and teaching efforts so far have explored points of convergence between ecocriticism and animal/ity studies and Southern studies, textual and bibliographic studies, and the literature of human rights.

Rinda West, who migrated from the eastern hardwood forest to the prairie of Chicago Wilderness, is professor emerita of English at Oakton Community College outside Chicago. She is the author of *Out of the Shadow: Ecopsychology, Story, and Encounters with the Land*, published in 2007 by the University of Virginia Press. She has also published numerous articles in journals, including the *Michigan Quarterly Review*, *Restoration and Management Notes*, and *Spring Journal*. Currently she is a landscape designer in Chicago. She serves on the board of the Midwest Ecological Landscape Association.

Chad Wriglesworth, who grew up in the Pacific Northwest, is an assistant professor of English at St. Jerome's University in Waterloo, Ontario. He was previously an Andrew W. Mellon Early Career Fellow and a James B. Castles Fellow with the Center for Columbia River History. He is currently working toward the completion of a project titled *Geographies of Reclamation: Writing and Water in the Columbia River Basin, 1855–2010*. He has recently published work on William Stafford, Raymond Carver, and Theodore Winthrop in *ISLE: Interdisciplinary Studies in Literature and Environment*, *Western American Literature*, and *Columbia: The Magazine of Northwest History*.

Dan Wylie is professor in the Department of English, Rhodes University, Grahamstown, South Africa. He has published two books on Shaka, the early Zulu leader; a memoir; several volumes of poetry; and articles on literature and ecology. In 2004, he launched a South African Literature and Ecology Colloquium, now moving into its sixth incarnation. The fourth colloquium's papers were published as *Toxic Belonging? Ecology and Identity in Southern Africa* (Cambridge Scholars Press, 2007). His recent book *Elephant* (2009) appears in the Reaktion Books animal series. Wylie was born and raised in Zimbabwe but has resided in Grahamstown, South Africa, since 1990.

INDEX